THE RISE OF
THE TALIBAN
IN AFGHANISTAN

MASS MOBILIZATION, CIVIL WAR, AND THE FUTURE OF THE REGION

NEAMATOLLAH NOJUMI

palgrave

IN MEMORY OF MY FATHER,

AND TO THOSE WHO LOVE

FREEDOM AND PEACE

IN AFGHANISTAN.

THE RISE OF THE TALIBAN IN AFGHANISTAN
© Neamatollah Nojumi, 2002
All rights reserved. No part of this book may be used or reproduced in
any manner whatsoever without written permission except in the case of
brief quotations embodied in critical articles or reviews.

First published 2002 by PALGRAVE™
175 Fifth Avenue, New York, N.Y.10010 and
Houndmills, Basingstoke, Hampshire RG21 6XS.
Companies and representatives throughout the world.

PALGRAVE is the new global publishing imprint of St. Martin's Press
LLC Scholarly and Reference Division and Palgrave Publishers Ltd
(formerly Macmillan Press Ltd).

ISBN 0–312–29402–6 hardback
ISBN 0–312–29584-7 paperback

Library of Congress Cataloging-in-Publication Data
Nojumi, Neamatollah.
    The rise of the Taliban in Afghanistan: mass mobilization, civil war,
    and the future of the regime / by Neamatollah Nojumi
    Includes bibliographical references and index.
    ISBN 0-312-29402-6 (cloth), ISBN 0-312-29584-7 (paperback)
    1. Afghanistan—Politics and government—1973–   2. Taliban
    I. Title.

DS371.2.N65   2001
958.104'5—dc21   2001044636

A catalogue record for this book is available from the British Library.

Design by Letra Libre, Inc.

First edition: January 2002
10 9 8 7 6 5 4 3 2 1

Printed in the United States of America.

CONTENTS

CHRONOLOGY OF EVENTS

1784	The establishment of the modern state of Afghanistan.
1973–1979	The establishment of the first Republic of Afghanistan.
April 27, 1979	The communist military coup d'etat.
December 1979	The Soviet invasion of Afghanistan.
1987–1988	The Soviet withdrawal from Afghanistan.
1987–1992	The emergence of the civil war and collapse of Najibullah's regime.
1992–1996	The establishment of the Islamic State of Afghanistan.
1996–2000	The rise of the Taliban movement and the establishment of the Islamic Emirate of Afghanistan.

List of Definitions and Abbreviations

ACBAR	Agency Coordinating Body for Afghan Relief.
AEC	Advisory Economic Council.
AGSA	Afghanistan Governmental Secret Agency.
Aimagh (Aimaq)	An ethnic group living in northern Afghanistan who speak Aimaghi, similar to Turkmani.
AIP	Afghan Islamic Press.
Alaqhadari	A governmental district.
Amir-ul-Muamanin	Religious or political leader in an Islamic community.
ANP	Awami National Party.
Baluch	An ethnic group living in southwest Afghanistan who speak Baluchi.
CAR	Central Asian Republics.
CAU	Central Asian Union.
CCP	Chinese Communist Party.
CIS	Commonwealth of Independent States.
Dari	A branch of Persian language that is popular in Afghanistan, mostly among Tajiks.
DeoBand	The traditional Henafi of Sunni Islam in DeoBand, India.
DRA	Democratic Republic of Afghanistan.
Ekhwan-al-Muslimin	The Muslim Brethren.
Enghalb	Revolution.
Fetwa	A Religious decree issued by a qualified Islamic scholar.
FNF	The Fatherland National Front.
GRU	Military secret service in the former Soviet Union.
Hazaras	An ethnic group of the Mongolian race, living in central Afghanistan. The language of this ethnic group is Hazaragi, a dialect of Persian Dari.
HIA	Harkat-e-Islami.

HIH	Hezb-e-Islami Hekmatyar.
HIK	Hezb-e-Islami Khaless.
HIM	Harkat-e-Islami Mohammedi.
HWA	Hezb-e-Watan Afghanistan (HWA in Persian and AWH in Pushto), The Homeland Party of Afghanistan, led by Najibullah.
ICP	Indian Communist Party.
IEA	Islamic Emirate of Afghanistan.
IMA	Islamic Movement of Afghanistan lead by Shikh Mohammed Assef Mohseny. IMA was influential among the Shia Muslims of Afghanistan.
IPA	the Islamic Party of Afghanistan. In Dari called Hizb-e-Islami, and I add the first letter of the last name of the leader of the party at the end to separate them. There are three parties with the same name: a) IPA or HIH led By Gulbadin Hekmayar. b) IPA or HIK led by Mowlwi Khaless. c) IPA or HIM led by Mawlawi Waghad.
IRI	Islamic Republic of Iran.
IRP	Islamic Republican Party.
ISA	Islamic State of Afghanistan.
ISI	The Intra-Service Intelligence of Pakistan.
Ismaili	Muslim Shia who live in northern and central Afghanistan.
ISP	In Dari called Jamait-e-Islami Afghanistan (JIA).
JIA	Jamaiat-e-Islami-e-Afghanistan, led by Burhanadin Rabbani.
Jihad	Struggle.
JIP	Jamaat-e-Islami-e-Pakistan, the Islamic Society of Pakistan led by Qazi Hussine Ahmed.
JUIP	Jamaat-e-Ulema-e-Islami-e-Pakistan, led by Maulana Fazl-ul-Rahman.
Junbish-e-Mili	A political and military front formed by General Dostam and Sayyed Hussine Nadery, dominated by the Uzbek and Hazarahs.
Kazak (Ghazagh)	An ethnic group living in northern Afghanistan and speaking Ghazaghi, similar to Turkmani.
KGB	State secret bureau in the former Soviet Union.
KhAD	The secret police under the PDPA rule in Afghanistan.
Khalifah	The highest political leader of Islamic community who may be also the religious leader.
Loya Jirga	The great assembly, also called the national assembly.

Maktabi	The Islamic fanatic section among Afghan Mujahideen who followed the revolutionary ideology that was adapted from the Muslim Brotherhood in Egypt and the Islamic Republic Party of Iran.
Mujahideen	The holy warriors, Afghan resistance against PDPA and Soviets.
Najibullah	Known as Dr. Najib, the former head of the Secret Service, the leader of the Watan Party, and the head of the pro-Soviet government in Afghanistan.
NATO	North Atlantic Treaty Organization.
NCC	National Commander Council.
NCS	National Commanders Shura, formed by major Mujahideen internal front leaders.
NIFDA	National Islamic Front for the Deliverance of Afghanistan.
NSF	National Salvation Front.
NWFP	Northwest Frontier Province of Pakistan.
OIC	Organization of the Islamic Countries.
Parcham	A faction within the PDPA who mostly speak Dari.
PDPA	The People's Democratic Party of Afghanistan.
Pir	The head of a Sufi group among Muslims.
Pushton	An ethnic group living in the southern and eastern part of Afghanistan who speak Pushto.
Qaum (Ghawm)	A group of people who are related to one another through a common language. Blood lineage can be a part of this kind of relationship but the main requirement to be a member of a Ghawm is that the language of that particular Ghawm be your mother tongue.
Qessass	Execution or death penalty, which would be carried out either by the victim's family members or by the local authority.
Qur'an	The Muslim holy book.
RAWA	The Revolutionary Women Association of Afghanistan, a grass-root political movement active among the Afghan women in the refugee-populated area in Pakistan as well as in Afghanistan.
RAO	Russian's state owned oil and gas company, known as GAZPRON.
RSA	Republic State of Afghanistan.
SAMA	Sazaman Inghalabi Mardom Afghanistan lead by Abdul Majid Kalakani.
SAZA	Jamait-e-Inghlabi Zahmatkashan Afghanistan led by Dr. Faiz.

SCN	Supervisory Council of the North (Shura-e-Nezar).
SDNA	Sazaman Democratic Nawin Afghanistan, The New Democratic party of Afghanistan (Hezb-e-Shola).
Shahadah	A Islamic phrase meaning martyrdom.
Shari'ah	The Islamic law.
Shora-e-Nezar	A political and military forum lead by Ahmed Shah Massoud in northern Afghanistan.
SIEIA	Shura-e-Inghalabi Etafagh-e-Islami Afghanistan.
SNA	Sazaman Nassr of Afghanistan, the Victory Party.
SSP	Sepah-e-Sahabah, a fanatic political party in Pakistan.
Taliban	The seekers; students who study at religious schools, armed political movement that holds a large portion of Afghanistan.
TCST	Tashkent Collective Security Treaty.
TTA	Transit Treaty Agreement.
UIFLA	United Islamic Front for Liberation of Afghanistan formed by the Taliban opposition forces.
UNDP	United Nations Development Programs.
UNHCR	United Nations High Commissioner for Refugees.
Uzbek	An ethnic group who lives in the north of Afghanistan.
Wahdat Party	Armed political party dominated by Afghan Shia in Central Afghanistan.
Walayat	A province.
Woleswali	A district in a province.

INTRODUCTION

THE APRIL 1978 COUP D'ETAT BY THE PEOPLE'S DEMOCRATIC PARTY of Afghanistan (PDPA) has become a jumping board for massive political, social, economic, and cultural changes in Afghanistan. The PDPA coup d'etat was followed by the Soviet invasion in December 1979, which lasted for almost ten years. The eruption of civil war in 1988 has opened another eventful chapter in the recent history of this country.

These changes were mostly the result of a very tense political and social environment in which sociopolitical events became the catalyst for change. For example, the April 1978 coup was the catalyst for the Soviet invasion (1979), and both were the catalysts for the Afghan civil war. Each event evolved and occurred because of previous events. The proposed political, social, and economic reforms of the PDPA have played an important role in the three tumultuous decades in Afghanistan's recent history. Through these reforms the PDPA attempted to move Afghanistan from a pre-industrial society toward a political establishment where men are free from exploitation.

To what extent was the PDPA able to wield their heavy reforms and bring them to fruition is a question that was answered by the events following the April coup. These events have shown that the PDPA, despite its ideological and organizational structure, was too far from the reality. The role of Islam, the complexity of ethnic groups, and their diverse languages made it difficult to cohesively govern or control many different social groups. In Afghanistan, people lived, traditionally, under communal codes of autonomy and individual freedom. The PDPA neglected the depth of these codes in the sociopsychology of the people, and such neglect resulted in the use of coercion in order to control and mobilize society into different governmental-made organizations.

By the early 1980s, the political interaction between Afghan communities and the PDPA-led government caused massive violent confrontations that dominated the political environment of the country. More than seven million people were forced to seek refuge in foreign countries; these people made up the largest refugee population in the world at that time. The Soviet invasion caused massive destruction of the farms and of livestock, and it changed the economic system of the country from self-sufficiency to dependency on foreign aid and international assistance.

After the Soviet invasion of Afghanistan in December 1979, the PDPA leadership and the Soviet advisors attempted to enforce their shaken authority and mobilize Afghanistan toward socialism, but this enforcement provoked resistance. This resistance was rooted in the confrontation between the PDPA reforms and the traditional social and political codes of Afghan society.

The theory of mass mobilization (chapter two) is the most important theoretical analysis in this study. The discussion encompasses the political, social, and economic interaction between masses and government. A clash occurs when the government attempts to mobilize and control all lives according to the political agenda of its leadership. I will, briefly, compare and contrast the situation in Afghanistan with the mass mobilization in China under Mao Tse Tung and the Communist Party and in India under the leadership of Mahatma Gandhi and the Congress Party. The aim of this comparison is to show the difference between the three models and to illustrate the effects of mass mobilization in Afghanistan and its scope of influence in the sociopolitical lives of the people.

The characteristics of the Afghan mass mobilization and its impact on the modern political parties and their political ideology are crucial to the contents of analyses. These modern political parties were categorized in three groups: the leftists (pro- and anti-Moscow); the radical Islamic political parties (the Ikhwanis and Wahabbis); and the nationalist/Islamic political parties.

The role of Afghan Mujahideen in the process of mass mobilization and their impact in the civil war are very important in helping to understand both sides of the conflict in Afghanistan. The internal division and external separation of the Afghan Mujahideen groups were fueled by the flames of violent confrontation. The lack of decisive leadership in both camps, the PDPA and the Mujahideen, created room for a third political movement to fill the gap between the masses and leadership in Afghanistan. In the course of decades of war and violence, the political leaders in the PDPA and in the Mujahideen organizations failed to provide a viable alternative. Neither side was able to form a political institution that represented the national interest of the Afghan people. Even though the majority of people participated in the process of mobilization, they always suffered from the absence of capable leadership to coordinate their efforts. Afghan Mujahideen leaders were too busy in party politics and personal hostilities in Pakistan and Iran. Neither the field commanders nor the external front of Mujahideen leaders were capable of leading the nation into the final stage of victory after the Soviet withdrawal.

The role of the internal front of the Mujahideen (mainly made up of the major field commanders) in the politics of Afghanistan is another outstanding phenomenon. In this case, the role of the National Commanders Shura (NCS) was very crucial to the outcome of political mobilization of the country. The failure of the field commanders to form an interim government in Afghanistan contributed largely to the eruption of civil war and external interfering. The NCS leaders, in particular Ahmed Shah Massoud, missed the only chance to incorporate the ex-governmental and Mujahideen forces into a larger political formation in 1992. Soon, the second phase of the civil war, a war between the Afghan Mujahideen factions, would shatter the country.

The rise of the Taliban in 1994 was an unanticipated event. They rose from the southern villages in Qandahar and the refugee camps in Pakistan. Their role in the political and military environment in Afghanistan was a new phenomenon in the history of this country. Studying the source of Taliban forces in the political and religious community in Afghanistan and Pakistan is necessary to understand the social background of the movement. To understand the organizational structure of the movement, one needs to know its leadership and rank and file. The Taliban military organization had an important role in the formation of the movement. There are many ex-military officers who participated with the Taliban, and the role of these Afghan ex-military officers was crucial to operating their military campaign.

Creating a portrait of the Taliban political strategies and military tactics will provide readers with a clearer image about the Taliban agendas. After the Taliban seized Qandahar, they understood the social and ethnic mixture of the region, and they attempted to manipulate the ethnic differences for their political and military gains. They rewarded those who cooperated and punished those who rejected them. The Taliban source of finance was important for the movement, with all its complexity of running a large army; they used captured weapons and external military aid in the formation of their army. The fall of Herat was an important military and political strategy for the Taliban, and this victory helped their move toward Kabul, which they seized in September 1996.

Since Afghanistan had never been controlled by religious leaders, the formation of an Islamic state led by clergies was another strange development. The Taliban supreme leader has a combined spiritual and political status in the Taliban high council as well as in the affairs of the people. The Taliban political ideology is a key factor that illustrates their attitude toward the issues of election, government, and political participation in Afghanistan. How the Taliban define legitimacy and authority is a very interesting part of chapter sixteen.

The Taliban victory in the northwest of the country, which resulted in their control of Mazar-e-Sharif, was very strategic. During this advance the Taliban gained control of 80 percent of Afghanistan and destroyed their political and military oppositions. Above all, Ahmed Shah Massoud, the former defense minister and the famous Mujahideen commander, was the only leader that was able to save the core of his fighters and mobilize them against the Taliban forces.

Current international and Afghanistan relations are also a crucial part of this book. Understanding the position of the countries sharing borders with

Afghanistan and the regional and international powers who are and will play roles in the political settlement of a future Afghanistan is a significant task, the essence of the national, regional, and international politics. A study of the peace building efforts by the international community as well as the people of Afghanistan completes this book. Examining the peace process in Afghanistan inherently embodies a dimension of the complicated nature of Afghan politics. In this regard, one may realize the current regional and international interests in regard to the situation in Afghanistan and, more importantly, the impact of Afghanistan in the regional stability.

I would like to thank the University Scholar Committee of Hartford University for their support during my primary work on this book. I would like to thank Bruce Esposito, associate professor in the University of Hartford history department, for his support when I was completing the first part of this book. I thank all those who allowed me to interview them, in particular those who are in Afghanistan and asked me to not mention their names. I also thank those who helped me edit and find resources to complete this work.

For my part, I hope this study becomes a useful source for those curious minds and passionate hearts who always desired to know what was really happening inside Afghanistan over the past three decades (1978–2000). I have spent more than ten years of my life in the Afghan resistance movement. I still remember those tough days and nights in the valleys and mountains of Afghanistan. Passing through the totally destroyed villages, crossing the cold water of rivers with damaged bridges, and walking through the narrow pathways that run through minefields were unpleasant ordeals to survive. After all these years, I can hear the joyful noise of the children who were playing in the village cemetery, the only spot that was clean from the land mines. I have the memories of many good friends whom I have lost in the smoky field of battle. The painful face of the Afghan soldiers who were forced to aim at their fellow Afghans has been included in my personal history. After all, when I decided to work on this book, I made a commitment not to unleash my personal sympathy for the sake of politics. In this regard I may not seem polite in my reporting and analysis, but I decided to be respectful and hold intellectual integrity as the highest honor of my study. I have used greatly my personal notes from interviewing local commanders, political activists, captured soldiers, government civil and military officers, and most importantly, the local communities inside Afghanistan and the refugees in Pakistan and Iran. I do believe that Afghanistan's case is unique for scholars and researchers to conduct scientific studies on social, political, cultural, and psychological aspects of social and political mobilization in times of violent confrontation.

CHAPTER ONE

HISTORICAL BACKGROUND

BECAUSE OF ITS GEOSTRATEGIC LOCATION BETWEEN THE PERSIAN Gulf, Central Asia, and the Indian subcontinent, Afghanistan has become a significant player in the world.[1] This geopolitical situation has not only created a capacity for the Afghan rulers to spread their authority toward the eastern and western present borders, it also has made Afghanistan a tactical target for regional and international powers to reach their strategic destination. These two elements were strong enough to shape governments that ignored the desire and will of the people.

The geographical features of Afghanistan have had a great impact on the cultural development of its people. An insufficient transportation system has impeded internal communication and, because of this, economic, social, and political integration has been very slow. Of the 25 million total population of Afghanistan, 20 percent live in urban areas and 80 percent in rural areas.[2] The mountainous features of Afghanistan make it necessary for many villages to be self-sufficient. They build their houses, grow their crops, and protect their community. Trade is primarily on the regional level, rather than national; for centuries the regional market economy was the primary source of commerce. Therefore, Afghanistan has never been able to integrate regional economies on a national scale.

Afghanistan's population is comprised of eight major ethnic groups (Pushtons, Tajiks, Hazaras, Aimaqs, Turkmen, Uzbeks, Kirghiz, and Baluchis) and dozens of small sub-ethnic minorities. While the main national languages are Dari and Pushto, there are between 20 and 40 different languages and dialects in Afghanistan.[3]

The relationship between all of these various ethnic and linguistic groups is based on two main points: ethnic identity and national identity. On the ethnic level the members of an ethnic group, in particular within a tribe, share "a common ancestor, a common leader and a common territory in a positive way and harbor negative attitudes toward members of other tribes."[4] There are Afghans who do not have a tribal background and who do not have a tribal identity, therefore their relationships with other Afghans are based on national identity. As Louis Dupree notes:

> In Afghanistan, besides the non-tribal Tajiks, there are many regions with mixed and partly detribalized populations as well as the urban centers with their immediate dependencies.[5]

Because of these unusual factors, the political system in Afghanistan took shape in a unique way. The tribes' chieftains, as the political leaders, came together traditionally when there was a national crisis, recruited their tribal forces, and led them in a united effort against the invaders. This traditional methodology allowed Afghan Khans or tribal chiefs to form the establishment of the modern Afghanistan state in 1747, by electing Ahmad Khan of the Abdali tribe through a *jirga*, or council.[6] The creation of the kingdom of Afghanistan was the direct result of the voluntary association of the tribal leaders who were legitimized by the support of the populace and religious leaders.[7]

THE POLITICAL ELEMENTS OF AFGHAN SOCIETY

NATIONALISM

The historical code of national politics that has formed national ideology in Afghanistan consists of nationalism, Islam, and modernization.

Nationalism brought the various ethno-tribal and religious communities together in a united effort against the direct external aggressions, but the need for such a united effort melted when the external threat disappeared. For example, in 1919 nationalism was at an all time high prior to the British defeat in Afghanistan and the subsequent independence of Afghanistan. After achieving independence nationalism plummeted when the political and ethnic factions began a bloody civil war. King Amanullah's regime collapsed, and he was forced to take refuge in Italy, where he eventually died.

Because Afghanistan always has been identified as a bridge for foreign powers to reach the wealth of India or the warm water of the Persian Gulf, this country has suffered through several invasions throughout the course of history. Struggles between the Afghan people and external forces make the national history of this land eventful. These struggles have created their own psychological, traditional, and sociopolitical elements within Afghanistan, which are an important part of Afghan cultural identification. The historical resistance to the external aggressors during the eighteenth, nineteenth, and twentieth centuries impacted the country and its people in all aspects. For example, Afghans held tightly to their cultural values and traditions; weapons became commonplace in almost all households. Afghans were very sensitive to foreign political influence as independence and individualism were very important values in their society. From this perspective, Afghans believed that their family, communal, and ethnic affairs were private matters and should not be displayed or advertised to outsiders. Nationalism has become an important part of their cultural identity.

Afghanistan has been the only country in the region to survive the political oppression of the colonial powers, secure its independence, and manage its internal affairs. From a sociopolitical point of view, life under colonial rule, in which all the decisions were made by the empirical government for the colony, is a lot different than living in a noncolonial society in which socially, culturally, and psychologically the people have greater freedom and independence to manage their daily lives. This is a very unique issue that has shaped significantly the sociocultural identity of the Afghan people. Since culture is a way of life for human society, the people of Afghanistan have been united by a cultural identity that makes them different from their neighbors and other Muslim communities around them. Therefore, nationalism presents the identity not only of the Afghan Muslims, who distinguish themselves from other Muslims and feel that they belong to the Afghan culture, but also of minority religious groups such as Afghan Jews, Hindus, and Sikhs.

ISLAM

When Islam became the dominant religion in Afghanistan, it inspired the need for national unity in a new way. In other words, Islam completed culturally the need for national unification of the numerous Afghan ethno-tribal populations. Now Afghan Muslims, who comprise the majority of the population in this country, will worship only one God. Therefore, one can argue that the national identification of Afghan Muslims is a combination of Islam and nationalism. Because, long before Islam, there were three dominant principles that formed the common foundation of Afghan society: honor, hospitality, and revenge. After Afghans chose Islam as their religion, these three principles stayed strongly functional within their Islamic religion. Hence, the cultural code of Afghanistan is a unique mix of Islam and nationalism. For example, in the political life of the nation, *jirga* is a historical tradition that was accepted long before Islam in Afghanistan.

After Islam was chosen as the religion, the issue of *jirga* fit into the principle of consultation in Islam. As stated in Suras 3 and 42 of the Holy Qur'an: "Those who harken to their Lord, and establish regular prayer; who conduct their affairs by mutual consultation; who spend out of what we bestow on them for sustenance."[8] This happened with the additional consideration that Islam combined the central code of *jirga* (which was based on ethno-tribal relationship) with the Islamic code of brotherhood. This melding decreased the ethnotribal confrontation and supported tribal and communal efforts in the creation of a nation-state, the federation under Ahmad Shah Abdaly. Islam has a deep role in the sociopolitical life of Afghanistan. In the internal affairs, Islam strengthened the principle of neighborhood with the notion of brotherhood. On the external front, the ideas of Jihad and Shahadah created a fearless belief of the protection of righteousness in one's life. (Jihad means holy struggle or endeavor against wrongness, and Shahadah means to be witness for the truth of such a struggle in which a Muslim will sacrifice one's belongings and one's self for the well being of one's human dignity.)

An important characteristic of Islam in Afghanistan is its philosophical impact on the Afghan local culture, which has enriched the traditional notion of individual freedom and communal autonomy. This impact goes back to the first century of Islamic history when the local communities in ancient Afghanistan resisted the Arab-Islamic armies for about a half-century. The resistance movement continued until the Afghan local communities decided willingly to adapt Islam as their religion. In this case, the Afghan local communities became Muslim by choice rather than by force. Local scholars and refugees fleeing the persecution of the Arab Khalifah were mostly responsible for the expansion of Islamic faith in Afghanistan.

In the second century of Islam, Muslims from Afghanistan and parts of Iran and Central Asia rose against the brutality of the Arab Muslim Khalifahs. The rise of Abu Muslim Khorasani, who incorporated the downfall of the Arab Amawiad dynasty in 754 A.D., brought the influence of the Afghani politicians to the Abbasid Islamic empire.[9] This influence allowed many intellectuals and scientists from Afghanistan and neighboring areas to contribute to the golden age of the Islamic empire during the Abbasid. Later, the 872 A.D. military campaign by Yaqub Laiss Saffari from Sistan, Afghanistan, which almost caused the downfall of the Abbasid dynasty, could have changed the ruling elite in the Islamic empire once again.[10]

Another important characteristic of Islam in Afghanistan is that the Islamic faith mostly was introduced by the local scholars, who were exemplary, knowledgeable individuals. For instance most Afghan Sunni Muslims follow Imam Abu Hanifah, who was originally from Afghanistan. Over time, these scholars became the most respected preachers who promoted tolerance and manhood. Names such as Mawlana Balkhi, Abdullah Ansari, Al Birooni, and so on are well known in Afghanistan as well as outside of the country. The teachings of these scholars enriched the understanding of peaceful life within the Islamic faith and later influenced *Sofi* and *Erphanic* ways of thinking. These ways of thinking, *tariqah*, were welcomed by the local communities in Afghanistan as well as in India, Iran, Central Asia, and Turkey. Historically, the impact of these teachings on society as well as on the ruling elite has been very significant. The establishment of the *Timuriad* Empire in Afghanistan, which formed one of the greatest civilizations in history, was the result of the contribution by the leading Afghani philosophers, scientists, artists, and political leaders such as Ali Shir Nawai.[11] The intellectual richness, particularly in northwestern Afghanistan, was so dominant that Mongol invaders and many other immigrants adapted the local civilized norms and culture and associated themselves with the local leading Afghani intellectuals.

Islamic faith, with its unique characteristics, has been an important element of social and cultural identity for the people of Afghanistan. This element of national identity has been obvious in the country while embracing non-Muslim Afghans such as Hindus, Sikhs, and Jews in the national social structure with great degrees of interaction and tolerance. These Islamic characteristics allowed secular political leaders to run the government with a high degree of understanding of the importance of faith in the life of its citizens. As a result the separation of mosque and state was an accepted practice in the country for many years. In contrast to other countries such as Turkey and Egypt, where Muslims form the majority of the population, the separation of mosque and state in Afghanistan has been the outcome of social and cultural development, rather than governmentally enforced measures. This social and cultural development makes Afghanistan different from its neighboring countries as well as the Middle East and North Africa.

MODERNIZATION

National independence and the development of a modern state are some of the most dominant principles in recent Afghanistan political history. Establishing a strong national military and social and political development was impossible without the use of modern techniques. The emergence of governmental bureaucracy, the urbanization of Afghanistan, the rise of the middle class, and the national desire for a more united Afghanistan with a centralized economy and political administration became very obvious during the twentieth century. Urbanization not only promoted modernization in a technical way, but it influenced the interests of urban politics in the governmental system of the country more than before. As a result, the structure of Afghan national politics was comprised of communal chieftains, religious leaders, the urban and rural middle class, and the commercial bourgeoisie.

Communal chieftains, or the important nonofficial elders, were community-based traditional leaders who, for the most part, did not submit to or comply with the interests of the government. They were concerned with the welfare of their own communities above all else. These nonofficial tribal and communal leaders who mostly did not hold any public office were the most important members of the Afghan national political system.

Because of highly ethnic and communal diversities and because of inefficient transportation and communications systems, the linkage between governmental centers (mostly located in the towns) and rural areas was very weak. Through the course of time, this geographical and ethnic situation created a social environment that was closed to outsiders. Many different ethnic groups lived together in the same territory, but each one had its own inside circle with different points of view and standards. Therefore, even while living in close proximity with other groups, each ethnic group was able to maintain their own identity, standards of conduct, and management styles.

Allegiance to one's ethnic group is very high; it is expected that members will support each other and honor fellow members. One's identity is established at birth; one is born into a community. According to Anthony Arnold and Rosanna Klass, "By being born into a particular local descent group an individual becomes a member of the ethnic group."[12] Since one particular ethnic group may have shared a territory such as a village or a valley with other ethnic groups, throughout time different ethnic groups (in some areas a religious group) may create bonds of kinship through marriage. As British anthropologist Hugh Beattie states: "Thus, at the village level kinship and ethnicity coincide."[13]

Geographically, there were many rural areas in the country that did not have a strong connection or interaction with urban centers. For example, in the north during the long winter it was very difficult to communicate with the outside world. The local mountainous roads were blocked by snow early in the season. Traditionally, the people who live in such areas have learned how to survive the harshness of the terrain and seasons. The local government's administrator's survival, and effectiveness as a facilitator of relations between the local communities and the central government, depended on his continued good relations with the people. Because of the self-sufficient nature of the rural communities, the government officers could interfere only if the people were agreed upon. Often the role of the central government in the daily affairs of the rural communities was marginal. Many villages not only produced their food without outside help but also managed their administrative affairs such as marriage, divorce, conflict over the land, and business. When there was an issue that the local leaders and citizens were not able to solve, it would then be time for government intervention.

In many cases the government was not able to conduct an inquiry without the help and cooperation of the local leaders. Usually, the government representatives, without the help from local leaders, were seen as outsiders.[14] For example, when there was a crime such as robbery or murder, the government representative, *woleswal* (the mayor or administrator for a group of villages) or *alaghah-dar* (a civil administrator), responsible for the administration of essential services (such as education, water distribution, and infrastructure repair) was called. Another important responsibility the *woleswal* carried out was implementing the draft system for men who turned 21. Dealing with the crime cases, the *woleswal* would send a soldier (unarmed) with a message or a statement to the local village leader. The local leader would cooperate with the police to arrest the suspect and escort him to the government location.[15] In some cases, the local community under the supervision of the local leaders would arrest the suspect and bring him to the *woleswali*, the government headquarters. In any situation such as a change in government policies or an emergency situation, the *woleswal* would contact the local leaders and these local leaders would keep the community informed through the local *jirga*.

Religious leaders were strongly attached to their local communities, and the majority of them belonged to the middle and lower social classes. Their support of political establishment was vital and their role in legitimizing the government was important. They never seized the government in Afghanistan, and traditionally they stayed out of politics. Local communities wanted to see religious leaders agree with the government's agenda. Through such a relationship the government could only operate effectively by receiving the seal of approval from the religious community. This relationship played a fundamental role in the national political system. Religion was strongly integrated in the daily life of the people.

After 1900, the urban middle class, relatively rural middle class, and the commercial bourgeoisie structured the most active political movements in Afghanistan. These political movements played the most significant role in the political events during the War of Independence in 1919 against the British and after. The agendas of the modern political parties were presented dominantly by the middle class, commercial bourgeoisie, and they had a great role in the decision-making body of governments.

Afghan government rulers always tried to balance their power between tribal chieftains, religious leaders, middle class, and national bourgeoisie by obtaining their support and agreement for the government policies. Such support occurred: mostly within the government through the participation of middle-class technocrats and the sons of tribal chieftains; or outside of the government through the satisfaction of the religious leaders and the cooperation of the community-based traditional leaders. For instance, in 1919 after Amanullah Khan became the king of Afghanistan, he maintained strong support from the Afghan educated middle class (the Constitutionalists and Nationalists) and eventually won the support and participation of the tribal chiefs, the community elders, and the religious leaders in the War of Independence against the British. In this war, the combination of Afghan political factions created such a strong movement that not only were the British defeated in the western frontiers, but an anti-British movement in India was also sparked.

When King Amanullah attempted to implement his radical-liberal social reform, he neglected the logic of such a power balance. King Amanullah and his urban educated colleagues tried to centralize the government authorities all over the country by establishing *Alaghadaris* in the rural area and supported them with the government forces. The objective of the central government was to impose the government decisions over the local community. This policy tried to abolish the traditional role of the tribal and communal chiefs and elders who had proved their outstanding positions during the War of Independence. Traditionally, these community leaders and tribal chieftains were always the intermediaries between the government and the members of the tribe or the community. As the Afghan historian Hassan Kakar states:

> This was the biggest blow ever directed against the institution of eldership and accounted for the major role played by the resentful elders in the subsequent dethronement of Amanullah.[16]

Regarding the role of religion in Afghanistan, King Amanullah enjoyed the support of the religious leaders on his decision to declare war on the British. The religious and community leaders had declared jihad on the British, and they personally participated in the war under the command of King Amanullah. King Amanullah introduced radical liberal reforms such as:

> Unveiling of women; the travel abroad of female students for higher education; the removal of the traditional right to betroth children; the dismissal of government officials who chose to have more than one wife; the changing of the weekly holiday from Friday to Thursday; the abolition of the prayer system (the system of following a religious leader) in the army; the suspension of allowances to the Ulema; the introduction of secular codes of laws along with the Sharia, which relegated the Sharia to a secondary place; and finally, the imposition of limitations on the almost unlimited discretion of the Qazi and Mufti (the Judge and prosecutor, respectively) in criminal matters . . . [17]

When he tried to enforce these policies he lost the necessary support and affirmation of his leadership from the religious community, thus leaving his administration impotent.

As a result of such political misbehavior, King Amanullah (with all his charisma and support) and his urban supporters could not stop the collapse of his regime. A wide range of rebellions flooded the capital, finally forcing King Amanullah to leave the country in 1929.[18]

Throughout the course of time, Afghan political ideology embodied elements of Islam, nationalism, and modernization, striving to achieve a coordinated and balanced structure. Government policies needed a strong tie to national ideology, which consists of Islam, nationalism, and modernization. The positive role of the national ideology would allow the political leadership to galvanize the government's political structure. However, the negative role could be very destructive to a political party or government. A sign of a successful political program is the one that secures the balance between these three political elements. In any extreme case, there has always been a great risk for the political parties as well as the governments. For instance, in 1919, when King Amanullah announced the independence of Afghanistan, the ideological collaboration of these three political elements created a massive physical force that mostly consisted of volunteers from all over the country against British military aggression. The religious leaders declared the movement a jihad against the British, and the soldiers were referred to as holy warriors. The nationalist sentiment for sovereignty brought many nationalists into a united effort against the British. The notion of establishing a modern Afghanistan brought many educated Afghans together for the cause of independence. The struggle for independence represented the Afghan national ideology, and Amanullah's acceptance and loyalty to this ideology allowed him to successfully lead the third Afghan-British war and secure Afghanistan's independence.

Later, when King Amanullah attempted to marginalize some of the political elements of Afghan society while initiating reforms, he lost control over the balance between the traditional political forces.[19] Because the king concentrated heavily on the modernization element without any proper consideration of the other Islam and nationalism, his government deteriorated quickly.

Indeed, modernization had been the most dominant theme of Afghan politics during the twentieth century. History has proved that modernization without social and political participation results in outcomes like those during Amanullah. Contrary to the demise of Amanullah's government was the fall of Habibullah Kalakani, known as Bacha-e-Saqhaw, who attacked Kabul and deposed Amanullah. Habibullah had formed a nonfunctional administration, which lasted only nine months. The main reason for his downfall was the neglect to balance elements of nationalism and modernization. Closing schools, calling back the Afghan students from abroad, and allowing religious leaders control over the national administration, led the country into a crisis over which Habibullah and his colleagues lost their heads.

The formation of a modern Afghan state under Ahmed Shah Abdali was the result of the ethnic and communal support, rather than an artificial establishment by the colonial powers. Modern initiatives have been the quest of the Afghan political forces during the twentieth century. If these initiatives take place in the spotlight of social, economic, and cultural requirements, local support as well as the participation of a variety of political forces would be encouraged within Afghan society.

In Afghanistan, the governmental leaders often have made repeated mistakes by neglecting the participation of the nongovernmental and private sectors while undertaking modern reforms. Government leaders have aimed to use public institutions as an enforcement mechanism by monopolizing the national resources for their unpopular social, political, economic, and cultural so-called modern agendas. They ignore nongovernment and private sectors of society who have the potential capacity and resources to incorporate modernization programs throughout the country. For instance, the formation of the mid-twentieth-century modern banking system was the successful achievement of the private sector in Afghanistan. Also, the efforts of leading private-sector individuals such as Abdul Majid Zabuli have helped Afghanistan to enter the international market economy.[20]

Thus, Afghan national ideology reflects the social, political, economic, and cultural reality of the people, and it must be taken into consideration by political leaders. Islam, nationalism, and the quest for modernization are the unifying foundation of many different ethnic, linguistic, and religious groups. Domination of one element over another threatens national unity and leads the nation into crisis.

CHAPTER TWO

The Theory of Mass Mobilization

MASS MOBILIZATION IS A METHOD THROUGH WHICH A CENTRALIZED political organization attempts to implement widespread changes in a society. The aim of this method is to create a state of progress and achievement in the social, economic, and political patterns of a nation. This can be characterized as political intervention in the process of the normal daily life of a society for the sake of a higher standard of living and nation building. The political incentive of mass mobilization is to create a massive force that speeds up the social development by changing the behavioral environment of people. These changes cause the social, economic, and political systems of a nation to take shape differently. Economic, social, and political mobilizations are three important factors that affect mass mobilization.

The economic target of mass mobilization is tapping the economic resources for the purpose of economic efficiency and decreasing the gap between rich and poor. The general strategy of economic mobilization can change the meaning of production, ownership, and property rights, generating a significant amount of change in a short period of time. The structure of this type of change is mostly collective and the sphere of its domain is very wide.

The social agenda of mass mobilization is to create a new social structure by modifying or breaking the theoretical borders between social classes and to decrease the gap between privileged and underprivileged by encouraging marginalized populations to rise up for social justice. During the process of social mobilization people are driven into a new social formation in which individuals are able to identify themselves within a social group rather than social class. Social status/standing is derived from the organization with which a person is affiliated. To achieve this, individuals must organize themselves into various groups or associations that represent their occupational skills and the way they interact with other social groups or social organizations. In this case, the importance of an individual depends on his or her role in the social organization, not on his wealth and ownership. For example, during the Chinese mass mobilization of the 1930s, the CCP (Chinese Communist Party) cadres were able to establish local administrations in many villages and towns. The heads of these local administrations were locally elected poor peasants, Red Army officers, and handicraft workers.

Compared to the pre-Communist era, in which the local landlord and the rich peasant enjoyed great influence over the local and regional administration, and the poor peasants and the handicraft workers had insignificant social status, under the CCP leadership, poor peasant leadership and Red Army cadres mostly came from peasant families, and they became influential members of the local administration while the local landlords were executed or lost their formal social status.

A more moderate example of mass mobilization would be the case in India under the leadership of Mahatma Gandhi. During this period, the majority of the population united against the British colonial control of India. The cause for independence created a significant solidarity among average persons in India. The social structure changed through continuous revelations from Gandhi's teachings. These teachings were able to break the social caste boundaries and decrease the gap between the marginalized people and the privileged ones and revolutionized the social status of untouchables cast by opening a door for their future prosperity on the social ladder of India. In this case, mass mobilization changed the way people behaved and opened to them a new social path.

The main objective of political mobilization is to challenge and change the meaning of authority by promoting political strategies that establish their own techniques and methodologies. These techniques are like sets of tools that have similar standards and designs but are used for different purposes. For instance, in China the political objective of mass mobilization was to create a track for the transition into socialism. Techniques to accomplish this task included stimulating the conscience of social class struggle, confiscating land, implementing land reforms, and establishing the Red Army. To implement the political objective of mass mobilization the CCP created mass organization to promote mass participation.[1] Mass mobilization cannot be achieved without mass organization and mass participation; they are absolutely essential elements. Through mass organization and mass participation in China, a country with a very high population rate, the government was able to move toward the creation of centralized leadership and a politically homogeneous society. In this effort, fueling the flames of social class conflict was the central target of this mass mobilization.

In India the main objective of mass mobilization was self-determination and independence. The philosophy of this objective was to foster the transition ability among the people to depose colonial rule and, at the same time, to build a just society with tolerance and social tranquility. The leadership was not attempting to stimulate the social class struggle among the people, but rather to modify the social differences by removing the traditional obstacles from the path of advancement and development of marginalized people. In this case, the leadership did not authorize the confiscation of private property; rather, they worked to establish social justice and self-rule by provoking the moral conscience of the people.

Mass mobilization in China under the leadership of the Chinese Communist Party and Mao Tse Tung and in India under the leadership of the Congress Party with the guidance of Mahatma Gandhi went through the same process but with two different strategies.[2] In China the formula of mass mobilization was as follows:

mass organization + mass participation = mass mobilization.

In this case, the movement started when the CCP was established as a political organization and grew with the establishment of the Red Army, the peasant crop, the working unions, the regional administration, the township, and the village local committee. Through this model, the creation of mass organization started before mass mobilization. In other words, mass organization was a mechanism that attempted to affiliate the people, as much as possible, with a variety of organizations to fulfill mass participation.

In India the formula was as follows:

mass participation + mass organization = mass mobilization.

In this case, people participated voluntarily against the colonial rule of India, and in the process of this voluntary participation they were able to form many different political organizations on the local and national levels. Thus, the leadership had to organize the people who were following Gandhi not only as a political leader, but also as a spiritual and holy man. Even though Gandhi was affiliated with the Congress Party, there were millions of people who were not affiliated with this party, in particular non-Hindus. However, many of these followers were later recruited by the Congress Party and other political organizations in a united front against the British colonials in India.

MASS MOBILIZATION IN AFGHANISTAN

Mass mobilization in Afghanistan had its own nature and organizational structure in which Afghan society was forced on a continuous path of fundamental changes. The massive changes started by a violent clash between the People's Democratic Party of Afghanistan (PDPA) regime and the masses. This front line crush between the people and the regime created a stormy dynamic force that not only drowned the mental and physical structures of different political parties, particularly the PDPA, but also twisted every single aspect of social and political life of the nation. The ideology behind this clash came from the conflict between those principles that were idealized by the PDPA leaders to revolutionize the social and economic order in the country and the Afghan national ideology, which was based on historical, social, and cultural principles that enabled different ethnic, linguistic, and religious groups to become a nation.

The armed struggle between the regime and its opponents overshadowed the social, economic, political, and cultural changes within society; violent interaction became one of the most distinguishing characteristics. In many cases, the massive mobilization was accompanied by severe destruction, displacement, and a great number of human losses.

The dynamic force of the conflict between the PDPA/Soviets and the general body of Afghan society played a significant role in the creation of massive changes in this country. Each side of the conflict had the ability to speed or impede the level of economic, social, political, and cultural changes. The most complex part of this process was the absence of a single centralized and organized leadership such as in China or India. For example, when one side of the conflict acted against their adversaries the response was an opposing reaction. This reaction was impulsive and instinctive in nature to survive; it was not a planned action. The aggressor responded, also without planning. Actions were constantly taken as a response, there was little time to create or initiate a strategic plan. In some circumstances the action of one side speeded up the changes in the other side, thus impeding the process of mobilization. Sometimes, the reaction of one side against the action of the other side created the same cause and effect.

There are differences between the Chinese and Indian cases when compared with the Afghan experience. In China, the central government led changes and mass mobilization was implemented under the central planning of CCP. During this period, the Chinese leadership knew where they were going and what they were doing. It was clear that mass mobilization plans were based on an ideology of Marxism/Leninism and that the strategy was to transform society from a pre-industrial structure into a socialist state, and from socialism to communism. The incentive for the massive participation was the auspice of mass mobilization for the working class.

In India, the British colonial government was an obstacle in the way of new changes for the country. So, mass mobilization acted as direct pressure on the colonial government to loosen up and subsequently give up government control. In this case, the Indian leadership under Mahatma Gandhi was aware of their tactics and strategies. The new ideological path of the leadership was nonviolent resistance until the collapse of colonialism. The masses were following the guidance of the leaders and accepted the nonviolent tactics as a proper tool to decolonize India. Therefore, the main aim was the transition of society from colonialism to independence and self-rule. The colonial government also was aware of such a strategy by the Indian leaders. That was the main reason that the colonial government attempted to maintain its rule in India with the use of military and police forces and by implementing some moderate reforms, although to no avail.

In Afghanistan at the beginning of the PDPA' s radical reforms, the leaders of the party and the government knew that they were implementing social, economic, and political reforms to transfer the Afghan society from pre-indus-trialism into socialism. But when the waves of mass revolt flooded the country, the PDPA and the governmental leadership lost control over the mobilization of society. In Afghanistan, mass revolt was the forefront of mass mobilization during which the PDPA government not only lost its direction but also lost many territories under its control to the opposition. The government was forced from an offensive position to a defensive position in military, economic, and political fronts.

Within the movement of the masses, there was no national or regional po-litical organization to lead the masses to a quick victory. In the primary phase of mass mobilization there was not an elite group to lead the masses in a profes-sional manner.[3] The professional leaders grew out of mass revolt and mass par-ticipation many years later. The mass revolt occurred in Afghanistan as a reaction to the PDPA government policies and use of force. The revolt started like a storm that flooded one village and then overran many towns and demol-ished the government's civil and military facilities in its path. After the forma-tion of local political armed groups, the political parties, such as Pakistani and Iranian-based Afghan Mujahideen groups, formed throughout Afghanistan. Even though these political organizations recruited thousands of people, the majority of these people did not believe in the political ideology of these parties.

The loyalty to the party was based on ethnic, linguistic, religious, and per-sonal characteristics of the leaders. For many local commanders, the political parties based in Pakistan or Iran were just the providers of tools and weapons for their fight. This became the main reason that many local and regional com-manders switched parties so often. In some cases, one local commander had the membership of several political parties at the same time and supplied his forces through different parties. In most cases many of these local commanders and party-affiliated individuals did not even know their parties' charters.

During the early months of the PDPA regime in 1979, mass revolt was in the process of shaping the local and national armed political organization. Mass revolt also caused mass fragmentation and severe internal conflicts within the PDPA leaders and their weak government. Many military officers and soldiers defected to the Mujahideen political armed groups and joined military opera-tion against the government. This severe political crisis exhausted the PDPA regime and caused the Soviets to invade and rescue their friendly regime from a total collapse.

The Soviet military invasion of Afghanistan extended the scope of mass re-volt in the areas controlled by the Soviet army and the pro-Moscow regime.

This extension stimulated a much larger number of Afghans to join the Mujahideen groups, and for the first time the Mujahideen regional armed political organizations were being formed inside Afghanistan. The Soviet invasion stimulated Afghan national ideology in the collision of Islam with the atheist political and military forces of the PDPA and the Soviets.

The Afghan resistance could be broken down into external and internal fronts. The external front was comprised of seven Pakistani-based political organizations (mostly Sunni Muslims) and eight Iranian-based political organizations (most of them Shia Muslim). In general, the Afghan external front attempted to lead the armed resistance inside Afghanistan, but was not successful because of conflict between the especial party interests and the general interests of the Afghan people. Like the PDPA, the external front attempted to avoid Afghan national ideology by breaking the traditional social and political structures of local communities to make them fit into the structure of their political party.[4] This attempt by the external front Mujahideen leaders impacted the resistance movement drastically.

The local communities were the main support system for the Afghan Mujahideen and provided them financial resources as well as food and fighters. Thus, the expectations of the local communities from the Mujahideen groups were to protect their historic, traditional, and communal interests from the intrusion of the central government and the PDPA. The members of these local armed groups were deeply loyal to their local commanders. Because they were members of the local communities, there was no rational reason as to why they would implement a policy to suppress their local interests for the benefit of a political party. So, when the political parties sent their loyal cadres, who were loyal to the especial interest of the party rather than those of the local communities, these cadres became the icon for an external interest. Often policies that were initiated by these party cadres were contrary to those of the local communities. And when they tried to implement these policies, they either caused more hardship to the locals, or the activities of these cadres turned into a secret network of conspiracy, terror, and propaganda against local leaders of the Afghan Mujahideen. Almost all of the Afghan political parties, Iranian- and Pakistani-based, were nuclear organizations, and many of their members were urban educated individuals. They did not have the social or educational skills to deal with the rural communities.

The external front desired to lead the local armed forces from outside the country while maintaining their political and organizational domain over the local communities. Many of these leaders never participated in a military operation against the Soviet army or in a military battle against the PDPA or the Soviet armed forces. From the point of view of the local resistance, particularly in a time of armed conflict, the leaders did not have enough charisma to encourage the local resistance fighters' sentiment in their favor. This was a weak spot that was used by the local resistance against the external political leaders.

In the military phase, because of the lack of transportation and poor communication, it was impossible for political leaders to oversee military operation externally. Most often, external leaders received information from news bulletins. They did not have the military, the organization, or the technology skills to command and control the military operations against the Soviet and PDPA armed forces from a distance. This situation created a gap between the external leaders and the field commanders over what type of leadership could answer the needs of local communities in the field.

The communal need for local leadership resulted in the emergence of outstanding local commanders and the creation of an internal front. Eventually these local commanders were able to mobilize their communities into significant armed political organizations on a regional basis. These local and regional armed political organizations established their own civil and judicial administrations, controlled the local commercial roads, and commanded their forces into battle. Under these administrations the daily problems of local life were solved, and in many parts of the country limited medical and educational facilities were provided. Even though these local armed political organizations were affiliated with the external front, they captured the attention of international aid sources and received financial, military, and food supplies directly, as well as through the political party.

Regional armed political organizations, such as the resistance groups under Ahmad Shah Massoud in the north, Ismail Khan in the southwest, and those under Mawlawi Haghani in the east, were able to contact each other and promote cooperation and joint participation in a larger military operation against the Soviet army and the force of the PDPA regime. This new mobilization caused a change in the balance of power in Afghanistan. The regional commanders ultimately were able to push their forces toward a more centralized formation. Ismail Khan conducted a conference in the town of Saghar, province of Ghor, in 1986 in which over 1,000 local commanders from all over the country participated. Its main purpose was to establish a centralized command system among local and regional commanders. Because the external front had failed to overcome the personal, ethnic, and linguistic conflicts among them and to form a coalition government, the internal front leadership attempted to solve the problem inside Afghanistan. This attempt resulted in the establishment of the Afghanistan Mujahideen National Council under the leadership of Maulwi Haqhani and Ahmed Shah Massoud in early 1992.

All the endeavors by the internal and external fronts could not unify the differences between the fronts of the Mujahideen groups. Moreover, there were many other issues, such as the priority of the leadership's personal and family interests over public interests that created a misunderstanding between the external leadership and the political armed body inside Afghanistan. Another factor that prevented a unified front among the Mujahideen was the Pakistani and Iranian influence that was followed willingly by some of the Afghan

Mujahideen external front leaders. Because of this lack of cohesive and dynamic cooperation among the Mujahideen leaders, the Mujahideen fronts never had an organized, centralized, and unified alternative to lead the resistance movement toward a resolution of the Afghanistan crises.

The Watan Party government under Najibullah deteriorated from inside. An organized collaboration of the Mujahideen under Commander Ahmed Shah Massoud and a segment of the regime, in particular forces loyal to General Dostam, led to its collapse in 1992. According to inside sources, at the time the Mujahideen external front leaders were busy with the formation of an interim government in Pakistan. Later the leaders of the external front were invited by Commander Massoud to come to Afghanistan and run the government. The external front, under the influence and encouragement of the Pakistani government, formed an interim government, which was officially recognized by the United Nations members as the Islamic State of Afghanistan (ISA).

Massive mobilization, which started right after the PDPA coup in 1978 and the Soviet invasion of Afghanistan in 1979 to 1988, has caused Afghan people to witness massive changes:

Prior to 1978, Afghan villages were inhabited by 80 percent of the total population, thus controlling the nation's economic base, of which its foundation was agriculture.[5] Therefore, the economic relationship between towns and villages was based on the urban dependence of the villages.

In a country such as Afghanistan, pressure directed at the cities from the rural areas is the most important military and political strategy of winning a war; because of the country's economic and social system and geographical features, the bulk of Mujahideen's economic resources (financial and food supply) came from local communities, in particular the rural areas.

Because of the agrarian nature of the Afghan economy, villages became very crucial in the economic life of the people. Agriculture was and is the primary source of economic activity, followed by animal husbandry. Prior to the PDPA coup, the value of Afghan currency was strongly related to the level of export commodities (largely agricultural products). The major economic activities in the urban centers concentrated on exports of agricultural products. Thus, the importance of the rural population as the main source for any political, social, and economic reforms was undeniable for all political organizations in Afghanistan.

From the PDPA perspective, massive mobilization was necessary to encourage radical progress in Afghan society. The masses lived in the villages; therefore, land reform was essential to breaking down the feudalistic system and pushing society toward fundamental mobilization. At the same time the PDPA announced numerous other revolutionary decrees to change the pattern of the traditional old system into a democratic system. Because of the politicized nature of these reforms, the reforms not only resulted in mass organization for the support of the PDPA regime, but fueled major disagreements amongst the masses. The stubbornness and brutality of the regime fueled the massive revolt against government. The clash between the masses and the PDPA regime shaped a political dichotomy that caused the PDPA to deteriorate internally and weaken externally. Anti-PDPA armed political organizations used this to motivate their membership internally and abroad.

The mass destruction of rural life by the Soviet military machine widened Afghan mass participation and mass organization. At the same time, Soviet strategy was to destroy the economic and social resources of Afghan resistance groups and secure the urban centers under their domination. By this strategy the area controlled by the Soviet army and the PDPA regime lost their internal economic support system. Massive Soviet aid changed the self-sufficient nature of economic life to extreme dependence on external aid. On the resistance side it was the same; massive international aid flowed to anti-Soviet armed political groups. As a result, the Afghan economy became vastly dependent on foreign aid.

The PDPA reforms attempted to identify the personal and social status of the population based on a class structure. Land redistribution was viewed as an effective tool for weakening the social status and domination of the landlords. The armed conflict between the government and the resistance provided many opportunities for fearless individuals who came from lower- or middle-class society to enter a new social status by achieving the rank of commander within the resistance groups or occupying a high position within the political party.

The massive destruction of rural life by the Soviet and PDPA armed forces caused millions of people to leave the country or become displaced by migrating into areas under the control of the Soviet and the PDPA regime. Five million external refugees and two million internal refugees changed the social structure of Afghanistan. Throughout this, the majority of higher social classes, in particular the landowners, were forced into much lower social positions, because they were not able to transfer their assets (land) abroad. Although a large percentage of PDPA members had a lower- or middle-class social background, they held important positions in the party and in the government.

One of the most interesting issues of the Afghan mass mobilization is the political parties' change of ideology. Before the PDPA coup in April 1978, the Marxist organizations were divided into three parts: the PDPA, with a Soviet orientation of Marxism/Leninism; the Labors Revolutionary Organization of Afghanistan, *Jamait-e-t Inghalabi Zahmatkeshan Afghanistan* (SAZA), under Dr. Faiz, with a Chinese orientation; and independent organizations such as Star (*Akhgar*), the People's Revolutionary Organization of Afghanistan, known as *Sazaman Inghalabi Mardom Afghanistan* (SAMA), under Abdul Majid Kalakani, and later under his brother Abdul Ghyom Dadfar (Kalakani). After the PDPA coup, SAMA was the most active leftist organization in many towns and cities in Afghanistan. This organization recruited many Afghan educated and government individuals. SAMA formed armed groups in the rural areas, in particular to the north of Kabul. But like other leftist organizations, SAMA found itself under the attack and pressure of the PDPA and the Islamic organization, especially by the Islamic Party under Gulbadin Hekmatyar and Islamic Unity of Burhanadin Rabbani. Another leftist group was the Oppressed Nation Movement (*Setam-e-Milli*) under Maulawi Ba'ess, a graduate of a religious school. This group was struggling for the rights of ethnic minorities against the so-called ethnic Pushton Tyranny. (It was the armed members of this group that held Adolph Dubs, the American ambassador of Afghanistan, hostage in 1978. They were all killed when the security forces stormed the building.)

There were other nationalist political groups such as Afghan Nation (*Afghan Mellat*) that believed in the establishment of a great Afghanistan and the reunification of Pushtonistan (northwest frontiers in Pakistan) and territories that were lost to the Soviets in the late nineteenth century. This group also believed in the supremacy of ethnic Pushtons. Yet none of these groups were recognized by Afghanistan's neighboring countries, particularly Pakistan and Iran. Therefore, they were not able to finance their operations or publicly use their political affiliations with their parties.

The Islamic organizations, both Sunnis and Shia, were divided into hard-liners and moderate organizations. The Iranian-based Victory Organization of Afghanistan (*Sazeman-e-Nassr-e-Afghanistan*) was the leading element among the Shia hard-liners, while the Pakistani-based Islamic Party under Hekmatyar was the leading element among the Sunni hard-liners. Both of these organizations claimed they were fighting for the establishment of a pure Islamic state in Afghanistan. The National Islamic Front of Afghanistan (*Mahaz-e-Meli-e-Afghanistan*) under Sayed Ahmed Gaillani and the Salvation Front of Afghanistan (*Jabha-e-Nejat-e-Mili-e-Afghanistan*) under Sibghetullah Mujadidi were the leading forces among the moderate parties. These two organizations supported the participation and leadership of the former monarch, Mohammed Zahir, who lived in exile in Rome. Among other Iranian-based Shiite organizations, the Islamic Movement of Afghanistan (*Harkat-e-Islami-e-Afghansitan*) under Mohammed Aassef Mohsseni was popular and more moderate. The Islamic Unity group under Burhanadin Rabbani moved between the hard-liner and moderate elements of the anti-PDPA Soviet and Islamic organizations.

Throughout their histories, the latter political organizations have changed their political ideology and organizational structure. The PDPA was forced to learn a very harsh lesson from its action and doctrines that resulted in the establishment of the Motherland Party (*Hezb-e-Watan*), and this party finally sunk into the sea of political mobilization in Afghanistan. The anti-PDPA and anti-Soviet leftist organizations such as SAMA were caught in a very confusing situation. They had to not only hide their organizational identities, but also their beliefs. As a result, many of the members and elements of these organizations melted into the mass mobilization stream, and their political ideology and organizational affiliations were wiped out. The hard-liners in these groups were caught in harsh situations, like pieces of wood sandwiched between sandpaper and scraped until they turn into powder. Currently, there is no evidence of any organized activities of these groups inside Afghanistan.

Among the Islamic groups, the hard-liners lost their political attitude and became more pragmatic. Many times they shifted alliances with moderate groups, and in some circumstances, even collaborated with ex-PDPA members. Many of the members and local commanders of these groups moved toward the middle of the political spectrum

Indeed, mobilization in Afghanistan sparked by revolt merged into mass participation. At this stage, armed political organizations were formed that attempted to recruit people in many different ways. The entire Afghan society, which was organized through ethnic, linguistic, religious, or political affiliations, became either for or against the PDPA regime and the Soviets. As a result of the conflict between the PDPA regime/Soviet forces and the Afghan Mujahideen, Afghanistan entered into massive political, social, economic, and cultural mobilization.

In Afghanistan, the ideological foundation of the PDPA and the Soviets was Marxism/Leninism, but the PDPA was never able to credibly or ably dominate Afghan society. In this case, the reforms and decrees that the PDPA launched during the first two years of government control were not successful; because of this the party deteriorated significantly. Although the PDPA interpretation of Marxism/Leninism was mixed with the local attitude of the PDPA leaders, this attitude also included characteristics of the nationalist and ethnic behavior of the leaders. For example, hostile relations between the *Parcham* and *Khalgh* leaders were rooted in the ethnic competition of each faction. Additionally, the conflict between Hafizullah Amin and Noor Mohammed Taraki was not based on their interpretation of Marxism/Leninism, but on their personal and sub-ethnic struggles over authority and control.

One may argue that Hafizullah Amin's resistance against the Soviet forces can be interpreted as a nationalist sentiment against the Soviet invasion of Afghanistan. This sentiment is also seen in Uzbek and Tajik members of *Parcham* who revolted against Dr. Najibullah's Pushton faction and collaborated with Mujahideen's internal front to tackle the Kabul regime. In many of these internal conflicts the factional, ethnic, linguistic, and personal interests were dominant over the ideological differences. In some situations, there was not a high degree of ideological differences between the hostile factions, but the nondemocratic and violent competition and rivalry were parts of their organizational structure. This rivalry became so extreme that circles of the same factions opened fire on one another and in some cases a group might join the Mujahideen group against other governmental factions. For example, the hard-liners of the *Khalghi* faction headed by General Shahnwaz Tanai attempted a joint, but failed, military coup with the Islamic Party under Gulbadin Hekmatyar in 1991.

On the opposite side, the Afghan Mujahideen created their own organization and expanded the scope of their activity rapidly and vastly. Despite this, and even though they were bound to their culture and controlled more than 60 percent of the country, they were never able to dominate Afghan society and implement their massive political, social, and economic agendas. Ideologically, all the Afghan Mujahideen proclaimed Islam as the foundation of their thoughts, but they had different interpretations of Islamic thoughts ranging from extreme to moderate. The general political ideology of the resistance movement against the PDPA and the Soviets in Afghanistan was a combination of Islam, nationalism, and the traditional values that people practiced in their daily lives.

The Islamic doctrines of *jihad* and *shahadah* were significant in changing the Afghan resistance groups into fearless fighters. Jihad gave them a moral duty to protect and defend their home and family. Shahadah prepared them to expect death and fulfill the duty of jihad. In this case, shahadah was a matter of graduation from the moral duty of jihad to be witness to the judgment day as a person who sacrificed himself for the sake of safety and peace within his brotherhood. Another moral principle was *Ghazi* (victor), which is rooted in Afghan traditional culture rather than Islamic doctrines. Being a *Ghazi* provided resistance groups, especially the commanders, high moral superiority in political and military leadership. To be a *Ghazi*, one has to be talented and able to plan, control, and lead the struggle by using the proper tools to win. A *Ghazi* believes in victory, not in death. When he dies, his death will glorify the victory. Therefore, a *Ghazi* will die fearlessly only after he takes down several of his enemies. A *Ghazi* develops a charismatic character among his community, which recognizes him as a devoted individual who puts his life in the line of fire to protect his community. In many situations, when the Mujahideen groups came back from their combat operations, the local people cheered them as heroes and *Ghazian*.[6] These three popular moral principles, rooted in the foundation of the Afghan Mujahideen belief system, enabled them to overcome adversities such as food and ammunition shortages and, most importantly, attack the Soviet army and its specialized units. The Afghan Mujahideen were not only able to crack down the military morale and machinery supremacy of the Soviet Red Army in Afghanistan, they were able to force them to withdraw from this country.

The question of leadership in this mass mobilization is an intriguing one. Throughout the continuous conflicts and clashes between the PDPA/Soviet and Mujahideen groups each side attempted to expand its domain as far as possible. Yet these attempts were not successful until the collapse of the Kabul regime under Najibullah in 1992.[7]

To describe the leadership and its role in mass mobilization in Afghanistan, one must concentrate on the interactions between the PDPA/Soviet and Mujahideen groups. These clashes became the source of a dynamic energy that filled the empty place of a national leadership, and the nature of this energy has remained the same during and after the Soviet invasion. Each side of the conflict desired to establish, maintain, and expand its authority within the Afghan community at the national level. The scope of this dynamic force was very flexible and adapted to changes in the military and political power balances. This dynamic force played the role of leadership leading society into different military and political stages. The impact of this force on the communal structure of Afghanistan was dependent on the numbers and levels of clashes between the warring parties. This impact could be destructive or constructive for the general population and created a base for subsequent events and changes in the future. In this case past events served as plans for future development and gave birth to many new changes in the sociopolitical and economic lives of the people. Thus, this dynamic force is the core point and the center of the conflict that massive social, political, and economic forces have mobilized around.

In the course of civil war, the structure of mass mobilization remained as dominant as it was during the Soviet invasion. Yet since the collapse of Najibullah's regime and the establishment of the Islamic State of Afghanistan, the structure of mobilization has changed temporarily. But the escalation of war between the forces led by Hekmatyar and by Rabbani/Massoud had forced the social and political mobilization back into its previous format. Once again, two rival and hostile powers divided Afghanistan, and their violent competition left the role of leadership vague.

In 1994, the emergence of the Taliban in Qandahar created a new leadership dynamic and softened the sharp edges of the structure for mass mobilization. The Taliban movement, under the leadership of the Mullah Omar Mujahid, reduced the gap between the masses and the political leadership in Afghanistan, which has existed since the early seventies. Mullah Omar's popularity as a Mujahideen commander and as a religious teacher gave him a significant ability to communicate with the local and tribal communities in southern Qandahar. This was the reason that many local communities, which were tired of years of violence and war, embraced the Taliban call for security and order.

After the Taliban movement captured Kabul in September 1996 and set up their ruling establishment as the only and true leadership of the country, the political gap between the movement and masses became wider. The Taliban introduction of decrees, which were rooted in the Taliban political ideology, conflicted with what they had promised in Qandahar. The introduction of religious police and their rigid military campaign against their opponents and use of non-Afghan forces were similar to PDPA doctrinal and political behaviors. As a result, many of the Taliban leaders, in particular their supreme leader Mullah Mohammed Omar, lost their connections with the mainstream forces that supported them. This development forced the Taliban to rely even more on the external support of non-Afghan fighters.

The rise of the Taliban and their military advance over 80 percent of the country destroyed the social and political bases of the many local, regional, and national political parties. Well-organized and well-funded parties such as *Hezb-e-Islami Hekmatyar* were crushed totally in Afghanistan and are now only active outside of the country. *Jamaiat-e-Islami* (JIA), led by Burhanadin Rabbani, was another political party that had dominated many Mujahideen controlled areas in Afghanistan, but has since lost its organizational structure. Ahmed Shah Massoud emerged as the most powerful leader and was able to rally forces around him to challenge the Islamic Emirate. Massoud's group is different not only structurally but also ideologically and politically. The JIA Maktabis have stayed mostly in Iran, although some have migrated to other countries. A segment of these Maktabis are active within the remaining official activities of the Islamic State of Burhanadin Rabbani in different countries.

As a result of such developments, the following formula illustrates the process of mass mobilization in Afghanistan:

mass revolt + mass participation + mass organization = mass mobilization.

VIOLENCE: A SOURCE FOR AUTHORITY

The use of violence by political organizations in Afghanistan affected all aspects of mass mobilization. The violent interactions created a hostile, rigid, and intolerable environment that fostered a culture of war.

From the early stages, when the PDPA launched its campaign to bring revolutionary changes in the social, economic, political, and cultural aspects of society, any anti-reform action counted as a reactionary sentiment against the Saur Revolution (military coup of April 1978). According to Article 27 of *The Basic Rights and Duties of Citizens* of the government revolutionary decrees, "no one may use democratic rights and freedom to the detriment of the Democratic Republic of Afghanistan (DRA) or the rights of other citizens."[8] In such a sociopolitical environment where the Revolutionary Council of the DRA is the highest body of state authority, and the PDPA is the vanguard of the working people, the party and the revolutionary council become the organs that make decisions for all the citizens. Once a decision is made, it is the obligation and the duty of the citizens to follow the order, and there is no higher body able to change that decision.

The DRA, under the Revolutionary Council and the vanguard doctrine of the PDPA, had authority to use violent forces, to expand and maintain its authority, and to hold the monopoly on those violent forces. The PDPA and DRA were self-appointed as the sovereign and nobles of society who had the right to rule and enforce order. In the words of Thomas Hobbes, "the sovereign's actions cannot be justly accused by the subject." But the critical issue with the DRA's authority in Afghanistan was the source of its legitimacy, which was not detailed in the constitution, or validated by a popular election, or understood through a mutual agreement between the "commonwealth and the sovereign."[9] This legitimacy came from the Marxism/Leninism-based ideolog-

ical belief of the leaders. Through this system the PDPA party managed its political relationship, which in some way involved "authority, ruling, or power."[10]

In the Saur Revolution, the PDPA took over political power through violent armed actions against the central government under President Mohammed Dauod. The level of armed forces involved greatly outweighed
nonmilitary participation; this was the reason that general information about
the leadership of the coup was not clear. The April coup was guided by two
military officers, Major Aslam Watanjar and Chief of Staff, Lieutenant Colonel
Abdul Qader. Obviously this was a nondemocratic approach to establishing authority and rule in the country.

The PDPA not only used violent action as a method to establish its authority in Afghanistan, but also attempted to use violent forces to introduce radical
reforms. The use of violence by the DRA government under the leadership of
the PDPA took place internally as well as externally.

Violence was used internally during the factional and sub-factional fighting over the control for political power and leadership within the PDPA party.
The inner violent struggle between the two PDPA factions, *Khalq* and *Parcham*, was constant and rooted in political, personal, linguistic, and ethnic differences. The violent campaign was started by these two factions of the PDPA
just after a few months of attaining government power. During the first wave of
the campaign the *Khalq* faction, under Noor Mohammed Taraki and Hafizullah
Amin, removed the *Parcham* members from key positions in the government.
The second wave of violence started with the *Khalq* victory over the *Parcham*.[11]
It was this bloody sub-faction fighting between Hafizullah Amin's circle and
another group under Noor Mohammed Taraki that resulted in the death of
Taraki and the rise of Amin as the secretary of the party and the head of DRA.

Violence was also used externally. On the eve of the PDPA coup and the
establishment of the DRA regime, the tolerance level with regard to non-
PDPA political organizations was almost nonexistent. Mass and secret arrests
of popular individuals and members of political parties who were not in agreement with the agenda of the PDPA were rampant. This violent campaign
against political opponents intensified after the mass revolt in the Herat
province and other parts of the country. For the safety of PDPA members,
many were armed or were protected by armed guards. Public appearances in
places such as schools and government offices, in particular in the provinces,
became popular and routine by the PDPA members.

After the Soviet invasion of Afghanistan, the violent campaign dominated
all Afghan lives. Under the new military strategy that practically stated "join
the DRA or be destroyed," alternatives for the opposition parties were nonexistent. Under joint policy that was officially called the Paternal National Front
and the National Peace, the general Afghan population had to locate physically
within the security zone marked by the DRA/Soviets or be destroyed by the
armed forces. Some took refuge in neighboring countries.

The Afghan Mujahideen also utilized violence. Internally, violent relations among the Mujahideen groups occurred over the control of leadership and military power inside Afghanistan. Hit operations, military ambushes, bombings, secret kidnappings, and terrorism became a routine part of some Mujahideen groups. Many famous Mujahideen commanders were assassinated by rival groups either inside Afghanistan or during their trips to Pakistan. Numerous famous Afghan politicians and intellectuals were gunned down while working in the refugee camps or while participating in nonmilitary activities in Pakistan.[12] This violent campaign was rooted outside Afghanistan among the external front leaders, yet became very flammable inside the country and involved many internal front commanders. The most extreme of all these hostile relationships was between *Hezb-e-Islami* under Gulbedin Hekmatyar, *Jamaiat Islami* under Burhanadin Rabbani, and *Herkat Islami* under Maulwi Mohammed Nabi Mohammedi's Pakistani-based groups. In one mass execution, the *Hezb-e-Islami Hekmatyar's* commander Sayed Jellal killed 30 high-ranking Mujahideen members from *Jamaiat Islami*, who were loyal to Ahmed Shah Massoud, in Oruzgan province. Among the Iranian-based Mujahideen groups, the fighting between the Nassr Organization and the *Shaurai Inqalabi Itefaq-e-Islami* killed hundreds of Mujahideen in the central provinces. Externally, violent interactions dominated the political relations between the PDPA and the Mujahideen groups. Within this political relationship, violence became "symbolically illuminated within a frame of extra-institutional protest" in which each side attempted to eliminate each other in all aspects.

There is a major difference between the violence directed by the DRA and the Soviets and the violence conducted by the Mujahideen groups during the Soviet invasion of Afghanistan. What distinguishes one from the other is the source of violent action and the question of legitimacy. From a fragmented point of view it is difficult to argue that there is a legitimate foundation for the violent behavior of each individual political party, both against the PDPA and against the rival groups. But, when we generalize the argument, we will see that the use of violence by the Mujahideen groups against the DRA and the Soviet army in Afghanistan was the people's response to the aggression of the DRA government. In other words, the DRA's campaign of violence produced violence as the only possible response from the people. For example, the mass revolt ignited when the DRA and PDPA leaders violated the system of life of the people without their consent; mass revolts such as in Herat occurred without any organized plan and political leadership. It was a protest against the DRA government's violation of people's traditional, communal, political, and economic rights. Therefore, there was consensus by the general population for the revolt against the state, which was deeply rooted in the people's will and citizens' rights.

As a result of such a development in Afghanistan, violent interaction between the political armed organizations and the professional armies, such as the Soviet forces and the DRA's military machinery, became one of the most important characteristics of mass mobilization in Afghanistan. Violent interaction between the government and Mujahideen groups left more than one million dead and severe destruction throughout Afghanistan. The use of violence by all parties created a warrior culture that nurtured the dynamic force to mobilize society in a very rapid and swift way. This rapid mobilization changed the traditional formation of people and mobilized society into different social, economic, and political structures.

CHAPTER THREE

TRADITIONAL POLITICAL SYSTEM

FOR CENTURIES THE SIGNIFICANT CODE OF POLITICS IN AFGHANISTAN was the principle of *jirga* (tribal or communal council) through which the members of a particular community or tribe could solve their problems. *Jirga* usually was conducted on a regular basis after the Friday prayers in towns and villages. On the national level, a *jirga* was called when there was an emergency situation or when the central government needed to make a crucial decision such as whether to enter into a war or with regard to the formation of the constitution. The national jirga, which was called the *Loya Jirga* (national assembly or great council), was comprised of local, regional, and national figures such as tribal chiefs and popular local and national individuals.

Generally, the essence of the *Loya Jirga* and its importance for the nation was stated in the former constitution, but there were no regular meetings nor specific durations between the meetings. Since the establishment of the Afghan modern state in 1747, the *Loya Jirga* has been recognized by all ethnic, linguistic, and religious groups in the country. In the course of history, the level of democratic participation of all ethnic and religious groups has many ups and downs. The *Loya Jirga*'s credibility as a traditional democratic national institution diminished in its effectiveness as the sociopolitical formation of the country decreased. This decrease was rooted in two nondemocratic developments: the domination of and monopoly over the decision of the *Loya Jirga*, mostly by the ethnic Pushton, the largest ethnic group in Afghanistan; and the domination of the central government over the process of the *Loya Jirga*.

The central government's intervention attempted to decrease the essence of traditional democracy in the formation of the *Loya Jirga*. In this case, the central government sent to the *Loya Jirga* those individuals and chieftains who were loyal to the ruling elite, thereby legitimizing its rule and domination of the *Loya Jirga*. Through this process, the *Loya Jirga* not only became an artificial organ of Afghan society, it also lost its democratic spirit as the united solidarity movement for the nation.

The foundation of the *Loya Jirga* was the local and communal *jirgas* in which people were discussing the important issues before sending their representative to the *Loya Jirga*. Usually, these representatives were aware of the hardships and communal interests.

When a representative or an ethnic or communal leader signed an article, it was like signing a contract between the local community and the rest of the country. In the case of war the local community would not only send their young men, they also provided food and supplies. The foundation of the local *jirga* was the local families. People discussed local issues within their families and then shaped their ideas behind the arguments in the local *jirga*. Family has a fundamental impact on the creation of *jirga* and family code is very strong within the community. Arnold Anthony and Rosanna Klass state:

> All males in the community participate in formal decision-making through a form of open meeting known as a jirga. Although only men actually participate and vote in a jirga, they do so only after consultations within their families, where women exercise an influence that is powerful even though it may not be publicly visible.[1]

The family code has been characterized as a cohesive unit that rejects external interference; this has inspired the external relations of the tribe or community. Cultural and political autonomy has had a sharp structure that was energized, historically, by individual independence within the tribe or community. Because of the strong familial ties between members, they felt responsible toward each other and enjoyed significant support. Community autonomy and communal freedom had a strong root in family autonomy. In many social and political areas of life, the nature of autonomy had a similar characteristic—the communal and tribal affairs were no one's business. At the tribal and community levels, all members enjoyed a type of collective right and security in contrast to other tribes. Such a sociopolitical environment provided a large amount of communal self-sufficiency that subsequently increased healthy relationships with other tribes and ethnic groups. Thus, tribal and communal interrelationships have not only articulated the economic, social, and cultural dimension of the tribesmen or the community members, but have also formed the political identity of the members. In other words, the tribe is not defined only as an economic, social, and cultural unit, it is also a political organization.

It is worthwhile to emphasize that this form of social and political structure has been very appropriate to the geographical nature of mountainous Afghanistan. If there was a problem within a family, that family would try to solve it first by family debate and consultation; only when the problem became more serious would they bring it to the local *jirga*. The *jirga* members were elected by the elders, popular individuals, religious leaders, and tribal chiefs. The chief of a tribe was the head of the *jirga*, usually a wise individual who earned the trust and the honor of the community. The most important social codes that shaped the moral values of the Afghan tribal community were three principles: honor, revenge, and hospitality. These principles have played a significant role in the internal life, as well as in the external affairs, of the tribes and communities.[2] Internally these principles increased communal hospitality and responsibility among the members of the community and involved them in a process of one for all and all for one. The membership rights of the community were respected fully by other members, and individual security of the members was protected.

Externally, these three principles had a great effect on intertribal and communal relations. If a tribe or community acted negatively toward another, under the principle of revenge, this action would be negatively reacted to. Because of the principle of revenge, there have been many hostile confrontations between Afghan families and tribes. However, in a situation of internal self-sufficiency the experience of workable mechanism, honor, revenge, and hospitality have been much more constructive than destructive in relationships between the Afghanistan tribes and communities. Each tribe has specific cultural and political rights that are respected by other tribes. The *Loya Jirga* has brought tribes closer and this fostered economic exchange, cultural tolerance, intermarriage, and political cooperation.

MODERN POLITICAL PARTIES IN AFGHANISTAN

The second decade of the twentieth century gave birth to many stormy political changes in Asia, including the collapse of the Ottoman Empire and the establishment of modern Turkey, the downfall of the Tsar's empire and the creation of the Soviet regime in 1917, and the British military defeat by the Afghans in 1919. All of these events occurred at a time when the Afghan nationalist movement was becoming very active against the British. The Afghan modern political parties appeared when the urbanization of Afghanistan developed and the rise of the urban middle class in the cities created a new way of political participation. Thus, cities became the main battlefield of modern political activists.

The first modern political organization, *halqa-ejawanan-e-Afghan* (young Afghans), was comprised of two societies, one led by Abdur Rahman Lodi and Mir Ghulam Mohammed Ghobar and the other led by Mir Sayyed Qassim Laghmani and Abdul Hadi Dawi. The political agenda of these two societies was based on the struggle for constitutionalism and nationalism, which was seen as modernization and independence of Afghanistan. Under King Amanullah's rule a new free political environment emerged, and many members of the young Afghan movement who were jailed after the assassination of Amir Habibullah (the last king before Afghan independence) were released.[3]

With new political change in government policy, after the promulgation of the constitution by King Amanullah (1919–1929) and King Nadir in 1931, the young Afghans were split into different factions. Radicalism became popular among some parts of these organizations, and as a result the government dismantled them. This government action resulted in the assassination of King Nadir in 1933.

THE PEOPLE'S DEMOCRATIC PARTY OF AFGHANISTAN (PDPA), ON THE PATH OF POWER

In 1955 a new liberal law was passed that promised free speech and free press for political parties. Several independent journals were published, each representing a political trend, and several of them were radical, including *Wish-e-Zalmayan* (Awakened Youth), a nationalist political party. Later, some of the Awakened Youth's leaders such as Noor Mohammed Taraki, a former member of the Indian Communist Party (ICP), and Babrak Karmal, an urban educated young man from Kabul, founded the People's Democratic Party of Afghanistan (PDPA) as a communist party.[4]

On January 1, 1965, the first secret assembly of PDPA with 27 founding fathers and one founding mother (Anahita) met in Noor Mohammed Taraki's house. The PDPA published their goals, portraying them as a struggle for the establishment of the national democratic regime in Afghanistan, and drafted a secret constitution that adopted Marxist/Leninist ideology as their official policy.[5] However, they did not go public with their policies and positions. The PDPA party received Soviet Union support from the day it was established and in return the PDPA adopted the ideological standards (anti-imperialism, the concept of the socialist bloc against the capitalists, and the support of anti-imperialist movements in third world countries) of the Soviet global vision.[6] Even though the PDPA membership was comprised of mostly educated, urban-based individuals who had in one way or another a familial and ethnic connection to the rural population, they were divided along the ethnic and linguistic lines of Afghan society.

As a result, the PDPA split into two factions: the *Parcham*, whose members mostly reflected the ethnic Tajiks and other minorities in the major urban areas; and the *Khalgh*, whose members came mostly from the Pushton ethnic group. Both of these factions believed in Marxism/Leninism and the Soviet global vision, but their public approaches toward democratic revolution and socialism in Afghanistan were different. The *Parcham* pursued a temporary collaboration with non-Marxists over the issue of power. Meanwhile, the *Khalqh* demanded pure revolutionary socialism and rejected collaboration with non-Marxists.[7]

From the beginning, the development and growth of the PDPA was geared toward two rigidly divided factions that ultimately caused the party to deteriorate. The conflict between the social and cultural norms and values of Afghan society and the basic ideological doctrines was the main reason for such deterioration. This ideological confrontation created a situation that caused the PDPA to operate from two antagonistic positions.

The party included communists with strong beliefs in Marxism/Leninism and a sense of loyalty to the Soviet Union as the father of socialism against imperialism. As article one of the PDPA 1965 secret constitution stated:

> The PDPA is the highest political organization and the vanguard of the working class and all laborers in Afghanistan. The PDPA, whose ideology is the practical experience of Marxism/Leninism, is founded on the voluntary union of the progressive and informed people of Afghanistan: the workers, peasants, artisans, and intellectuals of the country.[8]

But among the people, the PDPA betrayed their internal ideological positions, trying to convince people of their noncommunist and anti-imperialist identification and their struggle for a modern democratic political system in Afghanistan. As a result, PDPA had two identities at the same time: internally, a pro-Soviet communist identity that was secret from the public and masses; externally, a non-Communist and anti-Soviet identity that was their public face.

Socially, the PDPA leadership recruited their party members from the urban middle class who had traditional rural backgrounds. Particularly the *Khalqis* came from the lower social classes and remote areas of the country. Most of these members already knew what it meant to be poor or to be deprived from social and economic privileges. For these party members, living in a poor economic condition was the main reason to enter the party. Through the party literature and Marxist and Leninist ideology, the members dreamt about the glories of equality and social justice in an egalitarian way. This ideological fantasy built a theoretical illusion whereby the members, who struggled each day to survive, were not able to see the reality of the highly diverse and complex social fabric in Afghanistan. Yet Marxism/Leninism allowed the PDPA to see the social and cultural failings of Afghanistan that resulted from the poorly run feudalistic economic system. Therefore, revolution seemed the only way to change this backward and feudalistic system, raising the critical question: What kind of revolution would benefit the country and under whose leadership?

There were not significant numbers of workers (proletariat) to lead the society against the current establishment. According to the Lenin doctrine, in such a situation the middle class who accepted and believed in Marxism and Leninism should lead the urban and rural proletariat toward a revolution. Therefore, there was a need for a vanguard party to revolutionize the society under the direction of Marxist/Leninist philosophies and to control the state. After taking control of the government, the party's duty would be to lead society through a transition period into socialism and a communist form of government.

As a result of such a dialectic analysis of Leninism, one can see that government power is a necessary tool to change societies such as Afghanistan. To achieve these changes, communist party members worked within key government areas such as military, secret service, and police. This approach evolved into a tactical target for the pro-Soviet party. In many cases, this type of work and activity was conducted from within the government against the ruling group or class.

Despite the PDPA charter, the ability to lead Afghan society from a backward pre-industrial society through a transition period was the strategic target for the party, with the ultimate goal being a socialist state. According to Lenin's interpretation, human society entered a new age, the age of imperialism. In this age, the world was divided into two blocks: socialism under the leadership of the proletariat, and imperialism under the leadership of the bourgeoisie. Thus, the proletariats throughout the world are related to each other according to their social class interests, and at the same time all of the world's bourgeoisie are related despite their social class. These two groups are natural enemies, and the antagonism between them can be solved only through a social revolution. Through this interpretation, Lenin believed that a revolution can only be achieved under the leadership of the working class. In pre-industrial societies where there is not an active working class armed with the ideology of Marxism/Leninism, the vanguard party with such an ideology needs to lead society toward socialism.

Since Afghanistan's working class was only a small segment of the total population, they were also a small segment among the political organized forces of society. Moreover, they were much more under the influence of Afghan culture, tradition, ethnicity, and languages than Marxism/Leninism. Thus resulted the establishment of a vanguard party.

According to the PDPA's Marxist/Leninist orientation, for a society such as Afghanistan to complete the cycle of transition toward socialism, this society must pass through a democratic revolution. A democratic revolution is a tactical target by which the society, under the worker or vanguard party, enters onto the transitional period. This revolution tactically and violently disarms the bourgeoisie or ruling class, and the revolutionary party maximizes its power by controlling the state machinery. After the democratic revolution, the aim is to mobilize society massively. In other words, the aim of the prerevolution period is to maximize the power of the party by seizing the government's civil and armed forces. The aim of the postrevolution period is to mobilize the society toward socialism and communism.

A crucial tactical target for the PDPA was maximizing power, but what kind of political agenda would allow the party to seize political power or the government? Their agenda for the public provided them with the ability to increase their influence within society, but their agenda for the party acted against that influence. In any democratic party system in the world, the mechanism for maximizing power is the party's ability to address people's economic, social, and cultural interests within a timetable. In other words, a democratic party tries to line up its structure with the cultural ideology of society by representing the physical and ideological needs of the people. The political party becomes a part of society, but in an organized and collective way. When a party introduces bills to the public to decrease the economic, social, and political hardships, this is when a political party with a sharp and convincing view should be able to gain popular support and maximize its political power.

According to the above principles, maximizing power results in recruiting more and more party members and increasing the scope of its partisanship to deliver the party's message to the public. The physical structure of the party needs to be strong enough to gain the support of the masses and achieve their objectives. The masses are not marginal during the decision-making process because, by increasing the public support and the membership, there is a power-sharing mechanism. The relationship between the party and the people is not like the relationship between the ruler with his subjects or center and periphery. People are the main source of power, and without their support the political party cannot democratically maximize its power.

In a situation such as Afghanistan, maximization of power has the exact definition as above. A political party must line up with the economic, social, and cultural conditions of society, which is possible only through the voluntary participation of the people. The existing political party must represent the interests of three political elements: the tribal chiefs and the community leaders; the religious community; and the middle-class political activists or the associated government technocrats.

But the PDPA influence was conditioned by its leaders' ideological beliefs. It was easy to convince a person to join their efforts to change the deprived social, economic, and political conditions, but it was very difficult to persuade a person to reject his religious and cultural beliefs. In the long run, the PDPA could have had more influence over the social and political issues, but because of its ideological condition, new members were hard to attract. The PDPA did not have the support of the religious communities and was theoretically against the tribal chieftains and the communal leaders because of their feudalistic and bourgeoisie economic, social, and cultural positions. In the urban areas among the middle class, PDPA claimed to be the highest political organ and the vanguard of the working class and all laborers in Afghanistan who would transform a society from feudalism to socialism through a national democratic revolution. Logically and practically, the PDPA could not make any alignments with other urban political parties, even if they had similar agendas. The only alignment that could occur with another political organization would come if that political party accepted the PDPA leadership.

In the course of time, PDPA had three options: The PDPA had to act as a nuclear intellectual group with a publicly known Marxist/Leninist identification and with restricted activities only among the educated Afghan middle class. In this case, the main political activities would be theoretical research and argument within the party or through other Afghan leftists' publications. In order to become a political organization that could fit into the mental and physical body of Afghanistan, the PDPA needed to dissolve their Marxist/Leninist ideological agendas.[9] In this case, PDPA could represent the political elements of Afghan society in a democratic way and move toward gaining the support of the majority of the people. Therefore, the party's ideological norms and organizational structure would line up with the external activities or public influence. Then, the PDPA might have the capacity of maximizing power within the society by increasing membership and public support. As I noted in chapter one, prior to the PDPA coup in 1978, 85 percent of the Afghan population lived in the villages; the village population provided the main support for maximizing political power. As Anthony Arnold and Rosanna Klass write:

> For Afghans, the significant politics are those of the village, tribal or communal level, in which an ancient tradition of rough-hewn, town-meeting type democracy prevails. All males in the community participate in formal decision-making through a form of open meeting known as a jirga.[10]

In 1968, three years after the establishment of PDPA in 1965 with its Marxist-Leninist internal charter, there were only 500 workers employed in 15 production plants in Afghanistan, and only 10 percent of the population were literate.[11] Moreover, because of the Afghan cultural tradition, the lines between social classes were not clear. Much of the urban population had roots in the rural communities. The Afghan bourgeoisie had mostly a commercial status rather than an industrial one, and many of the commercial bourgeoisie were large landowners or came from families who owned large farms. In such social conditions, how can the minority working class lead society toward socialism? And how can a political party such as the PDPA, who reported a membership over 90,000 (yet really it was probably closer to 11,000 in 1980,[12] compared with 320,000 *mullahs*, or clergies[13]), lead the Afghan society through a transitional revolution into socialism?

Despite PDPA's Marxist/Leninist interpretation, the only possible way to achieve a national democratic revolution in Afghanistan was to take over the matters of the revolution as the self-claimed representative of the working class. The military coup of April 1978 was matched with the PDPA leaders' interpretation of Marxist/Leninist revolution in Afghanistan. By taking over the government forcefully and violently, the PDPA leaders thought they would be able to guard the workers from a pre-industrial socioeconomic condition, ushering the country safely into socialism.

In the internal party environment, democracy, as a mechanism of balance and achievement, was nonexistent. Again, according to the PDPA doctrines, the party leadership must be under one ideology, one party, and a democratic, centralist leadership. This party principle created an environment in which a member had to answer to the leader's question by saying yes or no; there was no middle ground or compromises. In other words, a member has to be on the side of the working class by accepting Marxism/Leninism or be sided with the enemy.[14] The low level of understanding of Marxism/Leninism by the party members often caused the internal confrontations of the two main PDPA factions, *Parcham* and *Khalgh*, and the lack of internal democracy. Because the limited publication equipment was under the monopoly of the central government, the possibility of allowing Marxist literature to be published in Afghanistan was very small. Moreover, the majority of PDPA members did not understand foreign languages such as Russian or English.

Most Marxist/Leninist literature was printed in Russian or English, while translated versions were published in Iran by the People Party (*Hezb-e-Todah*) and by the Soviet Communist Party in the Soviet Union. These translated versions were smuggled into Afghanistan through Iran or India, although they did not reach the nucleus of the party membership. Therefore, handwritten copies of the books were popular among the members. Lack of education also prevented many of the PDPA's general members from studying Marx, Lenin, or other thinkers' writings. In many cases, it was not an easy task for the members to digest the philosophy and economic and political statements of Marxist thinkers. Instead, many of the members' familiarity with Marxism and Leninism came from novels such as *Mother*, by Maxim Gorki. This low-level education of the PDPA membership created major dilemmas for the party.

Eventually the party was divided along ethnic and linguistic lines. Each ethnic circle within the party had an individual who was the first person to recruit other members from that particular ethnic group. Usually, such an individual was the charismatic leader among a particular ethnic group. For example, Karim Misaq, one of the executive members of the PDPA and later a member of the Revolutionary Council, came from the *Hazaras* ethnic minority. He was the main leader among the PDPA *Hazara* membership, and he had his own followers within the party. These members were more loyal to Misaq than to the party's main leaders. When the head of such a group or sub-faction changed his political position, no matter what the reason behind such a change, the ethnic loyal members followed the change. This is not to say that the members were unable to think for themselves, but they had a limited understanding of the political statements (which mostly came by word of mouth or in a short summary written by the head of a sub-group) to begin with. One should not forget that for many ethnic groups, the party meant an avenue toward power in which an ethnic group would be able to protect its economic, social, and political interests. To be safe and secure on this path of rivalry, it made sense to stick together, regardless of whether their actions contradicted the general will of the party or its ideology.

The limited studies and understanding of the social, economic, cultural, and ethnic reality of Afghanistan was the result of a poor educational system. Because of the monopolization of the educational system by the government, the bulk of the information, in particular information about the economy, society, and politics, was filtered by the Ministry of Education. Therefore, many issues and subjects were outdated. Yet the current social, economic, and political issues within the educational system were not addressed. Except for a short period of time in the early 1970s, the press was neither free nor independent. Only about a dozen bookstores in the country were selling books and magazines published in Iran and Pakistan. The majority of these books dealt with sports, science, and religion; it would be a surprise if any of these imported books dealt with Afghanistan. However, limited imported political publications of all kinds were in circulation within political parties, secretly and illegally. Now under such an educational and political environment, the PDPA members were studying Marxism and Leninism. Most of the leaders and sub-faction heads of the party discussed and argued their theoretical points of view behind closed doors. But after their discussions and arguments, they had great difficulty passing the message to their followers. These intellectual groups shaped the PDPA into three groups.

The leaders or heads of the major factions like Noor Mohammed Taraki, Hafizullah Amin, and Babrak Karmal were the individuals who had the most access to books and literature. They were able to express their opinions and define them in a way that could best exemplify the teachings of Marx and Lenin.

The sub-faction heads participated in the discussions, but many of these individuals were under the influence of the major factional leaders. This group was the bridge between the thinkers in the party and the common members. They were relaying the results of the debates and discussions of the party's leadership in a simple language to the lower ranks.

The ordinary members mostly did not have solid general knowledge or understanding of the theoretical and fundamental issues among the leadership. The incentive of being a member of the party was rooted in their social and economic condition. Many in this group were individuals who were marginalized in their political lives and deprived economically. Therefore, there was a large percentage of members that followed a specific leader or sub-faction head because of his personal characteristics. For this reason the members' adherence and loyalty to the party and its leaders was not ideological; rather it was founded on personal, ethnic, and linguistic trust.

In reality, a combination such as the above could fit with the socio-ethnic and political structure of Afghan society; it would also match the vanguard theory of leadership in a pre-industrial society like Afghanistan. When the vanguard party has the right to make decisions for the entire population, without an election or voluntary participation, it is not unusual for the leaders of the party to give themselves the right to make decisions for the members. Therefore, it is not necessary for the general body of the party to worry about the critical issues and complicated theoretical matters because the leaders will take care of them. One can argue that this type of loyalty was what allowed the factional leaders of the PDPA to brutalize not only the rival factions within the party but also their so-called ideological friends within the same faction. A good example of such political behavior is when Hafizullah Amin killed Noor Mohammed Taraki, the leader of his own *Khalghi* faction, and brutalized many others.

The main ideological confrontation between the PDPA leaders appeared when they had to answer the question of how they should implement Marxism/Leninism in Afghanistan. This ideological confrontation caused the PDPA in 1966 to crack into two factions after only 18 months of the establishment: *Parcham* faction under Babrak Karmal; and *Khalqh* under Noor Mohammed Taraki. *Parchamis* "criticized the Khalqis for being too openly and outspokenly socialist" and the *Khalqis* "accused Parchamis of betraying sacred socialist goals."[15] The lack of internal democracy was one of the major reasons why the party leaders could not tolerate one another within the same framework; this led to the assassination of Mir Ali Akbar Khaibar, a senior *Parchami* ideologue, by *Khalqhis* in the beginning of 1978 (before the coup). Nevertheless, both *Khalqhis* and *Parchamis* were unable to bring their case to the people. As a result, the PDPA tried to influence the government branches secretly. "PDPA targets consisted of journalists, media personalities, bureaucrats and military officers, particularly those trained in the Soviet Union, some of whom had probably already been singled out and co-opted by the KGB or GRU. Both *Parcham* and *Khalqh*, however, carefully avoided recruiting openly among state employees in sensitive positions (though both factions developed cadres of secret adherents) in order not to alarm the authorities."[16]

In the 1969 national elections, the two PDPA organizations participated as individuals rather than as party representatives; only Babrak from among the *Parchamis* and Amin among the *Khalqis* won a seat in the parliament. At this time, when the PDPA factions did not have any significant progress through the elections, they targeted two key political issues: the political conflict within the royal family, for example, the rivalry between the Afghan monarch, King Zahir, and Prince Dauod, an ambitious royal member; and the territorial confrontation over Pushtonistan, which lay between Afghanistan and Pakistan. As a result, in July 1973, General Mohammed Dauod, with the aid of key *Parchamis*, deposed his cousin King Zahir in a virtually bloodless coup, abolished the monarchy, and proclaimed a republic with himself as president. The establishment of the Republic of Afghanistan increased the Soviet investment in Afghanistan and the PDPA influence in the government's military and civil bodies.

But later, President Dauod, alarmed by the PDPA influence with the government, transferred his erstwhile *Parchami* allies into positions of political impotence. In 1976, he purged virtually all *Parchamis*, at least those he knew of, from his inner councils.[17] From its establishment, the PDPA had adopted the ideological philosophy of the Soviet Communist Party and was supported by the Soviet regime. Ideologically, the party was more Soviet-based than Afghan-based in its theoretical loyalty to the Soviet school of thought. Therefore, it was not surprising that the PDPA could not promise the national demands and needs in Afghanistan nor represent the social and political elements of the society. In this case, one can argue that the PDPA was ideologically much closer to the Soviet regime than to the Afghan political forces. Such logic caused President Dauod to purge the PDPA and secure his regime.

In 1976 and 1977, the Soviet Communist Party (CPSU) started wide-ranging activities throughout the Communist Party of India (PCI) and the Awami National Party of Pakistan. Their goal was to reunite the PDPA factions, thus securing and maintaining the Soviet influence in Afghanistan, and also to increase that influence by seizing power. By 1978, the CPSU had pledged $1.262 billion to Afghanistan, and there were more than 2,000 Soviet technical and economic advisers in the country.[18] President Dauod began to distance his regime from the Soviets and cultivate new foreign aid donors such as Egypt, India, Saudi Arabia, and Iran and, most significantly, he "declared his intention of making the Non-Aligned Nations Movement which was scheduled to hold a meeting in Kabul (6–9 May 1978) truly nonaligned."[19] He launched a filterization policy against the PDPA circles in the armed forces, which were under the influence of GRU (mostly *Khalqis*), and in the civilian administration, which was under the influence of KGB (mostly *Parchamis*).[20] As a result of President Dauod's filterization policy, 200 Soviet trained officers were removed from the armed forces in July 1974, and an additional 40 officers were dismissed in October 1975.[21] Under such government policy, Dauod not only dismissed the *Parchamis* from their ministerial posts, he also made more room in his cabinet for the conservative elements who were anticommunist. Moreover, Dauod announced the establishment of the National Revolutionary Front and the dissolution of the PDPA.

At the crowded funeral in Kabul for Mir Akbar Khaiber, the *Parcham* military recruiter who was assassinated, five key members of the PDPA, including Taraki and Karmal, were arrested. Hafizullah Amin, the *Khalqi* military recruiter, contacted Major Aslam Watanjar, deputy commander of the strategically placed Fourth Division, and Colonel Syed Golabzoi of the air force to move against President Dauod's regime.[22] The success of the coup became obvious when the air force Migs and SU-25s guided by the air force Chief of Staff Lieutenant Colonel Abdul Qader, a Dari speaking non-Pushton with loose *Parcham* ties, started to bomb the Presidential Palace. The military coup under the command of Hafizullah Amin in April 1978 violently ended

Dauod's life and his regime. This assassination left questions over what role the Soviets played in the coup operation. The PDPA relationship with the Soviets caused different speculations about the Soviets' role in the coup against the president Dauod.

The coup was extensively planned sometime in the past. When the Fourth Armored Division at 9:00 A.M. launched its attack on the Presidential Palace, the communication between the palace and the loyal military divisions, who had the ability to stop the coup, was concurrently being destroyed.

The electronic gear that controlled the palace missile batteries was not working when the air attack occurred.

According to Colonel Madhu Sameyran, the Indian military attache, "who had extensive contacts in the Afghan Air Force, there were 350 Soviet military advisors and technicians in Kabul."[23] Most of these Soviet advisors were "involved in the ground control and anti-air missile" training at Bagram, the main military airport in the country. Colonel Abdul Qader was leading the air attack on the Presidential Palace from this airport. It would be very difficult for the Afghan officers to operate the coup without the involvement of Soviet advisors. Even though there is not hard evidence to prove the direct involvement of the Soviets in the planning and operational stages of the coup, the above speculations make it hard to believe that the Soviet advisors in Kabul were not involved.

CHAPTER FOUR

The Democratic Republic of Afghanistan

THE PDPA COUP D'ETAT TOOK PLACE ON A THURSDAY AFTERNOON, April 27, 1978, when the office workers were off half of the day (in the Muslim calendar, Friday is the end of the week). During the weekend most government civil and military officers do not work, and the line of communication between the government ministries is very slow. The timing of the coup at the start of the weekend holiday had a great impact, as President Dauod was unable to receive adequate support from his well-equipped armed forces.

By the afternoon of April 27, the ground forces loyal to the PDPA seized the Ministry of Defense, the most important communication center for Dauod loyalists and Radio Afghanistan (national radio). At 7 P.M. the Radio Afghanistan broadcaster made a short announcement:

> For the first time in the history of Afghanistan the last remnants of monarchy, tyranny, despotism and power of the dynasty of the tyrant Nadir Khan has ended, and all powers of the state are in the hands of the people of Afghanistan. The power of the state rests fully with the Revolutionary Council of the Armed Forces.[1]

Shortly, another statement from the pro-coup elements was broadcast:

> Dear Compatriots! Your popular state, which is in the hands of the Revolutionary Council, informs you that every anti revolutionary element who would venture to defy instructions and rulings of the Revolutionary Council will be delivered immediately to the revolutionary military centers.[2]

At the time, these two important statements confused the general public, because the statements covered broad ideas such as the anti–Nadir Khan dynasty—power in the hands of the people—and also announced that the
Revolutionary Council was the highest body in the country and any act of dis-
obedience would be considered antirevolutionary.

Later events proved that such contradictions in early statements of the
coup leaders were the outcome of the PDPA's mentality in which the leaders of
the party believed that they were pursuing the people's interests. Through such
a mental fabric, power meant a self-styled leadership: PDPA leaders would be
chosen as heroic and charismatic individuals who would free the people from
tyranny and despotism. The psychological and theoretical foundation of such a
mentality was well established long ago in the principle of vangaurdism, within
the PDPA's interpretation of Marxism/Leninism.

When the first statement was broadcast, many political circles thought that
the PDPA might approach some sort of power sharing agreement with the
other political organizations, in particular with the anti-Soviet left or nationalists. There was not enough information about the identity of the Revolutionary
Council members, although the recognition of famous army officer Colonel
Abdul Qader made many think that the Council went beyond the monopoly of
the PDPA.[3]

In the second statement, one can see that the coup leaders are more certain
about their victory over President Dauod's loyalists. As a result of such cer-
tainty, the coup leaders are openly on the attack of any resistance group or de-
nial of the Revolutionary Council's guidance. In this statement the coup leaders
are not saying that all powers are in the hands of people, rather they are claiming that their hours-old regime is a popular state. In reality, this state had limited support from the masses and was under the control of a nuclear group of
the Revolutionary Council. At this stage of power, PDPA members were a minority group among the educated Afghans who controlled a significant segment of the Afghan people.

Moreover, if they did establish a popular state, then why would the leadership of the coup find it necessary to command their loyal elements to attack
those who were not in agreement with their guidance and to deliver them immediately to the revolutionary military centers? A popular state should not fear
its internal political opponents and should not follow a hostile strategy of using
armed forces against those who have differences within their political ideology.
Indeed, the PDPA and the coup leaders attempted to legitimize their military
and political actions by claiming the popular support of the Afghan people and,
more importantly, by legitimizing their hostile strategy against their political
opponents in the name of the people of Afghanistan.

Soon, this hostile strategy became the fundamental doctrine of the PDPA's
attempt to lead Afghanistan toward the future. This hostile strategy shaped a
psychological notion that the party not only used against its members, but also

became the status quo of PDPA's political behavior toward nonparty elements, in particular, against opposition groups.

THE STYLE OF MASS MOBILIZATION IN AFGHANISTAN

The mass mobilization in Afghanistan is a combination of the political behaviors of political organizations, in particular the PDPA, toward the general fabric of Afghan society. These political behaviors were strongly rooted in the type and formation of political ideologies of the political groups when they first engaged in public affairs. In general, the political ideologies of Afghan political parties were like security codes that allowed parties to drive their political vehicles onto the street with the masses, or to harmonize their political behavior with the path of mass movement.

Harmonizing with the masses provided the political groups the ability to expand their social and political activities and become an integral part of society's dynamic forces. Such integration allowed the political parties to play their roles by offering crucial resolutions when social, political, and economic crises hits. In a situation when a political party's ideology did not prove to be a secure entrance for the party to integrate with the masses, it isolated the activities of the party from the general movement of society. Thus, a conflicted interaction between the party and the masses emerged, creating clashes when the party attempted to move against the tides.

THE PDPA AND MASS MOBILIZATION

The political style of the PDPA to mobilize society was comprised of two types of interactions. Within the party, sub-factions were struggling for superiority and leadership control. After the PDPA coup, also known as the Saur Revolution, fundamental differences between the two PDPA main factions resulted in the further division of the party into two hostile rivals. Even though the Saur Revolution was completed by the action of military officers, the first cabinet of the Democratic Republic of Afghanistan was dominated by the civilian figures of the two factions. Out of 21 ministers, only a few were from the military, including Colonel Abdul Qader, minister of national defense, and Major Mohammed Aslam Watanjar, deputy prime minister. Among the members of the cabinet there were three dominant figures, Noor Mohammed Taraki, Hafizullah Amin, and Babrak Karmal. Taraki and Amin led the *Khalq* faction. (Because Taraki was the oldest figure of the *Khalq* leadership, he was the leader of the faction and one of the key persons among the founding fathers. He became the leader of the party and also the head of the Democratic Republic of Afghanistan.) Even though Taraki was the *Khalq* leader, his position was more symbolic. The main powerful leader in the *Khalq* faction was Hafizullah Amin who won and developed a loyal circle and strong ties to the military core of the *Khalq*.

Ideologically, *Parcham* was in favor of gradual approaches toward social, political, and economic reforms. Therefore, they attempted, tactically, to avoid appearing publicly, as Marxists and Leninists and instead to try to deal with political power in a diplomatic way. In the *Khalqi* faction of the PDPA, particularly among Amin's circle, the gradual approach was an opportunistic way of dealing with the Saur Revolution. Thus, to solve problems and to maintain control in the society, they used direct, aggressive, and irreversible actions, like the Soviets during the October Revolution. For *Khalqis*, Babrak and his *Parchami* followers in the government and in the party were the main challenge to the Saur Revolution. To implement economic, political, and social change in a revolutionary way they had to remove the obstacles and dominate their influence. In this case there would be one party and one ideology with strong leadership and without questions of revolutionizing society.[4]

Hafizullah Amin was the main and hostile rival of the *Parcham* leader, Babrak Karmal. His rivalry toward Babrak and to *Parcham* in general was rooted in his political interpretation of Marxism/Leninism and in the ethnic and linguistic differences between the two leaders. From the early days of the Saur Revolution, neither of these two leaders were comfortable with the other's influence in the cabinet. Many *Parchamis* accused Amin and his circle of Mir Akbar Khaiber's assassination, which deepened factional hostility. Khyber was the core *Parcham* leader, after Babrak Karmal, and was a longtime recruiter among the military officers. In the first five weeks after the coup, Amin's loyalists dominated the secret police and the ministry of interior. Reports indicated that Amin had a list of all *Parchamis* in the government and was monitoring their activities. In mid-June (six weeks after the coup) Amin launched an attack on the *Parchamis;* as a result many were arrested from the ministries, army, police, Radio Kabul, and Kabul University. Purification of the government by the use of armed forces allowed *Khalqis* to seize a more official position and to better influence the state. On July 5, *Khalqis*, under Hafizullah Amin, launched a coup against the *Parchamis* by posting the most important *Parchami* leaders to ambassadorships abroad. This included Babrak Karmal, Mahmud Baryalai (Babrak's brother), Nur Ahmad Nur, and Anahita Ratebzad. On August 17, Minister of National Defense Abdul Qader and the chief of staff of the army, Lieutenant General Shapur Ahmadzai, were arrested for attempting a coup against the *Khalqi* leadership.[5] This was the last attempt of the *Khalqis* to remove the remaining key figures of the *Parchamis* from the government before they focused on arresting and executing other political opponents.

When the *Khalqi* faction of the PDPA became the absolute power of the government, they began to purify the political institution of the country. *Khalqis* moved toward purification of Afghan society by eliminating their political opponents and those social and political elements that were a potential threat to the regime. "It detected enemies from all sides, from within and outside of Afghanistan, right wings of the political class, from ardent Afghan nationalists as well as from landlords and mullahs [clergies]."[6] The secret police (called AGSA under Taraki, KAM under Amin, Khad under Babrak Karmal and Najibullah) was established to monitor the behavior of all citizens of the Democratic Republic of Afghanistan. They made massive arrests. As the American author, Barnett R. Rubin, writes:

> Those arrested and killed included political leaders of the constitutional period (such as former Prime Ministers Moussa Shafiq and Nur Ahmad Etamadi); members of Dauod's family and other branches of the royal family; religious scholars and spiritual leaders (including, for instance, all the men of the Mojadidi family still in Kabul, by birth the leaders of the Naqshbandiya Sufi order); high school teachers and students, university students and professors, including leading scholars; lawyers and judges; government and diplomatic officials; military officers.[7]

It was not that long after the establishment of the DRA that a tense and fearful political environment dominated the Afghan political world. The whole political system was moving in a direction that was filled with political rhetoric and loud slogans of the PDPA zealous partisans and members. Many political figures who did not have a chance of public activities went into underground life or left the country. There was no security for jobs, private ownership, and education. In such an environment, the PDPA attempted to dislocate Afghan social, political, and economic features and fit them into a new identity.

THE DRA'S SOCIAL AND ECONOMIC REFORMS

On May 10, 1978, Radio Kabul broadcast Taraki's speech announcing the DRA agenda for social and economic reforms in the country. The reforms, known as the 23 basic lines of revolutionary duties, were aimed at bringing revolutionary changes to the traditional and historic lives of the Afghan people.[8] Many of the articles in this announcement came directly from the PDPA manifesto published in 1965. There was a high degree of political idealism that made the nature of the reforms vague and unrealistic. For example, the DRA regime announced that the national flag of the country had to be red rather than the traditional three colors (black, red, and green). This attempt not only altered any good in the benefit of the regime, it also created a national flag similar in style to the Soviets, thus representing Soviet influence in Afghanistan. Comparing Afghanistan in 1965 to Afghanistan in 1978, one finds a big gap in the country's social, economic, and political environment. Most of these decrees and reforms were finalized without a consensus or poll of the people. They were based primarily on ideological notions and political ambitions of the party leaders.

Politically, the PDPA was a small group (6,000 before the coup) compared to the total population of Afghanistan. Therefore, gaining the support of the masses was very crucial for their survival. In this regard, their social and economic reforms became highly politicized when they attempted to implement them. Technically, through these reforms the PDPA leaders planned to create mass organization to encourage the participation of the local community, as this would fill the gap between the regime and the masses and subsequently stabilize the central democratic government. In this case, mass organization was the only fruitful method that enabled the party and the state to complete the transition period from a pre-industrial society to socialism without entering capitalism. Theoretically, the DRA strategy for reforms was instituted utilizing this formula:

mass organization + mass participation = mass mobilization.

MOBILIZATION IN PROGRESS

In the eyes of the PDPA communist leaders, Afghanistan existed in the Asiatic mode of production (according to Marx, in Asia the production mode has little impact on changes within the society—the methods have remained constant for centuries), and the political, social, and cultural system was a historical barrier to further development toward socialism. Thus, the revolutionary middle class had to act as the vanguard of the workers and demolish the parasitic political system for fast transition into socialism. The PDPA introduced a controversial set of revolutionary reforms called, "Basic Lines of Revolutionary Duties of the Government of the Democratic Republic of Afghanistan on 9 May 1978."[9] Implementation and belief in the revolutionary decrees was not only holy for the PDPA members, it was the duty and obligation of all citizens of the Democratic Republic of Afghanistan. Article 32 of the Fundamental Principles of DRA states: "The defense of the Homeland and of the gains of the Saur Revolution, loyalty to its ideals and goals, and service to the nation are the supreme duty and sacred obligation of every citizen."[10]

Belief in the ideals and goals of the Saur Revolution was a part of the requirement to be a citizen; this was equivalent to defending the homeland.[11] Being a citizen required accomplishing the citizenship duty and obligation, which meant participating in the struggle with the PDPA to achieve the Saur Revolution gains. But the Saur Revolution leaders were not aware that in a predominant Muslim society with traditional historical and communal values, making people loyal to their ideals and goals of the April coup was far from reality. Their ability to achieve this goal was greatly underestimated.

Historically, the sentiment toward loyalty to the national government was weak in Afghanistan, and most of the time the ethnic and communal leaders were suspicious of the government. There was an ongoing resistance to the intervention of the national government in the affairs of the local community. Local autonomy and communal freedom were the traditional values that had been saved through the continuous struggle against the national government.

For example, the national government was not able to conscript young people from numerous local communities. In return, the official former governments preferred to have peace with the local communities rather than face insurgencies and communal revolts.

This revolutionary program brought almost the entire mental and physical fabric of Afghan society within reach of the reforms. The reforms were characterized as democratic objectives—abolishing and eliminating the feudal and pre-feudal social structures and making them fit into the noncapitalist development of Afghanistan.[12] The PDPA began an unprecedented intervention into the political, economic, social, and cultural lives of the entire Afghan people. Many of the reforms were undertaken without scientific studies of the macro and micro aspects of the prevailing social and cultural realities. The PDPA had no organization in the provinces; its cadres, small in number, were mostly urban and middle class. The regime therefore had to depend helplessly on the provincial and sub-provincial bureaucracy to implement revolutionary reforms, thus adding to their continued political/governmental impotence.

These revolutionary reforms were only the events in a mental revolution in the minds of PDPA leaders. They learned Marxism/Leninism through books and political journals, which was the reason the reforms were completed through a political analysis rather than social, economic, and cultural aspects.

Among the 23 revolutionary decrees, the literacy campaign and the land redistribution policy touched the heart of the social and economic life of Afghans.

LITERACY CAMPAIGN

One of the main objectives of the PDPA alternative for Afghanistan was to advance society toward modernization and industrialization, which they called a new society. To do this, there was a need to expand educational services and skilled labor forces, entrepreneurs, and professionals. Article 24 of the Fundamental Principles of the DRA states: "The state shows concern for young people and ensures them access to education and various professions. It will take the necessary steps for their ideological, moral and physical education and for their broad and creative participation in the building of a new society."[13]

Taraki called the literacy programs task a holy mission for the PDPA members, naming these members the children of history.[14] The DRA leaders proposed a five-year plan to increase the literacy rate from 10 percent to 50 percent of the total population. Through this plan, 1 million students of both sexes would be enrolled in literacy courses in the first year, 2 million in the second year, and 3 million in the third year. Combined with the one and a half million already in school, in three years Afghanistan would have 6 million students, giving Afghanistan one of highest literacy rates in Asia.[15] At the end of February 1979, the official sources (within the government) claimed that there were 180,000 students who were attending approximately 6,200 courses and being taught by 3,500 teachers.

For the PDPA leaders it was crucial to reach their educational goals, but they needed more research and scholarly studies on the social implication of a nationwide literacy campaign. The way the PDPA leaders approached the implementation of these plans was very ill managed, and the concept was far from the realm of success within Afghan society and its economy. New textbooks concentrated on the sincerity of the Saur Revolution and described the biographies of the leaders. Through all these books and texts, the DRA attempted to change the history of Afghanistan by calling the previous regimes of kings and presidents tyrannical.

The literacy courses were compulsory for all young adults of both sexes and they forced males and females to sit in the same classrooms. Traditionally, this was against the cultural values of the students. It was directly against the free will of the people, forcing them to be in the same room with strangers (particularly with members of the opposite sex). The majority of the teachers were young high school or teaching institution graduates who had limited experience with teaching. In some cases the loyal members of the party used police force to make people attend literacy classes, thus insulting the tradition and morality of individuals who had respected social positions in the local community. These actions became commonplace for many party militants. There were rumors about rapes within the classrooms and gossip about the dishonesty of women and girls in the literacy courses. Most likely, these were the main reasons that the bulk of the victims during the mass revolts turned out to be the literacy teachers. These issues were volatile among the rural population, and society was segregated for many centuries. Yet as a result, the important point here is not to question whether this DRA program was right or wrong, but how the voluntary participation of the people, in a way that they were able to enjoy themselves and see the benefits of being a literate society, would have affected the outcome.

The majority of Afghans did not have access to radio and television, or magazines and newspapers (except in the major cities). Working on the farms during the day with primitive agricultural tools did not require educational skills for the majority of the population. There was no electricity in the majority of the towns and villages. Sitting under the light of a primitive oil lamp in a dark classroom and listening to the biographies and history of the Saur Revolution bored many adult students and turned them off to the idea of continuing their education.

Members of the PDPA included a small minority of the 10 percent educated population in Afghanistan. Most of the party members and sympathizers came from the Training Teacher Institute, and many of these teachers became a part of the ministerial staffs and civil servants in the government. Yet there was not an adequate number of teachers to satisfy the need of the formal educational system. The Ministry of Education attempted to abolish exams and increase the enrollment rate.[16] In April 1979, the DRA started the expansion of high schools and training centers from 8,000 to 13,110.[17] Expanding the enrollment, without improving services, decreased the quality of education very rapidly.

Politicizing the formal educational system around the political ideology of the Saur Revolution concentrated on absorbing as many students as possible into the many different organs of the party. Affiliation with the PDPA organization created a corrupt atmosphere and caused many students to abandon the system. In many cases, a good student was the one who had a strong loyalty to the party, not the one getting high grades in math and science. In many exams there was a question about the biography or history of the revolutionary leaders in Afghanistan or in the Soviet Union. In the high-level educational system, party members and their families had priority for getting foreign scholarships, and many qualified graduates with high scores were discriminated against. Indeed, the number of students who were enrolled in the formal education system and training institutes was much higher than before the establishment of the DRA regime, but the quality of education for the general public was very poor.

A great impact of the literacy campaign on the general public was that this campaign provoked a large number of students to reject the strong and old path of politics in Afghanistan. This stirring created a mutual political communication that dealt directly with the authority and legitimacy of the political system. It expanded the political conflict between the PDPA and the opposition parties to every corner of society. With the political attitude and psychological behavior of the PDPA members, the literacy campaign was interpreted by many local communities as a method of control and intervention within the family and the community and a violation of the traditional values of the people. Therefore, in the time of the revolts and trouble against the regime, the literacy campaign fueled the flames of the war.

LAND REDISTRIBUTION

Decree Number 8 of the reforms announced the land redistribution policies, which were very foreign to the people. Article 19 of Fundamental Principles of the DRA stated land distribution objectives:

> The state takes measures for carrying through democratic reforms in agriculture in the interests of the broad masses of peasants and with their active participation; gives peasants the necessary assistance by providing them with bank credits; helps them to acquire farm machinery, selected seeds and chemical fertilizers and to market farm produce and raw materials; and supports and encourages the development of producers, consumers, and other kinds of cooperatives in the farming sector.[18]

The notion of land redistribution was an idea that the PDPA leaders adopted from Marxist/Leninist literature written by non-Afghan leftist theoreticians.

Generally, local communities and villages in Afghanistan were bound together by the ethnic and communal lines while the social class conflicts were very weak or nonexistent. The nucleus of industrial workers was strongly tied to communal and religious values, much more than to the idea of class conflict and struggles. The poor peasants in Afghanistan were the minority among the general population of the farmers. There was never a notion of revolutionary revolt and social conflict among these peasants; the sentiment of social class conflict was overwhelmed by the notion of ethnic and religious loyalty.

According to the UN report in 1988, the land distribution in 1978 and 1979 was noted as:

> 50% of the farmers owned their land and were self-sufficient or produced some surpluses, 25% were share-croppers and 25% were landless laborers. Large farms (over 100 ha.) hardly existed except in the south, for example in Farah province, the majority of farms were between 2 and 10 ha. in size, the average farm size being 3.3 ha.[19]

Moreover of the total 22 percent of arable land only 0.8 percent of the land was able to be farmed annually with crops; because of poor irrigation systems the rest of the arable land was not efficiently cultivable. A daring study showed that land redistribution was not the appropriate solution for the 25 percent landless farmers. In addition, the basic cultural and traditional values of Afghan society were based on the historical formation of their local communities: a strong faith in Islam and a firm belief in freedom, private property rights, and private enterprise, along with a largely self-sufficient structure of production that also produced surplus goods for the cities and enough goods to be exported. Most of the rural population was comprised of small independent farmers. Large land holdings were rare, especially for irrigated land where an average holding did not exceed 5 or 6 hectares (12 to 15 acres); for dry farming, land holdings might be large by Afghan standards at as much as 200 acres or more.[20]

Because the reforms were not formulated through a consensus or any democratic procedures, or through the cooperation of other political parties, the result was a system that was created by the top leadership without consultation with the local communities. Any rejection or complaints resulted in hostile reactions from the government authorities. Individuals who dared question the government's declarations were considered to be enemies of the revolution or pro-imperialism and feudalism.

The violent confrontation within the PDPA in the first two weeks of the coup between the *Parchamis* and the *Khalqis* resulted in the destruction of the *Parchamis*. Claiming to be the vanguard of the imagined working class, the highest political organ in Afghanistan created a deep and wide political gap between the party and society. In the social and political phases, the problem of the PDPA regime was that the policies and orders did not appeal to the Afghan population and lacked legitimacy; it soon became apparent that there was little support for their policies and programs. The PDPA regime altered the basic traditional ground rules that governed the relations between the state and microsocieties. They were attempting to avoid the standards implemented under the former King and President Dauod.

These ground rules largely consisted of norms of societal relationships between the Kabul-based Pushton political and military leadership and the Pushton microsocieties, and also between the largely Tajik bureaucratic/administrative elite and to some extent other minority microsocieties.[21] The PDPA isolated the traditional elements (Islam, nationalism, and modernization) of the political system in an attempt to create a stable power balance in Afghanistan. PDPA ideology was closer to the Soviet communist party rather than to the traditional and cultural values of its people. Thus, the PDPA became a self-authorized party that needed the military and economic support of the Soviet communist party rather than the support of the people of Afghanistan. The reforms resulted in the victimization of a society and the loss of many traditions and cultural values for the sake of mass participation to build an imagined new society. In this case, the PDPA's political interests were far from the interests of the Afghan urban and rural population, and they subsequently helped shape the following formulation:

PDPA political power + USSR military and economic support
= nonpublicly supported government.

VIOLENCE, THE LEADING ELEMENT OF MOBILIZATION

The reforms program under the leadership of the PDPA resulted in the unsuccessful implementation of the revolutionary agenda of the DRA. Because of the vanguard notion and political ideology of the party, the PDPA leaders and planners were not able to see their failures. They never accepted the defeat of the principles that were formulated years ago behind closed doors and without any scientific studies. Institutionally, there was no other higher organization to monitor or judge the PDPA activities and political behavior. They simplified their task as a political party, especially a vanguard one, and as a government responsible for its citizens, they worked to correct their actions and to find a practical and proper resolution to the problem they created.

The PDPA created an internal enemy and externalized the internal problem by blaming the failure of the reforms on imperialist agents, backward religious leaders, mercenaries of foreign powers, and so on. By doing this, the PDPA attempted to create an imaginary external threat to give them a legitimate reason to use violent force against its people. Mass arrests and executions, imprisonment of many scholars, religious leaders, and community nobles, and public violation of the traditional norms and values of the people destabilized the whole fabric of Afghan society. Indeed, the PDPA was able to continue its violent campaign to a limit, but in using violent forces the PDPA leaders pressed the social balance of Afghanistan far beyond their reach of control.

MASS REVOLT OF HERAT

On March 15, 1979, thousands of villagers and city households in Herat, in the northwest of the country, revolted against the regime. The riot started in the towns of Enjil and Gozarah by a stream of villagers carrying machetes, swords, old rifles, and wooden hitting sticks. They wiped out the local resistance of the government-armed posts, burned the government buildings and banks, and destroyed the telephone poles. The masses destroyed the police stations on their way to the city in a matter of hours. They burned the armored vehicles and the military tanks that were used by the PDPA armed units against the masses. The rebels demolished anyone who was inside the armored vehicles after reaching them and claimed the tanks.[22]

Riots erupted as armed PDPA members and the AGSA (secret police) opened fire on the people. More than 5,000 people were killed in 3 days. The rebels captured the city and the DRA provincial official asked the 17th Division of the Afghan army to fire on the city. The 17th Division not only refused to fire on the city, they opened fire on PDPA headquarters, in which the high ranking PDPA members and the Soviet advisors were discussing the dilemma. According to the rebel leaders of the 17th Division of Afghan military, none of the PDPA members or the Soviet advisors survived the attack.[23] As a result, the army revolted against the PDPA regime and after demolishing the PDPA members in the army, they embraced the mass revolt and distributed hundreds of automatic weapons to the mob.

For three days the city was out of the control of the DRA, until the air force started to bomb the city, focusing on the northern hillsides occupied by army rebels. On the fourth day, the mechanized division of the national army was able to open the route from Qandahar to the province of Herat. The armed forces were under the strict control of the PDPA officers who took over the city and the surrounding villages. Hundreds of people, mostly the communal nobles, were arrested. (The discovery of mass graves in Herat after the collapse of the *Watan Party* under Najibullah in 1992 provided significant evidence of mass execution. According to the official Islamic State of Afghanistan under Burhanadin Rabbani, many of the victims were alive while the bulldozer piled mud and soil over them.) In addition, the government sent a brutal special commando unit from the east of the country to Herat to disarm the rural population and restore order.[24] The mass revolt of Herat became the northern star of the uprising in Afghanistan. For the first time the locals were heartened by deserting military officers and the survival of the local political opposition in this area. In June 1978, fledgling resistance groups struck at police and army posts in remote parts of the country. Early areas of activity were in the provinces of Badakhshan, Bamiyan, Kunar, Paktia, and Nangahar.[25] A stream of discontented people saw the new government as a threat to their religion and way of life. A steady flow of deserters from the Afghan army began.

The increase of the 5,000 Soviet civil and military personnel demoralized the government. The Soviets had control over the Afghan bureaucracy and military, a large percentage of executions, and destruction of cultural values of society. Throughout the Afghan army, Afghan officers and soldiers could not serve under the brutality of the PDPA, while the government killed civilians. For example, on May 17, 1979 a motorized brigade of the Central Corps 7th Division sent to fight the rebel forces in Khost surrendered the entire unit to the Mujahideen. The defection of an entire brigade of, perhaps, 2,000 men, along with their armored vehicles and heavy weapons, was a serious blow to the government. Yet the most serious setback of the Afghan army against the PDPA government was the riot of the Asmar 38th Brigade of the 9th Division with 2,000 men in the summer of 1979 under Brigadier General Abdul Rauf Saafi, a non-party man.[26] As organized armed opposition surrounded the major cities, the PDPA regime almost lost control of the largest portion of the country.

During the 1978 to 1979 mass revolts in Afghanistan there was a political revolution to transform state structures but not social changes.[27] The revolt had a heavy impact on the structure of the society. A weak Marxist interpretation of Asian economic and social systems forced the PDPA regime toward a rapid downfall. When Marx turned his attention outside the European continent to Asia, the Middle East, and elsewhere, he discovered that his theory of European development did not apply. In this immense conglomeration of humanity (Asia), the precapitalist stages did not exist; there appeared to be no stages identifiable with the ancient and feudal modes of production. These civilizations seemed to be devoid of any internal mechanism for social change. There was no class conflict that would drive them from one stage of social development to the next.

Subsequent to this analogy, Marx introduced the concept of the Asiatic mode of production.[28] He argued that this was characterized by the unity and relative autocracy of agricultural and manufacturing production at the village level, and the existence of an autonomous and parasitic state, separated from the rest of society. He believed that this conservative social structure was responsible for the millennia of social and economic stagnation suffered by these non-Western societies. Finding no internal forces to move these societies forward, historically, Marx believed the external force of Western imperialism was required to move these societies from a social dead end. He eventually argued that "England has to fulfill a double mission in India: 1) destructive, 2) regenerating the annihilation of old Asiatic society and the laying of the material foundations of Western society in Asia."[29] Orthodox Marxism believed that capitalism develops, but does not do so evenly, continuously, or without limit. Lenin firmly believed that capitalist imperialism would give the colored races of the world the tools for their emancipation and that the incorporation of non-Western societies into the world economy through trade and investment should lead to their development.[30] But after the Soviet Union became the center of socialism against imperialism, this doctrine developed into Lenin's concept of neocolonialism and the cooperation of peasants and workers, who he called the village proletariat.

Because of the imperialist global market economy, national bourgeoisie has economic ties with capitalism as a part of that global market. Therefore, national bourgeoisie cannot establish an independent national capitalist system. Moreover, while there is not a significant working class in the Asiatic societies to lead society toward socialism, the revolutionary middle class who believes in the proletariat doctrine (Marxism/Leninism) can act as the vanguard of the working class by capturing the political power (the government) and providing the opportunity for workers to change from precapitalism into socialism without passing through capitalism.

This Marxist theory, when applied to the rapid downfall of the PDPA regime, highlights the middle-class membership who claimed to represent the working class and proletarians in Afghanistan. The PDPA became the instrument that was to lead the people toward socialism. This self-proclaimed position of representing the working class (the progressive force in society) caused the creation of a schism between the party and society as a whole, thus resulting in the accelerated failure of the PDPA. The PDPA was politically and ideologically polarized from the historical, traditional, and cultural values that dominated the daily lives of the Afghan people. Additionally, Soviet political and economic aid can be viewed as the external factors Marx required for social changes in an Asiatic society. In this case, Soviet economic aid and military intervention can be justified by PDPA leadership. They believed the outside impetus was necessary to continue their leadership.

However, the mass revolts against the PDPA regime in Afghanistan resulted in the emergence of strong political identities in the local communities and direct action, by the people, to change the political system in the country. Because of the absolute despotism, the only available option was an uprising; in this case, mass revolt was the alternative to political identity and remobilization of the political institution. When the masses flooded into the streets, when the army joined the rebels, and when hundreds of thousands of volunteers embraced the resistance, it became a very active political revolution that was aimed at destroying the PDPA regime.

PARTY DYNAMIC AND THE PDPA LEADERS

Dictatorship and totalitarianism were the only visible signs of the political attitudes of the regime, both within the party and toward the general public. One can argue, if the PDPA's leaders could not tolerate one another, how could they give any non-PDPA person a chance? Soon after the departure of the *Parchami* leaders, a new power struggle took shape within the *Khalq* leadership. This new power struggle was between Taraki, the *Khalq* faction leader, and Amin. Both of these leaders attempted to garner support from the other *Khalqi* leaders. Taraki was supported by the four prominent military officers: Watanjar; Lieutenant Colonel Shirjan Mazdooryar, the interior minister; Assadullah Serwary, the head of secret police; and Lieutenant General Gulabzoi. Amin had his own style of politics in which he endeavored to not only operate separate from the other PDPA circles but also attempted to work independently from the Soviets.

Amin's growing influence and style of political games concerned the Soviets who tried to play a supervisory role by pouring aid into Afghanistan. In particular, the Soviets were in support of Babrak Karmal's return to Kabul and the reunion of the PDPA faction. In this situation, the KGB was more supportive of Taraki's circle. This issue intensified the relations between the Soviets and Amin, especially when Amin started to act as an Afghan nationalist by claiming the establishment of Greater Afghanistan from the Oxus River to the Abasin. In a sharper comment, Amin summarized the Afghan-Soviet relationship as relations between two equal brothers.[31] The hostile relations between the PDPA factions in general, and among the *Khalqi* leaders, caused the Soviets to increase their involvement, not only in the general affairs of the country, but also within the power struggle between the factional leaders. As a result, the Soviet missionaries were arriving in Kabul one after the other to solve the internal problem of the PDPA and at the same time to help the regime against the ever-increasing armed political opposition that was controlling a significant portion of the country.

The Soviet mediation was not able to reunify the *Khalq* leaders or create a peaceful environment between Amin and Taraki's gang of four (Watanjar, Shirjan Mazdooryar, Assadullah Serwary, and Gulabzoi). Taraki was invited to Moscow by the Soviet leaders to develop a new strategy that included: the return of Babrak Karmal; a reunion of the *Parchamis* and the *Khalqis*; and sending Amin to an ambassadorial position abroad. Amin angrily rejected this new Soviet strategy. The gang of four convinced Taraki to participate in a plot to kill Amin while he was on his way to Taraki's headquarters for a meeting of peace and cooperation. They thought Amin would arrive only with the presence of Soviet Ambassador Pozanov, who personally guaranteed Amin's security. Serwary positioned two of his armed personnel to kill Amin when he entered the palace. But at the meeting it was Dauod Tarun, chief of the presidential secretariat, who was shot to death because he entered the palace before Amin.

Amin and his bodyguards retaliated and surrounded the palace with tanks in a matter of hours. The gang of four ran into hiding under the protection of KGB agents in Kabul, and the PDPA Central Committee announced the resignation of Taraki and the dismissal of the gang of four.[32]

The relations between the Soviets and Amin deteriorated swiftly; he was convinced that the KGB was aware of the plot. On October 8, in a meeting

with Communist ambassadors in Afghanistan (where the Chinese and Yugosla-
vians were in attendance), Amin's foreign minister, Shah Wali, openly said, "To
our great regret, the conspirators were assisted by the ambassador of a power
friendly to Afghanistan, by A. M. Pozanov of the Soviet Union, who helped
Taraki to entice the Prime Minister (Amin) into a trap."[33]

On October 10, Radio Kabul reported that Taraki had died from a serious
illness; he actually suffocated to death from a pillow placed over his face by
Amin's agents. Concurrently, Amin endeavored to achieve national reconciliation with the resistance groups and attempted to reach a settlement with the
Pakistanis in an important meeting scheduled for December 29, to reestablish
diplomatic relations with the United States. In the field of national politics,
Amin tried to convince the people that the brutality of the DRA regime was related to the gang of four and Taraki. He tried to blame Assadullah Serwary, as
interior minister, for all the killings and disappearances.

Therefore, the Ministry of the Interior announced in September 1979 that
it would publish the names of 12,000 people who had died in Kabul jails since
April 1978. It was revealed that torture was introduced under the tutelage of
the East Germans and Soviet KGB officers,[34] along with mass executions without trial. As Mark Urban writes: "in all [Afghanistan] about 50,000 to 100,000
people disappeared."[35]

THE SOVIET INVASION OF AFGHANISTAN
(DECEMBER 24, 1979)

When the pro-Soviet PDPA was faced with a clear-cut response to the attempt
to impose Marxism in Afghanistan, Moscow had another option besides invasion. They could backtrack and install a more pliable noncommunist front
while adopting, at the very least, a more gradual approach to the implementation of Moscow's regional agenda. Through such a step Moscow could convey
the idea that Islam and its associated traditions would no longer be targets, at
least openly. But this would have gone against the often-stated Soviet principle
of the irreversibility of the revolutionary process. There was no choice for the
aggressive global policy of the Soviets. Moscow was faced with a growing Muslim rebellion against the recently imposed Afghan communist rule and decided
that it had to invade in order to avoid a complete collapse of the Afghan communist regime, the loss of Soviet control, and the establishment of a hostile
government as its neighbor.[36]

The internal development of the PDPA, the rise of Amin, and the deterioration of friendly relations between Amin and Moscow caused the Soviet leaders to fear another Yugoslavia and a second Tito. Another possibility, which
Moscow feared, was that Amin would take actions like Sadat, and Said Valen-
tim Falin, then deputy director of the Central Committees International Department.[37] At the same time, the growing resistance could create a gradual

downfall of the PDPA regime or an internal settlement with cooperation from Amin, the opposition groups, and the West. In all scenarios, Moscow hard-line leaders, with the impact of the *Parcham* faction and their KGB supporters, felt threatened by the ongoing developments in Afghanistan. Finally, in December 1979, Moscow chose to send large numbers of Soviet troops to install another, even more trusted leader, Babrak Karmal.

A new chain of economic, social, and political reforms was introduced simultaneously with the Soviet occupation. Afghan media stopped calling the DRA a socialist country, or even holding out socialism as an eventual goal. Under the new leadership, the DRA proclaimed itself ready to respect, observe, and preserve Islam as a sacred religion. The national flag, dyed blood red under the *Khalqis*, reverted to a less provocative traditional red, green, and black. Land redistribution was downplayed and even reversed. An appeal was made to persons who only a short time before had been labeled class enemies, including independent entrepreneurs, landowners, religious figures, and traders. A number of political prisoners, most though not all of them *Parchamis*, were released publicly in the presence of the international press, though secret arrests of potential opponents continued unabated. The PDPA, under the safeguard of 85,000 Soviet troops, began to open the party to noncommunist individuals by introducing a new policy to broaden the base. Despite this, the National Fatherland Front (NFF) was set up in June 1981.[38]

In early 1985, when Mikhail Gorbachev became the head of the Soviet Communist Party and the USSR regime, Babrak Karmal was sent to Moscow for medical treatment, and Najibullah, the head of the grimy secret police, KhAD, was selected as the head of the PDPA regime in November. Moscow and PDPA policy was to bring new faces to both the party and the government to erase from the public's memory the brutality and unjust behavior of the PDPA. But any individual who entered the party and the government was colored by the organized and popular armed resistance groups and, as a result, lived under the armed security of the Soviets. In late 1986, after Najibullah returned from Moscow, he introduced the concept of a government-established national reconciliation that would include non-PDPA activists and some active resistance fighter leaders.

THE SECOND WAVE OF MASS REVOLT
(DECEMBER 1979 TO FEBRUARY 1989)

The Soviet invasion, the result of long-term Soviet economic and political investment in Afghanistan, was accelerated by the Afghan internal political and military changes in late 1979. The Soviet investment created economic dependence that put the political influence of the Soviet interests over the national interests of Afghanistan. The invasion of the Soviet army in Afghanistan increased the scope of the massive revolt and severely rattled Afghan society. The

Afghanistan crisis was internationalized and created a national and international effort against the Sovietization of Afghanistan. Therefore, the violence was nationalized and involved the general population of the country. All the state, civil, and military bodies came under the direct control of the Soviets. All the newspapers, magazines, book publishers, and sales were under the direct control of the government. All political parties except PDPA were outlawed. The curriculum at all levels of the educational system was changed to reflect Soviet interests, and thousands of Afghan children and students were sent to the USSR.[39] Mass arrests continued. According to the *UN Special Reporter,* over 50,000 political prisoners were distributed, as follows, between Kabul and the provincial prisons: 70 percent men, 15 percent women, and 15 percent young people. The heavy Soviet military attacks and bombings of populated areas under the control or influence of the Afghan Mujahideen left thousands of casualties. In the countryside, Soviet aircraft and ground troops also distributed antipersonnel land mines in inhabited areas, such as those used for grazing and cultivation and in villages. The troops also left mines in food storage bins, in mosques, under furniture, in fruit trees, and in fields. Large massacres of civilians, including the virtual annihilation of entire villages by special commandos, occurred with increasing frequency.

Soviet and PDPA strategy was the destruction of the social and economic base of the resistance, especially in the rural areas. This strategy forced the Afghan villagers to seek refuge in the area controlled by the Soviet army or take refuge in neighboring countries. Afghan resistance became more organized and it armed forces with modern and heavy weapons. By 1985, the Soviet army started losing its control over Afghan territories. The Mujahideen forces began to control almost three-fourths of the country, and the Soviets began to suffer heavy defeats.[40] To reach a solution, the Soviets had two options: deploying more troops or withdrawing its troops.

Given the determination and the human resources of the Afghan Mujahideen and the unfavorable regional and global circumstance, for the USSR to implement the first option, they would have needed to increase their troop deployment from the prevailing level of about 120,000 to at least a half-million. The result of this action would have been human and material losses, harder regional and international reaction, and further domestic backlash.

The second option would have been the Soviet withdrawal of troops from Afghanistan before being caught in a situation similar to the U.S. troops in Vietnam, with severe casualties and losses. With the presence of Soviet troops in Afghanistan, there was a greater possibility of the creation of a united and coordinated effort of Mujahideen commanders inside Afghanistan, particularly by the major centralized Mujahideen forces. Thus, Soviet planners were faced with a coordinated international effort against their presence in Afghanistan.

Inside Afghanistan, the Afghan Mujahideen armed forces were not only able to survive the military pressure of the Soviet Union, they were also able to mobilize and organize their forces into a more aggressive military movement. In several fronts the Mujahideen expanded their influence and control and, eventually, established their own administration. The Afghan Mujahideen movement emerged from a defensive position (hit and run) into an offensive position of attacking and controlling positions. For the Afghan Mujahideen, this new strategy decreased the Soviet military activities on the ground and forced them to mobilize in an effort to establish many military garrisons around the cities and along important highways. These units were kept very busy just protecting themselves from the ever-increasing Mujahideen attacks. In unusual cases, these military garrisons provided the Afghan army and the government militia with artillery and other long-range weapons.

In addition, the pressure from the international community increased dramatically. The Soviets began to feel the eyes of the world watching their actions in Afghanistan. The Olympic games of 1980 in Moscow will always be remembered for the U.S. boycott of the games, as well as the strong positions, written and oral, taken by many other nations.

These two factors magnified the domestic problems faced by the Soviet leadership: a declining economy as a result of the huge monetary investment in the Soviet military actions in Afghanistan; the growing public sentiment in opposition to the war; concern for the safety and welfare of the Russian soldiers; severe shortages of food and fuel; and the slipping Soviet position in the world of technology and science. Politically, the Soviet Union was going through major changes. The political disintegration of the Communist Party and the rise of Mikhail Gorbachev and his glasnost policy led to new policies that allowed the Soviet Union to begin withdrawing troops from Afghanistan, thus ending more than a decade of devastation and destruction. The war in Afghanistan drained the Soviet economy of millions of dollars and created strained international relations. Internally, the problems of the government were vastly accelerated by the war. The only possible solution for the Soviet Union was to begin withdrawing troops and redirect the funds that were once used for military might in Afghanistan to programs that would, theoretically, pull the Soviet Union back up on its feet. After several rounds of talks between the United States, neighboring countries, the Soviet Union, and the Kabul regime, the Soviet troops were forced finally to leave Afghanistan in 1988 and 1989.

CHAPTER FIVE

THE PHENOMENA OF CIVIL WAR IN AFGHANISTAN

SINCE THE WITHDRAWAL OF THE LAST SOVIET TROOPS FROM Afghanistan between May 15, 1988, and February 15, 1989, almost all of the political observers assumed that the pro-Soviet regime would collapse within a few months. This assumption did not become reality because of the absence of a united political and military organization that could lead the Afghan Mujahideen groups toward the establishment of a nationally accepted government. At the same time, the Afghan government under Najibullah was not able to provide a workable alternative for a peaceful settlement or gain more power to extend its control. The UN peace initiative on Afghanistan tried to foster the development of a positive environment for a peaceful transition of government, but this also failed. The internal interaction of Afghan armed political forces from the Afghan government and Afghan resistance factions left the UN peace plan without any power or ability to succeed. A bloody civil war shattered this already war-ruined country and forced the Afghans into larger fragmentation.

Studying the history and basis of the civil war in Afghanistan is a complicated task. There are so many factors and sub-factors that act as causes and effects at one time or another. The factors generated their own force, creating many reactions and adding to the extremely colorful events after the withdrawal of the Soviets in 1988. The ethnic complexity of Afghan society and the rise of armed local political power inside Afghanistan along ethnic boundaries caused a misunderstanding among many observers. These observers, such as the United Nations' former special Envoy to Afghanistan, Diego Cordovez, called the civil war after the Soviet withdrawal the "Afghan tribal disputes and blood feuds."[1] This conclusion on the civil war in Afghanistan came from authors who were not familiar with development studies in Afghanistan. First of all, using the words "tribal disputes" and blood feuds" to describe the ethnic conflicts in Afghanistan does not utilize the proper definitions. These perspectives illustrate, more, the way the author looks at the events in Afghanistan than the reality inside this country. Second, calling the ethnic conflicts and disagreement in Afghanistan tribal disputes is far from the ethno-social formation of this nation. In Afghanistan a tribe is a sub-ethnic group that lives usually in great peace and harmony with other tribes in the time of ethnic strife. One may argue that tribal disputes among the ruling elite such as *Ghalzais, Dorannis,* and *Mohammed Zaisis* before 1978 were very noticeable. This is a valid argument and one that may find many supporting facts in the modern history of this land. But the civil war in Afghanistan cannot be identified only as a dispute between the Afghan tribes. The civil war between Najibullah's regime and the Afghan Mujahideen was not only a tribal dispute or based on blood feuds. Both sides of the conflict enjoyed the common participation of many ethnic groups. There were Tajiks and Pushtons on both sides who were fighting harshly against one another. Indeed, tribal disputes were not a new phenomenon within the ethnic line of Afghan society, and there were many tribes who belonged to one ethnic group but sided with another in the conflict. This does not mean the civil war was based on tribal disputes.

In general, the notion that blood feuds fueled the civil war in Afghanistan is not true; however, historically in Afghanistan there have been instances of blood feuds. The concept of blood feuds has a deep root in the cultural tradition of revenge. Through this tradition (in particular among the Pushtons), there were situations where the people washed blood with blood. But this concept was not the only domain of cultural life of the people. There were always many different mechanisms used to stop blood feuds and implement some kind of settlement between two feuding parties. In the case of this current civil war, one can easily see the armed political groups changing sides and positions many times. They collaborate with the old enemy and fight against the previous friend. For example, in 1992 the Uzbek ethnic armed forces, led by General Dostam, sided with the forces loyal to Ahmed Shah Massoud, causing the collapse of Najibullah's government; in 1993, the Uzbek and Massoud forces opened fire on each other on all fronts.

In the wake of the Soviet withdrawal from Afghanistan, the concept of blood feud was popular in many political circles, in particular within the political environment inside Afghanistan. This fearful environment created a massive shift and transition among the local armed political groups, who were attempting to survive. During the years of war against the Soviets, armed local political groups were able to form a political identity that was secured by their social status. Now they, in particular the local leaders who provided financial backing and a group of loyal riflemen, wanted to maintain what they had developed. From a psychological point of view, many of the local commanders believed that they earned the title of being the local commanders or leaders by risking their lives and losing many loved ones.

The desire for survival was not based only on an environment of fear that was filled with blood feuds, it involved many other aspects of life of the local armed groups from both sides of the conflict. Despite all of these issues, many militia leaders and commanders, as well as the military officers and the civil servants of Najibullah's regime, collaborated with the local Mujahideen groups. This process was very obvious to the major organized Mujahideen groups. For instance, in 1987 and 1988 I worked as a nonparty political advisor in the southwest region controlled by Ismail Khan, a Mujahideen leader. The establishment of a civil and military administration to replace Najibullah's regime was one of the most critical tasks facing the Mujahideen in that region. I put together, with the significant help of an Afghan scholar, Gholam Rassul Poyan, a plan to run the local and regional civil and military administrations. One of the fundamental issues of the plan recognized the role of the Afghan technocrats who were working within the Najibullah government. In this case, there was a great need for a peaceful transition of government under the leadership of the Mujahideen. Ismail Khan generally agreed with the plan, although he made some changes, and later he introduced the plan to the planning committee. As a result of understanding the need for a peaceful transition, the southwest Mujahideen leadership, in particular Ismail Khan, committed themselves to declare general immunity for all individuals formerly employed in the Najibullah regime. I was nominated to write and print the charter of this declaration that the Mujahideen distributed all over the region. In the following weeks, I witnessed hundreds of military and civil government officers rushing to the Mujahideen headquarters to announce their willingness to cooperate and to work toward reconciliation. Many famous militia commanders and leaders, who once fought against the Mujahideen, such as Arif Barakzai, Dauod Jiwon, Aamer Said Ahmed, and Hakim Khan Baluch, came personally to the headquarters of Ismail Khan and registered their men and weapons.

Indeed, the possibility of blood feuds was recognized, and everyone believed that this would create bloodshed in the region. Yet the Mujahideen leadership strived to achieve a mechanism to prevent violence against defectors or former adversaries. Through this mechanism, the leadership agreed on a principle that emphasized a stable, national government that would allow people to bring their cause to a court of law and represent their position against those who committed the crime.[2] So, when Cordovez points to blood feuds as one of the most important causes of the civil war in Afghanistan, he is generally mistaken. Thus, the civil war in Afghanistan is not based only on the tribal disputes and blood feuds among the people of Afghanistan; it has a much wider range of causes. To illustrate the causes of the civil war in Afghanistan, one needs to go wider and deeper into the fabric and formation of this war.

POLITICIZATION OF ETHNIC GROUPS

As the crossroads of Asia, Afghanistan is the cross-connection of ethnic groups in the region. Historically, Afghanistan is a bridge between Southeast Asia, Central Asia, and the Middle East. With this in consideration, ethnic and linguistic groups from all over the region resided for centuries in this country and formed a nation state in 1748—many ethnic and tribal leaders came together as the representatives of their community and elected Ahmed Shah, from the *Durani Pashtun* ethnic group, as the head of state. This state was in the form of a federation that recognized the limited autonomy of each ethnic and tribal group.

There are eight major ethnic groups with many different dialects living in Afghanistan. The official statistics and figures on each ethnic group are not reliable due to the domination of the Pushton ethnic group within the government. Statistics obtained from scholars on Afghanistan are much more accurate and closer to reality than the statistics presented by the government. Prior to 1978, the eight major ethnic groups were Pushtons, Tajiks, Hazaras, Uzbeks, Baluchis, Turkmens, Aimaqs, and Kirghiz. Because of the crucial role of the first four ethnic groups in the civil war, I will concentrate more on them.

Pushtons live mostly in the southern and eastern parts of the country and comprise approximately 40 percent of the total population. Most Pushtons are Sunni Muslim, but there is a small sector who are Shia Muslim.[3] Pushtons dominate the government, in particular the armed forces, and their language (Pushto) is one of the two national languages in the country.[4] The eastern Pushtons in Afghanistan share ethnic and tribal cultures with the Pushtons in the Northwest Frontier Province (NWFP) in Pakistan. After the Soviet military invasion of Afghanistan in 1979, the logistical importance of Pakistan as the vital port for the Afghan Mujahideen increased.

In addition, almost 5 million Afghans took refuge in Pakistan, and the bulk of these refugees resided either in refugee camps or they mixed with the Pakistanis, particularly with the Pushtons in many towns and cities in the NWFP region, in particular in Peshawar. Peshawar and its suburbs became the location of military depots and training camps for the Afghan Mujahideen forces. In many aspects the Pushtons on the Pakistani side of the border appear to have very similar lifestyles with the Pushtons in Afghanistan; the only distinguishable aspect is the common use of *Urdo* words in the ordinary language of the people in the NWFP. War in Afghanistan brought many economic and financial opportunities for the people in the NWFP. At the same time that millions of weapons and tons of ammunition poured into this region, many international governmental and nongovernmental agencies opened offices there. Covert information-gathering operations by the western intelligence services and many news and journalist teams also located in this area. Pakistani military activities and military appearances in this region were the most active and intense in the history of Pakistan.

All these events created a large national and international concentration in this particular region that resulted in the important role of the Pushtons on both sides in the political and military events in Afghanistan.

Tajiks form about 30 percent of the population and mostly inhabit the northeast, the west, and some segments of the Kabul area. Tajik participation in the civil administration of the Afghan governments was outstanding for many years. They were popular in the market economy and trade, and Dari, the tongue of the Tajiks, has been the second official language of Afghanistan for many years. Before the 1978 coup, the Tajiks made up "the bulk of the educated elite and possessed considerable wealth . . . particularly in Kabul and Herat, they have significant political influence."[5] Educational opportunities and technical and professional skills helped educated Tajiks deal with politics and government, and, as a result, they had political influence in the country. This influence was very noticeable in the ministries and educational system, in particular at the University of Kabul.

Culturally, Tajiks are not a homogeneous ethnic group; they all speak Dari but each has their own dialect. They are divided into three dialect groups: in the west, mostly in Herat; in the northern provinces; and in Kabul. The majority of Tajiks are Sunni Muslim but there are also Tajiks who practice Shia Islam. The PDPA coup and the Soviet invasion forced many Tajiks to take refuge in neighboring countries. Because of the easy access to the Iranian borders, many people from Herat migrated to Iran, but the bulk of the northern and Kabuli Tajiks went to Pakistan

Hazaras formed 10 to 15 percent of the total population prior to 1978 and lived mainly in the central highlands.[6] The majority of Hazaras follow the Islamic school of Shia, although there is a small number of Hazaras who follow the Islamic school of Sunni. The Hazara language is Dari, a language that is similar to Kirghiz.[7] In the 1880s the central government, under the iron rule of Amir Abdul Rahman Khan, attempted to abolish ethnic autonomy in Afghanistan. Hazaras were among the first ethnic group that revolted against the central government forces. Later, Amir used the Pushtons and Uzbek forces to brutally crush the Hazaras. As Nassim Jawad writes: "thousands of Hazara men were killed, women and children were taken as slaves, and their lands were occupied."[8] This event caused the destruction of the Hazaras communal and social structure, and thousands migrated to Pakistan and Iran where they started a new community with different political identities.

When the Hazaras lost their fertile lands, they were forced to live in isolation in the dry mountains of the central highlands of Afghanistan. The Hazaras lived on the edge of the economic, political, and social system of Afghanistan; this forced many of them to migrate into the major cities like Kabul and form a large majority within the unskilled labor force. In the cities, the Hazaras became active in the economic and political life of the country, many joining the political parties and playing roles in the political game of Afghanistan.

Uzbeks form about 13 percent of the total population and live in the northern part of the country along the border with the former Soviet Union. Uzbeks are Sunni Muslim, speak Uzbeki, and are of Turkish origin, similar to the Turkman and Uzbeks in Turkmenistan and Uzbekistan. They are best known for their work with handicrafts such as producing *galim* (a kind of carpet); Karakul (sheepskin trade) helped Uzbeks develop their involvement in the economic life of the country by establishing entrepreneurial skills and leading to their involvement in the first Afghan industry, cotton production, and textiles. This involvement also enabled them to participate in the political and social life of Afghanistan with great enthusiasm and rigor.

THE PDPA AND ETHNIC GROUPS

For more than two hundred years, Afghanistan was ruled by rulers belonging to various Pushton tribes. After the establishment of the Democratic Republic of Afghanistan in April 1978 by the PDPA, Babrak Karmal, the leader of the *Parcham* faction and a non-Pushton, became the vice president. In the first four months of the April coup, there was a power sharing arrangement between the two PDPA factions, but this shared power collaboration collapsed because of the conflicts along ethnic and policy lines. One of the main reasons for the conflict between the two factions was the concentration of Pushtons in the *Khalq*, under Noor Mohammed Taraki and Haffizullah Amin and the gathering of non-Pushton ethnic groups such as Tajiks, Hazaras, Uzbeks, and Baluchs in *Parcham* under Babrak Karmal. As a result of such ethnic divisions within each faction, their social, political, and economic philosophies, with regard to interpretations of Marxism and Leninism for Afghanistan, differed.

Indeed, fighting over the control of power was an ongoing issue between the two factions. The *Khalqi* faction criticized *Parchamis* because of their weak participation in the coup. Only the air force, which was under Chief of Staff Abdul Qader, a Tajik from Herat who had a close relationship with Babrak and the *Parchamis*, participated in the coup.[9] All of the ground troops and the fourth mechanized army division were led by *Khalqi* officers. The level of participation did not reflect their ideological beliefs; rather, it was a tool used to monopolize the power by depressing their political opponents including their ideological comrades, the *Parchamis*. In this power struggle, the *Khalqi* leaders used the notion of ethnic supremacy to eliminate their political rivals. Once the non-*Khalqi* rivals were wiped out of important governmental positions, the notion of ethnic supremacy dominated the political environment of the PDPA. Indeed, this environment created its own psychological atmosphere that had a great impact on the social and political behavior of the *Khalqi* leaders. As a result, a personality cult of the leaders and their circles emerged within the PDPA, especially among the *Khalqis*, who opened fire on each other. This was the main reason behind the suffocation of Noor Mohammed Taraki by Amin's loyalists. After Hafizullah Amin seized power, he started a wide campaign against the non-Pushton resistance groups in the north of Kabul and in central Afghanistan against the Tajiks and Hazaras. Soon, after the death of Taraki, Amin conducted a military campaign to recruit thousands of young men from many Pushton tribes for entry into the Military Institute (*Harbi Pohanzay*) and the Special Police Academy (*Sarendoy*). A short time after the recruitment, he sent these young men to fight against the non-Pushton resistance. Although many of these young men had not received substantial military training, and, ideologically, they were not loyal to the *Khalqi* leaders, they found themselves in the middle of a battleground. Hundreds of these young men were killed or surrendered to the Mujahideen groups during this campaign in October and November of 1979. In general, Amin tried to bring the tribal groups into the heart of the Communist Party operation, thus creating close ties between the Pushton tribe and the leadership of the Communist Party. He understood the importance of the Pushton tribes on the eastern border of the country through which most of the logistical roads of the Afghan resistance passed.

When Babrak Karmal appeared as the president of the Democratic Republic of Afghanistan with the Soviet military invasion on December 24, 1979, it was the first non-Pushton person to become the head of state in two hundred years.[10] Babarak and his *Parchami* followers already witnessed the weakness of the monopolization of the political power under the *Khalqi* rule. Therefore, the *Parchamis* followed a different approach toward the formation of a broad-based political institution in the country. Under the pressure of Moscow, in particular when Mikhail Gorbachev became the secretary general of the USSR, Karmal agreed to broaden the base of his government. As a result, Babrak appointed about 12 non-PDPA members into the higher-ranking government. But most of these individuals were not Pushtons and many of them came from the Kabul bureaucrats. Theoretically, Karmal agreed with what Hafizullah Amin started when he began to create a constructive line of connection between the PDPA and the tribal and ethnic groups. Yet what was different with this approach was his refusal to give autonomy and flexibility to the Pushton tribes. Indeed, he recognized the autonomy of the non-Pushton ethnic groups during the party campaign known as the Fatherland National Front in the western part of the country.

Ethnicity was a crucial issue among the PDPA's sociopolitical agendas. In this regard, the party and its leadership were aware of the importance of ethnic roles in the political environment of Afghanistan. Through the course of time, the PDPA endeavored continuously to mobilize the ethnic groups throughout the country. There were three major organized efforts by the PDPA and DRA government that attempted to deal directly and explicitly with the ethnic groups and tribal communities.

THE MINISTRY OF TRIBAL AFFAIRS

The first attempt of the DRA government in dealing with the issue of ethnicity was establishing the Ministry of Tribal Affairs. The goal of this ministry was to bring the PDPA message to the tribal communities and in return gain their political support. This ministry was headed by a longtime *Khalq* member, Shah Mohammed Ziri, who had a Pushton background and was from the east. Ziri attempted to introduce the DRA reforms among the tribal population by providing economic aid and government services. This attempt helped the DRA to install its military and political cores in many remote area of the country.

Along with the Ministry of Tribal Affairs, the PDPA attempted to push forward the literacy campaign among the tribal communities. This campaign was filled with dramatic revisions of events and history. The PDPA's political interpretation of Afghan history was to present their party and governmental agendas in the most favorable light possible. Politically the PDPA made many promises to the tribal communities for a better standard of life but, in practice, there was not that much improvement in the daily life of these communities. These political activities among the tribal communities upset the traditional system of eldership by which the tribes lived for centuries.[11] The most important parts of this traditional system were as follows.

INDIVIDUALISM

The concept of individualism has a deep root in the history of ethnic and tribal communities. In Afghanistan, individualism has a great impact in the formation of the sociopsychology of the people and the community. Much of the communal and tribal pride deals with this concept. In the Afghan community, each person has his own space that connects him to the past and shapes his mental outlook in the present. Through such a mentality a person idealizes his future and endeavors to protect his pride and personal dignity. For example, verbally insulting a family member or a close friend will provoke a fistfight on the street. In a case of verbal insult on someone's wife, the person may risk his life and face very severe consequences. The psychological foundation of this kind of social behavior is based on the concept of individualism that that particular person interprets. Through this concept an individual, by punishing the instigator, protects his territory, his pride, and his privacy.

The concept of individualism has its own characteristics, details, and combinations in Afghanistan. This concept is different from the western concept of individualism; for instance, if a person verbally insults someone's family member, the possibility of a fistfight is very rare. The offended person may simply ignore the comment or walk away. In this case, the definition of individualism has a strong root in the social and psychological environment of a community. The main difference is that in western societies the concept of individualism has a narrower and sharper definition. In this society individualism can define things that illustrate the personal will of the people that establishes the dynamic core of the communal interests. In many cases, this concept is mixed with family and group philosophies. Traditionally, the core of this concept is seen in an environment where a person sees his will and expresses his interests.

Tribes usually run their affairs through a tribal administration called eldership. The eldership system is a process through which a tribal member earns honors and achieves a high level of loyalty and dignity among the people. To reach that level of communal respect, a member has to have sacrificed his own interests for the greater interest of the tribe. Historically, this respect and position is built and achieved throughout many years of life and great effort. An elder person who is the chief in the community is a highly respected individual, with great social prestige in the community. Commonly, the influence of elders in the community is not necessarily based on wealth or ownership of land or livestock, but rather on many different factors such as knowledge, compassion, bravery, family heritage, and the ability to solve problems. Indeed, to gain the position of leadership one needs to illustrate many of these factors collectively.

Prior to the PDPA takeover, leaders were the representatives of the local communities to the central government, and they mostly cared about their community's interests. Throughout the process of time, these representatives also became the interpreters of the central government's policies to the local communities. This does not mean that they prioritized the central government interests over the communities. For instance, when the central government chief city officers such as *woleswal* (mayor) or *alaqhadar* (chief district officer) in the rural areas wanted to introduce a government policy, they had to go through the traditional system. Inviting the local and communal leaders to a meeting in the government building (*wolesswaly* or *alaqhahdary*) was the first step. In these meetings the government chief officers attempted to introduce new governmental policies with respect to local community interests and draw a logical parallel between the policies and interests of the government and the ultimate benefits to the people. On several occasions, the local leaders invited the government officer to the main mosque for Friday prayers to talk with the people. After the local leaders presented the communal problems and hardships, the government officer would talk to the people in the mosque and represent the government's promises and support for the local community.

AUTONOMY

The concept of autonomy is very important in Afghanistan and this concept is rooted in the social and political history of this nation. The formation of the modern state system in 1748 was based on autonomous ethnic and sub-ethnic groups. This modern state was the result of a council led by a wise and popular individual, Saber Shah. In this council, the leaders of various ethnic and sub-ethnic groups agreed that Ahmed Shah Abdali (from his mother's side Alekozai and from his father's side Popalzai, thus demonstrating his own ethnic mix) would be the head of the federation of Afghanistan.[12] Each participating ethnic and sub-ethnic group was autonomous in its internal affairs and was responsible for providing men, food, lodging, and military supplies for the federal army.

The degree of autonomy was limited more in the reign of Amir Abdul Rahman Khan in 1897. Amir used military force to bring all the autonomous regions and the ethnic and sub-ethnic groups under the influence of the central government.[13] The military might exhibited by Amir resulted in many deaths and great bloodshed. Politically, Amir's activities vastly decreased the political autonomy of ethnic groups, but his absolute monarchy was not able to abolish the social autonomy of ethnic groups in Afghanistan. To date, the ethnic groups have been able to maintain their social autonomy, and they continue to have control over their internal affairs.

Twentieth-century autonomy in the years just prior to 1978 was based on ethnicity and economic self-sufficiency. Ethnic and sub-ethnic groups enjoyed limited autonomy from the central government. Most of the eight major ethnic groups in Afghanistan ran their ethno-communal lives without the interference of outsiders. The degree of ethno-communal autonomy was different among each group. For instance, the level of ethno-communal autonomy among the Pushtons was sharper and stronger than that of the Tajiks. Also, the level of autonomy was higher among the rural communities than among the people who lived in the cities.

CENTRALISM AGAINST INDIVIDUALISM AND AUTONOMY

The PDPA leaders widely used the exploitation of ethnicity to garner diverse ethnic support for the party, its policies, and its leadership. Recruiting members of each ethnic group was a major activity, but was vital for the party and the government. The recruitment mechanism often took place by educated individuals belonging to a particular ethnic group. These individuals conducted their recruitment efforts in secret, and their efforts led to the formation of a strong core within the party that recruited more people, finally filtering down to a party core among the members of an ethnic group. In many cases, this party core directly and indirectly endeavored to influence the communal decisions and ethnic affairs of the local people.

After the establishment of the DRA, the ethnic core of the PDPA approached the communal leaders in an attempt to influence and mobilize them within the party lines. Because the diverse party core was comprised of mostly young educated individuals, more often than not they did not have the ability to influence the leadership. Yet as they followed the party ideology that was based on Marxism and Leninism, they soon rejected the traditional system of eldership. The PDPA leaders did not accept the Afghan traditional system as a way of managing public affairs. As a result, the communal leaders and the religious heads who were the symbolic figures of the traditional system of eldership came under the political and, later, physical attack of the party and government.

PDPA and DRA activities systematically destroyed the traditional system of eldership and had detrimental effects on the very foundation of Afghan ethno-communal life, individualism, and autonomy. Under these activities, each member of the community or ethnic group should agree with the doctrines and policy of the party and the government. According to the *Inghalab-e-Saur* Editorial, any person who is not in agreement with these doctrines would be accused of being "anti-revolutionary and the representative of the despotic and backward feudalistic system."[14] These representatives could not fit within the party nor the revolutionary and democratic DRA because they would be considered representatives of the political and social elements that caused the backwardness of Afghan society. Therefore, these elements were identified by the PDPA ideological leadership as the enemy of the working class and all working people of Afghanistan.[15]

Considering the eldership system and all its elements as the enemy of the working class and anti–Saur Revolution, the PDPA created an internal enemy within Afghan society.[16] The creation of this internal enemy was rooted in their interpretation of historical materialism and new dialectic theory of Friedrich Engels. This theory argues that economy and market production are the leading elements of social changes within a society. The antagonistic relationship between the backward (feudalism and bourgeoisie) and progressive (proletariat and working class) forces has a profound effect on these social and political changes. This antagonistic relationship becomes a revolutionary war between these two forces. The backward forces fight to maintain their domain to impede economic, social, and political progress while the progressive forces strive to halt these impediments by mobilizing society internally.

In Afghanistan, the PDPA and the DRA considered themselves on the side of the progressive forces of society. They organized the party to be the leading organ in the struggle of progressive forces against the backwardness in Afghanistan. This theoretical interpretation of Afghan society by the PDPA positioned themselves and their government in a state of revolutionary war against the social, political, and cultural elements of Afghanistan. The strategic target of this revolutionary war was the mobilization of political forces to centralize Afghan society.

In Afghanistan, the concepts of individualism and autonomy were interrelated and formed the backbone of the eldership system. This system was a traditional organization that fit within the social and political fabric of Afghanistan. Ideologically, the centralization of political forces and mobilization of society by the PDPA functioned against the concepts of individualism and autonomy in

Afghanistan. In reality, Afghan society was forced into an internal war that planted the seeds of civil war into the soil of Afghanistan. The Ministry of Tribal Affairs was considered to be a tactical target by the DRA because of their efforts to mobilize Afghan society to conform with the ideological and organizational structure of the PDPA. The DRA and organizations such as the Ministry of Tribal Affairs were the tools used to force society into the party structure. The task of reaching this extremely difficult and complicated goal (fitting Afghan society into the PDPA model) was very overwhelming.

Because the PDPA was formed by a small portion of the Afghan population (10,000 in 1978), the ideological and organizational structure of the party did not have the capacity or the flexibility to recruit the majority of the population. In other words, the PDPA's ideological and organizational structure was like a large picture trying to fit into a small frame. To fit the picture into the frame, one must cut it from all sides while considering the picture as it was before. The PDPA followed a similar process, but they called the segment that fit into the frame progressive and revolutionary forces and labeled the parts outside of that frame backward and antirevolutionary.

Fitting Afghan ethnic and communal groups within the PDPA and the government created a nondemocratic political environment. In this environment the PDPA attempted to centralize Afghan society. Centralism abolished individualism and autonomy among the ethnic and communal groups. Individual freedoms and ethno-communal autonomy was the foundation of a democratic life and satisfied people's needs for freedom. One can argue that the Afghan society was enjoying democracy long before the DRA regime, as seen in the peaceful coexistence and high levels of cooperation among many different ethnic, linguistic, and religious groups within a territory. Members of these ethnic groups had individual rights within their groups. Indeed, these different ethnic groups were not only able to enjoy individualism and autonomy, they were also able to function, as Fredrik Barth writes, as "aggregated people who essentially share a common culture, and interconnected differences that distinguish this culture from all others"[17] and form a cohesive history together.

THE FATHERLAND NATIONAL FRONT

After the Soviet military invasion of Afghanistan and the takeover of the *Parcham* faction of the PDPA led by Babrak Karmal, the PDPA leadership and the Soviet advisors were aware of the importance of ethnic and sub-ethnic roles in the formation of the political system in Afghanistan. They witnessed the deterioration of the *Khalq* faction through a radical approach to mobilize Afghan society, led by Noor Mohammed Taraki and Hafizullah Amin. In this approach, the DRA regime endeavored to make the central government the only political institution of the country. The party and the government created many different organizations to connect the party with the masses. In doing so, the PDPA upset the traditional cycle of daily life, in particular in the rural areas, where more than 80 percent of the population resided. Yet this approach was unable to replace the traditional system of life with a new one. As a result, the traditional system of eldership that had functioned as a civic organization for many years lost its normal operation. This, in turn, created a chaotic environment that was filled with violence and military activities.

Politicization of ethnic and communal groups was like putting a stick into a hornet's nest without proper preparation. This political environment forced the DRA regime from an aggressive position into a defensive position and caused the disintegration of the party and government. The PDPA was divided into many different subfactions, and the government lost its credibility after the armed revolt of the government forces and their defection to the Mujahideen groups.

The PDPA, under the leadership of Babrak Karmal's *Parchamis*, planned to broaden the base of the government and recognize autonomy of ethnic groups. But because of the centralized government structure that they inherited from the *Khalqhis* under Hafizullah Amin, they were unable to change the political environment. The presence of Soviet troops in Afghanistan impeded any significant change for the benefit of the PDPA.

The establishment of the Fatherland National Front (FNF) in 1979 and 1980 was a new approach toward the recognition of ethnic and communal autonomy under the supervision of the PDPA and the Soviet advisors in Afghanistan. As Philip Taubman reports: "The gathering of the National Fatherland Front offered a look at a sometimes startling mix of Afghan tradition and Soviet-style Communism."[18] The strategic target of forming the FNF was to change the balance of power against the Afghan Mujahideen. This objective was comprised of two tactical targets.

The DRA regime attempted to broaden its social and political base among the people. Babrak Karmal blamed the *Khalqis* and Hafizullah Amin for all of the atrocities against the people of Afghanistan. He announced his respect for Islam and the religious leaders, and he attended the Friday prayer in the main mosque in Kabul. He met many ethnic and sub-ethnic elders and leaders and endeavored to open a dialogue with them about the role of the government. He announced that the decrees of reforms conducted by *Khalqis* were invalid, and he promised to return the confiscated lands and properties to their original owners.

Establishing the FNF broadened the politicization of ethnic and communal groups, especially when the DRA regime encouraged them to bear arms and form local armed groups as militia along with the government and Soviet forces. This policy was started by the creation of the local neutral areas such as villages, *woleswalis*, and *alaqhadaris*; it later spread all over the country. The people of any village and *woleswali* who agreed to remain neutral toward the Mujahideen and the DRA received government aid. Those villages who pledged their allegiance to the DRA not only received aid but also military protection. In this period of time, the structure of the DRA regime was comprised of the Soviet civil and military advisors, the PDPA, and the militia groups.

Massive military operations by the Soviet and DRA air and ground troops to mobilize forces became an important target of the PDPA. Through this target, the DRA and the Soviet planners in Afghanistan were approaching a systematic policy that offered Afghans, mostly in rural areas, the chance to cooperate or be destroyed. Being neutral and passive against the DRA and the Soviets in late 1981 and into 1982 meant taking away human and economic resources from the Mujahideen groups. In the course of time, most of the areas that were neutral found themselves in the middle of the fire. Many leaders of these areas helped the Mujahideen groups at night, but supported the government during the day. Areas that did not cooperate with the DRA and the Soviets were punished by severe bombardments and destruction of economic and communal life. This policy not only devastated the human and economic resources of the Mujahideen groups, it also destroyed the economic and social system of Afghanistan. Massive military campaigns of the Soviet and DRA air and ground troops forced millions of Afghans to take refuge in neighboring countries such as Pakistan and Iran, while a large group of people became internal refugees.

The formation of neutral and passive communities, in reality, became the social and military defense barricades around the DRA and the Soviets. These passive communities (that later became active against the Mujahideen groups) became the core of the PDPA political activities against the Mujahideen. When these passive communities became active against the Mujahideen by forming their own militia groups, they were confronted with an aggressive response from the Mujahideen groups. Eventually the issue of self-defense for these communities required DRA and Soviet military support and protection. Politically, these communities became isolated, and their channels of contact were limited to the DRA and the Soviets. Because of the security issue, the Soviets and the DRA planted a million land mines around these areas and controlled all communication and transportation. There were limited and secret activities of the Mujahideen groups in these areas, but the main channel of information and communication was under the control of the PDPA.

Destruction of the traditional social and economic system in Afghanistan damaged the economic self-sufficiency of the local communities and made the people heavily dependent on foreign aid. Areas under DRA and Soviet control depended on Soviet aid and protection, while areas controlled by the Mujahideen groups lost their internal, community-based economic supports such as food and money to finance their activities.[19] The increased volume of military operations between the DRA/Soviets and the Mujahideen devastated local economies; it was impossible to rely on domestic sources for purchasing arms and feeding armed groups.

The destruction of the economic system and the displacement of the local ethnic and communal groups caused the destruction of the traditional sociopolitical system in Afghanistan. The eldership system was severely damaged and many communal and ethnic leaders were jailed, executed, or sought refuge in neighboring countries. The local communities faced war against the aggressive DRA regime and Soviet military operations. Local ethnic and communal groups needed new leadership to guide them in this situation. This need, after the Soviet invasion, resulted in the rise of a new aggressive leadership able to fight smarter and better than ever before. This kind of leadership was comprised mostly of younger individuals who risked their lives in battle and heeded the call of the people for an armed defensive struggle.

The establishment of the FNF helped the Soviet troops to hide behind the Afghan army and militias in their military operations against Mujahideen groups. Creating a neutral zone by isolating villages made it easier for the Soviets to control larger segments of the Afghan population. This was important to the Soviets as they wanted to change the nature of the war from Afghans against Soviets to a war of Afghans against Afghans. From the Soviet point of view, this tactical aim would reduce Soviet human losses and decrease the anti-Soviet sentiment. In the long run, if the DRA and the Soviet planners were able to divide and fracture the Afghan people, the Soviet troops would have the ability to influence their interests in Afghanistan.

In general, the goal in establishing FNF was to bring the ethnic groups in line with PDPA philosophies and into the party structure. Even though Babrak Karmal was claiming that he had Pushton ethnic background, many of the PDPA members and leaders believed that Karmal used this proclamation of his ethnic heritage as a political tool to gain popular support from the Pushtons. The role of ethnic groups in the party created a gap between Najibullah, chief of intelligence of the government, and Karmal. Najibullah was a *parchami*, but also a Pushton who had developed strong ties with the Pushton ethnic groups in the east. Through a secret operation and the help of Chatty, a Pakistani communist who lived in Afghanistan for seven years and had a close relationship with Najibullah, Najibullah was able to send his message to the Pushtons on the other side of the eastern borders.[20]

Najibullah argued with Karmal to give him more room for the PDPA Pushton leaders and the prestigious Pushton ethnic leaders. In particular, Najibullah was aware of the important role the Pushton tribe could play on the eastern border in the aftermath of the Soviet withdrawal from Afghanistan. This argument was supported by the *Khalqh* faction under Gulabzoi and used against Karmal.[21] Keeping with this new Soviet policy under Gorbachev, that of the liberalization of the base of government in Afghanistan, Najibullah used the ethnic issue to persuade Soviet planners not happy with Karmal to remain the head of the Afghan government. On November 20, Radio Kabul announced Karmal's resignation as Afghanistan's president; it was broadcast that he was relieved of all his responsibilities by the revolutionary council "at his own request."

THE NATIONAL RECONCILIATION POLICY

Soon after he became the head of the DRA in May 1986, Najibullah introduced a broad-based policy that came with the waves of glasnost from the Soviets. Najibullah was aware of the national, regional, and international political environment, and he knew that the Soviet troops would leave Afghanistan sooner or later. Najibullah was the only realistic leader among the PDPA who dealt with national and international issues concerning Afghanistan. One can argue that he was the only Afghan leader who was aware of what was happening in Afghanistan, in the region, and in the global community.

For many years, Najibullah was the head of the KhAD, *Khedamat-e-Etal'at-i-Dawlati*, the state intelligence service known as the Afghan KGB and the backbone of the DRA government.[22] This position provided Najibullah a great opportunity to understand the circumstances within the Afghan ethnic and communal groups. He was not only able to contact the ethnic groups inside the country, he also was able to go beyond the eastern and southern borders, in particular, among the Pushton ethnic groups. His broad-based policy allowed non-PDPA individuals to take a role in the government. Through the National Reconciliation Policy, he sent his message to large numbers of important Afghans inside and outside the country. His government invested heavily in the Mujahideen commanders who did not have a strongly formed political ideology against the DRA by providing them with money, power, and weapons to fight their rival Mujahideen groups. This program caused a rise in ex-Mujahideen militia groups in many parts of the country. For the first time, in 1986 Najibullah removed the name of PDPA from the party and merged it into a broad-based party called the *Hezb-e-Watan Afghanistan*, the Motherland Party of Afghanistan (HWA). HWA was comprised of noncommunists and other individuals who were not affiliated with the PDPA. According to the Afghan official publication, HWA political ideology was not based on Marxism but rather on Afghan national and historical values and Islamic principles.

After Najibullah offered a peacemaking policy in 1987, he tried to win over potential peacemakers by renouncing communism, pledging commitment to pluralism and Islam, and subsequently he loosened controls on Kabul's opposition press and moderate dissidents. Najibullah's action indicated his political position was moving from radical communist beliefs of the far left to a more moderate middle-of-the-road policy. Sharing power and committing to pluralism and Islam was a serious ideological setback for the PDPA leaders who believed in the Saur Revolution as an irreversible event of Afghanistan history. This setback dismantled the notion of the vanguard party and the PDPA as the highest political organ of Afghanistan that was documented in the PDPA charter in 1978. In his press conference in May 1991, Najibullah stated: "If a political approach is not serving the cause of the people, then put it aside," and he added "my main responsibility as a politician is to move toward a positive direction, it is all I can do."[23] This ideological formation helped the HWA leaders to be more outgoing than before and able to approach ethnic and communal groups.

Under Najibullah's leadership the HWA in 1987 changed the name of the government from the Democratic Republic of Afghanistan to the Republic State of Afghanistan (RSA). These changes were essential for the former PDPA leaders to survive and were made in anticipation of the Soviet withdrawal from Afghanistan. As a result of this change, Najibullah allowed several non-PDPA members into his cabinet. Among those, Abdul Malik Khalighyar became the prime minister of Afghanistan. Khalighyar was an Afghan educated scholar and came from Herat province. He had strong ties to the ethnic groups in the *woleswali* of Kushk where he was born.[24] As prime minister, Khalighyar helped the RSA regime shrink the gap between the masses and the government. For instance in 1988 and 1989, Khalighyar's messengers, both inside and outside of Afghanistan, carried his message of reconciliation and cooperation. Under his guidance, hundreds of popular Afghan individuals from the village level to the national level and from inside the country, such as the local and major Mujahideen commanders, to the technocrats in exile all over the world were contacted. These messages were signed by President Najibullah or Khalighyar and received via Afghan embassies, consulates, and unofficial sources.[25]

Through the National Reconciliation Policy, President Najibullah announced national amnesty for all Mujahideen groups and attempted to open a dialogue with them. In May 1991, *The New York Times* reported that under the national amnesty, "Mr. Najib, as he was often referred to, promised to free prisoners who served four or more years of a seven year sentence, all prisoners sentenced to five years or less, all women in prison and any prisoners more than 60 years old."[26] But there were several problems for which the HWA and the Najibullah regime were not able to provide appropriate resolutions. Previously, Najibullah was the head of KhAD, a government organization that was responsible for the death, torture, and execution of thousands.[27] This was a counter-defect that counted against him directly and dismantled his strong role as the most knowledgeable and influential person in government leadership. This weakness in his character, as a person who was accused of thousands of deaths, gave his opposition a great chance to attack the National Reconciliation Policy and any political agendas introduced under his leadership. The RSA government was able to gain the cooperation of many Mujahideen groups through ethnic relationships, large financial and military support, recognition of ethnic and communal autonomies, and by using the conflicts between rival Mujahideen groups. According to Commander Ismail Khan, from 1987 to 1988 there were about 20,000 armed militias in Herat and neighboring provinces.[28] Prior to the Soviet withdrawal, these militia groups were the main force against the Mujahideen groups on all fronts. For example, in the fall of 1987, when I was visiting the western part of the city of Herat, I witnessed a military clash between the Mujahideen forces led by Commander Alawadin Khan, second in charge after Ismail Khan (the main Mujahideen commander in northwest), against the government militia forces under Amer Said Ahmed. Said Ahmed was a famous defected Mujahideen commander affiliated with the Islamic Society Party led by Burhanadin Rabbani. In this military clash, both sides called each other "Monafiq" (meaning those who betray Islam), and it was easy to hear the words "Allah-o-Akbar" (God is Great) from both groups when they attacked each other.

CHAPTER SIX

ZONAL DIVISION OF AFGHANISTAN

UNDER THE NATIONAL RECONCILIATION POLICY (NRP) FROM 1985 TO 1986, the name of the Ministry of Tribal Affairs was changed to the Ministry of Nationalities and Tribal Affairs. This change was associated with the Geneva Accord by which the Soviets agreed to withdraw its troops from Afghanistan. Under this change, the Republic State of Afghanistan (RSA) regime and the Soviets desired to broaden the government's social foundation and deal with larger concentrations of people—ethnic groups rather than tribes. Along with this change, the Soviet and the RSA leaders divided Afghanistan into seven zones, each with unique geographic, socioeconomic, and ethnic or tribal characteristics, and each was of different strategic importance to the Soviets.[1] Each of these zones had one deputy prime minister who had extensive authority working with a zonal committee comprised of military and civilian officers of both Soviets and Afghans. The main strategy of the zoning of Afghanistan was to secure the Soviet regional interests.

Dividing Afghanistan into seven zones would give the Soviet and the RSA regime the control and ability to use their military and economic sources in an efficient and useful way. Under this policy, the Soviet and the RSA government responded to each zone according to its importance to their short- and long-term strategies. In the short term, the security of the RSA regime was a vital tool for the long-term security and stability of the USSR's southern borders, in particular with regard to the spread of the Muslim insurgencies in Soviet Central Asia. Much of this zoning strategy remained on paper and was implemented roughly with the advent of each crisis. All the zones in the southern part of the Hindu Kush mountains remained under the increasing influence of the Mujahideen groups. Since northern Afghanistan borders Soviet Central

Asia, the three northern zones (the northwest, the north, and the northeast) were comprised of nine provinces that were vital to the Soviets. A large portion of the northwest province that was centered in Herat came under the influence of a famous Mujahideen commander, Ismail Khan, after several extensive military clashes. These clashes forced the Soviets and the RSA regime to reconsider the provinces of Shabarghan and Jowzjan as centers that might be able to keep the balance against Ismail Khan's forces. The north and northeastern zones became the focal point of the RSA and the Soviet efforts. Ethnically, these zones were less fragmented and were populated with the ethnic and communal groups who shared a high degree of ethnic and lingual affinity with Soviet Central Asia inhabitants.

According to Najibullah, "to strengthen the culture of these nationalities" the government should establish the Uzbek and Turkmen schooling curricula within the school system of the region. For this reason, the Soviets started publications such as *Yuldis* (The Star), *Girash* (The Struggle), and *Sab* (The Revolution) in the northern languages.[2] In addition to these publications, the Soviets began radio broadcasts and used new television capabilities to beam programs into northern Afghanistan in 1987. Many Uzbek and Turkmen families temporarily migrated from Soviet Central Asia to northern Afghanistan. This migration was a political attempt aimed at creating a more positive sociopolitical environment for the role of the Soviets in the region. These immigrant families brought a new concept of social and political life to northern Afghanistan.

Along with massive publications, radio, and TV broadcasting, the Soviets and the RSA regime appointed the most loyal and important officers in charge of the military posts to this region. General Jumah Asak, one of the most famous political and field commanders of the regime, was appointed to head the military administration (that was combined with the intelligence organization of the state).[3] Under his command, northern Afghanistan formed its own separate military structure and administration. The military ability of the armed forces improved dramatically as a result of the massive military aid and influx of military advisors. The military operations against the Mujahideen groups in the area were conducted in a very organized manner that used a combination of missiles, artillery, air force, and ground troops. These organized and notorious military operations forced the Mujahideen groups to retreat into the mountains around the northern centers, in particular Mazar-e-Sharif.

The Najibullah regime gained the cooperation of the *Setam-e-Meli*, a leftist political party who established armed organized groups in the north and were struggling against the supremacy of the Pushtons' rule in Afghanistan. (*Setam-e-Meli* planned and carried out the kidnapping of U.S. Ambassador Dub in 1978 that ended in the death of the ambassador and the kidnappers in a hotel in Kabul.) At the same time, the government was able to neutralize the Shia *Ismaeli* minority in the region, despite the fact that they were well organized and controlled their area through their armed forces under the leadership of Sayed Hussine Naderi, the religious representative of Aga Khan (the religious leader of the *Ismaeli Shia* in the world). This group eventually began to cooperate and assist the government.

In the civil administration of the north, Sayed Nasim Mihanparast, a very complex man (he worked as an Afghan government officer and as a Soviet military officer), was nominated as deputy prime minister.[4] Mihaparast was an important and well-connected official to Moscow. He was the brain behind the creation of a new province called Sar-e-Pol in April 1988. This new province was one of the richest in natural resources in the country, containing large natural gas and petroleum reserves. One of the incentives behind this effort was to change the regional social balance in Afghanistan and direct the economic resources of northern Afghanistan toward the social and political mixture with Soviet Central Asia. In late spring of 1988, President Najibullah appointed a new deputy minister, Najibullah Masir, to be in charge of northern affairs.[5] Still, Mihanparast remained the most influential person in the region.

Massive economic and technical assistance poured into these northern zones to promote economic stability and independence. The aim of this economic and technical assistance was to tie the local economy to the Soviet economy in Central Asia. On August 27, 1985, an agreement for Economic and Technical Cooperation was signed between the USSR and the RSA, which emphasized the economic, technical, and geographic developments of northern Afghanistan.[6] This new agreement brought numerous projects that were accompanied by thousands of the USSR technicians, mostly from Soviet Central Asia. Training centers in Mazar-i-Sharif, the capital of the Balkh province, recruited hundreds of young Afghans for training in numerous subjects. In December 1987 an agreement of energy and technical cooperation was signed between the province of Balk and the Republic of Uzbekistan. As a result of this agreement many Afghans were sent to Uzbekistan for educational and technical training. A new gas and petroleum pipeline, roads, and transportation facilities were to be built between the two areas. A new electricity line brought power into the province, and the job creation potential boomed in northern Afghanistan.

The agreement between the province of Balkh and Uzbekistan was unique in its kind. In the current history of Afghan foreign relations, this was the first time that the provincial authorities, who were a part of the central government, signed an agreement with a foreign state. In the beginning of the Soviet concentration of resources in northern Afghanistan, many observers thought northern Afghanistan could be a sophisticated base for Najibullah's regime to ward off the southern sect of the Hindu Kush (which was under the influence of the Mujahideen). But the August agreement between Balkh and Uzbekistan complicated the issue and created a very tense political environment in the region. Some argued that the development in the north would disintegrate Afghanistan as a united country and would change the geopolitical map of the region. Others argued that the Najibullah government, under pressure from the Mujahideen and with the support of the west (in particular the United States), would settle in the north and transfer the civil and military administration to Mazar-e-Sharif, thus losing control of valuable territory.

Indeed, the economic integration of northern Afghanistan with the Soviet Union was the main target of these activities in the north. From the Marxist point of view the economic development of society directly impacts political development; the economic integration of northern Afghanistan with the Soviet Union would result in the political integration of the region. Whether the Soviets were planning to formally annex northern Afghanistan into the USSR is still a question of much debate, as formal and direct annexation of northern Afghanistan would provoke the international community and would result in a higher degree of American involvement in the region. Moreover, annexation of the north would bring the southern Hindu Kush into the front line of an armed struggle that could involve Soviet Central Asian communities in a long-term war. This kind of war would be like a flooding river eroding its banks to reach new territories. There were logical and rational, short- and long-term objectives of the Soviet concentration in northern Afghanistan.

The short-term were objectives through which the Soviets attempted to increase the security of their southern borders with Afghanistan. The long USSR southern border with Afghanistan was dominated by the people who have great ethnic, linguistic, religious, and traditional similarities with the people who live on the Afghan side of the border. One of the most common political characteristics of the people on both sides of the border was that they were suppressed by the USSR. Traditionally, Afghanistan was officially or unofficially strong supporters of the Turkistan struggle against the Tsar and the Soviets.[7] According to the military sources in Afghanistan during the first stage of the Soviet invasion of Afghanistan, those USSR troops who came from the Central Asian Republics had more sympathy for the people of Afghanistan compared to the USSR soldiers from other republics. As a result, the Central Asian regiments were replaced by those who had a different nationality and religious background.[8]

If the Soviets were to be defeated, the result could be the development of a stable Islamic government in Afghanistan that would be perceived as a direct threat to the security of the USSR's southern borders. This kind of development would inspire insurgencies among the Central Asian nations against the Soviets, especially when such a government in Afghanistan could have U.S. support. Thus, southern border security was a prime focus for the USSR.

The long-term objective for the Soviets was to not only insure the security of the southern border with Afghanistan, but also to pursue regional objectives through the country. Northern Afghan Provinces, which became economically dependent on the local concentration of Soviets, lead also to a political dependency. Changing northern Afghanistan into an industrial and modern zone with a high level of productivity would have a great impact on the southern part of the Hindu Kush in this country and could facilitate Soviet regional interests. Northern Afghanistan could easily be used as an example of the Soviet generosity and good will for the people of Afghanistan. Theoretically, the Soviet concentration in northern Afghanistan would fit with the political ideology of the communist leaders by creating a modern, industrial, and pro-socialist democratic society as opposed to the backward and feudalistic southern and eastern parts of the country. This modern and socially oriented part of Afghanistan would operate as the base for the so-called revolutionary movements in Pakistan, Iran, and other countries in the region. By achieving these objectives in northern Afghanistan, the Soviets would be able to neutralize the sensitive nationalist, religious, and cultural feelings of the Central Asian nations for many more years.

Soviet concentration and the Najibullah government's efforts in northern Afghanistan were significant achievements for the Soviet interests in this country. This concentration has demolished the traditional social system of eldership in a large portion of the northern provinces. Much political attention was concentrated on the massive mobilization of the northern youths through numerous educational, developmental, and military programs. The government invested heavily to stimulate the youths by introducing liberal programs and sending them in large numbers to the Soviet republics for training. Also during this time, the University of Balkh was established and accepted high school graduates from all northern provinces. There was a big push to encourage the high school graduates to attend the army academy and join the army. The government started a massive campaign to enroll the Afghan youth in the armed forces. For example, in 1986 President Najibullah implored all the youth of Afghanistan to support the decision of the graduates of schools in Mazar-e-Sharif to voluntarily join the ranks of the armed forces. He called it a "shining example."[9]

The Soviet and RSA regime approached a unique methodology with the ethnic groups in the rural areas. They militarized the ethnic Uzbek into a unique military machine that soon became an important part of the Afghan army. The government was able to protect key positions on the highways, cities, and the natural gas projects with the fearless Uzbek militia and soldiers. Later, these militia were used against other ethnic groups in many parts of the country. The government's 18th army division, the number 1 *Sarandoy* units (the special armed forces working under the state intelligence agencies), and the air force units were deployed in the region and were heavily armed. The army and intelligence staffs received the highest government bonuses and commendations in the country. Indeed, northern Afghanistan, and in particular the Balkh province, became the safe haven for the former PDPA and loyalists of Najibullah's government.

CHAPTER SEVEN

THE AFGHAN MUJAHIDEEN AND MASS MOBILIZATION

AFGHAN MUJAHIDEEN GROUPS WERE THE MAIN POLITICAL AND military forces whose struggle resulted in the Soviet withdrawal from Afghanistan. The formation of the Mujahideen groups inside the country caused a significant impact on the social, political, and cultural mobilization of Afghan people. Since these groups themselves were the result of the mass mobilization in the country, they also have ideological and organizational status. The organizational and ideological mobilization of Afghan Mujahideen groups is one of the least studied aspects of the civil war. The leaders of the Afghan Mujahideen groups came from different personal, family, linguistic, and ethnic directions. In principle they had much in common but in practice they were very different. In general, both the internal and external fronts of the Mujahideen were the result of the sociopolitical mobilization of the country. As Anthropologist Frederick Barth states:

> The Afghan Resistance differs from most resistance and liberation movements in other parts of the world in that it is not based on a shared political ideology. It is not a centrally organized movement, and it is not animated by a vision of a new reformed society. Its roots are deep in folk culture, and consist of three major components: 1) A clear and demanding conception of individual honor and self-respect as a necessary basis for personal identity and value. 2) A desire to live by one's own local, highly diverse traditions and standards. 3) An Islamic conviction.[1]

Therefore, ideological and organizational ties were very weak among the Mujahideen political parties in Afghanistan. The most significant of the organizational relationship between the external and internal fronts was the importance of getting arms and financial support. During the three decades of war, there were numerous commanders who, at the same time, carried the membership cards of more than one party without the direct understanding of the political agenda of any of those parties. Almost all of the internal front commanders were operating without any specific command from the external front. This was the reason that several of them, such as Commander Massoud in the north, Ismail Khan in the southwest, and Molawi Haqani in the southeast organized large-scale military and administrative power operations that were out of the control of the external front. The loyalty of the armed Mujahideen was much stronger with the local leaders than with their external party leaders.

BACKGROUND

The Afghan resistance, known as the Mujahideen organizational formation, is rooted in political movements from 1968 through 1971. During this period, Afghanistan was dominated by waves of many different political organizations and circles. These political organizations were active within the government and segments of Afghan society. The political ideology of these groups originated in Marxism/Leninism, western liberalism, Islamic teachings, and nationalism. The majority of these political organizations were protesting for reforms and changes in the political institution of the country. The core of these groups was among the urban population, especially at the universities, high schools, and among the lower-ranking government employees.

After the military coup in June 1973 (under the leadership of Mohammed Dauod) and the establishment of the Afghanistan Republic, the new regime put pressure on the political oppositions and many prominent politicians were arrested. The collaboration and participation of the *Parcham* faction of PDPA in the coup, and later in the government, upset many political circles. Among others, the Afghan *Ikhwan-al-Mulimin* (Muslim Brethren) managed to organize secret activities against the regime. The group organized armed campaigns against the government in which they planned to assassinate several of President Dauod's cabinet members. Only one of the assassins hit his target, killing Minster of Planning Ali Ahmed Khoram.

Soon, many leaders and activists of the Afghan Muslim Brethren were jailed while others, such as Gulbedin Hekmatyar and Ahmad Shah Massoud, took refuge in Pakistan, where, under the support of Zulfikar Ali Bhutto's government, they obtained arms and ammunitions. (Also, among them were Burhanadin Rabbani, Maulawi Younos Khalis, Maulawi Mansoor, and Jalaladdin Haqani.) These individuals formed *Hezb-e-Islami* (the Islamic Party), a Pakistan-based militant organization led by Hekmatyar and Qazi Amin. The *Hezb-e-Islami* launched a military operation against the Dauod regime, in order to gain international support and national recognition in Afghanistan. In 1975, an armed group of Hizb led by Ahmed Shah Massoud crossed the border and

reached the Panjshir Valley (where Massoud was from) in an attempt to provoke the people into an armed uprising against the government.[2] The group
was not successful and was crushed severely by the government forces. As a result, some of prominent members including Abdul Rahim Niazi, a theoretician
of the brotherhood, were sentenced to death by the government.

During the Soviet invasion of Afghanistan, Mujahideen groups were comprised of two elements: the external front and the internal front.

The external front included those who were urban educated and had
strong ties to religious, ethnic-tribal, and linguistic populations within the
country. Almost all had a background of political activity; all took refuge in
Pakistan and Iran after the April coup.

The establishment of the Democratic Republic of Afghanistan, the widespread revolt against the regime in 1978, and the Soviet invasion in 1979
opened the road for expansion to the *Hezb-e-Islami* under Hekmatyar (HIH)
and Qazi Amin Waqad as the only organized Afghan group in Pakistan. The
support from the Pakistani government, the shared beliefs and activities of
Hekmatyar with Qazi Hussine, the leader of the *Jamaat-e-Islami of Pakistan*
(JIP), and their connection with the Muslim Brotherhood in Egypt provided
Hekmatyar great access to the Muslims in the Persian Gulf. Since *Jamaat-e-
Islami* of Pakistan had a great influence in the Pakistani government, in particular among the army, the political and personal connection of Hekmatyar
with Qazi Hussine had channeled the international aid to him. This strong
connection and closeness with the Pakistani government and JIP not only
helped the Hekmatyar to get the bulk of the international aid but also helped
him to monopolize the political activities in Pakistan by imposing political
sanctions and terror campaigns on moderate Mujahideen, nationalist, and
anti-Soviet leftist groups.

Hezb-e-Islami, under the influence of Hekmatyar, established one of the
most centralized political parties, a rarity in the political history of Afghanistan.
This highly centralized formation of the leadership and personnel control was
not only unrealistic with regard to the egalitarian notion of Afghan tradition, it
was in conflict with the social concept of individual freedom and communal autonomy of Afghan people, and it also did not tolerate different political opinions by other high-ranking members of Hezb. As a result, the fragmentation of
the party started with the departure of Burhanadin Rabbani, a former professor
of Islamic law of Kabul University, and Ahmed Shah Massoud, a former student at the School of Engineering. One may argue that the ethnic and linguistic differences between Hekmatyar, who was Pushton, and Rabbani and
Massoud, who were Tajik, played a great role in the disintegration of the Islamic Party. Eventually, the other Pushton breakaway group, made up of high-
ranking members including Qazi Amin Waqad, established a second
Hezb-e-Islami. This organization was the result of an attempt by Hekmatyar
to create a highly centralized political party under his leadership. Indeed, the

Jamaiat-e-Islami of Afghanistan (the Islamic Society of Afghanistan) under Rabbani recruited non-Pushtons, especially in the northern and western parts of the country.[3]

The external front was comprised of two factions: Seven of them were Pakistan-based groups, mostly Sunni Muslim, including the *Afghan Melat* who were not recognized by the Pakistani government; and eight of them were Iran-based groups, mostly Shia Muslim. The external front had a wide range of political and diplomatic activities with broad publications that were known internationally. Officially, the external front was comprised of the party bureaucracy and leaders of the general affairs of the Afghan Mujahideen, but practically they were only the food, money, and weapons distributors for the internal front. Many of them were never inside Afghanistan during the Soviet invasion and also never participated in any military operation. Some of them were large stock owners in the global banking system and enjoyed a luxurious lifestyle.

The external front leaders formed a new social element that became part of the political elite without holding government offices. This was a unique formation that was well organized, politicized (according to Afghan politics), and well connected to regional and international politics. In the course of Afghanistan's modern history, this was a new social and political development. There were always political leaders in Afghanistan who did not hold any government office or receive pay from the government, including the Afghan ethno-tribal and communal leaders under the eldership system or the political leaders during the reign of the Afghan monarch (1969–1971) and during Mohammed Dauod's presidency (1973–1978). But they did not have a wide scope of activities like the Mujahideen party leaders did during the Soviet invasion. The political elite outside the DRA government who formed the opposition groups (Mujahideen) were able to gain international support, in particular from western and Islamic countries.

This sociopolitical elite had its own political agenda for the social and political changes that would satisfy their personal, family kinship, and political interests. Most of the members of this political elite had interests similar to the party leader. In general, all the important divisions including the finance office and the military department were under the very tight control of the male members of the leader's family. The loyalty of these close family members often was not based on the political ideology of the party but rather driven by a combination of the traditional kinship concept and economic interests. Through these concepts, the active and powerful political and financial influence of the leader would secure the sociopolitical and economic interests of those family members.

In some cases, some of the close family members of the party leader in charge of key positions established their own circle of power and interests. Usually, the interests of this kind of establishment fit into the general interests of the party leaders. Because this type of leadership increased and spread within the party administration, the leadership was more safe and secure. In order for the lower-ranking family members to receive financial aid from the party they had to be registered with the party. This type of leadership allowed the leaders to retain ultimate control and domination over their party. In order to offer financial aid within the family circle, it was necessary to establish a wide range of investments through businesses, banks, and purchased property around the globe. Some of these circles were engaged in money laundering, racketeering, and international trade. Selling arms and ammunitions to Afghan and non-Afghan sources became a major source of financial revenues within these circles in the 1980s. The monopoly of arms distribution by these circles created a great deal of hardship for the local Mujahideen groups combating the Soviets and the DRA troops. Some local Mujahideen groups waited for months in their camps in Pakistan for arms and ammunitions. These long waiting periods often would devastate the entire group because of economic hardships or Soviet military supremacy. Therefore, many of these local groups were forced to sell a percentage of their weapons after they received them in order to survive. This hardship created another corrupt mechanism within the party operators by which the local Mujahideen, who were waiting to receive arms in Pakistan, had to make deals with their own party officers in charge of distributing the weapons. Corruption was inherent in this deal—if, say, group Y of the Mujahideen received 300 rifles and 60,000 rounds of ammunition, they would have to give up a portion of this cache to the distributing officers in return for a secured trip back to their base. The distributing officers would resell that portion of the weapons and ammunition, or give them to another group for personal, family, or party reasons.[4]

In addition to the Mujahideen political elite with family ties to the leadership, there was another very important part of the party cadre and officers. This part was comprised of those who were aware of the political ideology of the party and followed the party agenda intellectually. Among the militant groups, this loyal part of the party elite was called *Maktabis* (the educated ones), and they formed a political ring around the party leader. Often, the party's offices in different countries were under the control of *Maktabis*. This was very common among the militant Mujahideen groups such as the Islamic Party led by Gulbedin Hekmatyar, the Islamic Society led by Burhanadin Rabbani, the United Islamic Front headed by Mr. Abdul Rab-e-Rassul Sayaf (among the Pakistan-based groups), and the Islamic Victory (which later formed the core of the United Islamic Party led by Abdul Ali Mazary and Abdul Karim Khalili).

Among these Mujahideen groups, the *Maktabis* were also known as the *Ikhwanis* (the Brethren), whose roots can be found in the Muslim Brethren in Egypt. The literature of the Muslim Brethren founders and leaders in Egypt, such as Hassan Al-Bana and Sayd Qutb, was required party reading. It was widely studied and the subject of many intellectual debates; therefore, calling the *Maktabi* segment *Ikhwani* was not far from reality. Monopolizing the Mujahideen operation outside the country and influencing the armed groups inside were the most crucial objectives for the *Maktabis*. To fulfill this objective, they used financial support and weapons as tools. In many cases they desired to lead the Afghan struggle from afar, and, as a result, many of these people never participated in combat against the Soviets. The issue of influencing the local commanders and armed groups inside the country caused a negative environment of rivalry over control of the armed groups and territories. This rival behavior caused many bloody clashes between the armed Mujahideen groups inside Afghanistan. Thousands of Mujahideen fighters and hundreds of local commanders were assassinated or killed inside and along the border provinces of Pakistan and Iran.

According to the eyewitnesses and the Mujahideen local publications during 1982 to 1986, over 3,000 Mujahideen fighters were killed in Central Afghanistan between the Islamic United Revolutionary Council of Afghanistan, led by Sayd Ali Baheshti and his chief commander Sayd Hassan Jegran, and the Islamic Victory Party (*Sazeman-e-Nassr*). In another confrontation around the city of Herat between the Islamic Movement Party, led by Mawlawi Nabi Mohammadi, and the Islamic Society, led by Burhanadin Rabbani, 4,000 fighters and civilians lost their lives.[5] Armed clashes in the provinces of Helmand, north of Kabul (Shamalli), and other parts of the country created a river of blood and a war within a war.[6] All of these internal Mujahideen conflicts and fights helped the DRA regime and the Soviets maintain their control over the cities and major highways. These conflicts took away a lot of military and political pressure from the Soviet/DRA regime's civil and military organization in Afghanistan and, in some aspects, extended the Soviet presence in the country.

Indeed, the role of the external front of the Mujahideen in the struggle against the Soviets and the DRA regime had its own significance. Through the work and effort of this front, the Afghan Mujahideen publicized their cause internationally. Branches and offices of the external front in countries friendly to the Mujahideen operated against the DRA embassies and consulates and collected cash and goods in support of their efforts. In Pakistan and Iran, these offices recruited new fighters for the external front and supplied support like transportation and medical treatment for the wounded combatants. The external front opened schools and training centers in neighboring countries and enrolled Afghan children and teenagers. Mostly, these schools operated under the party officers who were aware of the political ideology of the party. Recruiting new members among the teenagers who would follow the political ideology of the party was an important task for those in charge. Hundreds of journals, magazines, brochures, and flyers were published and distributed in different languages domestically and internationally. Many seminars, conferences, meetings, and gatherings were conducted by the external front to show televised atrocities of the Soviet invasion of Afghanistan to the people around the globe. As a result of all these efforts and organizational structures, the political elite of the Mujahideen party expanded its influence over the daily life of the Afghans, thus, ultimately having an impact on all future decisions made for this nation.

The internal front was comprised of various armed groups led by local leaders and commanders and was the main force behind the Soviet and PDPA defeat in Afghanistan. The brutality of the PDPA and their campaigns against the traditional structure of society upset the social fabric of the country. This disruptive situation resulted in the mass revolt by people in many parts of the country. Many divisions of the army defected to the rebels and handed over their arms; moreover, they broke into the military depots and distributed ammunition and modern weapons among the people. In general, there was no organized leadership or political organization, there were only local grassroots resistance organizations working against the PDPA and the Soviet influence. In many cases, such as the mass revolt in Herat, thousands of villagers and urban dwellers participated with no leadership or previous planning. They were like waves that rose from the sea—they destroyed the PDPA stations and then returned to their valued land. Each time, these waves left behind footprints that became the essence of the local resistance groups against the PDPA and the Soviet army. In a matter of months, especially after the mass revolt in Herat, the local resistance organized their activities and guerrilla war to reduce the domination of the PDPA regime over the provinces. Even though many different leaders and organizations outside the country claimed responsibility for the events inside Afghanistan against the PDPA regime, they all happened without the aid of external political organizations or their leadership.[7]

Later, the organizational expansion and the need for weapons, ammunitions, and aid made the local groups and commanders develop a significant affiliation with the external political parties that were based in Pakistan or Iran. From a general perspective, the role of ideology as the impetus for affiliation by the local commanders with the external political leaders was very weak. In many cases, the local commanders were illiterate and did not know anything about the party agenda for the future of Afghanistan. All parties were talking about the fight against the pro-Soviet godless Afghan regime and the establishment of an Islamic government that would bring justice and tranquility.

Although, when studying the nature of Afghan resistance, one needs to be careful that the term Mujahideen does not define the struggle of only those groups based in Pakistan or Iran. There were groups who had loyal armed soldiers and commanders inside and external activities on the international level, or they worked within the Pakistan- or Iran-based Mujahideen parties. For example, soon after the PDPA coup, the People's Liberation Front of Afghanistan that recruited many leftist and nationalist activists initiated many armed activities in the cities and, at the same time, organized full-time armed resistance in the rural areas. The Revolutionary Council of the Islamic Union of Afghanistan, led by Ayatollah Baheshti and former army lieutenant Sayed Hassan (Sayed Jagran) in the central provinces of Afghanistan, and the Social Democratic Party of Afghanistan (Afghan Melat) garnered the support of many educated Afghans and technocrats belonging to Pushton ethnic groups. They were very active in the eastern provinces. The *Stam-e-Mili* (the National Oppression), which struggled for minority rights against the ethnic Pushton monopoly of the government's power, was a leftist group active in northern Afghanistan. One can argue that all these groups were struggling against the PDPA and later against the Soviet army, and each, in their turn, played a significant role in the formation of the Afghan resistance.

During the Soviet invasion, the separation of external and internal fronts prolonged the existence of the Soviet occupation and caused an increasing number of Afghan deaths and casualties and greater destruction of the country. The main reason for this destructive separation of the two Mujahideen fronts was the confrontation of the political ideologies within the Mujahideen political parties.

There was confrontation between the traditional leadership that had strong roots in the eldership system in the country and the current reality of community during the war. The reason behind this confrontation was the fast changes within the social and political fabric of the nation and the rise of new political and social identities for the ethnic and communal groups. These changes represented the new leadership that had different social backgrounds. The rise of the new ethnic and communal leaders within Afghan society was based on the need for a leadership that could satisfy the social and political demands of the people in a time of war. Many former ethnic and communal leaders had been jailed, killed, or took refuge abroad and became a part of Afghan refugees. The rise of the young or middle-aged males who had the nerve and courage to prove themselves against the oppression of the Soviets and the PDPA was an event to be heralded, since not all men can face such a difficult challenge. Most of the new leaders emerged in the form of Mujahideen commanders who fought bravely and guided their troops with skill.

Most of these leaders were lower- or middle-class farmers from the rural areas of the country. There were a significant number of educated people with an ethnic or *Qaum* connection to the villages who became commanders or influenced the local commanders. In many cases, the traditional leaders (if any were in the area) had to follow the political agenda of the local commander or, at least, cooperate with the group. This new social and political change disrupted the lives of those people who influenced society with their wealth and political connections. In the rural life, the influences that were based on wealth abruptly vanished, because economic influence was based on the ownership of the land and livestock. Both of these sources of wealth and influence were nontransferable; therefore, when these owners took refuge in neighboring countries they left behind all their resources.

In Pakistan the so-called moderate Mujahideen leaders were mostly traditionalist and desired to influence society in a traditional way. For example, Sayd Ahmed Gillani was the *pir-e-trighat* (the head of a sub-religious group) with a peaceful way of spiritual thought and was not involved directly with politics or the military. In many cases, this kind of religious group denounced violence and lived to promote peace and brotherhood. During wartime, these political leaders who were engaged in military and war activities needed new methods and new concepts of leadership. A *pir* was a savior for his followers, leading them from danger, and a *pir* was traditionally in the forefront of an ordeal. But now because of the unsecured and extremely risky situation inside Afghanistan, the *pir* was not able to save his followers from the Soviet-made bullets and was not able to fight on the battlefield.

As argued above, the objective of the *Maktabis* among the Mujahideen was to create a united and centralized leadership among the Afghan communities. In practice, this concept of leadership was parallel to the approach used by the PDPA after they took power. According to this concept, which attempted to be legitimized through the interpretation of the Islamic concept of *amir-ul-mua-manin* (the head of the Muslims), an Islamic society can achieve justice and tranquility under the guidance of an *amir-ul-muamanin*. Especially when Muslim lives and properties are under the attack of the *kafirs* (unbelievers), the protection of the Muslims and their properties is an Islamic duty.

In Afghanistan, the Islamic duty of the Muslims had been called jihad, in which the person who pursues this duty is a Mujahid (singular of Mujahideen) and he should voluntarily give his life and property for the sake of the brotherhood. The average Afghan does not have a problem with the general concept of jihad, but the most problematic issue was the question of leadership; *amir-ul-muamanin* allowed each political leader of the Mujahideen to claim that he is the legitimate one.

Despite the ethno-communal heterogeneity of Afghan society and the disintegration of the economic life of the people, it was impossible to force all ethnic and communal groups into one party under a single *amir-ul-muamanin*. This contradicted the social and political fabric of Afghanistan in the past and present and oppressed individual freedoms and ethno-communal autonomy. Moreover, most of the *Maktabis* who supported the enforcement of this concept worked in offices outside of the country. There was an empty spot for the political leadership inside the country to help groups cooperate and organize larger activities. Among the *Maktabis*, the Islamic Party under Hekmatyar was able to train its cadres and send the local armed groups inside to be directly or indirectly in charge of the group. The party was attempting to fit society into the party structural frame under the guidance of their *amir-ul-muamanin*.

The control and monopolization of the financial and military resources by the external front was an attempt to control the Mujahideen commander inside. For many local Mujahideen commanders this was artificial, and they wanted to take care of their affairs. The rise of the regional commanders within the Mujahideen organization inside the country was the subsequent result of the need for a practical leadership. During the Soviet presence there were four significant internal front divisions that formed their own organizations.

The northeast division was mainly dominated by the ethnic Tajik population, with a mixture of small groups of Pushtons who lived by way of mutual cooperation for many years. The two major highways connecting Kabul to Dushanbe and to Tashkent made the region a strategic site for both the Soviets and the Mujahideen. This important strategic location in the northeast became obvious after the concentration of the Soviets in northern Afghanistan. Through this concentration, the Soviets and the DRA regime made the north their jumping board to the northeast and northwest.

The assassination of the famous Mujahideen Commander Zabihullah in December 1984 allowed the Soviets and the DRA to push the Mujahideen back. After Zabihullah's death, under the command of Mawlawi Alam from Jamaiat Islami, the Mujahideen were forced to retreat to the southern part of Balkh province.[8] In the coming years, the Soviet/DRA troops attempted to secure the Salang highway that connected Kabul to the northern border with the USSR. These forces launched major military attacks on the headquarters of the Mujahideen leader Ahmed Shah Massoud. After six heavy military offensives by Soviet and DRA forces against Massoud units in Panjshir valley, he became aware that he had to stretch out his units to reduce the military concentration in the Panjshir Valley. For the Soviets and the DRA, Massoud was the main obstacle to establishing the security zone from Mazar-e-Sharif to Kabul. In 1984, the Mujahideen commanders from Badakhshan, Takhar, Kunduz (all in the northeastern zone), and Balkh (in the northern zone) formed a council under the leadership of Massoud.[9] This council, called the Supervisory Council of the North (SCN), unified the military and civilian administration of the north and was a strong rebellion against the Soviet concentration in northern Afghanistan.

Soon after, a new military and civil administration connected the north and the northeast through organized and well-planned military operations against the Soviet garrisons and the DRA military stations. Massoud knew that the ethnic and communal differences and the political party conflicts were strong obstacles in the way of establishing a unified force that could strike many enemy positions at the same time. So he opened a military academy at his base in Panjshir to train the volunteers from the other provinces in northern Afghanistan. He divided all of the Mujahideen groups in the SCN into three organizations: the central forces, comprised of the Panjshiris and the volunteers from the other provinces who previously fought with the local commanders; the mobile forces, Ghatah-e-Motaharek, mostly educated, well trained units who were operating out of the central bases (these units also served as a political messenger to the local community under the control of SCN and carried the political agenda of the council); the strike units, Ghatah-e-Zarbat, who were well trained and went through many battles with a great deal of military ability.[10] These units were generally engaged in reducing the Soviet offensives by hitting the vital cords of communication and transportation of the enemy.

Contrary to the *Maktabis* and the PDPA approach, Massoud did not attempt to make the local community fit within the organizational structure of the political party. He recognized the autonomy of the traditional organization of the local community and left them to run their daily affairs and give advice to the SCN leadership. In contrast with other Mujahideen parties, the SCN relied strongly on the local sources for the economic development of the region.[11] In the long run, most of the local community emerged as the main local support of the SCN agendas. The civil administration of the SCN was able to recruit many educated and skilled Afghans from many parts of the country, in particular from Kabul. The recruiting of skilled people increased the effectiveness of the SCN organization that was unique in Afghanistan. Even though most of the Mujahideen commanders in the SCN were affiliated with the *Jamaiat Islami* (the Islamic Society of Burhanadin Rabbani), the SCN ran its affairs independently from the party leadership in Pakistan.[12]

The center of the western region was the province of Herat, the location of the first mass revolt against the DRA regime. This province, located on the Turkman border of the USSR and the eastern border of Iran, was a strategic location for the Soviets and the DRA. The existence of the 17th military division and second main military air base in the country at Sheendand made this province a priority for Soviet troop concentration in Afghanistan. After the mass revolt of Herat, the 17th division doubled in size, and the 4th mechanized army division was stationed there.

During the first stage of the war, the Mujahideen groups in Herat gained ground on the DRA forces. But soon, the conflict between the *Jamaiat Islami* and the *Harkat-e-Islami* not only destroyed the cooperation and joint operation of the Mujahideen, it also devastated the political environment of the province. As a result of these armed clashes many Harkat commanders asked the DRA for military support and later defected to the government forces. In the middle of this chaotic chain of war, Ismail Khan, a former military officer who rebelled against the government with his men, started a wide range of activities that brought the forces loyal to *Jamait* under control.

After Ismail Khan formed a central unit, he established *Farghe-e-Amir Hamzah* (the Amir Hamza Division) that was inspired from his experience in the army and was comprised of five regiments (*ghund*), each with approximately 600 to 900 men in 1988.[13] Ismail Khan changed the military balance and controlled a large portion of the province of Herat. After he established a civil administration to deal with the daily affairs of the local people, he pushed toward the southwest and northwest provinces. His objective was to establish a regional organization in the southwest of the country and conduct larger scale military operations against the Soviet and the DRA government. From 1986, Ismail Khan encouraged the Mujahideen commanders from all over the country to establish united fronts through an organized council run by prominent Mujahideen commanders. Like Massoud and other regional leaders of the internal front, Ismail Khan knew that there was not that much hope for the unity of the external front and the party leaders in Pakistan and Iran. His objective was to establish a conference to offer a popular alternative for the people of Afghanistan. In the summer of 1987, hundreds of commanders and Mujahideen fighters from nine provinces, after long journeys, attended a conference in the *Saghar woleswali* of Ghor province. This conference was very significant;[14] it was an attempt by the internal front leaders to support the idea that a nationally known alternative for ending the war and the Soviet invasion of Afghanistan could be achieved by the internal front. Because this conference was so large it was not successful in establishing a central decision-making body within Afghanistan. According to Ismail Khan, at this conference the attending Mujahideen commanders agreed on general cooperation, exchange of information, and communication until the next meeting.[15]

Lying next to Pakistan, the major supplier of arms and finances to the Mujahideen groups, the eastern provinces were very crucial for both the Mujahideen and the Soviets and the DRA. The main supply route of the Mujahideen groups in the eastern provinces and around Kabul ran through this area. There were many attempts by the local commanders and internal leaders to establish a unified front like in the north, but it was very difficult because of great ethnic diversity and tribal confrontations. Mawlawi Haghani was able to form substantial military units and established a Shura Council in the Paktia province from 1986 to 1987. Even though this council changed the military balance against the DRA and the Soviets, it never created an organizational structure like the Herat or the SCN.

The province of Kabul was under the close military control of the DRA and the Soviets. The establishment of the security zone around the city caused large-scale military deployment and intensive bombardment on a daily basis against the Mujahideen groups. During the 1980s, commander Abdul Haqh, affiliated with *Hezb-e-Islami* (led by Mawlwi Khaless), attempted to create a regional Mujahideen organization. He established highly motivated mobile groups to strike Soviet and DRA front lines but was never able to form a civilian administration. The civil population around Kabul was devastated by the daily air attacks and military offensives by the Soviet and DRA armed forces. These heavy offensives forced the local population to migrate and leave many villages and towns around Kabul. Moreover, Abdul Hagh was less willing to bow to the ISI demands (as Massoud and Ismail Khan did); he operated independently from the party leaders in Pakistan. Because of Soviet and DRA concentration, manipulation, and the ISI in Pakistan, Abdul Hagh could not form a regional organization. The KhAD and the ISI were against the creation of a unified and centralized Mujahideen group built up around Kabul.[16]

CHAPTER EIGHT

THE FIRST PHASE OF CIVIL WAR

AFTER THE SOVIET WITHDRAWAL, THE EXTERNAL FRONT, UNDER THE pressure of the United States and the Pakistani military intelligence service, ISI, began to form an interim government to centralize the political and military operation against the pro-Soviet regime in Kabul. The first attempt resulted in a severe confrontation between the Iran-based leaders and the Pakistan-based leaders, and the external front leaders. This confrontation was fueled by the political conflict between the Iranian and Saudi Arabian regimes that were supporting particular groups on both sides. Therefore, this conflict raised the issue of power sharing between the majority Afghan Sunni and the minority Afghan Shia. Eventually, another dichotomy arose over the issue of ethnic confrontation. The external front could not reach a practical solution and weakened the unification of the internal front by injecting these contradictions inside the country. The external front marginalized the internal front's participation from its decision-making mechanism.

The marginalization of the internal front from the process of decision making created a gap between the two fronts. In reality, this gap prevented the Afghan Mujahideen groups from forming a united front against the Soviet/DRA regime. As a result, the Mujahideen groups not only lost the momentum needed to change the balance of power inside the country, the extension of the war caused immense physical destruction to the country and tremendous loss of human life. The lack of a cooperative and coordinated Afghan Mujahideen political and military organization caused the Mujahideen to fail to establish an interim government within or outside the country. As a result, when the Soviet troops pulled out of Afghanistan, the weak Afghan government, headed by Najibullah (who controlled 20 percent of the country), was able to maintain its existence for four more bloody years.

In such circumstances the Soviets supported President Najibullah's regime with $1.4 billion in arms during the first months of its withdrawal.[1] The Soviets did not leave the military domain entirely to the regime. Senior and middle ranking Soviet officers continued to participate in the planning and direction of all major military operations. In March and April of 1989, a heavy military campaign began on Jalalabad, under direct ISI supervision and with the participation of Mujahideen forces, mostly belonging to Hekmatyar with the support of the Pakistan military units. This military operation had the green light from the U.S. representatives in the area.[2] The main objective of this campaign was to capture a city close to the Pakistan border and transfer the interim government there for diplomatic recognition and international support, and while the first attempt was successful in capturing the outlying strategic garrison of Samarkhel, the lack of coordination with the other Mujahideen forces, both regional and nationwide, forced the campaign to fail. The Republic State of Afghanistan (RSA) regime rebuilt its economic, military, political, and moral position.[3]

These events brought the internal front to the clear conclusion that they had to decisively defeat the RSA regime without the external front. Because the Jalalabad campaign decreased the political and party confrontation among the external leaders, the three major Mujahideen internal forces, along with the other local commanders, started to create a centralized operation against the RSA regime. The military operations became active all over the country. The RSA government leaders saw the fast deterioration of their regime and the weakening of their power. All of this happened while the USSR, as the "bigger brother," fell apart with the crises of glasnost and the military coup of the conservative element within the Soviet government. *De Afghanistan Watan Hezb* (the Homeland Party, HWA) under the leadership of Najibullah was divided into many hostile factions over ethnicity and language. The regime and the external front of the Mujahideen agreed to the creation of a nonaligned government body to take over the government and establish a national *jirga*. All leaders of the former PDPA (now the HWA) and the military sought to assure their own survival by finding allies among the Mujahideen. In March 1990, a Pushton alliance formed when Defense Minister Shahnawaz Tanai and other *Khalqi* officers allied with Gulbuddin Hikmatyar and nearly overthrew Najibullah in a coup supported by the ISI.[4] In January 1992, the Uzbek forces of the government revolted against the government in the north under Uzbek General Abdul Rashid Dostam. The revolt enjoyed the support of the mainly non-Pushton, pro-Karmal forces in *Parcham*. Najibullah was arrested in the Kabul airport when he tried to escape from Afghanistan to India.

On April 26, 1992, Ahmed Shah Massoud's forces, in collaboration with Dostam's forces, seized control of Kabul almost peacefully. In Peshawar, the six leaders other than Hekmatyar finally reached an agreement on transitional arrangements. An interim government arrived in Kabul from Peshawar on April 29, 1992, and the pro-Soviet regime collapsed across the country.

A GAP IN POLITICAL LEADERSHIP

During the Soviet invasion, the mass revolt and organized struggle against the invaders was so strong that many Afghan political activists were calculating that the Soviet presence in Afghanistan would not last long. But it took almost ten years to force the Soviets from Afghanistan. The war resulted in almost one and a half million Afghan casualties, hundreds of handicapped individuals, thousands of orphans, and more than 60 percent destruction of the infrastructure system of the country. The extended Soviet presence in Afghanistan, the high number of human losses, and the severe destruction of the country made many wonder why the Soviet military presence in Afghanistan had lasted that long. Generally, studying Afghanistan from 1979 to 1989 would result in the three following conclusions that form the main reasons behind the extended Soviet presence.

MUJAHIDEEN'S MILITARY IMBALANCE

The imbalance between the military capability of the Afghan Mujahideen groups and the Soviets was a major factor in the long-term presence of the Soviets in Afghanistan. The Soviet army divisions in Afghanistan were one of the most sophisticated military forces in the world. The military leadership had a great deal of experiences from many battlefields and armed confrontations. The Soviet army fought in World War II successfully and learned how to play the regional and global military games. The most significant experience of Soviet military leaders was their successful campaign in the former Soviet Central Asia, where they suppressed a longstanding and popular resistance in the region. This campaign provided the Soviet military leadership with a handful of tactical and strategic approaches against armed resistance when they were fighting in Afghanistan.

In Afghanistan, the Soviet Army was well equipped and connected to the main military bases on Soviet soil. The Soviet air force and mechanized divisions were able to create long and extensive pressure on the Afghan Mujahideen groups. This pressure gave the Soviet ground troops great support and flexibility. This military sophistication devastated the newly formed local Afghan Mujahideen groups in any face-to-face encounters. The majority of the Mujahideen personnel consisted of the local farmers who did not have any military training experiences. The only trained individuals were the ex-Afghan army officers and soldiers who defected to the Mujahideen groups. In the first phase of the war, most rifles in the hands of Mujahideen were old weapons like the British Enfield, which were used in World War I. Soon, the local Mujahideen captured newer machine guns from the Soviets or received them from the Afghan army defectors; however, the lack of weapons, in particular anti-armored vehicles and anti-aircraft, was a major problem for many years.[5]

In 1982, the Soviet army and the Afghan government forces started a massive air and ground campaign against the Mujahideen groups in several key areas. Particularly in Herat and Qandahar, as *The Washington Post* reported, "the Soviet staged a brutal, block-by-block World War II–style assault."[6] According to Commander Ismail Khan, "the Soviet and Afghan military attack was very organized: First, air raids bombarded Mujahideen's positions; second, the artilleries hit the front line; and third, the ground troops were marching forward . . . and it was almost impossible to stop the Soviet campaign. We divided into two groups, one moved toward the Iranian border and I took my men and hit and run all over west and east of Herat."[7] In January of 1982, the Soviet and Afghan troops attempted to secure Kabul from the north, an act that resulted in a major military operation and damaged the strongholds of Mujahideen groups in the provinces of Parwan and Wardak. At this time, Soviet troops moved to secure the strategic Panjshir valley, the Mujahideen stronghold 60 miles northeast of Kabul led by Ahmed Shah Massoud.[8]

Even though the massive Soviet military campaign continued until 1984, the outcome was not to the benefit of the Soviets. The Mujahideen groups learned how to conduct military tactics and plans. In Herat, Mujahideen forces led by Ismail Khan were more organized and developed a core of devoted commanders. In Panjshir, Ahmed Shah Massud not only survived, he established the most well-organized and -trained Mujahideen group in the country.[9]

From 1981 to 1984, the military campaign of the Soviets and the Afghan government armed forces enormously damaged the country's society and economy. Thousands of villages were destroyed and millions of people were forced to become refugees in neighboring countries. This military campaign could not break down the Afghan Mujahideen; instead, it caused the Afghan Mujahideen to gain national and international support. Even though many local commanders were killed and Mujahideen groups were destroyed on the battlefields, the struggle against the Soviets and the DRA entered into a new stage. In this stage, the Afghan Mujahideen freed many parts of the country from the control of the Soviet and the DRA regime. Despite these new military and political developments in Afghanistan, the imbalance of military capabilities between the Mujahideen groups and the Soviets was an important factor when considering the long presence of the Soviet army in this country, although it cannot be considered as the main reason.

EXTERNAL INTERFERENCE

The interference of Afghanistan's neighboring governments, in particular Pakistan and Iran, in the affairs of Mujahideen groups has also been considered another major cause behind the long Soviet presence in Afghanistan. From the early stage of the war against the Soviets and PDPA regime, Pakistan and Iran became the headquarters of the political leaders of the Afghan Mujahideen groups, as well as the host of 7 million Afghan refugees. The Soviet invasion of Afghanistan caused the destabilization of the region. This regional instability resulted in U.S. aid to Afghan Mujahideen and also U.S. active involvement in Pakistan. The United States granted $1.5 billion in military aid, including 40 F-16s, together with another $1.7 billion in economic aid to General Zia.[10] This large military and economic package created an absolute rule by the generals of the Pakistani army. The United States also agreed with Pakistan to be the conduit of arms and supply to Afghan Mujahideen groups in Afghanistan. This development terminated the Pakistanis' moderate policy that was led by Pakistan's Foreign Minister, Agha Shahi, who believed in a diplomatic solution under UN leadership for Afghanistan. The monopoly of military and political powers by the generals led by Zia-ul-Alhaq formed a militaristic approach of Pakistan toward Afghanistan affairs. This approach enabled the ISI to influence the political armed struggle of Afghans against the DRA and the Soviets. Those Afghan political leaders with an ideological connection to the *Jamait Islami* or *Jamaat Uloma-e-Islami* (two political parties with extensive influence in the Pakistani government, in particular in the military), gained a larger share of U.S. and Saudi aid for the Afghan Mujahideen. In this case, the ISI became a very influential organization among the Afghan Mujahideen political leaders and party activists. The international aid to the Afghan Mujahideen and refugees was filtered by the ISI, and the distribution of aid among the Mujahideen groups was organized according to their cooperation and participation with the ISI's regional strategy. This situation weakened Mujahideen independence and reduced their success against the Soviet and DRA regime. By becoming a crucial military and financial filter, ISI was able to overrule the decisions of the Mujahideen political leaders on many critical issues. Furthermore, this development caused the Mujahideen political leaders to compete against one another for a greater share of the international aid. This competition created a hostile environment among the Afghan political leaders. As a result, political leaders who tolerated the influence of the ISI in Afghanistan received larger shares of international aid. In Pakistan, those politicians who acted against ISI control over international aid and expansion of ISI-allied Afghan leaders were assassinated or forced to leave Pakistan. Political leaders who were permitted by ISI to work in Pakistan became heads of the seven antagonistic political organizations until 1992.

In Iran, the two popular Mujahideen organizations, *Shura-e-Inghalabi Etafaqh-e-Islami Afghanistan* (SIEIA) and *Harkat-e-Islami Afghanistan* (HIA), were the most popular Mujahideen organizations among the Shia Muslims. SIEIA, led by Sayid Ali Bahishti and ex-military officer Sayid Hassan (Sayid Jagran), dominated central Afghanistan, especially Hazarahjat. HIA, led by Shaikh Mohammed Assef Mohseni, was popular mostly among Shia and some segments of Sunni Muslims all over the country. These two political parties struggled to maintain their political independence from the Iranian government, and this struggle caused their subsequent expulsion from Iran.

The condition of Afghan refugees was different in Iran in comparison to Pakistan. In Iran, Afghan refugees were not permitted to own property, travel freely, or run businesses. These restrictions were used by the government agencies to influence the Afghan Mujahideen and refugee communities politically. Soon, six new Afghan political parties emerged in Iran, and each attempted to gain military and financial support from different Iranian government factions. Because of Saudi influence on aid to the Pakistani-based Afghan Mujahideen, the Shia groups, in particular the HIA and SIEIA, were not able to receive direct international aid via Pakistan. The Shia groups also could not receive western aid due to the antagonistic nature of the diplomatic relationship between the Islamic Republic of Iran and the United States. This situation caused the further influence of the Iranian government over the Afghan Mujahideen political leaders and divided the Shia groups, causing confrontations between independent Shia groups and those loyal to the Iranian political and religious leadership. In the long run, this situation decreased the military and financial capability of the HIA and SIEIA. The Iranian influence was directed by the three governmental organizations: the Islamic Revolutionary Guard, the Ministry of Interior through the *Shura-e-Afaghanah*, and later, the *Sazaman-e-Italaat* (government intelligent service).

Indeed, the influence and interference of Pakistan and Iran in the internal affairs of the Afghan Mujahideen was another major factor that caused the Soviets to extend their presence in Afghanistan for ten years. But it cannot be said this was the main reason for the long presence of the Soviet forces in this country. Pakistani and Iranian interference weakened the unification of Mujahideen groups and reduced their cooperation. However, the Afghan Mujahideen commanders who became the leaders of the Afghan Mujhadedin internal front were able to form the locally and regionally based organizations and operate independently. With all the pressures that these internal front leaders received from Pakistan and Iran, they were able to safeguard their independence, and rely on the masses and their limited internal sources. The formation of the Afghan Mujahideen organizations inside Afghanistan also proves that the interference of Pakistan and Iran was not the main reason for the extended presence of the Soviet army in Afghanistan. The emergence of these local and regional organizations (led by Ahmed Shah Massoud, Ismail Khan, Mawlawi Haghani, Abdul Haqh, Sayid Jegran, and Haji Abdul Ghadir) occurred aside from the influence of Pakistan and Iran. These Mujahideen organizations, inside the country, were the main force against the Soviet and the DRA forces in Afghanistan.

MUJAHIDEEN'S WEAK LEADERSHIP

The weak political leadership of Afghan Mujahideen was the main reason for the extended presence of the Soviets and the survival of the dictatorial regime led by the PDPA in Afghanistan. This weakness was rooted in the personal characteristics, political ideologies, and organizational operations of their parties. The political ideology of these leaders followed mainly their personal, family, and party interest, and they interpreted them as those of Afghanistan's national interests. Generally, the political ideology of the Mujahideen leaders in charge of the external front activities divide into two categories: those who adopted their political ideology from non-Afghan organizations such as the Muslim Brotherhood in Egypt, or the Islamic Republic Party of Iran, led by Ayatollah Said Ali Baheshti; and those who adopted their political ideology in accordance with the social and political structures of Afghan society.

Among Pakistani-based Mujahideen parties, *Hezb-e-Islami* (Islamic Party or HIH) led by Gulbadin Hekmatyar and *Jamaiat-e-Islami* (JIA or Islamic Society) led by Burhanadin Rabbani followed the model of the Muslim Brotherhood of Egypt. Among Iranian-based Afghan political parties, *Sazeman-e-Nasr* (called NASR), the Victor Organization, led by Mir Husain Sadeqi, and later *Sapah-e-Pasdaran Inghalab-e-Islami Afghanistan* (the Islamic Revolutionary Guard of Afghanistan) followed the model of the Islamic Republic Party of Iran. Both the Iranian and the Egyptian models aimed to establish an Islamic state in Afghanistan under the exclusive leadership of these parties. In this case, all other Mujahideen parties must accept their charter and submit their political obedience (*baia't*) to them. The head of such a party acted not only as the supreme political leader of the country, but would receive the title of *Amir-ul-Muamanin*, or *Imam* (the sole religious leader of the Muslims after Prophet Mohammed).

The fact that HIH and JIA received a large share of the international aid helped these organizations to recruit thousands of Afghans from all social levels. The core activists of these two parties formed from educated middle-class Afghans with rural backgrounds. These activists formed the political elite of a party whose political ideology was developed by the ideas of the Egyptian Muslim Brotherhood's leaders and Abul Ala Maudodi of Pakistan. In Iran, the literature written by the Iranian revolutionary leaders was the ideological source for groups such as NASR. Activists who believed in the political ideology of the party and its leadership called themselves *Maktabis* (educated believers). These activists viewed the idea of party loyalty through a belief system based on ideology rather than ethnicity, linguistics, or kinship.

These political parties formed the most organized political activities in Afghanistan, in particular in Pakistan and Iran among the Afghan refugees. The Afghan followers of both (Iranian and Egyptian) models, in particular HIH and NASR, appeared to have strong ties to their host governments and the largest share of military and financial aid in comparison to the other political parties. Because of their rigid political ideology and extreme self-centralism, these political parties did not open their doors to the waves of newcomers. In reality, such an extreme self-centralism in addition to the adoption of ideologies not rooted in Afghan society clashed with the notions of individual freedom and communal autonomy. As a result, the HIH lost support among the local communities inside

Afghanistan and the number of the party members decreased. This situation produced a wide range of violent actions against those who left the party or were opposed to it. In central Afghanistan, Hazarahjat (Central Afghanistan), the NASR leadership in collaboration with the Iranian-led policy, devoted themselves to destroying the civil and military organizations established independently under the leadership of Ayatollah Sayyed Ali Beheshti and Sayyed Jagran.

The JIA, in comparison with the HIH, expanded largely all over Afghanistan. The main reason for this was the emergence of the famous commanders who became the regional internal front political and military leaders of the Mujahideen. Ahmed Shah Massoud and his close friends who were affiliated with the JIA were able to form a regional organization autonomous from the JIA. This regional organization did not follow the political ideology of the JIA or its organizational structure. Massoud's regional organization represented a new way of forming a political organization with respect to the notion of individual freedom and communal autonomy in Afghanistan. Thus, the local Mujahideen, with the support of Massoud's central forces, were able to manage their communal affairs with a great deal of communal autonomy. Soon after, these forces established the Supervisory Council of North (*Shurai-e-Nezar*). Finally, Massoud, who was a *Maktabi* at the beginning, moved from a self-centered organizational structure and fanatic political ideology to a more realistic and moderate position. Politically speaking, Massoud moved from the far right of political extremism to the center, which was based on a mixture of traditional and modern political views in Afghanistan.

In the northwest of Afghanistan, Ismail Khan was able to recruit many ex-military officers who defected to his forces. Soon, he confronted the JIA *Maktabis* in the region, causing the expulsion of the *Maktabis* from the Mujahideen controlled areas in the region. This expulsion of the *Maktabis* limited their activities inside Afghanistan and forced them to work only in JIA offices in Iran and Pakistan. Ismail Khan also established his regional administration in an area controlled by his forces, autonomously from the JIA. He went further by conducting national activities to promote the establishment of a united national front. For this purpose, he formed a successful Mujahideen conference in the province of Ghor in 1986. In a similar attempt, Massoud formed a national council of Mujahideen commanders in 1987 and 1988.

These two internal front leaders, Massoud and Ismail Khan, were able to force JIA leader Burhanadin Rabbani to accept more moderate approaches in Afghanistan. But Rabbani had acted to save his leadership by siding with both *Maktabis* and Massoud and Ismail Khan at the same time. This type of leadership created a grim environment full of conspiracy, propaganda, and sabotage, in particular by *Maktabis* against Massoud and Khan. This created a collaborative environment between the HIH regional activists, the ISI and Iranian-supported Afghan Shia elements as well as the Iranian intelligence service against Massoud and Ismail Khan. However, these efforts had different characteristics depending on whom they were dealing with. For example, in the northwest, which was controlled by Ismail Khan forces, the Iranian Government put pressure on him to allow Iran to build a bridge between central Afghanistan and Iran via Herat. Ismail Khan rejected this and limited the activities of those who were working for the implementation of such a policy. This act caused the confiscation of ammunition and military equipment being transferred from Pakistan via Iran to Afghanistan in 1985. Conflict developed between Iranian government and Ismail Khan–led forces, and according to this conflict, Iran supported any element that would reduce Ismail Khan's control of the area. As a result, the JIA *Maktabis* became the most active element against Ismail Khan's leadership in the region. Since the JIA *Maktabis* were not able to operate inside the country, they used the HIH and some element within the *Hizbullah* (a Mujahideen Shia group supported by Iran) to support their activities. In 1986, when most of the HIH forces in Herat joined the Kabul regime and took part in the military operations with the Soviets and government forces against Ismail Khan, the JIA *Maktabis* were still supporting and using these groups for their operation in the area.

In the north, Massoud was faced with a similar problem, with one exception: The area controlled was far from the Iranian border with Afghanistan, and therefore did not suffer from Iranian pressure. In addition, the political ideology of Massoud and Ismail Khan was far from that of the *Maktabis*. Both of these internal front political and military leaders believed in free elections, women's rights, freedom of speech, and an independent Afghanistan.

In Iran, the NASR was the most organized group among the Iranian-based Afghan political organizations. Later, with the support of the Iranian government, the Shia groups were able to form a united party called *Hezb-e-Wahdat Islami Afghanistan* (the Islamic Unity Party of Afghanistan, HWIA). *Hezb-e-Harkat-e-Islami*, led by Mohammed Assef Mohseni, and SEIA did not join the HWIA, and this caused them to be expelled from Iran. This expulsion forced these two parties to concentrate their activities in Pakistan and receive a small share of the military and financial aid independently and through the moderate Mujahideen parties (*Itehad-e-Seganah*).[11]

The leaders of the organizations that adopted their political ideology in accordance to the traditional social and political structure of Afghan society were comprised of: Sibghatollah Mojadadi, the leader of the National Salvation Front (NSF); Sayid Ahmed Gailani, the leader of the Islamic Liberation of Afghanistan; and Mawlawi Mohammed Nabbi Mohammedi, the leader of Harkat-e-Islami Afghanistan (HIA). These leaders adopted a moderate political ideology and recruited a large number of Afghan technocrats, ex-military officers, and civil servants. Many of these people were nominated into the bureaucracy of the party with no authority or power. Most of the important positions in the party were occupied by the leaders' family members, who often had little education and poor technical and professional skills. This ironic political situation led many of these technocrats and ex-military officers to leave Pakistan for Europe and the United States. Moreover, most of these leaders came from the upper social class, and their connection to and interaction with the masses were limited. This caused them to neglect the demands of the masses and fail to recognize the rapid changes in the social, political, and cultural structures of a country in war. In particular, these leaders failed to understand the emergence of the new leadership inside Afghanistan (the local and regional Mujahideen commanders) who acted on behalf of their communities. The majority of these new local Mujahideen leaders belonged to the lower social classes and ordinary farmer families who were aggressive in social and political changes in Afghanistan.

The monopoly of the organizational affairs of the party by the leaders and their families created an oligarchy that made their personal and family interests the primary goals of the organizations. This monopoly created a gap between the leaders who enjoyed a lavish lifestyle and the millions of Afghan refugees who lived under severe conditions in the refugee camps. Even though Gailani, Mohammedi, and Mujadadi, in comparison to the *Maktabis*, had more in common with the internal Mujahideen leaders, they were unable to achieve any workable solution toward the creation of a united effort against the Soviets and the PDPA regime. These leaders, in particular Gailani, encouraged former Afghan King Mohammed Zahir Shah, who was living in Italy, to come to Pakistan and form a general assembly of Afghans. According to the King's sources, he wanted to travel to Pakistan and visit the refugee camps but the Pakistani government would not issue a visa for him. This situation resulted in a chaos of leadership among the Afghan Mujahideen groups. The external front leaders could not introduce a functional agenda that might have brought them together in a united effort against the Soviet and the PDPA regime, yet they also strongly resisted the development of any formation of a national leadership by the internal front leaders inside the country. Therefore, the absence of a nationally acceptable leadership among the Mujahideen groups that could achieve resistance against the Soviets and the PDPA regime was the main reason that the Soviets were able to continue their military presence in Afghanistan for ten years.

CHAPTER NINE

THE FORMATION OF A THIRD MOVEMENT

THE WEAK POLITICAL LEADERSHIP OF THE EXTERNAL FRONT AND their failure to introduce a workable alternative for the formation of a united front against the Soviet-backed PDPA regime caused weakness of the internal front. This weak political leadership enabled the Soviets to extend their presence in Afghanistan and devastate the nation. Moreover, the control of international aid that was used by the external front leaders to keep the local commanders loyal to their parties forced the local resistance inside the country to make difficult choices. These difficulties arose when the military campaign of the Soviets devastated the Afghan villages and forced millions to flee the country from 1980 to 1984. The destruction of Afghan villages was a great threat against the local Mujahideen groups and severely limited their internal resources. At the same time the power struggle between the external front leaders against one another caused armed clashes between the local commanders all over the country. This situation forced some of the Mujahideen commanders to seek support from the Kabul regime against their rivals. These military clashes and this hostile environment caused the defection of many local Mujahideen commanders to the Soviets and the PDPA regime.

The Mujahideen inside Afghanistan suffered from shortages of food, medicine, ammunition, and weapons, and this caught the attention of international agencies. To make the aid more effective, a center independent from Mujahideen external front leaders was formed in Peshawar, Pakistan. This center attempted to build a direct bridge to the local Mujahideen groups and provided them with training camps, ammunition, and other supplies. Soon, the international humanitarian organization also formed the Agency Coordinating Body for Relief of Afghanistan (ACBAR) to channel their help directly inside

Afghanistan. These new establishments helped the internal front effectively organize their operation against the Soviets and the PDPA regime and form their own political organizations. Organizations like those led by Massoud and Ismail Khan opened their own training centers and expanded their activities.

After several major battles across the country in 1986 the internal front leaders formed regional organizations and limited the Soviet ground activities. The Mujahideen conference (known as the Saghar Conference) in 1986 sparkled the hope for a third movement that would finally form a new leadership to change the fate of the nation. Many political activists inside Afghanistan were witnessing the high number of casualties and the destruction of the country. These activists noticed that the people of Afghanistan stood between two hostile camps of political leaders: the People's Democratic Party (PDPA) leaders under the Soviet domination; and the Mujahideen political leaders in Pakistan and Iran. Neither of these two camps of leaders had any workable alternative to lead Afghanistan from such a political dead end. Therefore, the activities, mainly by grassroots politicians, with the cooperation and support of the internal front leaders, organized a new wave of political efforts.[1] This new wave spread out all over the country, and soon reached the Afghan refugees outside. Many politicians of both affiliations participated in this effort. This political movement began to form the foundation of a third movement in Afghanistan.

In the summer of 1987, Ismail Khan formed a conference joined by the regional commanders in western Afghanistan. He stated that the self-determination of Afghanistan is the most important factor to restore peace and stability, and he also rejected both the national reconciliation program by the Najibullah regime and the attempt by external Mujahideen leaders to impose a non-workable solution on Mujahideen commanders.[2] In the north, Massoud expanded his organization (SCN) and formed a wide range of dialogue with the local commanders. He established a line of communication between his forces and the famous Kabul commanders, Abdul Hagh and Mawlawi Haghani, in the southeast. These internal front leaders established a proper way of communication with one another.[3]

In May 1990 the National Commanders Shura (NCS), comprised of the major commanders, was formed to coordinate their activities at the regional and national level. Another meeting took place in June when the commanders heard one another's views and all agreed on a third meeting in October.[4] The NCS meting in October was one of the most significant political developments among the Afghan Mujahideen. A wide range of Mujhadedin commanders with different ethnic and political backgrounds and a large number of regional representatives gathered in Kunar, near the Pakistani border. As Steve Coll reported in *The Washington Post*, the internal Mujahideen leaders and the participants agreed to pass "a resolution against the ISI-sponsored strategy of a direct attack on Kabul by militia units based in Pakistan."[5] They agreed to avoid any premature attack on Kabul and to coordinate their forces to demolish Najibullah's regime in the provinces first. They divided Afghanistan into nine zones where the Mujahideen would establish their regional administrations after the capture of each province. In this case, the Mujahideen task was to cut off the internal resources and the external support roots of the regime and then capture Kabul. The intention behind this approach was to reduce human casualties and to destroy the capital. Soon after the Kunar conference, Massoud traveled to Pakistan and sent a delegation to the United States. The NCS presented their points in Washington and gained congressional support.[6]

The establishment of the NCS in reality was the third movement in Afghanistan that followed a separate strategy, different from the Afghan political leaders in Pakistan and Iran and Najibullah's national reconciliation proposal. The NCS almost filled the gap of political leadership that could have ended the Afghanistan crisis with less bloodshed and destruction. But the progress of the NCS movement was soon undermined.

From an earlier stage, when the regional commanders formed regional organizations and operated their military and political affairs independently, the external leaders feared losing their political status. They armed the smaller local Mujahideen groups in order to put pressure on the regional commanders. The *Maktabis* in particular attempted to sabotage the credibility and personality of the internal front leaders. In some cases, the *Maktabis'* hostilities against these regional commanders and internal front leaders were more extreme in comparison to their activities against the Soviets and the PDPA regime. For example, in *Jamaiat Islami* (JIA), a network of anti–Ismail Khan groups became active in most JIA offices in Pakistan and Iran.[7] Among many different anti–Ismail Khan activities, the most organized groups were *Afzalies*, led by famous Mujahideen commander Saffiollah Afzali. These activities were supported by Syyid Noorallah Emad within JIA offices and the *Niazis* led by Sayyd Ahmed Ghattali. This wide range of anti–Ismail Khan activities was incorporated within the government militia commanders and two radical Shia Mujahideen factions who were supported by Iran. At the same time, Massoud was engaged in a similar struggle with the *Maktabis* in JIA, led by Engineer Ayob, but Massoud was able to limit the scope of this kind of operation against him.

The fear of losing their political power and their personal interests made some Mujahideen external leaders support the militia commanders who were fighting along with the Soviets and the PDPA regime against the Mujahideen forces. Many of these local government militias received arms, ammunition, and money from the party leaders in Pakistan or Iran.[8]

In 1990, when the NCS leaders scheduled the October conference, Gulbadin Hekmatyar boycotted the conference and warned his field commanders against participating. Abdul Rab-e-Rassul Syyaf went along with the boycott; he also denounced the conference and asked his followers to avoid any participation. So, the opposition against the formation of NCS among the

Afghan leaders in Pakistan was very high. Other leaders decided to be silent about the formation of NCS and the statements made by Hekmatyar and Sayyaf. Prior to the formation of the NCS, Hekmatyar formed a special military force called *Leshkar-e-Eissar* (the Army of Sacrifice), who were fully trained and ready to be deployed south of Kabul. To support this plan, Hekmatyar forces transferred "forty thousand rockets and seven hundred trucks of ammunition" to the southern part of Kabul.[9] Hekmatyar's military plan was against avoiding a direct attack on Kabul, and he had already prepared a covert military operation with the *Khalqis* under General Shahnwaz Tanai. Even though this covert military operation was supported by the ISI and the Saudis and had the green light from the CIA, Hekmatyar forces were not able to break the security line in the southern part of the city when the *Khalqis* attempted the coup against Najibullah's regime.[10]

The establishment of the NCS made the ISI and the Saudi intelligent service nervous. After their vast involvement and investment in Afghanistan, any development out of their channel of command and control would jeopardize their interest in Afghanistan. Before the Kunar conference in October 1990, ISI director General Assad Durani tried to insist on attending the conference, but the NCS leaders rejected his request and announced the conference as an intra-Afghani meting.

General Durani was in a rage over the formation of NCS as a military and political force that was capable of lifting Afghanistan from its political dead end. In 1991, ISI attempted to undermine NCS by influencing the Mujahideen commanders who were close to the Pakistani border. The ISI, with the cooperation of the CIA, concentrated large military and financial resources with a large number of military advisors in the town of Khost, Paktia, to capture the Afghan government military garrison.[11] After a severe fight of Mujahideen forces under Mawlawi Haghani and Hekmatyar's groups, the Khost garrison was captured. Soon, General Durani, Hekmatyar's group, and Ghazi Ahmed Hussein, the leader of *Jamait-e-Islami* of Pakistan (JIP), visited Khost and celebrated the victory with local Mujahideen.

In principle, the military operation in Khost was within the NCS agenda of capturing provinces and establishing regional administrations. In strategy, however, this military operation was under the influence of Hekmatyar and ISI, and it was in conflict with the goals of the NCS. This military operation undermined the role of Mawlawi Haghani, one of the most important NCS leaders. Because of the influence of Pakistani military advisors, and ISI and Hekmatyar forces, Mawlawi Haghani was not able to coordinate the local Pushton community to establish a regional administration. In this operation a large amount of money was distributed among the local tribal leaders for their support of the military operation. The struggle over the sophisticated weapons and heavy artilleries between Hekmatyar forces (with the support of ISI officers in the region) and local armed groups created a more destructive environment that cracked the local leaders alliance under Haghani. This fragmentation of alliances was directly in the interest of ISI and Hekmatyar. The establishment of an organized regional administration would bring the Afghan technocrats and professionals into the region and would undermine the importance of Pakistan as a bridge for international aid to Afghanistan. Politically, the establishment of such local administration would provide a secure place for the NCS development, with easy access to the outside world.

In the north, the Ismaeli Shia militia led by Sayyd Nader Kaihani revolted against Najibullah. The Dustam Uzbek forces also entered in a severe fight against the *Khalqi*-led army division under General Juma Atsak and General Rassul that resulted in the defeat of Najibullah's army. These rebel forces joined the Mujahideen northern alliances of *Hezb-e-Wahdat* and Massoud forces. After the resignation of Najibullah on March 19, 1992, Mazar-e-Sharif fell into the hands of the northern alliance forces. In a matter of days, Kabul fell to the rebel army forces led by *Parchami* officers, in particular Mahmud Baryali, Babrak Karmal's brother, and his second cousin, and Najibullah's foreign minister, Abdul Wakil. While the northern alliances opened the way from Mazar to Kabul, General Mohammed Nabi Azimi, in charge of Kabul's military garrison, asked Ahmed Shah Massoud to enter Kabul and act as the head of the state. Massoud refused and contacted the external leaders in Pakistan to speed the formation of a transitional government. Najibullah was arrested when he was leaving Kabul for India. While the external leaders formed a cabinet, Afghanistan was in a tense situation without a central government.

The Sarandoy forces (security armed forces under the ministry of interior led by *Khalqis*) joined Hekmatyar forces in the south of Kabul. Soon, Hekmatyar and *Khalqis* planed to seize Kabul. This attempt caused Massoud's forces (who captured Bagram military air base) to peacefully enter Kabul on April 26, 1992, and secure the city. In Peshawar, the six external leaders, other than Hekmatyar, finally reached an agreement on a transitional arrangement. An interim government arrived in Kabul from Peshawar on April, 29, 1992, and the *De Hezb Watan* regime under Najibullah collapsed all over the country.

CHAPTER TEN

MISSING THE ONLY CHANCE

IN OCTOBER 1990, WHEN THE NCS EMERGED AS THE LEADING ELE-
ment for a third political movement inside Afghanistan, most of the Afghan
grassroots politicians, in particular the Mujahideen major commanders, had no
doubt that the external front leaders in Pakistan and Iran were not capable of
proposing a resolution to lead the Mujahideen forces inside Afghanistan. It was
also clear for many internal front leaders that all the efforts (from outside) toward the unification of the external front leaders by the friendly governments
(Pakistan, Saudi Arabia, Iran, and the United States) had failed.

With the quickening disintegration of Najibullah's regime, the quest for
leadership that would insure the participation of ethnic, religious, and political
groups in the national government was very critical for Afghanistan. Thousands of government military and militia forces aligned themselves with Mujahideen groups who had similar ethnic, linguistic, or religious backgrounds.
Most of the non-Pushton segment of the government's armed forces joined
Ahmed Shah Massoud in the north, while the Pushton segment joined Hekmatyar and Mawlawi Haghani in the east and Haji Qadir forces in Nangarhar.
All these changes occurred within days and none of the political and military
organizations were ready for such a rapid decentralization of Najibullah's
regime. The northern alliances headed by Massoud, General Dostam, Sayyed
Nader Kyani, and *Hizb-e-Wahdat* were able to control a large portion of the
country that extended from Mazar-e-Sharif to Kabul. Herat and the neighboring provinces came under the control of joint ex-government and Mujahideen
forces led by Ismail Khan. Qandahar was controlled by a mixture of Mujahideen and former government forces headed by Mulla Nagibullah Akhund.

The east and the southeast was controlled by the regional ex-military and regional forces led by Mawlawi Haghani and Haji Abdul Ghadir.

For a short period of time there were no military clashes, except some minor short battles, between the regional forces and the ex-*Khalqi* officers who aligned themselves with forces loyal to Hekmatyar in the north and west of the country. The regional commander acted as the head of military and regional organizations. The major Mujahideen commanders who formed the NCS in October 1990 were in charge of the regional commanders. Even among the northern alliance with the strong roles of General Dostam and Sayyid Nader Kyani (both former government militia commanders), Ahmed Shah Massoud was the most popular figure who also had an organized-mobile Mujahideen force under his direct command. Therefore, the NCS leaders could play a historic role in the formation of a national government in Afghanistan and enforce peace and security.

It was a golden chance for the NCS leaders to form their council in Kabul with a broader participation of the government ex-military and militia commanders and to integrate their forces with the ex-government forces into a national military. This kind of integration would keep the balance of the armed forces, and it would improve trust and alliances among them. In this case such a council would be able to not only ensure the security of Kabul, it also would be able to form the regional cooperation and solidarity in a higher level. The NCS could also form a joint task force for the security of Kabul, other main cities, and the borders with the neighboring countries. The presence of the regional commanders in Kabul itself could create a tremendous political force that would stop military attacks by Hekmatyar forces from the south.

Some Afghans with significant experience and knowledge of the behavior of the external leaders during the last ten years advised the internal front leaders to form a united effort without the direct participation of the external front leaders. For example, General Saffi, an ex-military general, advised Ahmed Shah Massoud on the formation of the NCS leaders in Kabul. General Saffi's proposal called for the establishment of a revolutionary council and argued for the formation of the national army under the major Mujahideen commanders, of which Ahmed Shah Massoud would be the chief. In this case, the external front leaders would be banned from entering Afghanistan until the national army was formed and the enforcement of peace and security was ensured.[1] At the same time General M. Nabi Azimi, in charge of the ex-government military division, insisted on a similar proposal. Ahmed Shah Massoud rejected both proposals and instead asked the external leaders to form a transitional government in Pakistan to be put in place in Kabul.

According to Ahmed Shah Massoud, he was worried about the military clash between the major ethnic and linguistic groups in the country, and he stated:

All the parties had participated in the war, in jihad in Afghanistan, so they had
to have their share in the government, and in the formation of the government. Afghanistan is made up of different nationalities. We were worried
about a national conflict between different tribes (Qhawm) and different nationalities. In order to give everybody their own rights and also to avoid
bloodshed in Kabul, we left the word to the parties so they should decide
about the country as a whole. We talked about it for a temporary stage and
then after that the ground should be prepared for a general election.[2]

Massoud's concept about the participation of the political parties in the formation of a new government institution proved wrong. The main weakness of this
concept was that Massoud exaggerated the political capacity of the external
front leaders. He miscalculated the political capacity of the Mujahideen commanders and the ex-government armed forces. He thought if the external front
leaders entered Kabul they would cooperate within a workable network to find
a resolution. In this case, if Hekmatyar did not agree with such a resolution he
would accept the majority, but he would not fire on Kabul. Massoud also followed the party line and his action promoted the JIA's partisanship, in particular by supporting exclusively Burhanadin Rabbani against other external front
leaders. It should have been clear for Ahmed Shah Massoud that the external
front leaders had not any alternative to form a national government, and the
animosity between them had many roots in the past. In this case, Massoud's
concept for establishing a national government was far from the reality of the
political and military fabric of Afghanistan.

In 1993, when Massoud witnessed the high level of animosity and the lack
of a political agenda among the external leaders who changed their political position in a matter of days and hours due to the military balance in Kabul, he re-
alized the sad reality of poor accountability of the political leaders. In his
interview by Sandy Gall, Massoud stated, "The leaders [of the external front]
have failed. The leaders have failed in both cases, militarily and politically.
Now it is time that the commanders should come to the forefront."[3] This real-
ization by Massoud came when Kabul was already damaged severely by Hekmatyar rockets, and the northern alliances had disintegrated. General Dostam's
forces and *Hezb-e-Wahdat* were allied with Hekmatyar and the balance of
power in Kabul was very fragile. Massoud forces captured the headquarters of
Hekmatyar in the southern part of Kabul, Charasiab, but the formation of a
new National Commanders Council never became a reality.

Indeed, the personal charisma of a nationally and internationally recognized Mujahideen leader like Ahmed Shah Massoud could have played a significant role in the establishment of a wider influence of NCS in Afghanistan.
Such an establishment would have promoted peace and security in the country.
In this case, the external leaders would not have had any other choice but to cooperate with the NCS. Unfortunately, the only golden chance for enforcing

peace, security, and the establishment of a national government was lost, and the birth of a third political movement was aborted in Afghanistan.

THE SECOND PHASE OF CIVIL WAR

After the arrival of the external front leaders, headed by Sebqhatollah Mujadidi in Kabul, they announced the establishment of *Dowlat-e-Islami-e-Afghanistan*, the Islamic State of Afghanistan. According to the Peshawar Accord on April 26, 1992, Mujadidi would be the head of the state for two months and then Rabbani for four months. At the end of the six months, the government would form a council to choose an interim government. This interim government would co-ordinate forces and prepare the political and military ground for general election. On April 28, the interim government appointed new ministers who belonged to the Mujahideen parties, and Ahmed Shah Massoud became the defense minister. With the arrival of this government, tens of thousands of armed groups entered Kabul. Each of these armed groups held an area of Kabul and established their checkpoints. Due to the absence of the central order, each of these armed groups became the ruler of their controlled territory.

Hekmatyar did not join the interim government, and he accused the government of being an illegitimate institution under the influence of the ex-communists and demanded that the northern militia under General Dostam leave Kabul. When the government appointed Ahmed Shah Massoud, his long-term rival, as the defense minister, Hekmatyar became more rigid against the Islamic State. On December 28, most of the leaders agreed to extend Rabbani's role as the head of the government 45 days. Rabbani's government formed *Shura-e-ahl-e-hal-wa-Aqhd* (Council of Resolution and Settlement). This Shura elected Rabbani as the president of the country, creating a tense environment between the opposition and the government. An armed clash broke out between the *Hezb-e-Wahdat* and government forces over the control of Kabul University. This armed clash extended to other parts of Kabul when Arab volunteers who belonged to Sayyaf's party became involved against the Shia population and the supporters of Wahdat. Soon, *Hezb-e-Wahdat* joined Hekmatyar against the government forces, and Hekmatyar forces were able to get closer to Kabul. Large scale fighting erupted all over Kabul and the military and political forces in Kabul divided along the ethnic groups: Hekmatyar with the ex-*Khalqis* Pushtons; Massoud supported mostly by the non-Pushton; Dostam supported by Uzbeks; and *Hezb-e-Wahdat* supported by Hazaras. Later, all these armed ethnic groups generally divided into two hostile groups: the government forces dominated by the *Shura-e-Nezar* (Supervisory Council) led by Massoud and Rabbani; and the *Shura-e-Hamahangi* (Coordinated Council) comprised of Hekmatyar, Dostam, and *Hezb-e-Wahdat*. The fighting devastated Kabul and thousands of people took refuge in Jalalabad and Pakistan. Moreover, more than 5,000 people were killed by the end of 1992.

On March 7, 1993, Saudi King Fahd sponsored a peace accord between the warring factions, mostly the ex-Mujahideen external leaders in Islamabad. All the participants agreed with a new proposal that appointed Burhanadin Rabbani as president and Gulbadin Hekmatyar as prime minister. Later King Fahd invited all the Afghan leaders to Mecca, and they swore in the Holy Kaaba to stand by their agreement. However, this agreement was never practiced effectively, Hekmatyar never held his official position as prime minister, and further fighting continued.

On June 25, the government forces led by Massoud attacked the opposition position in Kabul and captured their headquarters, Bala Hissar Fort, in eastern Kabul and the Maranjan, a strategic hill, east of the fort from which the opposition had frequently bombarded the city. During the next few days, *Harkat Mohseny* forces loyal to the government captured the Darulaman Palace that enabled them to take the Microyan Housing complex. The government forces pushed the opposition from around Kabul city and secured the city from the rockets and shelling.[4]

According to the International Committee of the Red Cross, the fighting was so intense that the hospital workers were unable to evacuate the wounded. More than half a million of Kabul's population fled the city. Some 3,000 were killed and 19,000 wounded.[5] This fighting devastated the remaining population and forced the people to live in refugee camps at the Sar Shahi, situated in a stony plain desert with a temperature of up to 48 degrees centigrade (118 degrees Fahrenheit), outside Jalalabad. There was no shade, little water, and barely enough food, and many of those who were able to reach Jalalabad had lost loved ones. The majority of these people were Afghan educated people who wished one day to be able to rebuild the country. As Ahmed Rashid reports, in the words of Del Jan, a widow with three small children, "I lived for 21 years in my house in Kabul. Now it is destroyed and my husband killed. These Mujahideen leaders are worse than the Russians, they are heathens." "We want a neutral government without these Mujahideen animals, a government that brings peace and cares for the people. Even Najibullah [the former communist president] would be acceptable now," said Ali Yar, a former professor at Kabul University, whose entire family was killed in Kabul.[6]

While the fight over power was ruining Kabul and left a large number of casualties, the rest of Afghanistan was controlled by the regional powers. In Nangarhar, the local forces established a Shura and elected Haji Ghadir, a former Mujahideen commander, as the governor of this province. In the north, Dostam and Ismaeli Shia commander, Sayyad Nader Keyani, controlled Balkh, Faryab, Jowzjan, parts of Kunduz, and Samangan. In the west Ismail Khan disarmed the local Mujahideen and militia groups and controlled Herat, Badghis, Frah, and Ghor. Most of the regional forces sided with one or the other hostile forces, either the government or Hekmatyar.

Later, Dostam and government forces clashed causing Dostam and Hekmatyar to form an alliance against Massoud and Rabbani-led forces. The armed conflict among these groups shattered Kabul and neighboring areas, causing more causalities among civilians and forcing thousands to flee the capital in many directions. Massoud-led forces pushed the opposition forces from Kabul city and reduced the attack on Kabul by Hekmatyar's long-range rockets and artilleries. These events caused the Islamic government under Burhanadin to become occupied with fighting Hekmatyar forces and to slip into a wider military clash with Dostom and *Hezb-e-Wahdat*. As result, the government lost its credibility to run the country as a whole and provide security for its citizens.

At the end of 1993, Afghanistan was controlled mainly by five regional political armed forces. The north was under the control of Dostam with the support of *Hezb-e-Wahdat* and the Ismaeli Shia. The east was under the control of Nangarhar Shura led by Haji Qadir. (Nangarhar Shura did not take part directly in the armed conflict between Hekmatyar and Rubbani.) In the southeast, Paktia was under the control of Mawlawi Haqhani with the presence of armed groups loyal to Hekmatyar. The west was under the control of Ismail Khan, who was neutral in the beginning, but became an important supporter of Massoud and Rabbani in the following years. Kabul and areas north of the capital were controlled by Massoud's forces. In reality, Afghanistan was divided into regional and local forces that ran their administrations independently from the government leaders in Kabul. The most important element that sustained the connection between Kabul and the local and regional forces was the financial support sent by the Rabbani and Massoud to these local groups. This financial support came in the form of cash that was printed in Russia and transported to Kabul.

Following the collapse of Najibullah's government, those political and military forces who identified themselves as the Watan Party lost their political identities. The new social and political environment in Afghanistan forced them to search for a new political identity. The ex-government forces attempted to fit within one of the political and military formations of ex-Mujahideen groups. This search for identity brought a new combination of forces that mobilized society on a larger scale. The extremist *Khalqis*, such as Aslam Watanjar, worked under the leadership of Gulbadin Hekmatyar, an extremist Mujahideen leader who advocated the establishment of a pure Islamic government in Afghanistan.

The *Parchamis* and other non-Pushton segments of the ex-government forces attempted to save their semi-political and military autonomy while working under the leadership of Ahmed Shah Massoud and Burhanadin Rabbani. Because of the dichotomy of political ideology between the *Maktabis* (*Ikhwanis*) and Massoud's within *Jamaiat Islami* (JIA) under the symbolic leadership of Burhanadin Rabbani, the integration of ex-government forces was not as concrete as it was in Hizb-e-Islami Hekmatyar. When Hekmatyar forces fired on Massoud-Rabbani forces in Kabul, the ex-government forces within JIA attempted to rescue their military and political organization. For example, forces under General Dostam remained neutral because they were not sure who was going to win the war. This neutrality did not last long and forced those led by Dostam to change positions many times; consequently, they became an important part of the political game in Afghanistan.

In general, the Mujahideen leaders who had a greater legitimacy base than the ex-governmental elements for establishing a national government lost their credibility. They victimized the victory of a nation that had lost too many and suffered so much for their personal, ideological, and ethnic ambitions. The political and military shift by the armed political groups in many directions decentralized the social and political structure of the country once again. The cycle of violence and the massive mobilization of the nation in an unclear direction with no popular leadership continued.

CHAPTER ELEVEN

THE RISE OF THE TALIBAN

IN 1994, QANDAHAR WAS UNDER THE CONTROL OF THE EX-MUJAHIDEEN and ex-government forces led by Molla Naqibollah Akhund, a former commander loyal to JIA Rabbani. Because of its location between Herat and Pakistan, Qandahar became an important commercial center in the country. Herat and Qandahar formed the most important part of the commercial road connecting Gulf countries to the Pakistan market. Numerous caravans carrying commercial goods passed through Herat and Qandahar every day. This commercial road contributed large revenues to the regional authorities in Herat and Qandahar. The control of this lucrative commercial road became an important issue for the regional and local armed groups. The area between the city of Qandahar and the town of Speen Buldak at the Pakistani border came under the control of the local armed forces belonging to Gulbadin Hekmatyar. These local armed forces established their own checkpoints to maintain political power and secure financial resources. All commercial owners and travelers had to pay a large amount of cash to these local groups. These checkpoints became a destructive barrier for the commercial businesses and the local people. The commercial businesses had to pay duty to regional authorities in Herat and Qandahar as well as booties to these checkpoints. If a commercial vehicle refused to pay, there was no guarantee that the commercial goods would reach their destination. At the same time, travelers not able to pay were beaten up and held in captivity until their family and relatives were able to pay. There were reports that the armed guards of these checkpoints dishonored young Afghan women and young boys.

During Benazir Bhuttos's second term of office (1993–1996), the Pakistani interior minister, General N. Babar, established an Afghan Trade Development

Cell to facilitate Pakistan connection to Central Asia. In this case, Babar wanted to use the military transportation company that was created to ship arms from Karachi to the Afghan borders for Afghan Mujahideen during the Soviet occupation. The majority of the truck drivers were Pakistani ex-army officers. In August 1994, a 30-truck Pakistani convoy accompanied by the several ISI officers crossed the border into Afghanistan to reach Turkmenistan. There were several military and ISI officers, such as Colonel Imam, a prominent ISI field officer, on board. This convoy seemed suspicious and was held by the local armed groups headed by Mansur Achekzai, Ustad Halim, and Amir Lalai, who were now controlling the road between Qandahar and Pakistan. The action of these groups upset many businesses on both sides of the border in addition to the Pakistani government. In early September, an armed group comprised of religious students who called themselves the Taliban, rose up and answered the local communities' call for justice. The Taliban, commanded by Mullah Omar, helped the local disputes and carried out military operations against the brutalities of the local armed groups. The Taliban were supported by the local villagers and the business communities, in particular in Quetta. In October 1994, about 200 Taliban fighters rallied at the border on the Pakistan side. Consequently, they were able to cross the border and take control of Spin Buldak from Hekmatyar's men. In Spin Buldak, a large depot of arms was captured by the Taliban and facilitated their military need to push forward toward Qandahar. They opened the way toward Qandahar and released the Pakistani commercial caravan from the hand of the local armed groups who controlled the road. Soon this group increased their ability by getting transportation and human support from the Pakistani government and marched into Qandahar. The Taliban convinced Mullah Najibullah (the most prominent commander in Qandahar, who was in charge of 2,500 soldiers) to surrender. The Taliban captured a large quantity of arms, including numerous armored vehicles, artilleries, and most importantly, six Mig-21 fighters, and several helicopters. They took control of the commercial road between Qandahar and Pakistan and disarmed the local armed groups. In a matter of days, they seized the military garrison and administration in Qandahar and kept the commercial road secure and free for exports and imports as well as for the travelers.

In September 1994, the Taliban established their administration in Qandahar and organized their military campaign toward the surrounding towns and provinces. They brought the province of Helmand under their control and approached toward Zabul and Farah. In the long years of war in Afghanistan, Helmand became the regional center of opium cultivation. The annual production of hundreds of tons of opium made this province the most important economic center of Afghanistan. Controlling Helmand was crucial for the Taliban movement, and they completed the task very rapidly.

THE ORIGIN OF TALIBAN

The word "Taliban" originated in Arabic. Its singular form, is Talib, which means seeker. In the course of time, the singular form, combined with the Dari ending -*alef* (a) and -*noon* (n), shaped the plural form Taliban, the seekers.[1] After the PDPA coup and the Soviet invasion of Afghanistan, numerous religious schools (*madresah*) that were funded by the Gulf countries, in particular Saudi Arabia, were established along the Afghanistan borders in Pakistan. These religious schools were controlled by the two powerful Islamic parties in Pakistan: *Jamaat Islami Pakistan* (JIP), led by Qazi Hussien Ahmed; and *Jamaat-e-Ulema-e-Islami Pakistan* (JUIP), led by Maulana Fazl-ul-Rahman.

In the 1980s, JIP was very influential among the Pakistani army, which was one of the most important political forces behind General Zia-ul-Haqh. The JIP interpretation of Islam was close to the ideological line of Muslim Brothers (in Egypt) funding leaders such as Hassan-al-Bana and Sayyid Qutb with a mixture of Maududi's political ideology. Some segments of the JIP also accepted the Saudi's school (*maslak*) of Wahbiat. JIP had a wide range of connections with many revolutionary Islamic activist groups around the globe, in particular with the Egyptian organizations. JUIP was more traditionalist, and most of the Madaris under JUIP followed the Deobandi denomination and were funded by the Saudis.[2] "Fazlul Rahman and his party were long-term supporters of Bhuttos," especially when Binazir Bhutto became the prime minister of Pakistan in 1994.[3] JUIP was originally sponsored by the government of Pakistan to counterweigh the Awami National Party (ANP), a nationalistic Pushton separatist party in the Northwest Frontier Province of Pakistan (NWFP).

In the 1980s, hundreds of Afghan refugees in Pakistan joined the religious schools in many parts of the country. Religious schools became the most attractive centers for many Afghans in the refugee camps in Peshawar and Quetta, the center of Baluchistan. Attending these religious schools was a source of income for many families. The schools provided free room and board for students and a monthly salary by which the students supported their families. Most of the refugee camps in Peshawar and Baluchistan were located far from the towns; therefore, finding jobs was almost impossible. For the Afghan families, sending their male children to these religious schools was an opportunity to secure the future of their children. Since refugee camps became the main source of the Mujahideen activities, the Afghan Mujahideen parties became very active in the refugee camps.

Afghan Mujahideen groups, in particular *Hezb-e-Islami* led by Hekmatyar and *Jamaiat-e-Islami* led by Rabbani, and some circles in *Hezb-e-Islami Khales* and *Harkat Islami Mohamadi*, were involved in these religious schools. Some of these Mujahideen groups established their own schools with the support of the JIP or JUIP. Generally, Hekmatyar's party and the *Maktabis* (hard-liners) faction in JIA under Rabbani were affiliated with the *Jamaat-e-Islami* (JIP). The close relationship of Hekmatyar and Qazi Hussien Ahmed, the leader of JIP, helped Hekmatyar to gain a wide range of access in the Pakistani government, in particular with the ISI. These connections helped him to get the largest portion of the international financial and military aid directed to Afghan Mujahideen. The support of the JIP and the access in the military leadership of Pakistan helped Hekmatyar to form the most organized armed and political group among Afghan refugees, as well as make large investments in businesses in Pakistan. Hekmatyar's affiliation with JIP and the Muslim Brotherhood in Egypt directed hundreds of the volunteers from the Islamic countries, in particular from the Arab nations, to Afghanistan.

During the Afghan conflict, the religious schools in Pakistan, in particular those attended by Afghans, were affiliated with the war. Many graduate students and also teachers routinely participated in the armed struggle against the PDPA and the Soviets. In the beginning, students from these schools went to Afghanistan to manage the religious affairs (*tabliqh*) of the Mujahideen groups. Over the course of time, many of these students received military training inside Afghanistan and in Pakistan. Some of these students became full-time armed activists inside Afghanistan and formed local groups. There were many who became members of the JIP or JUIP in Pakistan and participated in political-religious activities in many parts of Pakistan, in particular along the Afghanistan border.

The ideological formation of Taliban has historical roots in the emergence of the mushrooming growth of thousands of *Madresah* across Pakistan. A secret survey conducted by the government of Punjab in 1997 showed the growth of only one sectarian organization started in 1987, called *Sipah-e-Sahaba Pakistan* (SSP), the Prophet Companion's Guards, based in Muridke (Sheikhupura district). This organization runs 28 centers in Punjab, 2 centers in Baluchistan, 3 in interior Sind, and 43 in Karachi. This study also showed that "there were 2,512 functioning deeni madresahs, representing all schools of sectarian thought in Punjab."[4] Most of the Taliban leaders came from *madresahs* run by JUIP, in particular from *Jamiat-ul-Uloom-al-Islamiyyah* located in New Town, Karachi. This *madresah*, run by Maulana Mohammed Yusuf Binori, has 8,000 students from different nationalities. Three of the six members on the council of the Taliban leadership came from this *madresah*. Mullah Mohammed Omar Mujahed also is affiliated with this *madresah*. During the Taliban defeat in Mazar-e-Sharif in 1997, he spoke with Binori to send more Talaba to Afghanistan.[5]

The Taliban leader, Mullah Mohammed Omar Mujahed, is the supreme head of the Taliban movement. He is a *Durani* Pushton, either *Popalzai* or *Noorzai*, and was a religious teacher in a local *madresah* prior to the Soviet invasion. He became affiliated with the JUIP,[6] and like many other Hanifi Mowlawis in Afghanistan, reportedly followed the Deobandi school of thought based in India.[7] Mullah Mujahed then became a commander of Mohammedi's party in the Arghestan district in the province of Qandahar. He commanded a group of local Mujahideen over the control of the strategic location north of the Qandahar-Chaman Highway. He fought the militia forces led by Esmat Muslim over the control of these important areas. In his fight against the Soviets, Mullah Omar lost one eye. After the fall of the Kabul regime led by Najibullah, Mullah Mujahed returned to his religious activities by becoming the head of a local *madresah*. He was disgusted by the ex-Mujahideen leaders who were fighting over power and causing a large number of human casualties and the destruction of what was left from the Soviet invasion.

Most of the leaders of the Taliban who are now working in key positions in Afghanistan are graduates from the religious schools in Pakistan. For example, the governor of Jalalabad is a former student of *Jami'ah Haqqanih*, Akora Khattak Peshawar. The present judge of Jalalabad High Court and its Qazi are scholars of another *madresah* in Peshawar. Taliban representative to the United Nations, Maulana Abdul Hakim, graduated from the *Binnori Town madresah* in Karachi. The Taliban ambassador in Islamabad, Muhammad Masoom Afghani, graduated from *Dar-ul-Uloom Karachi*.[8] The Taliban's affiliation with the JUIP helped them to gain massive support from Pakistan. This support was based on the personal and political friendship of Maulana Fazl-ul-Rahman, the spiritual mentor of the Taliban in Afghanistan.[9] The Taliban alternative for the educational system of Afghanistan followed the same direction as in Pakistan by establishing as many *madresahs* as possible. Like Pakistan, these *madresahs* can attract large funds from Saudi and other Gulf countries, and, subsequently, can create a massive political force that can influence national and regional politics. Thus, establishing *madresahs* in each area captured by the Taliban forces was a primary target of their agenda.

The formation of the Taliban has strong roots in the second phase of civil war between the ex-Mujahideen groups in Afghanistan. The chaotic situation inside Afghanistan created a deep gap between the political leaders and the general public. In reality, the Taliban movement emerged in a gap between the general public and the Mujahideen leadership after 1992. This gap was the direct result of fighting over political power by these leaders in Kabul and their failure to form a nationally based government. This absence of a nationally accepted leadership allowed the Taliban to emerge strongly and aggressively. In other words, the absence of a nationally accepted political leadership opened a space in the political affairs of the nation for a third movement rather than the two warring hostile factions, Hekmatyar-Khalqis and Rabbani-Parchamis. When the Taliban declared their cause to establish peace, security, and the formation of a national assembly, many local communities in Qandahar that were suffering from the war became supportive of the Taliban cause. The Taliban proclamation fit largely with the need for a third political movement to guide Afghanistan out of the civil war.

The formation of the Taliban associated the power struggle between the JUIP and JIP and "a turf battle between ISI and Interior Ministry in Islamabad during Benazir Bhutto's second term"[10] in Pakistan. In 1993, the ISI's control and autonomy over the Afghanistan operation and its failure to influence the newly established government in Kabul was criticized by the Interior Minister, General Babar. Pakistani government circles such as the ISI and the Interior ministry were afraid of an active independent Afghanistan. The fear of the establishment of a nationalist government in Afghanistan, which could form one of the most skilled armies in the region, and the existence of a large weapon surplus, would be a nightmare for the Pakistani leaders. This fear was amplified by Pakistan losing its regional strategic location against the communist threat. A part of its strategic interests, Pakistan's influence in Afghanistan aimed to justify its regional interest against India.

THE SOCIAL ROOTS OF THE TALIBAN

The bulk of the Taliban forces came from the Baluchistan *madresahs* on the Pakistan side of the Afghan border. They were recruited from the refugee camps into these religious institutions. Most of these students originally came from rural areas in Qandahar, Helmad, Zabul, Frah, and some from Nimroze and Gazni. Becoming refugees in Pakistan for long periods of time caused these students to be disconnected from their social, cultural, and economic bond with Afghanistan. Many of them were very young when they arrived in Pakistan, and they had not experienced the historical and national pattern in which their ancestors lived for hundreds of years. These young Afghan boys, with minds ready to learn and adapt to the world they were living in, were like a fertile land for those who wanted to plant the seeds of their political ideologies. Indeed, establishing the *Deeni madresahs* became a financial source for the Pakistani and Afghan political parties by which they mobilized forces within the Afghan and Pakistan societies.

Soon, the Afghan Mujahideen parties (the external front) established numerous *madresahs* all across the borders in connection to the refugee camps. In this effort, *Hezb-e-Islami Hekmatyar* (HIH), *Jamaiat-e-Islami Rabbani* (JIA), *Hezb-e-Islami Khaless* (HIK), and *Harkat-e-Islami Mohammedi* (HIM) were serious about establishing *Deeni madresahs*. HIH and JIA *madresahs* were influenced by the revolutionary political ideology of the Muslim Brothers (*Ikhwan-ul-Muslemin*), Mawdodi, and by some degree the Wahabiat. Later, *madresahs* that belonged to the Sayyaf party came under the direct influence of the Wahabiat school of thought that was funded by the Saudis. *Madresahs* controlled by the HIK and HIM followed the traditional school of *Ahl-e-Sonna-wa-Jamah* (traditional Sunni Islam). In these schools, HIM was able to run the largest *madresahs* in the Baluchistan region that recruited thousands of refugee boys who feared for their lives, rescuing them from hunger, homelessness, and anxiety. These young Afghan boys had spent more of their lives at school than with families and were searching for an identity that would satisfy their psychological needs and help them to find salvation.

The psychological needs of these young students were rooted in a war environment that was politicized by many different factions. There were important concepts driven by the psychological notion of the young folks in the refugee camps. Among all, the most important were the concepts of jihad and *shahadah* (holy war and self-sacrifice). These concepts were rooted deeply into the devotion to Islam and the battle against atheist forces in Afghanistan. For many of these Afghan youngsters, attending jihad was considered the highest honor of bravery and personal salvation. This highest honor stimulated their quest for a *mujahed* identity, fighting one of the world's superpowers. The concepts of jihad and *shahadah* became dominant in the refugee camps and the *Deeni madresahs* during the years of the Soviet invasion of Afghanistan. A large percentage of these students came from families who had lost at least one loved one in the war, in particular a male member such as a father or brother. In this case, the social behavior and personal attitude of these students were very different from those who attended religious schools during peacetime in Afghanistan. Most of these young students felt obligated to continue the path of those martyred in the war. At the schools, attendance in the armed struggle also had been preached as a religious duty. Thus, these students received military training when they were in religious services for the local Mujahideen groups inside Afghanistan. In this regard, the military training became a regular part of the curriculum of these religious schools. In many cases, Islamic beliefs in jihad and *shahadah* made these students fearless fighters on the battlefield (in particular when such beliefs were combined with revengeful feelings toward those who killed members of their families, bombed their villages, and forced them into refugee camps). For example, during the Soviet invasion, the Taliban forces led by Mollah Nassim Akhundzada became the most feared Mujahideen group in Helmand. They not only vanquished the PDPA and Russians in the territories they controlled, they also became harsh on their rival forces belonging to Hekmatyar. The core Mujahideen forces led by Mollah Nassim were 1,500 *talibs* who called themselves the sacrificers.[11]

Generally, the students attending religious schools in Pakistan did not lead a comfortable life; they had to be in school many years and go back and forth to the front line in Afghanistan. The uneasy lives of these students, their observations of the misery of millions of Afghans in refugee camps, and the severity of Mujahideen life inside the country made them familiar with the harsh reality of war. Moreover, the teaching of Islam that emphasizes brotherhood among Muslims and the support and sharing of wealth with fellow Muslims in the time of severity gave these students a sense of devotion for the sake of God. At the same time, when a *mujahed* was killed in battle against the Soviets, it was the *talibs'* duty to complete the funeral ceremony. In the term of daily prayer (Muslims pray five times a day), it was these *talibs* who stayed in front of the prayers to conduct *namaz* and preach after. In many areas, local *mollahs* and these *talibs* became the judiciary core of the local Mujahideen groups, and these cores issued the degree of punishment against the war and civil crimes. All of this made these religious students become sincere in politics and play an important role in the power game among the Mujahideen parties.

During the war years, these Afghan religious students engaged in politics, looking for a faithful leadership to fit with their psychological needs and also fit with the Islamic doctrines of honesty, devotion, and self-sacrifice that they learned at schools. But when they observed the external front leaders of the Afghan Mujahideen in Pakistan who had luxurious lives, large investments, corrupt administrations, and family and personal privileges, many of these students lost their optimism for the Afghan political leaders. For example, in the 1980s there were a large number of the religious schools established by HIM in Baluchistan. According to Taliban sources, Maulawi Mohammedi was not able to satisfy the psychological needs of these students and the teachers due to the corruption of his family members, in particular his sons. Both students and teachers became attracted to the character of the JUIP leader, Mufti Mahmud, who followed the *Deobandi school.* In these religious schools, the leaders of JUIP, in particular Mufti Mahmud, became much more influential than the Afghan leaders, such as Maulawi Mohammedi.[12] The JUIP, under Mufti Mahmud and later under his son Maulina Fazl-ul-Rahman, influenced many religious schools that were established by the external front of Afghan Mujahideen. They also recruited many Afghan students into their own administrated schools. This shift of leadership among the religious schools established by Afghans had changed the local loyalty of the Afghan students. As a result of this change of students' loyalty from a local base to a regional base, they found themselves affiliated more with the JUIP Pakistani leaders than the Afghan Mujahideen external front leaders. The leaders of JUIP became the ideological mentors of the Afghan *Talibs* and gave the Afghan students and teachers an avenue to enter the regional political game. This ideological affiliation between the Afghan students and teachers in the *Deeni madresahs* gave birth to their political alignment with the political circles in Pakistan.

CHAPTER TWELVE

THE SOURCE OF TALIBAN FORCES IN AFGHANISTAN

THE AFGHAN TALIBAN FORCES ARE COMPRISED OF THREE CATEGORIES. One category consists of the *talibs* and *mollahs* who graduated from the religious schools or from the local seminaries in the rural areas in Afghanistan. Before the PDPA coup in 1978, most of these *mollahs* and *talibs* lived in mosques all over the country, and they were among the first social groups that were harassed by the PDPA regime. In the later stages of the war, many of these *mollahs* and *talibs* joined the Mujahideen groups, and some became Mujahideen commanders. A segment of these *mollahs* and *talibs* remained in Afghanistan and continued their religious services for the local communities. Those who left the country attended religious ceremonies and schools in Pakistan and, to a lesser extent, in Iran. When the Taliban movement started, these *mollahs* and *talibs* joined the movement and became loyal members of the movement.

The second category consists of those *mollahs* and *talibs* who took refuge in the neighboring countries, in particular Pakistan, and attended schools there. This group is comprised of two segments.

One segment attended the religious schools that were established and run by the Afghan Mujahideen external front who had studied similar subjects and curriculum in the official religious schools in prewar Afghanistan. The main subjects in these schools were Quranic studies, general principles of the Islamic law, and Arabic language. Most of these students and their teachers were active in the local Afghan and non-Afghan communities in Pakistan. Many of these students followed the teaching of the JUIP with the Deobandi interpretation of Islam and were trained by the Pakistani military sources. The first group of armed Taliban who crossed the border into Afghanistan was comprised of these groups and followed the religious call of the Afghan Taliban leaders to restore order in Afghanistan. The religious call of restoring order in Afghanistan by the Taliban leaders, in particular Mullah Mohammed Omar, was rooted in their desire to establish Islamic justice and end the civil war. This call was supported by the JUIP leaders in Pakistan and those military and political circles who were allied with JUIP. In reality, this religious call to restore order was interpreted by the Taliban to enforce the rule of Islamic law (*Shari'ah*) in Afghanistan. This development was a shift in the political ideology of the Afghan religious students from pure devoted fighters against the atheist forces to the enforcement of order and security in Afghanistan.

Those who attended the religious schools established and controlled by JUIP and studied a curriculum different from the one taught in Afghan religious schools in Pakistan formed a separate group. The school's curriculum run by JUIP was comprised of religious subjects such as *Kafia* and *Sharhe Jami* (Arabic grammar), *Muhjtassarul ma* and *ani Duroosul Balagah Miftah-ul-Uloom* (philosophy subjects), *Sullam-ul-Uloom*, *Meerzahid Mulla Jalaal*, and *Mulla Hasan Qutbi*, and *Sharhe Tahzeeb* (Mantiq, logic subjects), and *Sarf* (syntax). The curriculum of these schools also included some secular subjects such as political science, international studies, economics, and foreign languages like Urdo and English.[1] This group of Taliban is the core of the high-ranking leadership who run the Taliban's administration inside Afghanistan and manages their international affairs. They not only have prominent positions among the Taliban in the country, they are also the most important core connecting the Taliban with Pakistan and other external supporters. The affiliation of these core leaders with the JUIP provided a network of contacts with the local and international Muslim activists who follow the Deobandi school of thought.

Another group of participating Taliban are those Pakistani students and JUIP activists who work in both civil administration and military rank of the movement.[2] This group came from many parts of Pakistan, in particular from the Baluchistan and Sind provinces of Pakistan. Cooperation and support of this group was an important element for the Taliban in recruiting new fighters who shared belief and faith with the Taliban. The recruitment of new fighters created a wave of mass participation of the Pakistani religious students in the politics of Afghanistan. For example, on August 10, 1997, the parents of a 13-year-old Pakistani boy named Marouf Ahmed filed a lawsuit against a JUIP school in Karachi. They accused the school of sending their young son to support the Taliban in Afghanistan. "I was only introduced to jihad through speeches of my teachers but now I know what jihad actually means. I have seen the Taliban fighting enemies," Marouf told reporters. According to Sharfuddin Memon, a leader of the local Citizen-Police Liaison Committee in Karachi, "there are 600–700 Pakistani boys who had been sent by religious schools to

Afghanistan."[3] There are many activists whose school of thought is either rooted in Wahabiat, Muslim Brothers of Egypt, or *Salafis* working with the Taliban. According to Taliban sources, these elements of the Taliban are in the minority, and the majority of the Taliban forces are those who believe in *Adlah Arbaah* (the four Sunni schools of Islam).[4]

The Taliban military forces formed another group that was divided into two sections. In 1990 to 1992, when the influence of the non-Pushton factions of the ex-PDPA members and the northern militia dominated *De Hezb-e-Watan* led by Najibullah, many of the Pushton officers of the army, particularly the ex-*Khalqis*, feared losing their position in the power game of the country. The military coup led by Shahnwaz Tanai against Dr. Najibullah in 1990 was rooted in this power game among the political forces in Afghanistan. Even though Tanai's coup failed, a large number of the army officers defected to Hekmatyar and were organized and supported by the ISI. After the Taliban disarmed Hekmatyar forces, these officers, including Tanai and his group, were recruited into the Taliban army units. According to an Afghan source, there are over 1,600 ex-*Khalqis* working with the Taliban. The Taliban also attempted to recruit the ex-army officers who were refugees in Pakistan, in particular those who had ethnic Pushton backgrounds. These officers, like Molla Bore Jan, an ex-PDPA officer, became the core of the Taliban army and were familiar with the use of advanced military air and ground machines.

The second part of the Taliban armed forces was comprised of the ex-Mujahideen commanders and personnel who fought the PDPA and the Soviets in Afghanistan. This group had battle experience, but in small scale military operations; therefore they operated under the leadership and guidance of the Pakistani army officers. The ex-Mujahideen groups and commanders became a significant source of local support for the Taliban in the areas under their control. The majority of this group had neither any other source of income nor any professional skills rather than fighting. In the past, these groups enjoyed the U.S./Saudi financial support. But with the Soviet withdrawal and collapse of the Najibullah regime, the Mujahideen parties lost this international financial support. Now, working for the Taliban provided them with privileges, especially for those commanders who worked for the Taliban opposition and switched sides, receiving a large amount of cash.

THE TALIBAN ALLIANCE AND PAKISTAN'S FORWARD POLICY

Pakistani military leaders and the ISI's Afghanistan Bureau were involved in Afghanistan for decades. The direct involvement of Pakistani military leaders and the ISI began with a failed coup led by the Muslim Brothers of Afghanistan against President Dauod in the spring of 1974. After the coup crashed, many of the Muslim Brothers escaped to Pakistan, where they received direct support from Zulfiqar Ali Bhutto's regime. As Anthony Davis writes: "President Dauod's strident support for the cause of Pushtunistan—an irredentist vision of a greater Afghanistan embracing Pushton tribal lands in Pakistan, was feared by Pakistan's leaders."[5] The Pakistani military, led by the commander of Pakistan's Frontier Corps, Brigadier Nasirullah Babar, became involved in Afghanistan's internal affairs. Babar has been the leading advocate of Pakistan's forward policy—direct intervention toward Afghanistan. "I told the government we must have some elements to influence events in Afghanistan in case there was trouble," Babar later explained.[6] Soon, a group of Afghan Ikhwanis (Muslim Brothers), led by Gulbadin Hekmatyar and Burhanadin Rabbani, were recruited and supported by the Pakistani government against President Dauod's regime. These Afghan youths were sent to the Cherat Army camp near Peshawar, where they received courses and military training "dressed in the uniforms of Babar's Frontier Corps—ostensibly Pakistan from the tribal areas."[7] Hekmatyar and Massoud were among those trained in Pakistan, and the ISI armed 30 of these young Afghans, commanded by Ahmed Shah Massoud, to attack the Afghan army stations in late July 1975. This group was destroyed mostly by the local Afghan community in Panjshir valley with the government support. Later Babar recalled the operation as a success and he stated, "I told Mr. Bhutto it is time we conveyed a message to Dauod."[8]

After the PDPA military coup in 1978, General Zia-ul Haq and his military circle were looking for a strategic ally in post-Communist Afghanistan to provide Pakistan with strategic depth in its struggle with India and a bridgehead for Islamic revolt into the Muslim underbelly of the Soviet Union. Gulbadin Hekmatyar's long-term connection with the Pakistani elements and his revolutionary pan-Islamism incorporated the political ideology of General Zia and mirrored the beliefs of several senior ISI officers, such as General Hamid Gul. In this case, Hekmatyar's large, well-organized Hezb party became the favored vehicle for Zia's vision in Afghanistan. When the Soviet troops invaded Afghanistan in 1979, the political ideology of General Zia dominated the Pakistan government, and ISI became massively involved in Afghanistan. As Anthony Davis states:

> The ISI under the command of Lt.-General Abdur Akhtar Rahman, a close confidante of then-president Zia-ul Haq, intended to run the conflict in a hands-on fashion. "Not only did ISI serve as the sole conduit for U.S. and Saudi-funded munitions reaching the Mujahideen parties," recalls one Western analyst, "ISI officers were also closely involved in planning and directing operations." Indeed, the ISI came to see the Afghan war as its own, with the Mujahideen viewed as valiant but ill-disciplined warriors serving as the sharp end of a strategy made in Islamabad. As Brig. Mohammed Yousaf was later to write of his 1983 appointment as director of ISI's Afghanistan Bureau: "I was now cast in the role of overall guerrilla leader."[9]

The arrival of large amounts of international aid, particularly that from the United States, to the hands of the Pakistani government made the ISI a custodian of the Afghan Mujahideen leaders. Even after General Zia, this situation enabled the ISI to not only put pressure on Afghan leaders, but also give political muscle to the ISI leaders to filter out the Afghan political activists, in particular in Pakistan. This situation led the ISI to act against any Mujahideen organization both inside and outside who wanted to run the war against the Soviets in accordance with Afghanistan interests. Politically, the pressure of ISI on the Afghan leaders in Pakistan disabled the Mujahideen external front to coordinate their activities according to what was going on inside the country in the battlefields. On the international level, the Mujahideen external front leaders failed to represent collectively the Mujahideen's view on the future of Afghanistan. This failure of Afghan political leaders abolished their role in the Geneva Accords, where Pakistani diplomats and the United States represented Afghanistan. This disability caused a destructive gap between the Mujahideen political leaders in Pakistan and the field commanders inside. This situation resulted in the formation of the Mujahideen regional organizations that were able to manage their political and military affairs in accordance with the political, social, and military situations inside the country. However, it is interfering in the affairs of Afghan Mujahideen, preventing the formation of nationally based leadership in Afghanistan.

The emergence of these regional Mujahideen armed political groups inside Afghanistan became a serious threat to the regional strategy of the ISI. The ISI attempted to influence the Mujahideen internal front leaders through the control of weapons, ammunition, money distribution and also through those Afghan political parties who had close ties with the ISI. The ISI was against any direct communication between the Mujahideen regional leaders and commanders. For a long period of time when any regional commander wanted to communicate with a commander in another region, he had to contact Pakistan-based radio communication stations to pass along his message. Finally, the Mujahideen leaders inside Afghanistan exchanged information and communication equipment during the *Saghar* conference conducted by Ismail Khan in 1986.

The activities of the ISI came under pressure by the diplomatic efforts of the United Nations after the withdrawal of the Soviets in Afghanistan. In this period of time, the ISI pushed a military solution against Najibullah's regime in Afghanistan. The ISI supported the military coup led by Shanawaz Tanai and Gulbadin Hekmatyar against Dr. Najibullah in March 1990. The defeat of this military coup was a big blow to the ISI's regional strategy and caused more pressure from the nonmilitary political leadership of Pakistan on the ISI. The formation of the NCS of Afghan Mujahideen in Kunar was the most important political development against the ISI's regional strategy. Through this council, the Mujahideen internal front leaders were able to deal with the fate of the Afghan nation together, without the influence of the neighboring countries.

These new political and military developments in Afghanistan forced the ISI to organize a military plan with forces belonging to *Hezb-e-Islami* Hekmatyar against Najibullah's regime. This militaristic plan aimed to capture Kabul and was in full force when the governments of Pakistan, Iran, Russia, the United States, and the rest of the Mujahideen leaders in Pakistan agreed to the UN peace plan. On the eve of the successful implementation of the UN peace plan in Afghanistan, the ISI, through Hekmatyar and non-Afghan volunteers, led hundreds of trucks loaded with weapons and fighters to the southern part of Kabul. This military deployment of the ISI and Hekmatyar concerned other political armed forces within Najibullah's government and the Mujahideen forces, in particular Massoud units. A secret military operation, with the direct support of the ISI and planned by the Hekmatyar and the ex-*Khalqis*, in particular the Interior Minister's *Sarandoy* forces, aimed to capture Kabul and install Hekmatyar as the head of the government. This secret military plan forced Massoud and his allies to move into Kabul. This military buildup caused the UN peace plan to remain only on paper forever.

After the collapse of Najibullah's government in 1992, the ISI attempted to use the conflict between the armed forces toward the formation of a coalition force under the leadership of Hekmatyar against Massoud-led forces. For this purpose, the ISI and other Pakistani leaders visited General Dostam and other ex-Mujahideen leaders who were in Pakistan. The main political hope for the ISI was to unite the southern Pushton Heartland under the leadership of Hekmatyar and overrun Kabul. But the formation of the regional political and military organization, in particular the Nangarhar Shura within the Pushton population of the country, dismantled such a hope.

THE POLITICAL SHIFT IN
PAKISTAN'S FORWARD POLICY

The collapse of the Soviet Union and the emergence of the new republics in Central Asia forced the Pakistani leaders to shift their strategy toward Afghanistan. The Bhutto government followed a market-oriented policy rather than a militaristic tactical approach toward Afghanistan. Contrary to General Zia, the Bhutto administration attempted to influence Afghanistan because of its importance as an economic highway connecting Pakistan to the Central Asian market rather than a base to support the Islamic revolts in the region. Pakistani leaders also wanted to use Afghanistan as a strategic support base in future military conflicts against India. Thus, this strategy was a combination of General Zia's vision of pan-Islamism and Bhutto's market orientation policy. These two visions forced the military leaders of the Pakistani army and the ISI to unite their efforts to influence and control Afghanistan, this crucial economic highway.

Indeed, Pakistan has viewed the Taliban as the closest ally toward its strategy depth in the region, and for this reason Pakistani leaders support the Taliban massively. The failure of the ISI attempts via connected Afghan-Mujahideen groups to overcome Najibullah's government and capture Kabul alarmed the Pakistan leadership. In 1993, Interior Minister General Nasirullah Babar and his military and political allies established a new agenda for Afghanistan. This new agenda, called Pakistan's depth strategy, had three ultimate goals.

The first goal was to pacify the threat that could rise from a strong Afghan government. In this context, such a government in Afghanistan might pursue the cause of independent Pushtonistan and the rejection of the Durand line. In time of conflicts, this government could form an alliance with India and cut off Pakistan from the Central Asian Republics (CAR), a crucial energy source and a prosperous regional market economy. Influencing Afghanistan's national politics by selecting who should run the government in Kabul became very critical for Pakistani circles. Thus, an ethnic Pushton ally in Afghanistan would help Pakistan integrate the Pushtons on the other side of the border and make them important in the process of Afghan forward policy. Achieving such a goal would reduce the future tension over the Durand issue and could create a psychological integration of the Pushton population in the Pakistani state.

Another priority of the depth strategy was to rescue the collapsing economy by providing economically efficient energy to the fast growing population of Pakistan and having free and fast access to the CAR. The CAR's energy and market economy would not only help Pakistan economically, it also would provide a free hand for this country to compete with Iran and India in the regional power game. In this case, Pakistan would be able to contain Iran's influence in the CAR as well as eliminate this influence in Afghanistan.

The third goal was to contain India in the Kashmir fronts with the avoidance of friendly government relations between India and Afghanistan. Using the Afghan soil as a camping ground for the Kashmirin militants would help the Pakistani army to balance its position against India in that region. According to sources in Pakistan, in the past five years (1995–2000) 60,000 to 80,000 Pakistani nationals were trained in Afghanistan and went back home.[10] This circumstance helped the Pakistani leaders to use these forces in Kashmir as well as in Afghanistan. In addition to this, many Islamic militants from around the world gathered in Afghanistan and participated in battles in Afghanistan, Kashmir, and the CAR. All this would be different if there were friendly government relations between India and Afghanistan.

There were three political circles behind this new Pakistani strategy. One was led by General Nasirullah Babar. Babar as the minister of interior had strong links with elite circles in the Pakistani army. Babar was the mentor of the new agenda for Afghanistan and also was one of the most experienced senior army officers in regard to Afghanistan. His experiences and connection to the Army elite was key to achieving the Pakistan strategy-depth agenda in Afghanistan. Babar was able to gain the support and cooperation of ISI elite officers in charge of Afghan policy. Benazir Bhutto, the leader of the People's Party of Pakistan (PPP), who was serving her second term as Pakistan prime minister, represented another political circle within the Pakistani strategy. Bhutto's wide connection with the prominent political leaders, in particular in her party, was an important source of support for Pakistan's forward policy toward Afghanistan. JUIP leader Maulana Fazl-ul-Rahman, who supported Bhutto and also was one of the most influential political leaders in NWFP as well as Baluchistan, led the third political circle. JUIP was running hundreds of religious schools in many parts of Pakistan. Fazl-ul-Rahman was a mentor for many Taliban and most of the Taliban leaders graduated from schools controlled by his party. Fazl-ul-Rahman was the main supporter of the Taliban in Pakistan and the Taliban were able to draw out thousands of students for their military campaign against the United Islamic Front for Liberation of Afghanistan (UIFLA). In this regard, JUIP provided the Taliban with grassroots support in Pakistan. In addition to this, it was Fazl-ul-Rahman who organized the hunting expedition for the Saudi princes in Qandahar in the winter of 1994 to 1995. In this expedition Prince Turki, the head of Saudi intelligence, met with the Taliban supreme leader Mullah Mohammed Omar Mujahed, and he expressed Saudi support for the Taliban. In this hunting trip, the Saudi princes donated cash and also left behind several luxurious jeeps and hundreds of pickup trucks. Later, the Taliban made good use of these trucks by breaking through the supply lines of Ismail Kahn and chasing his forces in many directions.

The coalition of the above three circles extended Pakistan involvement in Afghanistan, and it added the civilians' participation as well as the military and ISI in the affairs of Afghanistan. Subsequently, this coalition of forces created massive support for the implementation of the Pakistan forward policy toward Afghanistan, and the Taliban alliance with Pakistan benefited from this development greatly.

In the Pakistani government, the ISI became suspicious of Bhutto's administration in dealings with Afghanistan; the ISI leaders viewed the Taliban as yet another Benazir Bhutto ploy to reduce its role in Afghan affairs. With the emergence of the Taliban movement in southern Afghanistan, the military rather than ISI was put in charge of Pakistan involvement in Afghanistan.

Eventually, the remarkable success of the Taliban forced the ISI to co-opt itself into training and guiding the Taliban ranks.[11] This friendship and political affiliation between the Taliban leadership and JUIP resulted in the military support and training of the Taliban forces by the Frontier Constabulary Corps, a paramilitary force of the Interior Ministry and the *Sibi Scouts* of the Pakistan army.[12] In the eyes of the Pakistani leaders, the Taliban forces in Afghanistan became new political and military allies that would pacify an Afghan nationalist threat against Pakistan. In this case, such a political armed force would influence the national government in Afghanistan and provide secure access to the Gulf and Central Asian market.

Having access to the Central Asian market became very crucial for the economic growth and industrialization of Pakistan. The importance of this access was highlighted when the discovery of oil and natural gas demanded ground transportation. For Pakistani leaders, controlling the economic road between Central Asia and Pakistan became an important task. In this case, the establishment of a national government, in particular a nationalist one in Afghanistan that could have firm control over the economic highway connecting Pakistan to Central Asia, would not be acceptable to the Pakistani leaders. Therefore, the disintegration of the Afghan Mujahideen and the local and regional armed and political groups during and after the Soviet invasion can be viewed in the interest of the Pakistani forward policy toward Afghanistan. Establishing a government with passive military ability in Afghanistan under the influence of Pakistan was considered the most favorable alternative for Pakistani leaders.

CHAPTER THIRTEEN

TALIBAN TACTICS AND STRATEGIES

WHEN THE TALIBAN FORCES CROSSED THE BORDER AND CAPTURED Spin Buldak, they asked the local armed groups to lay down their weapons and surrender. When the local groups resisted, the Taliban used their full military forces to implement their objectives. One of the most effective tactics used widely by the Taliban was influencing the political, ethnic, and family conflicts between the local armed groups. After they captured Qandahar, they announced their cause of fighting the corrupted local and regional armed groups for Islamic convictions to establish peace in the country.

Many local communities greeted this conviction and cause; they also supported the Taliban movement in Qandahar. After controlling Qandahar and Helmand, the Taliban laid their plan to conquer the whole country step by step. Soon, the Taliban found themselves between four armed forces: the northwest forces led by Ismail Khan; the northeast forces led by Ahmed Shah Massoud; the east forces under *Nangarhar Shura* and led by Haji Abdul Qadir; and the north forces led by General Dostam and Afghan Shia factions. If the Taliban wanted to move toward Kabul, they were not secure from Ismail Khan, who was a strong ally of the Rabbani-Massoud group. Moreover, to approach Kabul they needed air support, especially since they did not have enough fighter jets.

To reduce resistance against their ambitions, Taliban leadership announced that the goal of their movement was not to pursue political power or control the government but to restore peace and security in the country. They also announced that when peace and security was achieved in Afghanistan they would allow the people of Afghanistan to form a national Islamic government. The call for peace and security and an end to the civil war was a long desire for

Afghans inside and outside, and this declaration was a perfect match. This Taliban leadership's political call for peace and security not only deactivated many political groups in Afghanistan, it also successfully created a confusing environment among the remaining political groups. Moreover, the Taliban's affiliation with the JUIP and the Pakistani military (who were out of the ISI's control), prevented information from getting through to the JIP- (led by Qazi Ahmed Hussein) and ISI-connected Afghan factions. As result, the scope of confusion about this new movement was wide, and wider among the politicians and general public in Afghanistan. This confusion provided a great environment for the Taliban to move forward and influence many areas across the country.

Years of civil war and the bloody clashes between the ex-Mujahideen groups in Kabul had disturbed the lives of millions of Afghans and made them desperate for peace and security. Opening the commercial roads between Afghanistan and Pakistan and disarming the local armed groups were positive political and military tactics that helped the Taliban approach Qandahar and Helmand in a matter of weeks. In all these areas, the Taliban made agreements with the local communities that if they submitted their loyalty to them, they could continue their normal lives. At the same time, they integrated the local armed forces under their military organization and supported them with a generous cash flow that came from external sources.

In Qandahar, the economic activities were based mainly on trades and some agricultural products, but in particular opium production. The absence of a central government after the collapse of the Najibullah regime made export and import the most dominant sectors of regional economy. Commercial goods were arriving from the Persian Gulf and Central Asian countries via Herat to Kandahar. At the same time many commercial goods arrived from the port of Karachi to Qandahar in transit status and were illegally exported back to Pakistan. This commercial-based economy created an influential social class with strong financial abilities. However, the existence of the local armed groups on the commercial roads was very costly for the traders. Numerous checkpoints run by local armed groups interrupted the commercial movement in the region. After the capture of Qandahar by the Taliban, it was an important positive development for the traders to enjoy the security, and the Taliban to have such strong financial support.

In Helmand, the Taliban supported Abdul Wahid, the head of the Boghran district, against a stronger armed group led by Abdul Qhaffar Aakhondzadah. After a round of negotiation, Aakhondzadah agreed to give up Leshkargah, the capital of Helmand, to the Taliban forces and return to his town, Mossa Qalah. After the Taliban seized the capital of Helmand, they asked Aakhondzadah to surrender and put down his arms. Aakhondzadah refused to do so, and severe fighting erupted between the two sides. Aakhondzadah and his allied local group was not able to stop the Taliban and so retreated to Ghor to take refuge in the territories controlled by Ismail Kahn. The Taliban controlled Helmand

and expanded their authority over this province. Helmand was a strategic location near their headquarters, Qandahar, and this province also had a great economic incentive for the Taliban. Helmand's economic activities were based mainly on opium cultivation, and thousands of people were engaged in farming and trading. As Ahmed Rashid writes: "According to the UNDCP, Afghanistan in 1997 produced 2,800 tons of opium, half of it in Helmand."[1] Helmand and southern Qandahar regions produced more than 60 percent of Afghanistan's opium.[2] The Taliban administration collected a 10 percent tax from opium cultivation, which was a good source of local revenue. Since the control of the Taliban, opium production has increased rapidly, and more fertile land has been cultivated. Helmand soil is very fertile for agriculture and can harvest about 20 pounds in two and a half acres, compared to Burma (the Golden Triangle), which harvests 5 pounds in the same portion of land. It is a good cash crop for the local landowners and also for the buyers on the other side of the Afghan borders in Pakistan. Securing the opium harvest and transportation not only provided the Taliban with significant financial support, it also encouraged the landowners to support the Taliban rule in Afghanistan. The fact that the Taliban controlled Helmand was not only an economic opportunity, but also a strong source of political and social support on both sides of the border.

In late 1994, the Taliban forces moved toward Zabul and in a rapid military move, soon invaded Ghazni, the stronghold of Qari Baba (allied with Rabbani), whose force was attacked by armed groups loyal to Hekmatyar. The Taliban were able to defeat Hekmatyar forces, and because Qari Baba was a Rabbani supporter, the Taliban disarmed his forces and controlled the area by January 1995. In February, the Taliban defeated forces loyal to Hekmatyar in the province of Logar, and in a matter of days they captured Maidan Shahr, the capital of Logar. On March 10, the Taliban forces seized Karte Seh in Kabul after they disarmed *Hezb-e-Wahdat* forces and asked the government leaders to surrender. In the following days the government forces fired on the Taliban and recaptured the area. On March 13, the leader of *Hezb-e-Wahdat*, Abul Ali Mazari, and several central committee members of the party were killed by the Taliban, and on March 19 government troops pushed back Taliban forces to Char Asiab, where the Taliban disarmed Hekmatyar forces. After the Taliban seized many provinces along the way to Kabul they finally announced their intention to establish a pure Islamic government in Afghanistan. Meanwhile, they expanded their controlled territories toward the west by capturing Farah and Nimroz and approached Herat.

THE TALIBAN ADMINISTRATION

The current Taliban political bureaucracy is the result of a three-stage developmental process. The first stage was started in 1994, when the Taliban leader, Molla Mohammed Omar Mujahid, rallied forces around him in southern Qanda-

TALIBAN TACTICS AND STRATEGIES

har and finally controlled the province. In this stage, the Taliban appeared as an armed political organization with very loose organizational skills and an identified political agenda for the country. The second stage of bureaucratic development took place when the Taliban seized Kabul and announced their administration as the government of Afghanistan in September 1996. In this stage, the key Taliban members were appointed to the important positions of the government. All the appointees to the government ministries occupied their position under the title of acting ministers. These positions were temporary and were subject to change in the near future, which indicated that the leadership was not sure about the individual capability of the appointees or the faith of their administration. During this three-year stage, the Taliban expanded their military and civil administration over almost 80 percent of the country and enforced their way of Islamic law.

The Taliban faced many obstacles in all fronts of their affairs both nationally and internationally. On the national level, they either crashed or pushed back their armed opposition groups. On the international level, they rejected the international critics concerning the violation of human rights, in particular the critics who commented about the status of women in Afghanistan. The Taliban ban on women's education and public activities, particularly working in the programs run by the international NGOs, has inspired international condemnation. During this stage also, the Taliban faced severe diplomatic problems connected to the existence of Osama bin Laden in Afghanistan. Taliban support of bin Laden resulted in U.S., and later, UN, sanctions against the Taliban-controlled area in Afghanistan.

During the second stage, the Taliban political bureaucracy was run by two major councils: Inner Shura was comprised of six members and led by their supreme leader, Mollah Mohammed Omar Mujahed. The Central Shura was comprised of nine members, in addition to the Taliban's liaison officers in Pakistan and later in other countries. The Central Shura was under the control of the Inner Shura and their members were in charge of important ministries. The Taliban Leaders who worked in the key administrative positions were as follows:

- Amir-ul-Moamanin, the Supreme Leader: Mullah Mohammed Omar.

Members of the Inner Shura:
- Mullah Mohammed Rabbani.
- Mullah Ehsanollah.
- Mullah Abbas.
- Mullah Mohammed.
- Mullah Pasani.

Members of the Central Shura:
- Mullah Mohammed Hassan.
- Mullah Noor-al-Din.
- Mullah Wakil Ahmed.

- Mullah Mohammed Malang.
- Mullah Abdul Rahman.
- Mullah Abdul Hakim.
- Mullah Sardar Ahmed.
- Haji Mohammad Ghaus.
- Massom Afghani.
- The Taliban Liaison Officer in NWFP: Abdul Rahman (Rashid) Zahid.
- The Taliban Liaison Officer in Quette: Mohammed Masoom.[3]

The above Taliban leaders were the key figures in the military and civil administrations in Afghanistan, and each of these key figures had his own circle operating at the local level. These leaders did not personally attend the front line against their oppositions, and they enjoyed a degree of autonomy in the region they were controlling. In terms of format and responsibility, the Inner Shura had an organization similar to the PDPA, known as the Afghan Communist Party (1978) and the National Security Council during President Mohammed Dauod's term as president (1973–1978).

In the Islamic Emirate of Afghanistan (IEA) under the Taliban rule, all the appointees and all the important decisions had to be approved by the Inner Shura. For instance, after the Taliban captured Kabul in September 1996, the Inner Shura (located in Qandahar) appointed a supervisory council comprised of seven members to be in charge of Kabul:

- Mullah Mohammed Hassan Akhund, vice chair
- Mullah Mohammed Rabbani, second in charge of the Taliban leadership
- Mullah Mohammed Hassan
- Mullah Mohammed Ghous, third in charge of the Taliban leadership
- Mullah Syed Ghayasuddin Agha
- Mullah Gazil Mohammed
- Mullah Abdul Razzoq

These members supervised the civil and military affairs in Kabul although it was not necessary for them to hold government office. This council contributed to the decisions made in Qandahar, but their main objection was to make sure that those decisions were carried out by the local and regional administrations in the area connected to Kabul. In reality, the members of the Kabul council were the movement's core in the military and civil administration, and they endeavored to reflect the movement's political ideology in the daily life of the government. Generally, the leading members of the Taliban movement were active in many parts of the country, and sometimes they held offices.

The third stage of bureaucratic development has been taking place since October 1999 and continues through 2001. During this stage, the Taliban leadership introduced massive changes in their bureaucracy and made the title of the government ministries permanent. They attempted to use the Afghan constitution that was formed during former Afghan King Mohammed Zahir's reign, with some pervasions and changes.[4] These massive changes occurred when the IEA's bureaucracy was struggling to reshape their diplomacy due to the U.S. and UN sanctions. On the national level, the IEA leaders faced the reorganization of the United Front Liberation for Afghanistan (UIFLA) forces as well as the subsequent economic difficulties imposed by the sanctions. The new changes in the IEA's administration were announced via Radio Shariah, the Taliban's national radio network, in a decree issued by the Taliban supreme leader Mulla Mohammed Omar Mujahed. These changes were as follows:

1. Mulla Wakil Ahmad Mutawwakil (Mullah M. Omar's principal spokesman) was named as foreign minister;[5]
2. Mulla Mohammad Hasan Akhund was named deputy to the head of the council of ministers Mulla Mohammad Rabbani;
3. Mulla Qudratullah Akhund was named minister for information and culture;
4. Mulla Amir Khan Muttaqi was named head of administration in the council of ministers in Kabul;
5. Mulla Abdul Razzaq (the former deputy defense minister) was appointed interior minister;
6. Mulla Khairullah Khairkhwa was made governor of the Herat province bordering Iran and head of the southwestern zone that also includes the provinces of Badghis, Farah, Nimruz, and Helmand. (Khairkhwa has risen through the ranks after a humble beginning as one of the Taliban spokesmen in 1995 to 1996);
7. Mulla Noorullah Noori (former governor of the Laghman province) was promoted to a powerful office overall in charge of the northern zone provinces. He would also serve as governor of the Balkh province with its capital at Mazar-i-Sharif;
8. Mulla Biradar, one of the four founders of the Taliban Islamic Movement along with Mulla Omar, Mulla Abdullah, and Mulla Rabbani, was named vice chief of the Afghan Army and head of the country's military air bases;
9. Mulla Ubaidullah was named defense minister;
10. Mulla Raauf Akhundzada was named corps commander for Kabul;
11. Mulla Abdul Salam Rocketi (former corps commander of Jalalabad) was appointed corps commander for Herat;[6]
12. Mulla Said Mohammad Haqqani (former head of administration in the council of ministers in Kabul) was appointed Afghanistan's ambassador in Pakistan; and
13. Mulla Saeedur Rahman Haqqani was appointed deputy minister of public affairs in Kabul.[7]

There were many motives for these massive changes in the administration, including warding off the wide range of anti-Taliban diplomatic activities of the UIFLA, which had received significant attention from the international community during the U.S. and UN sanctions. These massive changes illustrated the IEA's commitment for holding political power and strengthening their military organization against the UIFLA. In the meantime, the Taliban government sent diplomatic delegations to many countries around the world. According to sources close to the Taliban, they even proposed the expulsion of Osama bin Laden from Afghanistan in return for their recognition by the United States and the removal of the UN-imposed sanctions.

In the IEA bureaucracy, most of the governors are the Taliban key members who are not only in charge of provincial civil administration but also supervise the military organization. One of the differences between the Taliban administration and the previous governments is that their headquarters is located in Qandahar, and important decisions are made there. In this case, the capital of the country is Kabul even though the headquarters of the movement is in Qandahar. The availability of modern communication makes this type of operation functional; in particular, the interconnection of the IEA's telecommunication with Pakistan makes possible widespread activities in the area under Taliban control.

The IEA's administration has a fluid structure that was shaped in accordance to their military expansion in different parts of the country. This shapelessness of the Taliban's bureaucracy provided the leadership to be mobile and also had a positive impact on the formation of their administration. Even though the shapelessness of the Taliban bureaucracy is rooted in the nature of their movement, this administration was functional within the nature of Afghan social organization. As Charles Fairbanks writes about the unshaped administrations, "It [shapelessness] can have opposite effects in different circumstances. Shapelessness can be used to increase central control of bureaucracy."[8] In theory, a shapeless bureaucracy is contrary to Max Webber's famous analysis in which he insists on the importance of fixed official jurisdiction in accordance to the rule of law.[9] In the case of the IEA, the usage of modern communication makes the leaders aware of the front lines and keeps their civil and military operation within a general framework and within the guidelines of the inner and central shuras.

One should not forget that the shapelessness principle of bureaucracy can have a negative impact on the functionality of an administration such as the division of command and control and the weakness of the central leadership. Since the IEA's administration was in the first stage of its formation, this stage can be interpreted more like a revolutionary process rather than the process of a political bureaucracy. In this stage, the Taliban attempted to control the government bureaucracy and use the statecraft to dominate their political agenda in Afghanistan. Because of this revolutionary nature, the main concentration of the bureaucracy was on military affairs, while providing services to the local community had secondary importance.

THE FALL OF HERAT

Herat before the Taliban.   After the collapse of Najibullah's government on April 19, 1992, the government forces unconditionally surrendered to Mujahideen forces led by Ismail Khan. Herat became the administrative center of the region and comprised the provinces of Herat, Badghis, Ghor, Farah, and Nimroze. Ismail Khan integrated and appointed his Mujahideen officers in the regular army, many of whom had worked at the rank of Mujahideen in the local administration. Soon, he started to disarm all warlords and former government militia groups in the region, in particular in the province of Herat. In addition to the government administration, Ismail Khan organized a city council comprised of the popular nongovernment individuals with different ethnic, religious, and political backgrounds who could bring greater civic support for the administration. The local police force and the border frontier corps were reestablished and massive UN-led de-mining programs became active in the area. The roads were opened and security was enforced in the provinces that helped trades to expand and the economy to grow. The security of roads and cities caused the businesses to boom and provided people with thousands of new jobs. In 1995, there were about 150 shopping centers in Herat, more than in the entire country at that time.[10]

The existence of security and the booming economy attracted thousands of Afghan refugees to return home and many others who were running away from the civil war took refuge in this province. Numerous reconstruction programs led by the United Nations and other international NGOs became active in the area under the control of Ismail Khan. An Advisory Economic Council (AEC), comprised of Afghan professionals and led by Aziz Ludin (former professor at the economy school in Kabul University) and Gholam Rassul Poyan (a notable Afghan scholar), was formed. AEC was the only professional circle in the country in which its members were skilled educated Afghans who finished their degrees from Kabul University or studied in Europe. AEC introduced several development plans for Herat, including a residential housing plan for the city and the construction of a green belt, around the northern part of the city, that would block the famous 120-days wind. Historically, this long blowing wind had a severe negative impact on people's health and on agriculture. Blocking this wild wind would improve the social and economic lives in the region. Above all, these two plans became law, and any resident who wanted to build or construct anything needed to have a permit from the *sharwali* (mayor's office).

Herat became the commercial center of the region and emerged as a cosmopolitan city in the country. New private enterprises began to shape the economy in a new way with rapid growth that resulted in new services to the local communities. Many skilled Afghan individuals who had worked in the Iranian factories returned and started small industries. More colleges, such as the college of engineering and the medical school, were added to the University of Herat. The public schools that had been closed in many provincial towns reopened for both boys and girls. The University of Herat became an active academic center for the region as well as for hundreds of students from many parts of the country. For the first time in the last two decades, reconstruction of the historical sites, with the help of international agencies, started. According to the Herat's Health Department in 1995, there were more than 300 medical doctors in the city, and half of these doctors were women.[11] But the high population density created a lot of difficulties for the local administration. Since the local administration's financial strength was based on the local revenue, the shortage of health services, transportation, housing, drinking water, and educational facilities became very obvious.

Herat's Role in Peace Activities.   In the process of war and peace in Afghanistan, Herat's strategic location as a commercial center for the region and a door to Central Asia and the Persian Gulf gave this province an important geopolitical position. Ismail Khan's political and military role in regional development became important; he was under pressure from both Pakistan and Iran. Pakistan was not happy with his support of Massoud and Rabbani against Hekmatyar, and Iran was demanding more authority for the pro-Iranian political elements. To make the pressure effective, Pakistan made it difficult for international aid to reach Herat. Meanwhile, Iran expelled Afghan refugees into the province of Herat in towns that were already overcrowded. The whole region was heavily dependent on the importation of food and fuel from outside, and from this point, Herat was very vulnerable in time of conflict with the neighboring countries. The neighboring countries could threaten the peaceful lives of the people and the regional stability under Ismail Khan.

The continued civil war in the country, in particular around Kabul, and the involvement of the neighboring countries caused Ismail Khan to believe that without the establishment of a national army and a national government it would be impossible to enjoy long-term regional stability. Therefore, he sent delegations to the warring factions and invited them to an intra-Afghan peace negotiation. For this purpose, Ismail Khan traveled to Kabul, and as Ahmed Rashid reported, he was "pushing a peace plan that has the approval of the UN and Pakistan. He called for the president [Burhanadin Rabbani] to be replaced by a leadership council that would choose a neutral interim president. But Rabbani played for time, and while discussing peace he and his military chief Ahmed Shah Massoud were preparing for war."[12]

In July 1994, Ismail Khan put together a national conference in Herat to which he invited all the Afghan leaders, the heads of the warring factions, and notable Afghans from abroad. For this purpose, he sent a civilian airplane to

Germany to bring several hundreds of notable and intellectual Afghans who lived in the United States and Europe back to Afghanistan. About 4,000 people with different political, ethnic, and religious backgrounds attended the conference for ten days. The participation of the Afghan intellectuals and notables, such as former Prime Minister Mohammed Yossuf, from outside of the country, and many of the local leaders and ex-Mujahideen commanders, from inside, created a productive environment for a peace settlement. At the beginning of the conference, the local political activists, in particular those of the JIA, attempted to influence the conference by gaining support for the pre-prepared proposal in which they attempted to condemn their political opponents. The proposal was rejected immediately by Yossuf and other notable Afghans, creating a tense situation. Ismail Khan agreed with Yossuf, and they were able to move the conference in a positive direction to improve solidarity and cooperation between Afghans. At this conference, the Afghan intellectuals and notables expressed their opinions directly and freely to the public for the first time since 1978. This conference proposed a plan for the formation of a national army and the establishment of the *Loya Jirga*. A committee of several notable Afghan technocrats was formed to open dialogue between the warring factions in Afghanistan.[13]

Problems and Prospects in Herat.   Most of the ex-Mujahideen external front leaders who were based in Pakistan and Iran had not attended the conference, and many of them were fearful of its results. In particular, they were afraid that if the conference could gain the support of Iran and Pakistan, they would have no choice but to agree with its subsequent outcomes. At the same time, the Pakistani elements who wished to influence the political establishment in Afghanistan were also afraid of losing their influence in this country. Iran was not happy with the presence of large numbers of Afghan intellectuals and technocrats who were educated in the west. According to Mowlawi Mansoor, the governor of the Paktia province (1992–1996), he had been warned by the ISI not to attend this conference.[14]

Inside the country, General Abdulrashid Dostam and Gulbadin Hekmatyar were not happy about the conference; they declared it a JIA conference that tried to save Rabbani's regime. At the end of the conference, Rabbani arrived in Herat, where he stated in his speech that he was aware of the conference idea and supported the resolutions. By this speech the JIA leadership attempted to use the conference as a source of legitimacy for their influence in Afghanistan. This attempt created a passive mood among the participants and produced a great deal of propaganda against the conference and Ismail Khan.

The main reason for the fall of Herat was rooted in the conflicted nature of the local military and administration of the region that distracted the solidarity and cooperation among the military and political leadership in the region. This local inner-conflict goes back to the days of jihad against the

Soviets. Ismail Khan ran his forces in a military organizational structure like those in the formal armies. Ismail Khan's forces were organized in a vertical format and included the head of the group and the head of several committees who were appointed by the head of the group. Even though Ismail Khan was an army officer, he was a man of the people who was not following any political party in Afghanistan. Often JIA proclaimed him as one of its members, but Ismail Kahn continuously enjoyed a great deal of freedom from the JIA party agenda. But this freedom never convinced him to form another political party, since he believed establishing a new political party would not solve the problems in Afghanistan.[15] His traditional belief as an educated Afghan army officer was based in the people and the country rather than in a political party. This type of political ideology could not fit in the framework of the JIA's political ideology and its charter.

The revolutionary political ideology of the JIA asked the activists to work for the establishment of a central leadership such as the one in *Hezb-e-Islami*. In this case, the JIA claimed a self-selected representative for the people. According to their interpretation, the Muslims in Afghanistan should follow their leadership because they are "the sincere and ardent protector of brilliant Islamic teachings."[16] This type of ideology led the JIA *Maktabis* to believe that the field commanders inside Afghanistan must follow their leadership. They attempted to control the political and military operations inside the country from their offices in Pakistan and Iran. The emergence of the local and later regional military and political leaders such as Ismail Khan and Ahmed Shah Massoud with a high level of autonomy created a dichotomy within the JIA's rank and put the *Maktabis* against the regional field commanders.

Ismail Khan resisted the *Maktabis'* orientation of politics in the region, and this was the reason he formed a traditional *shura* comprised of the local *mawlawis* called *Shura-e-Uloma*, led by Maulwi Mohammed Omar Shahid, a notable Afghan clergy. Later, the *Maktabis* attempted to influence the local community by opening religious schools in the region. These schools were funded by Saudi Arabia, and soon the local Mujahideen found out that the volunteer Arabs were teaching Wahabiat *maslak* in these schools. The *Shura-e-Uloma* condemned these activities and banned those teachings and the books that dealt with this *maslak*. In 1985, Ismail Khan rejected the financial aid of the Saudi representative, Abdullah E'azam, and expelled him from the region. Since then, the JIA *Maktabis* united against Ismail Khan and armed the local Mujahideen groups against him. In the following years, they aided the government's militias to challenge Ismail Khan's influence in the territory. All these anti–Ismail Khan activities were accompanied with a segment of the pro–Iran *Hezbullah* and another Shia faction that was led by Abdul Ali Massbah, who became a member of Rabbani's cabinet in 1992.[17] Mainly, the *Maktabis* in the JIA against Ismail Khan were incorporated into two groups, *Afzalis* and *Niazis*.

After the collapse of the Najibullah government, Ismail Kahn followed his nonparty politics, thinking it may help to cool off the levels of contingency with the two hostile factions within JIA and other local groups. Therefore, he appointed Colonel Azizullah Afzali as head of the police force, Sayyid Ahmed Ghatally (*Niazi*) as head of the provincial secret service, Gholam Yahya Siawshon (a former government militia commander who was supported by both *Afzalis* and *Niazis*) as the mayor of Herat, and Sayyid Mahbub Katib (from Hizb-u-llah) as the second in command of the police forces. Ismail Khan wanted to keep the army integrated, and for this reason he appointed his second in charge, General Alawadin Khan, as the head of the army and General Mohammed Zaher Azimi (ex-Mujahideen commander of Harkat Muhseni) as the head of the border patrol forces (the Jandarms).

From 1992 until the fall of Herat in September 1995, a massive and organized campaign against Ismail Khan was formed within the local and regional administrations. This campaign was connected with the two important heads of the government, Sayyid Norullah Emad, the second in charge of JIA after Rabbani, and Sayyid Ishaqh Delju, the minister of education and a former member of the Hekmatyar central committee. Both of these individuals were from Herat, and they were able to coordinate a political force comprised of *Afazalis* and *Niazis* from the JIA and the former activists of the HIH (*Hezb-e-Islami Hekmatyar*) in Herat. After the peace conference in Herat, the level of activities against Ismail Khan by the *Maktabis* was increased. Ismail Khan's forces pushed back General Dostam's forces that attempted to capture Badghis while at the same time Khan sent arms and ammunition to support Massoud in Kabul. Ismail Khan's involvement in the conflict between Hekmatyar-Dostam against Rabbani-Massoud reduced his administrative and military ability. With this involvement, Ismail Khan slipped into the civil war that he had attempted to avoid so many times.

In March 1995, the Taliban forces captured Farah, one of the provinces controlled by Ismail Khan, but on May 10, Ismail Khan's forces recaptured Farah from the Taliban forces. Fighting on two fronts against Taliban and Dostam forces redirected all the revenue sources toward war and caused the price of food and other commodities to go up. The rise of prices and fast growing inflation rates upset people. Those who worked for the regional administration had a difficult time feeding their families. In a similar situation, low-ranking military officers and soldiers suffered from the severe economic condition, providing a ripe situation for Ismail Khan's oppositions to strike and also file complaints against him in Kabul while he was on the front lines against the Taliban and General Dostam. According to local sources, the ISI and Iranian intelligent services influenced some elements of the local administration in the area controlled by Ismail Khan. There were many government employees, particularly in the local intelligence service and police, who received indirect cash from Pakistan and Iran, as well as from Ismail Khan's rivals in Kabul and the Taliban. In my interview with one of Ismail Kahn's secret service officers in Herat, the Taliban and the ISI were distributing large amounts of cash via their circles in the region.[18] This cash distribution was used to bribe some key figures in the civil administration as well as in the military. The second in charge of the governor's office, Haji Mir, and also, Moulawi Khodadad, an influential preacher of the Friday Masque and the head of the regional justice department, became active secretly with the pro-Taliban circle in Herat against Ismail Khan.

On the Taliban side, the front line against Ismail Khan–led forces was quiet during the summer of 1995. The Taliban, through the Pakistani brokers, received Dostam's cooperation. As result, a technician team arrived in Qandahar via Pakistan to repair the fighter jets left over after the fall of Najibullah's regime.[19] Soon, the Taliban MiG-21 fighter jets were ready for air operation, and they forced down a charter Russian Il-76 transport aircraft carrying ammunition from Albania to Kabul on August 3. In the same style, the Taliban fighter jets forced down the Aryana Boeing–727 that was carrying commercial goods from the Persian Gulf to Jalalabad. The Taliban launched a massive recruitment from NWFP and Baluchistan as well as from Paktia and Logar and set up many training camps in Qandahar. Thousands of ex-Mujahideen fighters were recruited by Mawlawi Ehsanullah, the Taliban commander in Khust, with the help of ex-Mujahideen commander Mawlawi Jalaladin Haqqani. All of these recruited fighters were dispatched to Kabul and Qandahar.

In this severe circumstance, Ismail Khan's focus was on the front lines against the Taliban, and he and his famous main commander Nassir Ahmed pushed the Taliban forces back. After months of heavy fighting, Ismail Khan's forces seized Musa Qala, now Zad, approached Grishk, the capital of Helmand, and pushed the Taliban back toward Qandahar on August 25, 1995. Later Ismail Khan described that a large group of the ex-Mujahideen from Qandahar and Helmand who were recruited and armed by the Rabbani's government in Kabul were sent to his aid. Ismail Khan led his forces in a three axes military operation, via the main road to Grishk and in two flanks. At the same time, Rabbani's government, under the influence of Ismail Khan's arch rivals, discharged him from his official positions as the governor of Herat and chief general of the armed forces in the southwest of Afghanistan. In response, Rabbani appointed a high council that included Ismail Khan's arch rivals, Emad and Delju. In parallel with the formation of the high council in Kabul, the Qandahary and Helmandi forces, armed and sent by Rabbani, left their positions on the front line without informing Ismail Khan or Nasir Ahmed. Soon, the Taliban forces deployed a massive mobile force using the Saudi donated pickup trucks and attacked Ismail Khan's forces on the main road. These Taliban pickups that were armed with ZU anti-aircraft, cannons, and BM-21 multiple-barreled rocket launchers ambushed Ismail Khan's units and cut off their over-stretched logistics and supply routes. In heavy fighting commander Nasir Ahmed was killed mysteriously. Ismail Khan, who was in the battlefield and was walking along with his troops while receiving an intravenous serum because of exhaustion, lack of sleep, and dehydration, called for a general setback.[20] Forces led by Ismail Khan were set back with heavy casualties, and the Taliban forces recaptured Grishk on August 26. Ismail Khan gathered his forces and repositioned them several times, but the lack of support reduced the morale of his men. The new council arrived in Heart and was controlled dominantly by Ismail Khan's rivals—*Afzalis, Niazis,* and *Ikhwani Shia.* The new council stopped sending army personnel who supported Ismail Khan to the front line, where his forces were defeated several times and had not eaten for 36 hours.[21] On September 4, the Taliban captured the Shindand military air base, while General Dostam's planes bombarded the Herat airport and city. The Taliban launched an offensive on Herat the next day, and Ismail Khan retreated to Iran. The Taliban canceled classes at Herat University. They later reopened them only for boys, but closed all schools for girls. The Taliban, who considered photography and painting un-Islamic, blacked out the magnificent art and miniatures of the City Hall, which was the decades-long work of the famous artists Ustad Mashal and Mohammed Ali Attar.

Many reasons can be considered for the fall of Herat under the Taliban forces. One is the self-style leadership of Ismail Khan that caused the absence of a regional armed political organization like the one led by Massoud or the Nangarhar Shura. This style of leadership prevented him from allocating the trained, professional, educated, and prominent individuals in the regional administration. Khan failed to pay attention to the Economic Council of Herat. Members of this council were treated poorly, and their advice and critical thinking on a variety of issues were dismissed. In contrast, unskilled and corrupted opportunists were appointed to key positions in the administration. Compulsory conscription was another factor that created massive disappointment among the local population. In the eyes of many local communities, the cause of the civil war was not clear. The absence of a political organization comprised of trained political analysts in the administration caused an illusion in the mind of people. All the above factors played their respective roles in the downfall of Ismail Khan. But, according to the current documents and other sources in Afghanistan, the main reason for the fall of Herat can be rooted in a secret operation of the *Ikhwanis (Maktabis)* of *Jamaiat-e-Islami* within the Burhanadin Rabbani's regime. This secret operation coincided with the military operation of the Taliban against Ismail Khan. Some internal sources stated that this correlation was the product of the ISI's link with the JIA *Maktabis* who may or may not have been aware of the ISI's covert operation. The Taliban's offense on Herat was one of the most significant military operations on Afghanistan soil after the Soviet invasion. According to western intelligence reports this military operation was conducted with massive external support.[22] As Zalmay Khalilzad, the Director of the Greater Middle East Studies Center at the RAND Corporation states:

Credible reports said that Islamabad appears determined to keep the Taliban adequately supplied. On several occasions Pakistani aircraft, including C130s, have flown supplies to Kandahar for the Taliban, and Pakistan may have helped the Taliban service capture military aircraft and recruit pilots. Independent reports said trucks had crossed into Afghanistan with supplies intended for the Taliban.[23]

Whether or not the operation against Ismail Khan was coordinated by the ISI is not clear, but the events show that there was a logical connection between the Taliban secret operations and those of the *Afzalis* and *Niazis* in *Jamaiat-e-Islami*. In any event, Pakistan's diplomatic activities in the region indicate that its leadership was in close contact with the outcome of western Afghanistan's operations, particularly in the fall of Herat on September 5, 1995. For example, on September 7, Pakistan's President Farooq Leghari visited gas-rich Turkmenistan to discuss building a pipeline across Afghanistan to the Indian Ocean. According to Reuters: "Leghari, on his first ever visit to Central Asia, held talks with Turkmen President Saparmurat Niyazove while angry Afghan demonstrators attacked the Pakistani embassy in Kabul."[24] Days after the fall of Herat, General Nasirullah Babar, with a large group of Pakistani officials, led a road show from Quetta to Qandahar to Herat and back. Reuters reported that this group crossed into Afghanistan to show their Pakistani flag and accepted greetings, encomiums, and offers of Islamic support from friendly loyalist Afghans.[25]

In 1996, Allawadin Khan united with Ismail Khan to form a guerrilla force to attack the Taliban's position in the southwest region. Allawadin Khan led a group of new fighters in the remote area of Herat, but was assassinated by one of his guards and his body was transported to the city under the Taliban forces, where people undertook a respectful funeral. Months later, Ismail Khan reentered Afghanistan from Iran with armed guerrillas and attacked the Taliban's position in the north part of the city. He and his group reached Badghis and began organizing their forces in the area controlled by General Dostam's forces. He then attacked the Taliban position in Badghis.

THE FALL OF KABUL

The fall of Herat by the Taliban was the most significant change in the power balance against Rabbani's government in Kabul. This change secured Qandahar, the headquarters of the movement, from the most serious threat by Ismail Khan's forces and allowed the Taliban to concentrate their military deployment on the southern front toward Kabul. By controlling Herat, the Taliban were able to secure the transit road connecting Pakistan to Central Asia, which was also a political victory for attracting external support and attention.

On June 1, 1995, the Taliban crushed the remaining forces belonging to Ismail Khan in the province of Ghor and captured its capital, Chaghcharan.

This military victory completed the Taliban control of southwest Afghanistan. The Taliban established their administration in these newly captured territories and opened the transit trade between Pakistan and Turkmenistan. For one year, the Taliban strengthened their military and civil administration muscle and prepared their strategic plan to seize Kabul. According to this plan, they avoided a direct approach on Kabul from the south and decided to make a shortcut through the area connecting Afghanistan and Pakistan. This way, they would be safe and secure from behind and would also be able to mobilize their forces via Pakistan. This shortcut would also make the best use of the political gap between the *Nangarhar Shura* led by Haji Ghadir and Rabbani's government in Kabul. *Nangarhar Shura* controlled the eastern province of Afghanistan with a large military machine.

During the Soviet invasion of Afghanistan and Najibullah's regime, the eastern province of Afghanistan, particularly Nangarhar, received the largest portion of military equipment and facilities. As a result, the area held one of the largest military organizations in Afghanistan that not only protected the province, but also could stop a large-scale military campaign against Kabul. After the collapse of Najibullah's government, all these facilities fell into the hands of *Nangarhar Shura,* and these facilities made Shura one of the four most powerful militaries and political forces in Afghanistan. The *Nanagarhar Shura* chose a neutral position in the civil war and endeavored to improve the civil life of the region through trade and the activities of the United Nations and NGOs. In this effort, the *Shura* restored security and stability in the area under its control. However, large waves of refugees who were running from the killing fields of Kabul created a tense environment in the area, particularly after the fall of Herat. As a result, Rabbani's government in Kabul attempted to get the *Shura*'s support against Hekmatyar and later against the Taliban. Even though the *Shura* held its neutral status in the civil war, the fall of Herat made the leadership of the *Shura* nervous. According to regional sources in Afghanistan, the leaders of the *Shura* believed that the Taliban would not attack the *Shura*'s controlled area. The *Shura* had a neutral position in the civil war, and more importantly, the eastern Pushtons shared a great deal of traditional beliefs in Islam, which conflicted with the Ikhwaniat and Wahabiat. The eastern Pushtons also shared a common language that has deep roots in their shared ethnic background. According to these common ethnic, linguistic, and Islamic traditions, a military campaign by Taliban forces was not anticipated by the *Shura*'s leaders. Therefore, the Nanagarhar *Shura* planned to continue its neutral position until the Taliban and Rabbani government settled through a peace treaty or one lost power to the other. In either situation, *Shura* leaders could participate in the central government through a coalition with the winning side. Moreover, the Shura was counting on its military strength to defend its territory from either the Taliban or Rabbani's government.

The Taliban leaders were aware of the *Shura*'s military capacity, and they recognized the political gap between the *Shura* and Rabbani's government. They thought that if there was a direct attack from the south on Kabul, Rabbani and Massoud may get the support of the *Shura* forces. In that case, the Tajik-led Rabbani forces would combine with the Pushtons and would not only reduce the support of the Pushtons for the Taliban, but also would pose a serious military threat. Thus, the Taliban leadership planned to seize Nanagarhar as a military tactic toward capturing Kabul. The Taliban knew that the level of the eastern Pustons' resistance against them would be less than the Tajik forces led by Ahmed Shah Massoud, who had a different ethnic and linguistic background.

On September 5, 1996, the Taliban launched a massive offensive in eastern Afghanistan and captured part of Paktia that was controlled by Hekmatyar forces. In this military campaign, the Taliban seized the largest *Hezb-e-Islami* arms depot in Afghanistan, which supported other *Hezb* groups in the region. The Taliban appointed their governor in the province and established a local administration. On September 11, the Taliban forces approached Nanagarhar swiftly and promised limited autonomy to the local sub-ethnic armed forces within the Taliban's framework. The Taliban captured Nanagarhar without any serious resistance and discharged the *Shura* by appointing their own governor. Haji Qadir fled to Pakistan and claimed he surrendered Nanagarhar to the Taliban to avoid civilian deaths. Thousands of people ran away to the Pakistani border, including those who ran from Kabul, but the Pakistani authorities closed the border to avoid the establishment of new refugee camps on their soil.

Capturing Nanagarhar was a successful military tactic for the Taliban, and it opened the road toward Kabul.[26] The Taliban's victory in Nanagarhar was the second major victory after Heart, and it was vital for launching an offensive on Kabul. They seized all the military garrisons and police forces, as well as all the arms depots that were intact after Najibullah's regime and were not wasted in civil war. According to a source close to Taliban who was an eyewitness, "250 tanks of excellent Russian make fell into the hands of the Islamic militia in Jalalabad."[27] On September 13, Taliban forces entered the province of Lagman and soon captured Mehtar Lam, the capital. Seizing Lagman allowed the Taliban to seize Kabul from three directions—from Logar, Nangarhar, and Lagman—and the only way open for Massoud's forces was from the north of Kabul through the provinces of Kapisa and Parwan. On September 22, Taliban forces moved into Kunar to avoid any cooperation between rival Pushtons and Massoud's forces against them. After they seized eastern Afghanistan, the Taliban worried about the formation of an alliance between Massoud forces and General Dostam. If such an alliance was reached, there would be a possible deployment of General Dostam's forces in Kabul that would abort the Taliban campaign on Kabul. In the case of such a deployment, Massoud might have been able to help the Taliban's Pushton opposition in Kunar and compose a joint military operation from two directions: from Kunar and from Kapisa, which could impose a severe setback to the Taliban.

The Taliban did not want to waste time or give the implementation of such an alliance between their two opposition forces a chance. On September 25, the Taliban launched an offensive toward Kabul and captured the town of Sarobi, 31 miles east of Kabul. The Taliban organized their forces, built up their support system, and attacked Kabul on September 27. Massoud forces and the head of the government military and the civil administration retreated to the north, fearing heavy civilian casualties. On the same day, the Taliban armed units entered the UN compound in Kabul and executed Najibullah while he was under UN protection, along with his brother Shahpur Ahmedzai.

CHAPTER FOURTEEN

THE POLITICAL IDEOLOGY
OF THE TALIBAN

THE STATE FORMATION BY THE TALIBAN MOVEMENT WAS BASED ON their interpretation of the Islamic principle of *Khelafat*. In accordance with the Taliban, Mullah Mohammed Omar Mujahed, the leader of the movement, is *amir-ul-mumanin* (the leader of believers), which makes him respectable among all Muslims in the world. In Afghanistan, the *amir-ul-mumanin* also is the *khalifah*, who rules the territory under his control in accordance with the Islamic law, *shari'ah*. All Muslims and non-Muslims who live in such a territory are obligated to obey the *Khalifah*. A *khalifah* is selected by a small council of leaders who have religious capacity and communal trust. Despite Taliban interpretation, issues such as elections are not a lawful way for selecting a *khalifah* and forming a *khelafat*. Previously, the Taliban criticized the ex-Mujahideen leaders for not following the Islamic way of forming a government. As a close source to the Taliban, Mohammed Mossa from the *Darul Ifta-e-Wal Irshad* writes:

> Thus the selection of a Khalifah, the formation of a government was extremely sensitive and important in those blessed days of long ago [the first thirty years of Islam after the Prophet Mohammed], and here in the present times the Mujahideen were asked to form a government in installment! This was the biggest mistake, as it provided an opportunity for creating disturbances to every enemy of Islam. Another greater mistake was that Khalifah was purposely not mentioned anywhere, faithfulness to the shahadah's (martyred) blood had demanded the use of terms Khalifah and Khelafat instead of president and prime minister. A Khelafat should have been established based upon the golden rules of Sharee'ah, but this was not so.[1]

The parliamentary system of government or a more conservative model of a government in which the head of the government is elected through a general election, was not acceptable to the Taliban. With this in mind, the Taliban rejected any moderate interpretations of *Shari'ah*, and criticized the JIP led by Qazi Ahmed Hussine. As a Taliban source states:

> Maudoodi Jama'ah (group) by the name of Jaha'at-e-Islami in Pakistan, which keeps announcing at the top of its voice that it has brought Islam to Pakistan. When the Taliban implemented Islam, one of its [JIP] leaders, in an interview to the BBC said that the Taliban-implemented Islam was not correct, that the Taliban had implemented their own interpretation of Islam. This shows that these people [JIP] are deceiving the people of Pakistan with their claims of bringing Islam to the country, for when Islam was implemented they denounced it for being wrong. Now who knows which kind of a modern Islam they are advocating the Jama'at-e-Islami, or other people who criticize the Taliban-implemented Islam actually want a religion which has no substance, which is Islam in name only.[2]

The JIP was the most important political party involved in Afghanistan before the rise of the Taliban. Several Afghan ex-Mujahideen leaders like Hekmatyar and Rabbani had very close connections with the JIP. Both the leaders and the political ideologies of their parties were shared on state, revolution, and society. In addition to the disagreement over power and politics, the Taliban criticized these Afghan leaders and their parties for their ideological ties with the JIP. The Taliban also criticized Iranian leadership and their interpretation of Islam and disagreed with the revolutionary aspect of the Islamic Republic. The Taliban considered the Iranian interpretation of Islamic law incomplete and called it a "headless, baseless Islam."[3]

Some Afghanistan observers argue that the Taliban's rejection of the JIP, the *Wahabis* and the Iranian interpretation of Islam was more in theory rather than in practice. There are individuals among the Taliban who follow the JIP or Wahabiat ideologies, but because of the external support of Pakistani elements and Arabs, in particular Saudi Arabia, they tolerate the differences. In this case, it is true that the Taliban political ideology differs from those of *Ikhwanis* (*Maktabis*) and *Wahabis*, but the outlook of these differences is more political rather than ideological. Therefore, if there was no political threat by the ex-Mujahideen leaders against the Taliban, the ideological differences would be very limited.

According to the Taliban, establishing an Islamic state means enforcing the *Shari'ah* in the land of Afghanistan and bringing security and peace to the people. This was a religious duty for the movement, and the leadership was devoted to such an establishment. In an interview with Mufti Jameel Khan, the Taliban supreme leader, Mullah Mohammed Omar, stated the goal of the movement as follows: "To end the mischief in the country, to establish peace and security, to protect life, wealth and honor and to enforce the sharei'ah, do jihad against the leaders who were devoted for power, and endeavor to make the land of Afghanistan an exemplary state."[4]

LEGITIMACY AND AUTHORITY UNDER THE TALIBAN

The Taliban enforced numerous law decrees according to their interpretation of *Shari'ah*. To make sure that these decrees were implemented in Afghanistan, they established a religious police. The main objective of the religious police is to carry out what is decided in the court of law of the country and conduct punishment. In accordance with the Taliban, the *ameer-ul-mumineen* is a political leader who has a legitimate authority over the people living in a territory controlled by his followers. Obeying *Ameer-ul-Mu'mineen* is *fardh* (God's demand and must be practiced), and it is based on the law of God. Because the principle root of obeying the *ameer-ul-mumineen* is the law of God, anyone who refuses *bai'at* (oath to obey), and opposes him, "will be called a rebel according to *shari'ah*. It would be a *fardh* to execute him [or her]. Moreover, if the *Ameer* called the people to jihad, it is also *fardh* for all qualified Muslims to follow his order and bare arms against those who are enemies of the *Ameer*."[5]

On September 30, 1996, Wakil Ahmed, the Taliban spokesperson, stated to reporters in Kabul that "women should not report to work, they should stay home." In a similar line of order, a source of the Taliban stated:

> In the areas under the Taliban government every kind of wickedness and immorality, cruelty, murder, robbery, songs and music, TV, VCR, satellite dish, immodesty [be purdagi], traveling [women] without a mehraum [immediate blood related person], shaving-of or trimming the beard [among male adult], pictures and photographs, interest, have all been totally banned.[6]

To implement these decrees, the Taliban formed an organization called *Amr-e-Bil M'arouf Wa Nahi Anil Munkar*, the General Department for the Preservation of Virtue and the Elimination of Vice. This organization, headed by Maulwi Qalamuddin, "has thousands of informers in the army, government ministries and hospitals who monitor foreigners and Western aid agencies."[7] Most of these informers are teenagers and recent graduates of the Pakistani *madresahs*. The young members of this organization patrol the streets with long sticks, making sure that the people go to mosque at the time of daily prayers, women are covered from head-to-toe with a garment (*bughrah*), and men have not shaved their beards.[8]

Capital punishment is widely enforced for all cases dealing with manslaughter, and this type of punishment is usually in the form of *qisaas*, through which a male member of the victim's family carries out the execution.[9] Under the Taliban rule, this type of punishment takes place in public, in the presence of the victim's family.[10] All Afghan families have to pay *zakat* (similar to income tax), and the landowners and farmers have to pay *ushr,* 10 percent of their agricultural products. Under the law, "gambling, betting, pigeon-flying, dog-racing, sodomy are strictly forbidden."[11] Thieves are subjected to surgical amputation of their hands and arms and adultery is punished by stoning to death in the eyes of the public.[12]

THE TALIBAN'S SECOND STRATEGY AFTER KABUL

The fall of Kabul at the hands of the Taliban was a most significant victory and gave them national and international political and diplomatic identities. Completing these identities was dependent on their military and political abilities to restore their administration all over the country. But it was not an easy task for the Taliban because of the two most powerful and well-organized forces led by Ahmed Shah Massoud and General Dostam. The Taliban leadership attempted to make a deal with General Dostam by offering him a share in the government and recognizing his credibility. At the same time, the Taliban chased out Massoud's forces the day after controlling Kabul. The Taliban followed a double-sided strategy to fight their oppositions. On one side, they attempted to reach an agreement with General Dostam, or if an agreement was not possible, at least stop him from supporting Massoud. On the other side, they pounded Massoud, their immediate enemy, with all of their power. In Taliban calculation, if they could destroy Massoud, General Dostam would have no other alternative than to put his arms down and join the Taliban.

The massive Taliban forces ran over northern Kabul with little resistance and deployed forces all along the towns and villages toward Panjshir valley, where Massoud and his loyal forces took position. The Taliban forces were able to block the southern entrance roads to the valley that connected Massoud to his main supporters, the Tajik population in the north of Kabul. On October 1, 1996, Sher Mohammed Istanikzai, the Taliban deputy foreign minister in Kabul, claimed to have trapped Ahmed Shah Massoud in Panjshir valley. Istanikzai also emphasized that the Taliban did not have any animosity toward General Dostam and that they would not fight his forces. The Taliban decided to finish off Massoud, and they issued a "surrender or die" ultimatum to him.[13] But Massoud's response was to fight the Taliban, and he organized his forces in his homeland, Panjshir valley, where he had fought the Soviet and the PDPA forces.

Many observers who were following the Taliban development in Afghanistan had no doubt that Massoud would not survive in the fight. Massoud was squeezed from several directions in the Panjshir valley by his former ally General Dostam from the northwest and by the Taliban from the southeast. All his connections to the outside world were cut off, and there was no hope for any support from outside the territory he was controlling. Massoud ordered the populated Panjshir valley and the surrounding area's civilians to be evacuated and put his core force into position ready for fighting. At the same time, he endeavored to make peace with General Dostam and pushed for a new alliance with him. According to General Dostam's sources, the general publicly announced that his forces would remain neutral, and he warned the Taliban to stop their advance toward the north, particularly toward the north side of the Salang highway.

On October 5, the Taliban forces advanced into Panjshir valley, 90 kilometers northeast of Kabul.[14] Heavy fighting ensued, and the Taliban captured some ground from the Massoud forces. Even though the Massoud forces deployed heavy military machinery, the ragged mountains of Panjshir valley and its narrow roads reduced their impact on the ground. As a result, Massoud changed his military tactic and strategy. He expanded his units around the area to reduce the Taliban's pressure on the valley, and in the meantime he moved back inside the valley to drag in the Taliban forces inside. Then he combined his fire with the support of artilleries and rocket launchers while one of his units moved behind the Taliban and cut them off. This was one of the military traps Massoud had used many times against the Soviet and PDPA forces in the area, but this time, his military operation used new guerrilla warfare—mobile units with the support of heavy weapons. Massoud forces opened fire from front and back on the Taliban forces. The Taliban forces, who had been very confident in their fighting against Massoud's men, were not able to get support from Kabul. The heavy fire from many directions made the Taliban lose control and command of their forces, and hundreds were killed or captured.

The war in the Panjshir valley was a blow to the face of the victor forces of the Taliban, and this created a crack in their military morale. This victory for Massoud was very crucial because, until that moment, it was not clear on whose side General Dostam was on. Even though this military victory was very small on a national level, it was enough for Massoud to reach an agreement with General Dostam, which allowed Massoud to use Dostam's controlled territories against the Taliban. When the Taliban noticed that it was impossible to capture Panjshir valley through a direct military attack, they decided to mobilize their forces from several directions. They advanced north of Salang Highway to cross the area controlled by General Dostam's forces and cut off Panjshir valley from the north. This move caused tension between General Dostam's forces and the Taliban. The Taliban had become suspicious about the relationship between Massoud and Dostam, especially when they failed to gain his support in the war against Massoud. On October 30, 1996, they declared jihad on Dostam. This situation resulted in the formation of a new political and military alliance between Massoud and Dostam.

On October 31, northern Kabul witnessed the heaviest fighting since the Taliban took over Kabul.[15] Associated Press reported that the Taliban forced the local people in the north of Kabul to work for them and support them against the oppositions. This forced work, combined with the arrests of many suspicious supporters of Massoud, increased the discomfort of the local people. Taliban forces wanted to teach the local people a lesson, so they struck the village of Sur Cheshma, causing heavy destruction and casualties. An uprising was reported in the town of Jab-ul-Saraj, 60 miles north of Kabul, against the Taliban, and this uprising was followed by the advance of Massoud-Dostam forces toward Kabul. Massoud captured the town from the Taliban, and his forces, with the support of Dostam units, recaptured the strategic air base of Bagram. These military activities concerned the neighboring counties and caused a wave of diplomatic efforts to enforce a cease-fire. Abdul Rahim Ghafoorzai, Rabbani's deputy foreign minister, stated the opposition's demands for the demilitarization of Kabul, and the pullout of the Taliban from that city; but the Taliban requested a cease-fire first.[16]

In January 1997, the Taliban forces started an organized offensive against Massoud and Dostam and recaptured several towns, including Charikar. Taliban forces conducted a house search to disarm the local people, and this resulted in massive arrests of suspicious individuals. The war in the north of Kabul and the uprising of the people in Jeb-ul-Seraj caused the Taliban to lose the trust of the local communities to the north of Kabul. To avoid further revolt, they forced people to leave the towns and villages. Thousands of civilians, caught in the middle of the battlefield, took what they could carry with them and headed to Kabul in severely cold weather. The United Nations High Commissioner for Refugees (UNHCR) reported that "the arrivals, mostly from Charikar, raise the total of displaced people from front-line areas north of Kabul since January second to 50,000." UNHCR officer Terry Pitzner told reporters in Kabul, "I believe that the situation of living for these people will be a nightmare."[17]

The massive displacement of people in north Kabul, and the fleeing of thousands more from Kabul toward Jalalabad and Pakistan, brought new shifts in the social fabric of the people in Kabul. This massive displacement brought a new range to mass mobilization that created a new political formation and military development in the area. Most of the people who fled Kabul were non-Pushton and were replaced by the arrival of a large number of Pushtons, from both sides of the southern borders between Afghanistan and Pakistan. These new arrivals, combined with the disappearance of women from the streets, girls from schools, bans on art, music, cinema, and photography and the appearance of a large number of bearded men have changed the outlook of Kabul, once famous in Afghanistan for its liberal orientation and cosmopolitan life.

CHAPTER FIFTEEN

THE TALIBAN ADVANCE
TOWARD MAZAR-E-SHARIF

WHEN MASSOUD'S DOSTAM'S FORCES ADVANCED ON KABUL AND captured the area north of the capital, the Taliban opened another front to reduce the concentration of forces against their front line in Kabul. In early November 1996, the Taliban advanced into the province of Badghis, northeast of Herat, which was controlled by Dostam forces. For the Taliban, advancing northeast was a significant military tactic that held two goals.

Attacking northeast of Herat, which was closer to Dostam's mainland, could force Dostam to pull out his forces fighting the Taliban along with Massoud to the north of Kabul. In this case, the Taliban would be able to balance the battle and use their forces more effectively. Also, the northeastern section of Herat was closer to the Taliban heartland in Qandahar in comparison to Kabul, and they could mobilize their forces and strongly support the front line.

If the Taliban were able to open the road toward the province of Balkh and its capital Mazar-e-Sharif, they would be able to destroy Dostam and cut off Massoud's only supply line and connection to the outside world. In this case, the Taliban would be able to seize Massoud's forces and bring northern Afghanistan totally under their control. In this case, the Taliban also would complete their second strategy of finishing off their oppositions totally.

The Taliban's offensive on Badghis, bordering Herat, was successful in the beginning, but the deployment of fresh forces by Dostam made the Taliban's advance difficult. The Taliban attempted to use the Pushton ethnic population of Badghis against Dostam, but this plan was counterattacked by Dostam's Uzbek forces. As a result, thousands of residents, especially the Pushton population, were forced to leave their towns and villages in Badghis. At the same time, a similar approach toward the non-Pushton population was implemented by the Taliban, and this ethnic demobilization of the population caused the displacement of thousands of people who fled the war to take refuge in Herat. After months of severe fighting, the Taliban seized Badghis on October 25, and deployed fresh troops along the Murghab river. On November 20, 1996, Mullah Yar Muhammad, the governor of Herat, told the Pakistani-based Afghan Islamic Press (AIP) that 50,000 people had been displaced by fighting in the neighboring province of Badghis, and many of them lacked food or shelter against the harsh winter.[1]

Seizing Badghis was very crucial for both sides of the conflict because if the Northern Alliance forces could control this province, they could then launch an offensive on Herat. If the opposition controlled Badghis, they could cut off the Taliban from the transit road to Central Asia. This control could also provide the opposition significant access to Iran, which was supporting them against the Taliban. Capturing Badghis was a great victory for the Taliban, and now they could easily attack the northeast area of the Murghab River on the other side of Safid Koh. From a logistical point of view, the Safid Koh (White Mountains) that separate northern Afghanistan from the southwest, and particularly the gorge of the Sabzak area and the Murghab River, were a main obstacle for the Taliban. Soon after the Taliban forces crossed these natural barriers, they launched an outstanding attack on the province of Faryab and captured Qaysar.

The rapid advance of the Taliban army and the concentration of their forces worried the Northern Alliance. To reduce this concentration on northern Afghanistan, Massoud's forces launched an offensive on the Taliban front in the north of Kabul. Both sides exchanged ground, but the Taliban held their position. At the end of December 1996, the Taliban movement controlled three-fourths of Afghanistan, and significantly, they controlled the passage highways that connected them to Pakistan. These highways provided the Taliban a substantial capability to connect with their supporters in Pakistan and other parts of the world. The Taliban fought the opposition on a 50-mile front in the north of Kabul and along the border of Badghis and Faryab in the northeast of Herat. For the opposition, which had a poor logistic and communications system, keeping up in a battle that stretched from the eastern part of Afghanistan to the northern areas was a very difficult challenge.

During the spring of 1997, Ismail Khan, who was in exile in Iran, recruited his former ex-Mujahideen forces and created a network on the western and northern parts of Herat. He entered Afghanistan and crossed the province of Herat, which was under the massive control of the Taliban, to reach the area controlled by Dostam. Soon, Ismail Khan and his fighters were positioned on the front line in the Faryab area and were engaged in fighting Taliban forces. According to one of the local sources, Ismail Khan planned to create a network of guerrillas on the north strip from Faryab to the Iranian border and spread a mobile military operation against the Taliban. His goal was to recapture Herat and at the same time put pressure on the Taliban through advancement into the province of Ghor. Ismail Khan's popularity in the region, particularly in Herat, could result in a severe threat to the Taliban's position in the area and could reduce pressure on the front line in Kabul. Ismail Khan was famous for conducting such military operations against the Soviets and the PDPA in the region and had seized the center of Herat and Badghis in a similar method during the Soviet invasion.

Throughout the spring, the Taliban ran a significant secret operation to use a dispute between the opposition leaders against one another. The Taliban concentrated on the personal gap between Ismail Khan and General Abdul Malik Pahlawan, second in command of the Uzbek forces. The Taliban reached a secret agreement with Malik Pahlawan with several goals.

They planned to disarm Ismail Khan, who was with a group of his fighters in Malik-controlled territory, and hand him over to the Taliban. If Ismail Khan was able to flee the area, it would be very difficult for the Taliban to catch him again. In this case, Ismail Khan would be a serious potential threat to the Taliban in the area. Finishing off Ismail Khan was a strategic victory for the Taliban and could safeguard their rule in the region, particularly in the province of Herat.

The Taliban and Malik agreed to not only open to the Taliban the road toward Mazar-e-Sharif, the capital of Balkh, but also to provide them with passages and logistics, in case the military needed his forces along with the Taliban against the opposition. In accordance with this plan, Malik, who wanted to be the supreme leader of the Uzbek forces, dismissed his rival General Dostam and disarmed those units who were loyal to the General.

In the beginning of May, Malik's units took control of the entrance to Mazar-e-Sharif, and the Taliban forces moved swiftly into some parts of the town and seized many positions in several areas. The Taliban foreign minister, Mullah Mohammed Ghaus, endeavored to establish a new local administration that would operate under the Taliban's direct control only. The issue of the direct control of the Taliban and the disarming of the local forces scared many, including the Uzbek forces led by Malik. On the third day of controlling Mazar-e-Sharif, Ghaus put together a press conference and said to reporters, "all the ethnic groups together will make one government."[2] But the political and military environment was very unstable, and there was a fearful environment on all sides. Among all ethnic groups, but the Hazaraz in particular, those belonging to the *Hezb-e-Wahdat* were more suspicious about the Taliban. This suspicion was rooted in the 1995 events when the Wahdat leader, Abdul Ali Mazari, was invited by Taliban commander Mulla Borejan to the south of Kabul to balance the front line against Massoud's forces. The Taliban not only did not support the Wahdat, but they disarmed them. Days later, the Taliban arrested Mazari and the members of the Wahdat central committee and killed them in March 1995.[3]

The men and women of Hazaras in Mazar-e-Sharif bore arms and took positions in their houses. When the Taliban forces entered the area to disarm and control them, they fired on the Taliban from many directions. This happened while Mullah Mohammed Ghaus was talking about the formation of a Taliban-controlled government in Afghanistan. Soon, the units belonging to Massoud joined the fight and opened fire on the Taliban; this action caused the low-ranking Uzbek officers who were not happy with the development in the area to turn their weapons and open fire on the Taliban forces as well. As Kenneth J. Cooper reports:

> Within a couple of hours, ethnic Uzbek and Tajik troops loyal to the Taliban's professed allies now enemies once again sneaked along roofs and sidewalks behind the Pushton Militiamen, firing rocket-propelled grenades at them. In the confused overnight street battle that followed, Taliban detachment of 3,000 was forced from the city and Ghaus disappeared.[4]

This was a nightmare for the Taliban since in capturing Kabul, the massive losses and casualties were disastrous. Hundreds of Taliban soldiers were killed in the battle, and thousands were captured by the opposition forces. The number of Taliban captured by the opposition, which was estimated at more than 3,000, was the first of its kind during the decades of war. The Taliban forces also retaliated while they retreated from Mazar-e-Sharif by firing on hundreds of civilians. "In one village inhabited by the Hazaras, 50 civilians were killed, and many other Uzbek civilians lost their lives."[5] The New York Times reported: "Some 100,000 refugees from the fighting in Afghanistan have fled to the country's northern border and could start entering Tajikistan."[6]

According to the sources inside Afghanistan, the Taliban's goal in capturing Mazar-e-Sharif was to move swiftly toward the Massoud-controlled area after seizing Balkh. For this reason, they used massive deployment of forces in the area. When the Taliban came under fire from many directions, they were not able to mobilize their forces and lost commanding control of their troops. This situation caused hundreds to be killed, and thousands ran away without any direction, only to be later captured by the opposition. Some sources believe that the Taliban advance toward Mazar-e-Sharif destabilized the social structure of the region and caused a severe ethnic cleansing. The Taliban opened fire on the non-Pushton civilian residents while retreating, and this act caused a hostile situation between the northern Pushtons who were cooperating with the Taliban and other ethnic groups. This hostility that was rooted in the politicization of ethnic groups in the north caused the largest number of casualties and human loss in this area since the withdrawal of the Soviets. Thousands of Taliban who were captured by the oppositions were mistreated and a large number were executed. According to the UN team visiting northern Afghanistan, "more then 1,000 of an initial total of 1,680 Taliban prisoners from the Shiberghan jail alone were systematically murdered. The team also visited villages near Mazar and Qaisar district where they heard reports of massacres of local Shias and Uzbeks by Taliban or pro-Taliban Pushtons troops."[7]

The Taliban's defeat in Mazar-e-Sharif created a new political and military development in Afghanistan that caused a new wave of mass mobilization in the area. This event changed the political and military positions of the Taliban; it also produced new shifts in the military organization and political leadership of the opposition. The events of Mazar-e-Sharif also formed a different political and diplomatic environment at the regional level, particularly among the countries bordering Afghanistan.

AFGHANISTAN AFTER THE TALIBAN DEFEAT IN MAZAR-E-SHARIF

The Taliban lost the most significant chance of establishing a national government under their leadership. As a result, the opposition not only survived, but also formed a new alliance called the National Islamic Front for the Deliverance of Afghanistan (NIFDA). This new alliance was comprised of "former military chief Ahmed Shah Massoud, Uzbek leader Malik Pahlawan, Shiite Muslims belonging to *Hezb-e-Wahdat*, former Prime Minister Gulbuddin Hekmatyar, Ismaeli Muslims and a royalist party led by Pir Ahmed Gailani."[8] The Taliban rejected the new alliance and attempted to negotiate only with General Malik to break through the newly formed alliance. But Malik's spokesman, Humaun Powzie, said that if the Taliban wanted to negotiate they would have to negotiate with the Islamic Front.[9]

Meanwhile, the NIFDA was not trusted by General Malik even though his men were holding thousands of Taliban prisoners. The *Hezb-e-Wahdat* controlled a large portion of Mazar, which was not tolerable to Malik, and therefore a hostile situation developed between the two groups. According to inside sources, *Hezb-e-Wahdat* and Massoud helped General Dostam, who was in exile in Turkey, to return to Afghanistan. General Dostam, with the support of *Wahadat*, was able to push out General Malik, who went into exile in Iran. Later, General Dostam clashed with Wahdat forces, and they reached an agreement over the control of Mazar-e-Sharif. After the return of General Dostam, the NIFDA was comprised of four main groups: the forces led by Ahmed Shah Massoud; the Uzbek Army led by General Dostam; Wahdat forces led by Karim Khalili; and Ismaeli Shia forces led by Sayyd Nader Kiani. On the political front, NIFD increased its diplomatic activities and attempted to form an interim government with a broader base. In a council of political and military leaders of the NIFDA, Abdul Rahim Ghafoorzai, vice minister for foreign affairs and the representative of Rabbani's ousted government in the United States, was selected as the prime minister. He planned to form a new political combination by including several Afghan technocrats in his cabinet. A week before the final formation of the interim government's new cabinet, Ghafoorzai, Engineer Hashimi (an influential ex-Mujahideen commander who controlled Bamyan), Sayed Amin Sajadi, a key member of Wahdat, and several other important figures were killed in a plane crash between Mazar and Bamyan. As a result, the NIFDA was not able to put together this proposal, as Ghafoorzai had been working on it.

On the military ground, the conflict between Uzbek generals Malik and Dostam reduced Uzbek potential military forces and took away the military credibility they had before. After Dostam returned from exile, the Uzbek leaders endeavored to reorganize their forces and extend their civil administration. They united their forces and improved their political position as one of the most important armed political groups in Afghanistan. Dostam endeavored to rebuild his military and civil administration and at the same time he managed to strengthen his diplomatic relations with Uzbekistan, Iran, Turkey, and Pakistan. Life in Mazar-e-Sharif became normal once again, the United Nations and some international NGO's reopened their offices, and the waves of refugees returned. Schools, Balkh University, and local administration started to function, but this time not as organized and productive as they were before the Taliban's attack on Mazar.

Hezb-e-Wahdat became more influential among the Hazarahs and organized its forces on a larger scale. New developments among the Hazarahs after the Taliban defeat in Mazar-e-Sharif created a new social, political, and military solidarity. According to the sources belonging to this ethnic group in Afghanistan, this solidarity was like a new political movement that had strong roots in their sociopolitical survival rather than the political ideology of *Hezb-e-Wahdat* leadership. In this new political movement there were many Hazarah intellectuals and community leaders who did not believe in the political ideology of Wahdat Party. Many of the Hazarahs who were teaching at the schools and Bamian University were not loyal to the political ideology of Wahdat's leadership. This new leadership also was not united by ideology; however, they were working together in accordance with the current sociopolitical situation. Another important factor that contributed to the influence of the Abdul Karim Khalili faction among Hazarahs was their control over foreign aid. This foreign aid, in particular from Iran, helped a segment of the leaders to maintain their monopoly over the Hazarah-run military and administration.[10]

Among the Afghan population in central Afghanistan, the Ismaeli Shia armed forces, led by General Sayyd Jafar Nader Kiani, emerged as an important armed political group in the Taliban opposition side. During Najibullah regime, Ismaeli's forces organized themselves and became active in the power game of northern and central Afghanistan. General Kiani was an important member of the Junbesh Shamal along with General Dostam. Later, he established a good relationship with Ahmed Shah Massoud in the region. Afghan Ismaelis are one of the most organized ethnic and political groups in present-day

Afghanistan. They have a vast line of connections with the Afghan Ismaelis all over the world, from which they get their financial and technical support.

After the defeat in Mazar, the Taliban attempted their largest effort to get help from the religious schools in Pakistan. They recruited hundreds of fresh students, in particular from the Baluchestan area, and sent them to the front line in northern Afghanistan. At the same time, they advanced north via the Salang area, but this time Massoud launched a heavy offensive on the Taliban six kilometers from Jabul Saraj.[11] The Taliban held their positions on all fronts and advanced to central Afghanistan via Laghman. But the Hazarah forces held this advance at the gate of Bamyan and later pushed them back from the area. The Taliban sealed off all the entry roads to central Afghanistan, which created a severe shortage of food and supply. Finally, the Taliban leaders offered to negotiate with the opposition leaders and in doing so requested the release of the Taliban prisoners. In September 1997, Reuters reported: "Wakil Ahmed Muttwakil told Reuters that the offer by Taliban leader Mullah Mohammed Omar was made last week in the first phone contact with Ahmed Shah Massoud."[12] General Dostam was the first to agree with releasing hundreds of his prisoners, and soon, more Taliban prisoners were released by *Hezb-e-Wahdat* and Massoud.

Indeed, the Taliban's defeat caused Ahmed Shah Massoud to emerge as the most powerful Taliban opposition leader in Afghanistan. Massoud saved his forces and kept his military and political operations intact and while overcoming the JIA leadership and party activists, in particular the *Maktabis*. Most of the political officers, in particular in India, Europe, and North America, were more loyal to Ahmed Shah Massoud than the JIA or Burhanadin Rubbani. (Only the JIA offices in Iran and some in Persian Gulf countries controlled by the JIA *Maktabis* were not.) This group of JIA members (*Maktabis*) in Iran was influenced mostly by the *Afzaly* faction led by Sayyd Noorallah Emad. This faction was involved in coordinated political activities with an inner faction of the Iranian government that dealt with Afghanistan. For the first time, this group conducted their activities among the Afghan refugees in the region in the absence of their arch rival, Ismail Khan.

Through the emergence of the Taliban in Afghanistan and the rise in power of *Jamaat-Uloma-e-Islam* in Pakistan, Gulbadin Hekmatyar lost his support. Hekmatyar's armed groups were among the first to be crushed by Taliban forces in Afghanistan. The Taliban operation against Hekmatyar forces resulted in the severe loss of his military and political capability in Afghanistan. The loss of support from Pakistan, and the crush of his well organized and loyal commanders by the Taliban in Afghanistan, made Hekmatyar baseless in this country. His only commander, Bashir in Laghman, played a double role between the Taliban and Massoud to save himself. According to Taliban sources, Laghman's influence is great, and Hekmatyar no longer has any role in the political development of the province.

In 1996, Hekmatyar moved to Iran and established his main base there. This move as a Pushton leader was very risky for him and his party; it could cause Hekmatyar to lose his support among the Arab Muslims who are not happy with the Iranian government. According to *Issar Haqh* of HIP publication in Iran, Hekmatyar's transition from Pakistan to Iran was the only functional alternative. In Iran, the JIP *Maktabis* and the HIH activists who have a similar political ideology are active in a coordinated effort to influence the population who are living in the area controlled by the Northern Alliance, in particular, in Mazar-e-Sharif. JIP activists, especially the Afzali faction, are concentrated among the Afghan refugees to promote their political ideology in preparation for the time when they return to Afghanistan.

The main route to northern and central Afghanistan is through the area controlled by General Dostam's forces, and Hekmatyar's activities ran through this area. Both General Dostam and *Hezb-e-Wahdat* endeavored to have Hekmatyar in the region to balance their political ability with Ahmed Shah Massoud. According to some observers in northern Afghanistan, Hekmatyar's main objective of being active among the northern alliances was to be able to recruit his former activists and organize them into a new political and military movement in the region. He also wanted to use the Iranian support against his arch rival, Ahmed Shah Massoud, to reduce his influence and power among the northern leaders. The political strategy of JIA *Maktabis* in Iran, HIH of Hekmatyar, and the *Hezb-e-Wahdat* has been incorporated with the Iranian government's policy toward Afghanistan. Through this policy, Iran wants to increase its influence in Afghanistan beyond the Shia and non-Pushton populations of Afghanistan. For this purpose, Alluadin Brojerdi, the special envoy of the Iranian government in Afghanistan affairs, traveled to Mazar-e-Sharif to discuss the results of the diplomatic efforts between Pakistan and Iran over the issue of Afghanistan in June 1998. According to the National Islamic Front for the Deliverance of Afghanistan (NIFDA), Brojerdi tried to persuade the NIFDA leaders to accept Hekmatyar's participation in their effort against the Taliban. This source stated that Hekmatyar could reorganize his forces and position them north of Kabul and northeast of Badghis. If Hekmatyar gained the agreement of the NIFDA leaders, in particular Massoud and General Dostam, HIH, under his leadership, could play another round of military and political roles in Afghanistan.

Some of the Afghan politicians argued that the participation of HIH and Hekmatyar would endanger the credibility of NIFDA, and they advised the northern leaders to avoid any agreement that allowed HIH membership. These politicians offered as example Hekmatyar's armed conflicts with Rabbani's government, in particular the bombardment of Kabul, which cost thousands of lives and started the bloody civil war after the collapse of Najibullah's regime.[13] But HIH criticized the ability and credibility of NIFDA and the lack of a workable alternative toward the establishment of an interim government or a popular political and military front. HIH proclaimed that the participation of this party and its leadership in NIFDA would make the opposition win the military and political game over the Taliban.[14] But at the same time, Hekmatyar stated at the University of Balkh in Mazar-e-Sharif that his party struggles to complete the Islamic revolution in Afghanistan. In this vein, he did not support a policy that wanted to share power with those who did not follow the path of Islamic revolution in Afghanistan. Hekmatyar excluded former king Zaher Shah from such a group, and he argued that the issue of *Loya Jirga* and the king's participation in the current political events of Afghanistan was an American-made policy. "Through this policy, the US wants to impose Zaher Shah on Afghan people," he stated at the Mazar-e-Sharif University.[15]

Ahmed Shah Massoud argued, "we need to gradually expand this war"[16] and drag the Taliban into many different battles that would increase their military losses and their costs. Since most of the financial aid to the Taliban comes from Pakistan, this country could not afford to keep its aid to them in the long run. Seizing a large territory by the Taliban forces may be possible in the short term, but the Taliban would not be able to maintain their rule in those areas. Therefore, Massoud's alternative was a long-term fight against the Taliban through large scale mobile military and political activities. Such a plan would damage the Taliban's ability to form a government under their direct rule, and this would reduce their foreign support on which they were dependent. For this reason, Massoud's representative in India, Abdullah Abdulah, proclaimed that their forces were able to seize Kabul but that they wanted to reduce the concentration of forces on one front.[17] Ahmed Shah Massoud attempted to convince the Pushtons, who were against the Taliban, to join him in a united front. He helped the Pushtons in Kunar, loyal to Haji Abdul Qadir, the former leader of *Nangarhar Shura*, to revolt against the Taliban. On March 19, 1997, a large arms depot was blown up by the anti-Taliban elements around Jalalabad.[18] This explosion caused a large military concentration of the Taliban in the area. The revolt was suppressed by Taliban forces and Haji Qadir was forced by the ISI to leave Pakistan; he went into exile in Germany, but returned in the following year to fight the Taliban.

THE TALIBAN'S NEW ADVANCE
IN NORTHERN AFGHANISTAN

The Taliban's defeat in Mazar-e-Sharif not only caused the loss of hundreds of its fighters, it was also an extreme blow against their political and diplomatic position among the international community. This event reduced the possibility of the Taliban becoming the official government of Afghanistan. To establish a national government they needed to control the land and manage the affairs of the people, as well as meet the basic human rights that were declared in the United Nations charter of human rights and freedom. In 1997, the Taliban controlled two-thirds of Afghanistan, but their defeat in the north showed their weakness. Because of this, and also because of the reluctance of international financial institutions to fund the pipeline project, oil companies such as UNOCAL conditioned their operation on the establishment of an internationally recognized government in Afghanistan.

Throughout this, the Northern Alliance emerged as an equally important military and political force in Afghanistan. The Northern Alliance attempted to use this military victory politically and continued their proclamation as the rightful government of Afghanistan. But the Northern Alliance was not able to put their military victory to use toward the creation of a stronger and more cooperative military and political front against the Taliban. The political gap between the Uzbek forces was widened after General Dostam returned from exile in Turkey. This political gap expanded into the military clashes between the Uzbek forces and caused the exile of General Malik to Iran. Publicly, General Dostam became the supreme military leader of the Uzbek forces once again, but in reality, there was internal conflict between those led by General Gulai, Malik's brother, and General Dostam. This political conflict that circled around the personal interests of the Uzbek leaders kept the Northern Alliance leaders busy with their internal problems and reduced their efforts in national and international activities. This conflicted situation between the Uzbek forces provoked the disagreement of local communities under their control. Many areas suffered from the lack of security and the abuse of power by the local armed forces who came down harsh on civilian populations. According to eyewitnesses, some of the local armed forces in Mazar-e-Sharif became bandit-like groups who financed their expenses by controlling commercial roads connecting Afghanistan to the Hiratan port in Uzbekistan. This kind of behavior caused unrest in the local communities, particularly since the lack of security was disturbing the Hiratan Highway.

Taliban leaders waited patiently for a ripe moment to strike on the northern forces and take advantage of the conflict between the Uzbek leaders. They opened a wide range of communications with those who were not happy with the Uzbek leadership, and at the same time, they invested financially in the unhappy commanders under the control of Uzbek leaders.

The Taliban deployed a large number of forces across the front line against the opposition troops in the provinces of Badghis and Faryab. According to western aid workers in the area, the Taliban fighters shot dead in execution style around 600 Uzbek villagers in Faryab. After a month of fighting, the Taliban military advanced farther north, and captured Shiberghan and Sar-e-Pul, 35 kilometers (15 miles) from Mazar, the main natural gas reserves in Afghanistan.[19] On August 8, 1998, the Taliban forces attacked the Uzbek position and advanced rapidly toward Mazar-e-Sharif, seizing the city. Radio Sharia, broadcasting in Kabul, claimed, "the Taliban forces have taken full control of Mazar-e-Sharif and its airport, and there is complete peace and stability in the city now."[20] The Taliban supported their ground and air forces without the direct cooperation of the loyal Uzbeks. In contrast to their previous campaign, the Taliban relied on the Pushton ethnic groups in Balkh and used their members as local guides. Since these Pushtons lived in harmony for hundreds of years they not only avoided taking part in the hate killing of other ethnic groups by the Taliban fighters, they protected their Hazara neighbors from the Taliban rage. Radio Sharia also announced that the Taliban leader, Mullah Mohammed Omar, had ordered "the immediate enforcement of the Islamic law over Mazar-e-Sharif, and the general amnesty to the opposition forces."[21] According to Taliban sources, many local commanders had not fought, but they surrendered their forces to the Taliban army and opened the roads.[22] But reports from Afghanistan indicated that many of Uzbek commanders were bribed by the Taliban. *The Frontier Post* in Pakistan reported that some well-known opposition commanders, including Abd-ul-Rahim, Abdul Manan, and Tila Mohammed, along with their fighters, joined the Taliban. In the Kundooz province the prominent pro-Dostam commander Abdul Qadir along with his 500 fighters joined the ranks of the Taliban. In another development Mohammed Usman Salikzada, once a strong ally of General Dostam and ex-governor of Mazar-e-Sharif, sent a delegation to the Taliban and expressed his willingness to join them.[23]

In the western part of Mazar city, the Taliban bribed an Uzbek commander to leave the western road to the city open to the Taliban forces. Over 1,000 Hazaras main forces were faced with a surprise attack by the Taliban. The Hazara fighters, who were under siege from all directions, resisted until their last bullet, and only around 100 survived and reached Bamyan. Taliban fighters, riding on their pickup trucks in many parts of the city, opened fire on any moving creature. A revengeful operation for their last year's losses in Mazar was launched against the civilian population and among other non-Pushton ethnic groups; Hazaras were targeted deliberately. Taliban fighters did a door-to-door search and shot the males of the families or slit their throats. According to eyewitnesses, hundreds of women were kidnapped and became concubines for the Taliban fighters. The narrow streets of Mazar city were covered with dead bodies and blood, and the local residents were not allowed to bury the corpses for a week. Stray dogs ate the human flesh and the smell was noticeable from far outside the city. The UN and ICRC estimated the total deaths in Mazar at around 5,000 to 6,000, but the local sources claimed a much higher number. A group of Taliban fighters led by commander Mullah Dust Mohammed Niazi, accompanied by the Pakistani anti-Shia militants of *Sapah-e-Sahabah*, entered the Iranian Consulate and asked eleven Iranian diplomats and one journalist to go in the basement. The Iranians thought that the armed group came for their protection and so obeyed the order. A moment later the armed Taliban lined them up and executed them all together.

The third day after seizing Mazar-e-Sharif, Taliban forces advanced farther northeast and captured the province of Talghan, cutting off the supply line of the opposition in Uzbekistan.[24] The *Hezb-e-Wahdat* forces retreated to Bamyan, and Massoud's forces along with other opposition leaders in the area moved back into the Badakhshan region. On August 12, Massoud deployed new forces on the border of Takhar and Talaghan to stop the Taliban.

THE FALL OF BAMYAN

Bamyan is one of the most significant historical heritages of ancient Afghanistan, and it is dominated by ethnic Hazarahs. In the ancient history of Afghanistan, Bamyan was the center of Buddhism, and in the eighth century A.D., it was an important pilgrimage stop on the Silk Road. The 114- and 165-foot-high Buddha statues that are carved into the sandstone mountains of Bamyan are the symbolic identity of this province. Historically, the central Afghanistan people ran their affairs with a great deal of autonomy. In 1893 the Hazarahs revolts were suppressed by the Iron King, Abdul Rahman Khan, which resulted in the killing of thousands of Hazarahs and the exile of many more into other provinces or in the neighboring countries.[25] This event left a deep scar in the memory of the Hazarahs and kept them distant from the Pushton rulers of the country. Even though the Afghan constitution declared equal rights for all citizens of Afghanistan regardless of their ethnic and religious background, often the Hazarahs have suffered simply because of who they are.

The Taliban moved to central Afghanistan via Logar and wanted to finish off the Wahdat forces in that area. But the Taliban offense on central Afghanistan created a large solidarity among the Hazarahs, which helped them to hold back the Taliban's offensives three times. During this rigid time, there were attempts by Abdul Karim Khalili's faction of *Hezb-e-Wahdat* to utilize Iranian aid for their control of the party. However, *Hezb-e-Wahdat* became a political and military front for the Afghan Hazarahs in Afghanistan rather than a political party that could be monopolized by Khalili faction. Previously, Wahdat leadership had incorporated successfully the local commanders, prominent community leaders, intellectuals, and educated Hazarahs who were neither loyal to the Khalili leadership nor believers in the policy of the party. In most cases, the resentment against the factional monopoly and rejection of the Iranian influence among the Hazarah intellectuals and communal leaders stayed very high. This development encouraged the leaders to expand the membership of the Central Council of the party up to 80 people, including 12 women. It was the first political party after the PDPA that welcomed women in its central council. Most of these women were educated, and some of them, like Humaira Rahi, a famous poet, taught previously at Kabul University. All of these events led the Afghan Hazarahs' political forces into a new, moderate political and social mobilization. This new mobilization directed the Hazarah professionals to build up the skills of civil societies. They established Bamyan University along with a significant number of schools for boys and girls. In return, the

Taliban blocked all the roads and entrances to central Afghanistan, creating a severe shortage of food and other basic needs. Despite the rejection of the United Nations and international NGOs of the Taliban military campaign, the Taliban continued the Bamyan siege and prevented the arrival of any outside aid, in particular foodstuffs. After months of air raids, the Taliban launched a decisive attack on Bamyan that was not faced by outstanding resistance from the population. The main forces of the Hazarahs fighters, in particular *Hezb-e-Wahdat* forces, along with thousands of civilians retreated to the mountains and several local commanders surrendered to the Taliban. Taliban forces seized the city on September 3, 1998, but stayed away from the civilian populations. On September 18, the Taliban, who considered the Buddhas statues un-Islamic, blew off the head of one of the Buddha statues with explosives and fired rockets at Buddha's groin, destroying the delicate design of the statue. Since July 1998, the Taliban jets already had bombed the sandstone mountain that held the statues several times, causing cracks on the niches.

The Taliban military was successful in the north, capturing the stronghold of both the Uzbek and the Hazarahs and destroying their military organization, as well as their social support bases. This gave the Taliban control of their Islamic Emirate of Afghanistan in almost 80 percent of the country. In the meantime, Ahmed Shah Massoud, the only leader of the northern opposition, reorganized his forces and challenged the Taliban on both political and military grounds. In the dust of the Iranian deployment of forces at the Afghan border, Massoud took advantage and launched numerous well-organized attacks on the northeast of the country. His forces captured a large territory bordering Tajikistan, imprisoned about 2,000 Taliban solders, and reopened his connection to the outside world. On December 7, 1998, Massoud invited all the remaining anti-Taliban commanders to the Panjshir valley for a strategic meeting. Here, the commanders formed a new military and political organization called the Islamic United Front for Liberation of Afghanistan (UIFLA). At this meeting the commanders appointed Massoud to be the military commander of all anti-Taliban forces in Afghanistan.

CHAPTER SIXTEEN

THE ROAD INTO THE FUTURE

IN THE EYES OF THE TALIBAN LEADERS, ESTABLISHING THE ISLAMIC Emirate of Afghanistan (IEA) illustrated their control over the civil and military administration in the country. Theoretically, the Taliban were successful in adapting the charismatic role of their leader Mullah Mohammed Omar to their interpretation of Islamic principle of governing, the Islamic *Khelafat*. They attempted to build a legal administration and judicial system based on this so that the personal role of their supreme leader would dominate within this system. From this stand, the Taliban endeavored to influence Afghan society by enforcing their rule as the legal government of the country. Such an endeavor by the Taliban leaders made them mobilize their activities on four fronts.

THE MILITARY FRONT

In 1998, after the Taliban brought the city of Mazar-e-Sharif under their control, they held their front lines around Kabul and maintained control of the city. They moved to central Afghanistan via Logar and planned to finish off the Wahdat forces in that area. But the Taliban offense in central Afghanistan created solidarity among the Hazaras, and this solidarity helped them to hold back the Taliban's advance for a short period of time. Consequently, the Taliban blocked all the roads and entrances to central Afghanistan, causing a severe shortage of food and other basic needs in the opposition-controlled area. In northern Afghanistan, the Taliban advanced closer toward the province of Faryab, strengthening their military position. The Taliban built up their military machine and formed a very effective military organization that used the art of mobile military operations brilliantly. The use of modern communication resulted in a victorious command and control. The tactical consistency of logistics, supplies, and reinforcements provided the Taliban a well-structured connection between the front lines and the support area. Indeed, all this was not expected from the semi-militia and ex-Mujahideen commanders. The core military officers in the Taliban army are Pushton ex-military officers of the former Afghan army. According to western intelligence sources, the Taliban enjoyed the cooperation and military aid of the ISI and the Pakistani army field officers, whose aid has been very effective in forming organizational structures, communications, logistics, and military plans. The Taliban established several military training camps, in southern Afghanistan and Kabul, where they trained new arrivals from the Deeni *Madresah* in Pakistan.

In the meantime, the Taliban opposition, the United Front forces, maintained their firm control over 20 percent of strategic locations, stretching from the Uzbekistan border to the north of Kabul. Among the opposition leaders, Ahmed Shah Massoud organized his core forces and expanded his influence westward and eastward. His forces mobilized their operations in the form of guerrilla tactics, while creating underground activities in the Taliban-held areas. The United Front forces also channeled military aid from Iran, the Central Asian Republics, and India.

The escape of Ismail Khan from the Taliban jail in Qandahar in April 2000 was interpreted as a significant victory for the Taliban opposition. If Ismail Khan, a prominent politician and a Mujahideen hero against the Soviets, is able to rally forces around him in the southwest and northwest of the country, the military balance against the Taliban may shift swiftly. His influence among the local communities in the province of Herat is especially critical to the Taliban's normalization process of their administration. Herat currently is one of the most important geopolitical areas under Taliban control. If Ismail Khan could take Herat, he would take away a significant commercial center that connects Pakistan to Central Asia and the Persian Gulf via land routes. This province also serves as an important strategic supply route to the Taliban forces in the north. Losing Herat would jeopardize their control in the north of the country and would extend the front line massively. Importantly, the majority of the people living in northern and western Afghanistan are Tajiks, Uzbeks, and Hazarahs, and they are forming the main forces of the opposition groups against the Taliban.

THE DIPLOMATIC FRONT

The Taliban attempted to gain international support and recognition for their administration in Kabul. In September 1996, Sher Mohammed Abbas Stanakzai, the acting foreign minister of the Taliban, visited Washington. He met with top officials of the Clinton administration to argue unsuccessfully for U.S. diplomatic recognition of the Taliban. The Taliban representative at the

United Nations, Abdul Hakim Mujahid, also endeavored to convince the United Nations to recognize the Taliban administration in Kabul as the legitimate government of Afghanistan. Taliban activities in the United States also aimed to be in control of the Afghan embassy in Washington. After a round of internal conflicts between second secretary Seraj Jamal (pro-Taliban) and Yar Mohammed Mohabbat (pro-Rabbani), the head of the embassy, neither faction was able to establish a fully recognizable operation in place. U.S. State Department spokesman John Dinger warned both sides of their diplomatic status in the United States.[1] In November 1997, Taliban leader Mulla Mohammed Rabbani attempted to gain Saudi Arabian king Fahd's support for Taliban membership in the Organization of the Islamic Conference (OIC).[2] Despite the support of Saudi Arabia, the United Arab Emirates, and Pakistan, who recognized the Taliban administration as the government of Afghanistan, they were not able to obtain full membership.

The Taliban administration sent delegates to China, Japan, Indonesia, and Malaysia to convince these countries to provide economic investments and diplomatic recognition. The Taliban's internal policies toward women and political opponents cost their administration a heavy price. Many countries, including the members of the OIC, criticized Taliban policies for shutting down girls' schools and banning women from any public work. These policies caused the cancellation of many international humanitarian activities by NGOs and the United Nations, who had employed a large number of Afghan women before Taliban rule. Many of these organizations who hired non-Afghan women from the Islamic countries criticized the Taliban, but these critics were responded to harshly by the Taliban. Several international aid organizations threatened to cancel their programs in the Taliban-controlled territories. These threats created a conflicted situation, in turn causing a negative diplomatic environment against the Taliban in the international communities. The Taliban's arrest of Eimma Banino, the head of the European Organization delegation in Afghanistan, while she was visiting and filming a women's hospital in Kabul created a massive diplomatic critique against the Taliban. On November 18, 1997, in the presence of Pakistani Foreign Minister Gohar Ayob Khan, U.S. Secretary of State Madeleine Albright condemned Taliban policies toward women and she reasoned her condemnation because of the Taliban approach to human rights, calling the Taliban's treatment of women despicable. She also said: "Their [Taliban] general lack of respect for human dignity is more reminiscent of the past than the future."[3]

The Taliban's attempt at normalization by changing the titles of the members of their cabinet from "acting" to "direct ministerial," as well as appointing a dozen new faces in October 1999, was interpreted as a major shift in this direction, but one that occurred too late and unproductively. The Taliban were under a double sanction by the United Nations and the United States, which created severe diplomatic problems. In February 2000, a Taliban delegation headed by

Deputy Foreign Minister Abdul Rehman Zahid held threadbare discussions with the authorities of Germany, Switzerland, France, Denmark, Holland, and Belgium in a bid to find a way for lifting UN sanctions against the Islamic Emirate.[4] The Taliban delegation accused the west of airing wrong information about the Islamic Emirate. These discussions proved to be in vain, and this delegation did not receive European support to remove either sanction.

The Taliban's association with Osama bin Laden, as well as other fanatic organizations such as those in Pakistan, Central Asia, and the Persian Gulf countries, raised severe diplomatic problems for the Islamic Emirate. These diplomatic difficulties forced the Taliban administration into deeper diplomatic isolation. Even though the Islamic Emirate did reestablish its diplomatic relationship with the Islamic Republic of Iran despite the execution of the Iranian diplomats in Mazar-e-Sharif, this reestablishment gave the Taliban only land route access to the Persian Gulf.

THE POLITICAL FRONT

Taliban leaders have endeavored to gain political support from the local communities inside the country. According to sources inside Afghanistan, the Taliban offered a handsome amount of cash and aid to each commander if he turned against the opposition. The financial ability of the Taliban helped them to be widely successful in this policy. But many local commanders took advantage of the hostile situation between the Taliban and their opponents. These local commanders made promises to both sides occasionally to receive money and arms. War politics became a great business for many local commanders in territories controlled either by the IEA or the UIFLA.

The Taliban political front was not as united as the military front against their oppositions, and the movement struggled to appoint one political leader for the whole movement. The long continuation of war against the oppositions and the need for a workable civil administration created several gaps between the Taliban leaders. At the beginning of the movement, the Taliban leaders never mentioned that they were struggling to establish an Islamic government under their leadership. They thought that seizing the country would be a fast and rapid process, and they would be able to restore peace and security in a short period of time. But this was a simplistic understanding of war and politics in this country where one may enjoy a military victory but may not be able to govern. In addition, governing a country devastated by years of war and bloodshed with a complicated political environment such as Afghanistan's was not an easy task. All these factors severely damaged the Taliban united leadership, which may have agreed on principles but was falling apart more and more.

The existence of the non-Afghan fanatic Muslims and their affiliation with the government agencies of the Islamic Emirate has influenced a rigid political approach toward other political parties. The Taliban administration was not able to reach any major political settlement with the opposition. Moreover, the Islamic Emirate has continued an ethno-nationalistic approach toward other ethnic and religious groups, which created a high level of mistrust and hatred between ethnic and religious groups. This situation resulted in yet deeper animosity among the population. This high level of hatred and animosity among the population itself has become an obstacle against the normalization process. After all, the Islamic Emirate is not ready to share the political power with the oppositions, and the Taliban leaders use the military option as the only alternative to normalize their politics in Afghanistan.

THE ECONOMIC FRONT

The Islamic Emirate's military and civil administration depends largely on foreign aid and partially on internal revenues. Taliban authority attempted to attract foreign investments in Afghanistan, but the continuation of civil war emerged as a serious barrier. The Taliban improved trade with Central Asia, which brought along some financial support for their administration. Still, they had a great deal of difficulty with the trade line that connects Afghanistan to the Persian Gulf countries via Iran.

The administration endeavored to exploit the mine reserves in the area controlled by the Taliban, but the lack of financial and mechanical ability caused the outcome to be very marginal. Maulawi Ahmed Jan, Minister of Mines and Industries, argued, "we have enormous mineral, oil and gas resources which should interest foreign investors. We will give land to anyone who wants to build a new factory."[5] This is a remarkable investment incentive by the Taliban for foreign investors, but any interested party has to build its roads, provide its electricity, and construct its housing. In some cases, the primary cost of a project was too high compared with the running cost of a project, which damaged the generous Taliban investment incentive. For example, in 1997, Qari Abdul Rashid, a commander of the Taliban in charge of the marble mine in the Helmand province, sent samples to China. The Chinese response was optimistic, but until now, there has not been any action from the Chinese investors. The mine has no engineers, no equipment, and no electricity, only 500 men using picks and dynamite struggling to make the mine profitable.[6]

In the meantime, the Taliban sent a delegation to the southeastern Pacific countries to stimulate investment in Afghanistan. Because of the political instability of the administration and the continuation of civil war, this effort did not realize any significant results. Another dilemma that the Taliban faced was the poor planning organization through a centrally coordinated economic leadership. Most educated and professional Afghans had left the country in the course of Soviet invasion and, in particular, when the Najibullah's regime collapsed and the civil war started. The shortage of trained and skilled professionals in the Taliban administration is still very severe, yet the administration has not organized a plan or direction for the economic development and reconstruction of Afghanistan. As Ahmed Rashid reported: "The Finance Ministry can barely put together a budget, and not just because funds are scarce. The ministry has no qualified economists: the minister and his deputy are mullahs with a madresah education. The ministry's own budget for the fiscal year that began in February 1979 was $100,000."[7]

The domestic revenue that came from opium cultivation was not a stable financial resource, and there was great pressure from the international community on this issue, making the cultivation of opium more difficult. Moreover, the opium cultivation created international smuggling and illegal activities, often concentrated around the Afghan-Pakistani border. This concentration has caused a chaotic environment in the regional economy and resulted in the addiction of millions of people in neighboring countries, particularly Iran and Pakistan, as well as Afghanistan. This chain of illegal activities contributed largely to the corruption of the governments and the increase of the crime rate in the region.

Since controlling Kabul, Taliban leaders have attempted to convince the international financial institutions to recognize their rule in Afghanistan. The main purpose of these attempts is the construction of the natural gas and oil pipeline that connects Central Asian natural resources to Pakistan. The American oil company, UNOCAL, which controls 80 percent of the project, agreed to start the project as soon as possible. But the mistrust of the lending agencies played against this agreement. As a result, in 1988, UNOCAL officially announced that until the establishment of a government recognized by the international financial institutions, they will stop any effort toward the implementation of the project and will not negotiate with any faction inside Afghanistan.[8] Taliban leaders attempted to use the competition between UNOCAL and the Argentinean company Bridas to put pressure on UNOCAL. This attempt divided the Taliban leaders into two parts: the Qandahar-based leaders under Mullah Mohammed Omar who support UNOCAL; and the Kabul-based leaders under Mullah Mohammed Rabbani who support Bridas. This conflict caused the Taliban, the largest military and political force in Afghanistan, to not have a unified strategy for the pipeline project. After the U.S. missile strike against bin Laden's camps in Afghanistan, UNOCAL stopped all its planned activities in Afghanistan. Under the U.S. sanctions, American-based businesses and corporations are not allowed to conduct business in the areas controlled by the Islamic Emirate of Afghanistan.

The absence of skilled professionals dealing with the pipeline project in Taliban's administration has been very obvious. According to the oil companies dealing with the pipeline, the Taliban agenda was more concerned with their political view and their faithfulness for their rule in Afghanistan, and because of this, the Taliban were not able to provide a proposal that consisted of a technical and scientific analysis. The Taliban's negotiating team with the oil companies was comprised of nine *Mullahs* and one engineer. In their proposal, the Taliban insisted that the company who wins the contract "must also build roads, electricity grids and telephone networks. Provide free gas to cities and drill for oil and gas."[9] How to implement these requests was not clear in the proposal. Most Afghan observers argued that even though the oil companies agreed with the Taliban proposal, the non-Afghan professionals would be in charge of implementing such a project in Afghanistan. In this case, they would implement the projects in a way that serves the oil companies and the non-Afghan investors' interests rather than the interests of Afghanistan. The Taliban's proposal not only attracted the oil companies, it also caused the oil companies to criticize Taliban programs. One oil company executive quipped, "we are not in the business of running a country."[10]

In April 2000, the Islamic Emirate joined a feasibility project for establishing a rail link between Pakistan, Afghanistan, and the Central Asian states to promote trade, tourism, commerce, and industry through an overland route. Within this project, the Pakistani railway network would be extended to Qandahar and Herat from the Chaman rail terminal on the Pakistani-Afghan border. This extension through western Afghanistan would enable Pakistan to get linked with the Central Asian states at Khushka, Tajikistan. This connection would provide quick access via the already existing rail links with other Central Asian states. The cost of this project—an 800-kilometer-long track from Chaman to Khushka—was estimated at $600 million. Since the Pakistani railroad connection to the Afghan border is not prepared for such a busy network, there are needs for improvement on the part inside Pakistan.[11] The cost for this improvement has been estimated at $100 million, causing Pakistan large financial difficulties. Pakistan is under severe pressure by the international financial institutions to continue with the project, and the Pakistani economy suffers largely from an enormous deficit. Therefore, the implementation of the railroad project is out of the financial feasibility of the participating countries, and the growing opposition in the north, in particular within the new activities by Ismail Khan in the area, reduces the feasibility of this project.

The continuation of war in Afghanistan and the imposed UN-U.S. sanctions has forced the local administration to ignore opium cultivation in the area under its control. Opium has become the most secure cash crop for farmers.[12] According to a UN report in 1997, since the Taliban movement seized power in Kabul, there has been a rapid increase in the production of poppy. According to the United Nations Drug Control Program in Afghanistan, "Taliban has leveled the *ushar,* a 25 percent tax on all agricultural production. This brought in $15 million a year from the $60 million Afghan growers and traders earn from opium exports out of a business worth $40 billion in Europe alone."[13] The estimated generated revenue from the Golden Crescent is worth $90 billion internationally.[14] Drug production and trafficking has created massive social, political, and economic problems in pre-industrial as well as in industrialized countries. Aside from its social and political destruction, the economic cost of drug control programs and antidrug operations has already diverted billions of dollars from the productive sectors of industrialized countries and has deprived pre-industrial countries from economic development.

In addition to the Golden Crescent related networks, another large network of illegal cross-border activities has emerged in the area. Under the Transit Treaty between Pakistan and Afghanistan a massive illegal smuggling network has developed. Both of these illegal networks has created a criminal economy in the region. As Ahmed Rashid reported: "The total transit trade last year between Afghanistan and Pakistan and on to other countries in the region was worth up to 4.5 billion dollars, equivalent to half [of] Pakistan's annual exports."[15] From this transit trade the Taliban receives only about $100 to $130 million every year. This criminal economy has created an artificial system of exchange in smuggled goods across the Afghan borders, but it could collapse with the improvement of border security in the neighboring countries. The revenue from this criminal economy may help the Islamic Emirate to support their military campaign against the United Front forces in the short run, but it would never establish a stable national economy. The poor economic condition of the country and the unstable economic system would cause further political instability in the country, and the Islamic Emirate may never have the chance to become a normal and functional administration.

Indeed, the military success of the Taliban against their oppositions may increase their political and diplomatic capabilities, but whether the Taliban are capable of forming a civil institution to run the country is not certain. The governing ability of the Taliban is dependent on their political and administrative efforts to promote ethnic, linguistic, and religious participation of Afghans in the central government. In this case, the establishment of a coordinated and centralized government with increasing participation of skilled Afghans would be crucial for this nation. Moreover, all this may happen only when the Taliban and the Northern Alliance settle peacefully.

A normal administration can exist only when there is a legal authority in place and a government that rules society correctly. Legal authority relies deeply on a functional bureaucratic administration that is fundamentally dominant through knowledge.[16] The rationale behind a system of legal authority relies on its technical and professional knowledge that makes the administration functional. By providing services to the public and extracting revenue a government can promote statehood. Serving the public would promote the correct way of ruling society, and it would allow the administrative staff to interact with people in accordance to the law. In this situation, the administrative staff and their supervisors are not going to be responsible to one person; rather, they would follow the law of the country. When a government system enjoys a knowledge-based administration, bureaucracy can expand the knowledge of its officers. This expansion of knowledge increases the legality of authority.

FRAGMENTATION IN THE TALIBAN LEADERSHIP

Enforcing the decrees issued by the Taliban supreme leader in Afghanistan was a difficult task and it has caused divisions between the leaders. Even the Taliban were able to recover from their military defeat in Mazar-e-Sharif in 1997, but it has left a deep impact on the psychology of the movement as well as on the political behavior of the leaders. These difficulties and the impact of the war has forced the Taliban leadership to be fragmented into three groups: the conservatives (Qandahar-based leaders), the moderates (Kabul-based leaders), and the religious police.

The conservative group is loyal to the supreme leader, Mullah Mohammed Omar, who is responsible for the religious and political edicts for the area controlled by the Taliban. Mullah Mohammed Omar is a heroic character among his followers as a Mujahideen commander during the Soviet invasion of Afghanistan. The first group of his armed men were those who fought with him against the Soviets and the Communist regime in southern Afghanistan. Mullah Omar also taught at a *madresah* in the remote area of Kandahar where he was greatly respected in the local community. Most of the close individuals working around him were those who studied in the traditional Deeni schools in Afghanistan and were associated with the semi-rural life. He had not wanted to have a direct connection with the foreign journalists or diplomats, in particular those from the western countries. There were also Talibs and Maulawis working with him who studied in Pakistan, and they wanted to use the traditional leadership against those who blocked their way to key positions in the administration. The division of leadership had caused the traditionalist mullahs and talibs to be threatened by the moderate circles. This forced the conservatives to rally around the Taliban supreme leader, Mullah Mohammed Omar, and use his authority to stop the influence of the moderates. This group also does not want to share power with any other political faction in the country, and they oppose the idea of elections, parliamentary government, women's public work, and the education of girls.

The moderate group is headed by Mullah Rabbani, the Taliban leader in Kabul who studied in Pakistan. Mullah Rabbani has been engaged in most of the diplomatic and foreign policy of the movement. Rabbani is the second most powerful leader after Mullah Mohammed Omar. In Kabul, the Taliban's health minister, Mullah Mohammed Abbas, is the most moderate and outspoken Taliban leader. Mullah Abbas has opposed many edicts that have come from Qandahar, and he has attempted to reform the policies concerning women in Kabul's hospitals. Through this reform, Mullah Abbas has changed the principles and let women doctors and nurses continue working in the hospitals. Mullah Abbas was for the establishment of a shared government with other political groups in Afghanistan. As John F. Burns states: "He [Mullah Abbas] favored a peace agreement to allow elections and the formation of a Parliament representing all Afghans, which would decide what kind of Islamic society the country would have."[17]

Mullah Abbas, a former merchant, has been considered by sources close to the Taliban as a reformer, a leader that understands the current situation in Afghanistan, and one who is familiar with the international development of science and technologies. Working toward a peace settlement and sharing power with other political groups in the country is an idea that fits within the sociopolitical fabric of Afghanistan. In the long run, if the Taliban are able to defeat their opposition militarily or if the civil war continues, the moderate leaders of the Taliban would be more qualified to get the popular support from the local communities and the movement supporters in the cities. Since the movement heavily depends on foreign aid, without a recognizable government, the Taliban leaders must establish an administration that will serve the nation.

Mullah Abbas is the leading moderate figure among the Taliban movement, and he calls his opposition within the Taliban leadership the hard liners. He argues that the hard-liner Taliban, led by Mullah Mohammed Omar, "don't want to analyze our situation properly. Either they can't, or they don't want to. In either case, the result is the same."[18] Without a proper understanding of the current social, political, and international relations, it is very difficult to govern a society.

According to sources close to the Taliban, Mullah Rabbani, the head of the administration in Kabul, had agreed to the peace initiative offered by the U.S. officials. Included in this peace initiative is the issue of *Loya Jirga* and the participation of the former Afghan king Mohammed Zahir Shah. The hard-liner Taliban are against this peace initiative for Afghanistan, and they argue that a proper government for Afghanistan is the establishment of an Islamic *Khelafat*, run by an Islamic Amir. In this case the supreme leader of the Taliban, Mullah Mohammed Omar, would be the living Amir for Muslims in Afghanistan.

The third group among the Taliban are those who formed the organization called the Department for the Promotion of Virtue and Prevention of Vice, headed by Maulvi Kalamadin. Officially, this department should be a part of the administration and work under the supervision of the Justice Department, but as Maulvi Kalamadin said to a reporter, "we are an independent organization and we don't take advice from the Justice Ministry or the Supreme Court about what we should implement."[19] The goal of this organization is to implement *Shari'ah* law according to the organization's interpretation of the Islamic law. This organization has recruited hundreds of young students who attended religious schools in Pakistan and Afghanistan. These students are obligated to report all non-Muslim and un-Islamic personal and social behaviors that do not fit within the guidelines of the organization. The members of this organization are patrolling streets, government buildings, military stations, and residential areas to enforce the law.

Maulvi Kalamadin argued that the reason the Soviets invaded Afghanistan was the absence of *Shari'ah*, and he states, "we fought for Shari'ah and now this is the organization that will implement it."[20] So far, this organization has issued many different decrees, including that men should not shave their beards and women should not appear on the streets without a blood-shared relative. In a later decree by this organization, shops should not sell makeup, and women should not wear high-heeled shoes. In his interview with Ahmed Rashid, Kalmadin said: "Stylish dresses and decoration of women in the hospitals are forbidden. Women are duty-bound to behave with dignity, to walk calmly and refrain from hitting their shoes on the ground which makes noises."[21] These decrees, issued by the religious police, are increasing in numbers and have touched all aspects of public life under the control of the Taliban. For example, during sport tournaments, onlookers are not allowed to clap their hands. Instead they have shouted *Allah-o-akbar* (God is great), and both the audience and players must pray together at times during the games. The head of the Taliban religious police, Maulvi Kalamadin, argued that the Taliban will eventually allow girls to attend school and women to work. However, until there are separate transportation, school buildings, and government offices to prevent contact between genders in public, girls and women will stay home.

Politically, the religious police are closer to the hard-line Taliban under Mullah Mohammed Omar than to leaders like Mullah Abbas and Mullah Rabbani. These kinds of mentalities are also more obvious in the Justice Department. For example, Taliban Attorney General Maulwi Jalilullah Maulvizada states that the Taliban must follow the *Shari'ah* law and do not need a constitution, because *Shari'ah* is the only constitution.[22] To this end, many Muslim critics from around the world, including in Iran and Saudi Arabia, did not change the edicts issued by the Taliban conservative leaders. According to some reports, the radical edicts by the Taliban leaders in Afghanistan created a tense situation between them and the *Ulema* in *Darul Uloom Deoband*, the origin of the Taliban spiritual source. These *Ulema* believe that the Taliban have gone beyond the meaning of the spirit of Islamic teaching on women and other issues.[23] But the Taliban argued that the Deoband institute deals only with theoretical issues, and that they have never practiced *Shari'ah* in society. In basic principle they feel they are on the same path, but there may be some differences within the applications. At the same time, the Deoband chief mufti Mohammed Zafeeruddin has rejected the Taliban ban on flying kites and women wearing white socks.[24]

CHAPTER SEVENTEEN

AFGHANISTAN IN THE INTERNATIONAL SYSTEM

THE ADVANCE OF THE TALIBAN IN NORTHERN AFGHANISTAN AND THE control of Mazar-e-Sharif alarmed the region, particularly the neighboring countries. Central Asian countries worried about a boost in the Islamic extremism in their countries with the support of the Islamic government under the control of the Taliban. Years of the Soviet's religious, linguistic, and ethnic suppression in Central Asia kept the seeds of freedom, independence, and self-determination beneath the soil. The Soviet retreat from Afghanistan watered these seeds and provided an environment in which to grow. In these newly formed independent countries Communism had lost its attraction long ago, but the western liberalism was too wild and too foreign for the Central Asian nations. Thus, a third alternative was something other than Communism or liberalism. In such an environment, the Muslim activists, who politicized Islam long ago, inspired Central Asia and established access to the Afghan Mujahideen after the PDPA coup in 1978 and the Soviet invasion in 1979.

PAKISTAN'S POSITION BEFORE 1992

During the Soviet invasion of Afghanistan, Afghan Mujahideen groups, in particular the HIH, led by Hekmatyar, and the JIA, led by Burhanadin Rabbani, were the main supporters of the Islamic Resistance Party (IRP) in Tajikistan. Hundreds of Afghan Mujahideen became involved in a cross-border political armed operation in northern Afghanistan. On May 13, 1988, reports indicated that "there was wide circulation of audio cassettes, video films, etc. to spread radical Islam in Tajikistan. Works of Maududi, the founder of *Jamat-e-Islami*, Said Qutab, and *Jamal Din Afghani*, the noted Muslim revolutionary, were translated into Russian and printed at Peshawar and then smuggled across Afghanistan into Tajikistan for wide circulation."[1] Later, it became clear that the Afghan Mujahideen groups conducted their operations with the active guidance and assistance of Pakistan's ISI in Central Asian countries that bordered Afghanistan. In 1988, the Deputy Chairman of Tajikistan's KGB, Belousov, openly accused Pakistan ISI of carrying out a subversive program code-named M to destabilize the sociopolitical situation in Central Asia.[2]

After the collapse of the Soviet empire, Central Asia emerged as a vital market for the economic development of Pakistan, which was facing extreme economic shortages. Pakistan could sell its goods and services in this market, and would benefit by providing access to the Central Asian nations to the Indian Sea. This emergence changed Pakistan's strategy toward Afghanistan and the regional development. During the Cold War, Pakistan's strategy toward Afghanistan concentrated on the issue of Pushtonistan and its border conflict, the Durand Line. With the end of the Cold War, and the emergence of the new Central Asian states, Pakistan was among the first countries in the region to realize the importance of this new development. Therefore, the Pakistani leaders expanded their strategy beyond the border problems with Afghanistan and the issue of Pushtonistan. This expansion made the Pakistani leaders look for a long-term ally in Afghanistan.

Pakistan pursued its attempt to increase its political influence in Afghanistan, particularly regarding the process of establishment of a national government in the country. During the Soviet invasion and the existence of the PDPA regime, Pakistani leaders simply were following General Zia's ambitions when he politicized Islam for the creation of a massive political force in the region. The goal of this politicization was to create a pan-Islamic movement in the region, and General Zia wished to play the role of a heroic leader in such a regional movement. This role would be similar to that of Gamal Abdul Nasser in Egypt, through which he attempted to facilitate the Arab nationalism under the banner of pan-Arabism for the unification of the Arabs and the establishment of a greater Arab state. General Zia's doctrine was based on a religious interpretation of such a political movement in the region, and he desired to give Pakistan a leading status in this movement and use Afghanistan as the front line to support and arm the Islamic resistance in Central Asia against their Soviet-style governments.

General Zia's forward policy toward Afghanistan looked to solve the conflict over the Durand line and the issue of Pushtonistan through the establishment of a friendly government in Afghanistan that would be dedicated to the pan-Islamic movement in the region. In this case, the border issue and the ethnic environment would be stable under the banner of the Islamic brotherhood. The issues of nationalism and political independence would lose their meaning;

the solidarity of the Muslim brothers would be the main objective. Despite this strategy, General Zia and his circle in Pakistan were invested in *Hizb-e-Islami* led by Gulbadin Hekmatyar as the closest regional ally for the movement. This investment and alliance caused the Pakistan leaders to support a stronger role for Hekmatyar in the newly established government and greater domination of the HIH in Afghanistan. Pakistani leadership under General Zia not only insisted on avoiding the growth of those Afghan political movements not devoted to the pan-Islamic movement, they also rejected the existence of such political force on Pakistan soil. Pakistan government circles gave the green light to those Afghan activists who believed in the pan-Islamic movement to open fire on many Afghan popular politicians and scholars in Pakistan who were against pan-Islamism. This green light produced random mass kidnappings, mysterious disappearances, and assassinations against those Afghan politicians who did not leave Pakistan.

In Afghanistan, the emergence of the Mujahideen regional power under the political and military leadership of commanders such as Ahmed Shah Massoud, Ismail Khan, Maulawi Haqhani, Haji Abdul Ghadir, and Abdul Haqh was an event the Pakistani leaders had not anticipated. These regional military and political leaders ran their affairs independently; they did not operate under the direct control of the external front of the Mujahideen. These Mujahideen commanders (internal front leaders) did not follow the pan-Islamic doctrine led by General Zia and his Afghan allies, but they embraced many Afghan political activists who were under the pressure of the pro–pan-Islamic parties, both in Afghanistan and Pakistan. The emergence of the Mujahideen internal front leaders challenged General Zia's forward policy and the pan-Islamic doctrine in Afghanistan.

THE PAKISTAN POSITION AFTER 1992

After the Soviet withdrawal from Afghanistan, which was followed by the disintegration of the Soviet empire and the emergence of the newly independent Central Asian nations, the Pakistan leaders noticed that pushing the pan-Islamic doctrine through armed struggles against the Soviet aggression in Central Asia was not viable anymore. Instead, they recognized Central Asia as a vital economic market for Pakistan and changed their approach toward these new countries. Pakistan started to conduct new diplomatic relations and looked forward to having access to this market with full power. Also, it defined Afghanistan as a supporting base for its conflict against India. This new approach toward Central Asia changed the nature of the Pakistan policy from an armed struggle into a market-oriented one. Pakistan leaders knew that reaching Central Asia without Afghanistan was impossible; therefore, the establishment of a friendly and trustworthy government in Afghanistan became one of the most crucial tasks for Pakistan. This was one of the most important reasons

Pakistan leaders rejected a joint government comprised of the *Hezb-e-Watan* (led by Najibullah) and the Mujahideen Parties.[3] In this regard, a larger influence in the Afghanistan government would be more fruitful for Pakistan, and a government comprised of *Hezb-e-Watan* and Afghan Mujahideen with the significant influence of the Mujahideen internal front leaders could result in an independent Afghanistan. An independent Afghanistan with a sophisticated army, dominated by those political and military leaders who were not committed to Pakistan pan-Islamism, would be considered a serious threat. Such a government could cut off Pakistan from Central Asia in the event of conflicts. Or, at a time of conflict with India over Kashmir, Afghanistan may join India. Therefore, the Pakistani leaders attempted to use all their diplomatic, political, and military forces to reject Najibullah's government and also prevent Mujahideen internal and external front leaders from opening a dialogue with Najibullah.

After the fall of Najibullah's government, and the establishment of the Islamic State of Afghanistan (ISA), Pakistan's pro–pan-Islamic leaders, in particular in the ISI, attempted to expand their influence in the ISA by supporting Hekmatyar against the Afghan government led by Sibqhatullah Mujaddidi, and later by Burhanadin Rabbani. The main factor for supporting Hekmatyar against the ISA was the influence of ex–Watan Party political and military forces, in particular forces led by General Dostam, and also the Mujahideen-led forces by internal front leaders, such as Massoud, Ismail Khan, and the Nanagarhar military and political leaderships. If these forces formed a central government and a united national army, it would be almost impossible for Pakistan to influence Afghanistan. In this kind of development, Pakistan would not only face the reality of a strong, united, and independent Afghanistan, it might be restless from the issue of Pushtonistan and the border conflict with Afghanistan.

Since the Soviet/PDPA alliance from 1978 to 1988, Pakistan alliance with the Taliban has formed the most powerful external influence in Afghanistan. Even though the Pakistani/Taliban alliance has much deeper and broader elements in comparison to those of the Soviet/PDPA, in the eyes of the Afghans, the legitimacy of such an alliance is almost the same as the previous. The deep and broad connection between the Taliban and the different government ministries and the civilian local communities created an ever-increasing impact in the social and political behavior of many Pakistanis. The Taliban enforcement of *Shari'ah* in Afghanistan became an exemplary model of governing for many Pakistanis who were suffering from years of corruption and mischief on the part of government. This situation caused the emergence of *Tahrik-e-Taliban* (the Taliban movement) in Pakistan. In this regard the Talibanization of Pakistan and the rise of Islamic fanaticism has become an obvious phenomena.

Pakistani involvement in Afghanistan has created a severe pressure on the economic system of the country. The emergence of the Golden Crescent as the second largest opium producer in the world has caused the formation of the internationally organized drug trafficking and crime syndicates. The smuggling mafia under the Transit Treaty between Afghanistan and Pakistan (TTA) has created massive cross-border operations. These operations were conducted every day under the watchful eyes of the local and national authorities in both countries. Both the Golden Crescent and the smuggling mafia have created a multi-billion dollar industry in the region that has financed the war in Afghanistan and also is destroying the Pakistani infant industries massively. The destruction of Pakistani infant industries makes Pakistan fall behind in the industrial development, economic growth, and social progresses. Indeed, Pakistan's long-term involvement in Afghanistan would weaken its economic and political stability and also jeopardizes its regional security.

IRAN'S POSITION

After the Soviet invasion, the Islamic Republic of Iran (IRI) became a home for around 2 million Afghan refugees as well as a support base for the Afghan Mujahideen, particularly the Shia groups. During the Soviet's campaign in Afghanistan, Iran provided the Shia groups, mostly Hazaras, with limited military and financial aid. The hostile relations between Iran and the United States prevented western aid from being sent to the Afghan Shia Mujahideen groups, even though there were popular Afghan Shia groups who rejected Iran's interfering in the affairs of Mujahideen (although because of this they were under severe pressure from Iran). While the main objective of Iranian involvement in Afghanistan was to contain the Soviet threats from its border, most of the Iranian energies were wasted in the process of influencing the Shia Mujahideen leadership in accordance with the Iranian regional and theological agendas.

After the PDPA coup (1978) and the Soviet invasion (1979), the Iranian Revolutionary Guard controlled Afghan Mujahideen affairs. This involvement influenced the younger Shias, mostly Hazaras, causing a serious gap between the traditional and popular Shia Mujahideen leaders and these younger revolutionaries who attended religious schools in Iran. The Iranian Revolutionary Guard and the clergy leaders supported these younger leaders who fit with the Iranian regional policies and also followed a similar ideological doctrine. This interfering in the affairs of the Mujahideen caused massive fighting between the traditional and the revolutionary Shia leaders of Mujahideen. Above all, the long years of fighting between the pro-Iranian *Sazeman-e-Nassr* (SN) and the traditional group of *Shora-e-Islami Etefaq-e-Inghalab Afghanistan* (SIEIA), led by Ayatollah Bahishty, had cost thousands of lives. In all of these clashes, the Iranian clergies and the Revolutionary Guard supported the SN. This Iranian interference led to the fragmentation of the Shia Mujahideen groups that were supported by Iranian circles as the principle of divide and rule. In addition, Iran also supported the Afghan hard-liner Mujahideen known as the *Ikhwanis*, such as Hekmatyar and those in the *Jamaiat Islami Rabbani*.

Over time, in addition to the Revolutionary Guard, other government agencies such as *Etelaat*, the security service *Bunyad*, and the *Wazarat-e-Keshwar*, ministry of interior, were involved in the affairs of Afghan Mujahideen. Each of these agencies attempted to push their agendas in Afghanistan while getting credit at home. Later, the Iranian government became sensitive to the U.S. and Saudi influence among the Pakistani-based Afghan Mujahideen groups. Thus, after the withdrawal of the Soviets from Afghanistan in 1988, Iran moved toward normalization of relations with the Najibullah regime in Kabul. Since then, the IRI supported the idea of a united position of the Shia groups and encouraged these divided factions to form a united organizational structure that was later called *Hezb-e-Wahdat*. The main reason for this shift of policy was the Iranian desire to protest the U.S. and Saudi influence in the coming Mujahideen government in Afghanistan. The IRI recognized the Islamic state formed by Afghan Mujahideen leaders and later supported the Rabbani-led government. IRI support for the Rabbani government intensified after the Taliban captured Herat in 1995.

Pakistani alliance and Saudi recognition and financial support of the Taliban in Afghanistan forced the IRI regime to aid the anti-Taliban alliance. The fall of Mazar and the execution of the Iranian diplomats by the Taliban fighters intensified the level of hostilities between the two governments. IRI deployed 200,000 of the Revolutionary Guard forces on the Afghan borders to invade Afghanistan if necessary. The moderate Iranian leader, Sayd Mohammed Khatami, and their pragmatic approach toward Afghanistan had prevented the troops from crossing the border. The UN activities led by Lakhadar Brahimi reduced the tension and the Taliban leader agreed to release the Iranian truck drivers who were captured in Mazar as well as send the bodies of the executed diplomats to Iran. In May 1999, President Khatami visited Saudi Arabia after almost 30 years of diplomatic confrontation between the two countries. Khatami assured Saudi Arabia that there was no threat to the Saudi security in the region. In regard to the United States, Khatami was for a dialogue between the civilizations.

In the region, Iran competed with the Pakistani influence in Central Asia, in particular over the pipeline projects. Iran lobbied the Clinton administration to give the green light to the international financial institution and the oil companies to run the Caspian oil and natural gas through Iran to the Persian Gulf as well as to Pakistan. The war in Afghanistan and the emergence of the Golden Crescent created massive smuggling of weapons and narcotics problems. The IRI invests billion of dollars each year fighting drugs and smuggling from Afghanistan and Pakistan. The cross-border smuggling into the Iranian soil increased not only the high numbers of addicted individuals but also caused drug-related crimes and corruption. The Iranian moderate leaders endeavored to normalize their relations with western countries. To this end, Khatami visited Germany in June 2000 to expand diplomatic and economic cooperation between his country and the European Union. Iran views the Afghanistan crisis as an issue that they can use to bargain with the United States and other regional countries.

In June 1998 U.S. Secretary of State Madeleine Albright told the Asian Society in New York that the critical role that Iran plays in the region makes the question of Iran-U.S. relations a topic of great interest and importance. Iran has the desire to play its role as an important regional power, and from this perspective, Iranian leaders support the anti-Taliban forces in Afghanistan.

SAUDI ARABIA'S POSITION

Among the Islamic countries, Saudi Arabia was the strongest supporter of the Afghan Mujahideen against the Soviets during the 1980s. Saudi Arabia's official and unofficial financial support for the Afghan Mujahideen helped to facilitate the war against the Soviets and the PDPA regime. It was Saudi Arabia's funding in combination with the U.S. financial aid that financed the Afghan Mujahideen group's struggle as well as provided a needed balance against the Soviet's funds for the war. In 1980, the Saudis agreed to match the U.S. funding to the Afghan Mujahideen dollar for dollar. As Samuel P. Huntington states:

> Between 1984 and 1986 the Saudis gave $525 million to the resistance, in 1989 they agreed to supply 61 percent of a total of $715 million, or $436 million, with the remainder coming from the United States. In 1993 they provided $193 million to the Afghan government. The total amount they contributed during the course of the war was at least as much as and probably more than the $3 billion to $3.3 billion spent by the United States.[4]

How much of these massive funds reached the Afghan field commanders who were the main force responsible for the defeat of the Soviet military campaign in Afghanistan is still unclear. Generally, these funds went to the ISI accounts and were distributed to the Peshawar-based Afghan Mujahideen political party accounts. This distribution was determined according to the level of alliances of a political leader with ISI.

In March 1990, the ISI convinced Saudi Arabia's chief of intelligence, Prince Turki Al Faisal, to back a military operation against Najibullah. This military operation was a combination of the coup by Shahnawaz Tanai from the inside and forces led by Gulbadin Hekmatyar from the outside. Saudi Arabia provided Hekmatyar with $100 million, but despite this, the coup failed and Tanai escaped to Pakistan.

During the Gulf War from 1990 to 1991, with Operation Desert Shield and later Desert Storm by the U.S.-led forces against Saddam Hussein taking place, the Afghan *Ikhwanis* including Hekmatyar stayed on the side of Saddam Hussein.[5] Years of Saudi political influences and billions of dollars of investment in Afghanistan evaporated in a short period of time. Moreover, the Afghan *Ikhwanis* supported or sympathized with the Saudi Arabian dissident,

Osama bin Laden. Then in 1992, Saudi Arabia's closest political leaders in Afghanistan, Abdul Rab-e-Rassul Sayaf and Gulbadin Hekmatyar, fell into a political and military hostile confrontation. Hekmatyar allied with the *Hezb-e-Wahdat* and Sayaf supported the Rabbani/Massoud forces. From the Saudi perspective, Wahdat was considered a pro-Iranian political party; therefore, its alliance with Hekmatyar was against Saudi Arabia's regional interest. In other words, Hekmatyar's and Sayaf's followers used the Saudi money to kill each other on the streets of Kabul, which benefited Saudi Arabia's regional rival Iran.

In 1994 and 1995, the JUIP leader lobbied successfully to convince Prince Turki to support the Taliban, resulting in the hunting expedition of Saudi princes to Qandahar. Later, Saudi Arabia provided financial aid, transportation, and fuel to the Taliban advance toward Kabul, and Prince Turki was among the first prominent statesmen that congratulated the Taliban in Kabul in 1996. In Saudi Arabia, the Wahabbi Ulema community (which is forming the most influential political group in the Kingdom's foreign policy) was introduced to the Taliban leaders by Mawlana Fazl-ul-Rahman. As a result Grand Mufti (*Mufti-e-Aazam*) Sheikh Abdul Aziz Bin Baz, the chairperson of the senior Council of Ulema, along with other influential members of the council such as Minister of Justice Sheikh Mohammed bin Jaber, supported the Taliban. This support influenced the government structure of the Taliban that resulted in the establishment of the department of the Prevention of Vice and the Protection of Virtue in the Taliban administration. This type of organization in the government was considered by the Saudi *ulema* in conjunction with the Wahabbi principles. Another source of support for the Taliban was the Saudi Delta Oil company, which was holding about 80 percent of the shares with UNOCAL in the pipeline projects in Afghanistan. The combination of such a support system within and outside of the Saudi government was very important for the Taliban to finance their massive and costly military campaign against the United Front forces in Afghanistan.

In 1998, the Taliban and Saudi relations became murky over the anti-Saudi activities of Osama bin Laden in Afghanistan. Bin Laden was accused of bombing the U.S. embassies in Kenya and Tanzania, which killed Americans as well as other nationals. Saudi Arabia's request for the deportment of bin Laden was rejected by the Taliban supreme leader Mullah Mohammed Omar. The Taliban leader supported bin Laden's call for the U.S. withdrawal from the Saudi soil and declared him a guest of the Afghan people. The Taliban leader argued that handing bin Laden, a guest, over to the Americans was against Afghan tradition. This position created tensions between the Saudis and the Taliban, and it also caused personal insult to Prince Turki by the Taliban leader Mullah Omar. Since then, the Saudi leaders have stopped their support for the Taliban, and this has caused further isolation of the Islamic Emirate among the world community.

THE CENTRAL ASIAN REPUBLICS' (CAR'S) POSITIONS

After the collapse of Najibullah's regime the Central Asian states were worried about the formation of a radical Islamic state in Afghanistan. Most of the government leaders in these countries were searching for a way to avoid the exports of Islamic fanaticism into their territories. On November 4, 1992, in a meeting of the Central Asian leaders, Russian Foreign Minister A. Kozyrov agreed that the Russian 201st Motor Rifle Division should remain in Tajikistan to patrol the border with Afghanistan. On July 13, 1993, the Commonwealth of Independent States (CIS) led by Russia were shocked by a Tajik rebel attack that killed 25 Russian soldiers. This border incident caused the Russians to reinforce their troops on the Afghan border in Tajikistan, and President Yeltsin described the Tajik-Afghan border as "the frontier of Russia."[6] The situation in Afghanistan created a wave of Islamic fundamentalism and aggressive armed political movement to flow from the south (Afghanistan) toward the north (Russia). These waves of armed political movement forced Russia to reappear in Central Asia, and made the statesmen of these countries more open to this reappearance.

Afghanistan could provide the CAR a short and affordable land connection to the outside world. The CAR desired to export their natural resources to the south and southeast Asian market, but the war in Afghanistan became a destructive barrier. Among the CAR, Uzbekistan is a major player in the region, and the Uzbek leaders supported the forces led by General Dostam against the Taliban. Uzbek President Karimov addressed his people in a TV speech:

> He [Dostam] defends a very important sector which in essence defends the north of Afghanistan from the arrival of the Taliban. If we really want to prevent a further escalation of the war, if we want the war currently under way to end, for the parties to the conflict to sit down at the negotiating table including the Taliban, then we must do everything possible so that Mr. Dostam can hold on to the Salang.[7]

Because Uzbekistan has been a major player in the region, this country also is under a more serious threat by the Islamic militant groups based in Farghana. The bomb explosions that shocked Tashkant in 1998 and killed several people was a serious alarm to President Islam Karimov.

The successful advance of the Taliban in northern Afghanistan and the total destruction of the Dostam stronghold made the CAR leaders very nervous. President Askar Akayev of Kyrgyzstan called an emergency meeting of the government ministers to take serious security measures in the Gorno-Bdakhshan region of Tajikistan. This strategic region that creates a buffer zone between Afghanistan and Kyrgyzstan was congested by the Tajik Islamic rebels for many years. As a result, 5,000 Russian troops were positioned in high alert on the southern border of Kyrgyzstan. Tokayev, Kazakhstan's foreign minister, called the CAR leaders for "an appropriate political measure."[8] Tajikistan President Rakhmanov expressed his "grave concern" over the border security. The Taliban success in northern Afghanistan might impact the situation in Tajikistan and reignite the bloody civil war in this country. Among the CAR leaders, President Niyazov did not expect any complication in relation to the Taliban victory, and he offered to be a peace broker in Afghanistan. He stated:

> Turkmenistan, in view of its internationally recognized neutral status, is completely ready to cooperate in the constructive efforts of the Afghan people, the international community and the UN in establishing peace and stability in the state as soon as possible.[9]

All these concerns took place after Afghanistan had been used as a training camp for the Central Asian Islamic militants groups. During civil war in Tajikistan, Afghanistan was the main supply route as well as training base for the Tajik rebels. The long and bloody civil war in Tajikistan was an important example for the CAR leaders to take all the necessary measures to prevent such a destructive war in their homelands. Later, the war in Chechnya, which many political circles in the CAR sympathized with, created a confused situation. The Taliban support of the Chechen rebels and the bin Laden connection with Al Khatab fighters developed into a tense situation in the region. These connections and support overshadowed the Chechen legitimate struggle for freedom and self-determination. The involvement of Afghanistan in Chechen affairs and the fear of the bin Laden connection gave an advantage to the Russian troops and perhaps allowed them to get away with brutalizing the Chechens in Grozny and other parts of Chechnya. This escalation of war in Chechnya and its connection to Afghanistan provoked the Russians to enforce their influence southward toward Afghanistan. As result the CAR slipped increasingly into the sphere of Russian interest in the region.

CHINA'S POSITION

China shares a border with Afghanistan on the northeast corner of the country. The China Xingjan populations, dominated with Turkics and Tajiks, have common language, history, and culture with those on the Afghan side of the border. China's confrontations with the former Soviet Union and its alliance with Pakistan directed its foreign policy to support the Afghan Mujahideen against the Soviet invasion. Chinese-made Kalashindovs and anti-air machine guns were very popular among the Afghan Mujahideen. When the Taliban captured Kabul, China attempted to have normal diplomatic and economic relations with the Taliban-controlled government. The Taliban sent a delegation to China to open economic and security relations. In February 1999, China and the Taliban signed an agreement on economic cooperation as well as the training of the Taliban military forces. The Chinese announced that they had agreed to start direct flights between Kabul and Urumchi.[10] Some observers argued that there was a possibility that China would develop its relations with the Taliban on the model it had applied in the case of Myanmar's military junta.

The Chinese cooperation with the Islamic Emirate became alarming with regard to the cross-border arms and drugs traffic. Xingjian/Shanghai became one of the important and popular routes for narcotic trafficking. Soon, many of the Uighur ethnic groups educated in Pakistan reached Afghanistan and joined other militant groups in the training camps. The members of the National Movement of Uighur Muslim and the Xingjian Liberation Front became active in Afghanistan. The Chinese government has accused these groups of several bombings, kidnappings, and attacks on the border guards. Several Uighurs from China were among those who were captured in 1999 by Ahmed Shah Massoud's forces.[11]

China's competition in the CAR has become more obvious than before, and the country has improved its relationship over economic cooperation and regional security. Since Soviet disintegration in 1991, Chinese-manufactured goods dominated the CAR markets, and this domination has increased while Russia suffers from an economic collapse. China is becoming a major player in the CAR, and its position encouraged the neighboring CAR countries, including Kazakhstan, Kyrgyzstan, and Tajikistan, along with Russia, to form a security pact. This security pact, known as Shanghai Five, allowed China to help the CAR members on security issues and also provided the CAR members with greater economic cooperation with China. Indeed, regional security is the main concern for China, and the activities of the Uighur militants and separatists under the Islamic Emirate of Afghanistan is in contrast to the Chinese national security.

RUSSIA'S POSITION

After the Soviet withdrawal from Afghanistan in 1988 and the collapse of the Najibullah regime in Kabul in 1992, Russian foreign policy toward Afghanistan has experienced a lull and a confused moment. This lull was the direct result of post-Soviet internal and regional problems in Russia as well as their embarrassment and traumatic defeat in Afghanistan. Afghanistan contributed greatly in the disintegration of the Soviet empire while the Soviets also contributed massively to the destruction of the political, social, economic, and cultural systems in Afghanistan. Such long-term destruction has become the underlying factors of the post-Soviet civil war and the continuation of external interfering in Afghanistan.

Among the regional member states, Russia has benefited mostly from the continuation of civil war and the absence of law and order in Afghanistan. The Soviet invasion of Afghanistan that was considered a national trauma for the people of Afghanistan created a negative notion among Afghans as well as other nations about the Soviet leaders. Since Russians comprised the dominant force as well as the core political and military elite in the Soviet system, logically such a negative notion was directed toward Russia. In the eyes of Afghans, Russia was more responsible than any other member of the former Soviet Union for the grave human tragedy in their homeland. This kind of notion could and would find its way to the international courts to condemn Russia and seek compensation for the damages caused by the Soviet military forces in Afghanistan.

The Afghan civil war and the interfering of Pakistan and Iran in the factional fighting has created a smoky and diluted environment in which the destructive conduct of the Soviets/Russians during their military invasion has begun to disappear from the eyes of the public in Afghanistan. In the course of civil war, in particular after the formation of the Islamic State of Afghanistan, the high level of political violence and violent crimes against civilians made the Afghan public opinion sympathetic to the pro-Soviet leaders such as Najibullah.

In addition, the rise of Islamic fanatics in Afghanistan, rooted in a popular uprising against the communist coup and the Soviet invasion, was considered an Islamic threat by the Russian leaders.[12] This has become a catalyst for Russia's internal and foreign policies. Russian leaders attempted to exaggerate the Islamic threat against their southern borders and provoke public opinion to gain popular support for the government policies. This exaggeration helped the federal troops invade Chechnya in 1994 and 1995, which ended disastrously for Russia.[13] Russian leaders endeavored to depress the sentiments of autonomy and self-determination among the non-Russian ethnic groups, in particular in the southern republics. For this reason, Russian leaders condemned the Chechens' call for self-determination and attempted to suppress it in a Soviet style.

After the capture of Kabul by the Taliban, Russian leaders became very serious about the new developments in Afghanistan. Russian Prime Minister Viktor Chernomyrdin arrived in Almaty for a meeting with CAR presidents on October 4, 1996. The Almaty conference resulted in the formation of common objectives toward the Taliban victory in Afghanistan:

> The Flame of war is approaching the borders of the CIS states, and this creates a direct threat to the national interests and security of these states and of the CIS in general and destabilizes the regional and international situation. We declare that any activity which undermines stability on the borders with Afghanistan is unacceptable. Such activity, no matter who is responsible for it, will be regarded as a threat to common interest and . . . will meet with an appropriate response.[14]

The Taliban takeover of Kabul and especially their advance toward northern Afghanistan caused the Russian's notion of Islamic threat to dominate Russian media. Along with this domination, the Russian leaders attempted to manipulate the situation. For example, President Yeltsin's security advisor, General Alexander Lebed, stated:

> Their [the Taliban] plans include making part of Uzbekistan including Bukhara, one of Islam's holy places, part of the Afghan state. They will join with detachments of the Tajik opposition leader, Sayid Noori. They share the same faith. They will then sweep away our border posts.[15]

At the same time, Lebed asked the Russian government to intervene decisively in Afghanistan and bail out Rabbani's regime. In most cases, this rhetoric was groundless and used to influence personal politics in Russia. There is no evidence that the Taliban claimed the takeover of Bukahra or other parts of the CAR territories. In all of their official statements, the Taliban talked about the reunification of Afghanistan under their Islamic Emirate. As the Taliban announced their official position: "The Islamic Emirate of Afghanistan wants the establishment of friendly relations with all countries in the world, especially the neighboring and regional countries, on the basis of accepted international principles, peaceful coexistence and non-interference in the internal affairs of other countries."[16] But, the Russian approach toward the Afghan Taliban issue continued in the mass media. On October 1, 1996, a *Rassiskaia Gazeta* editorial stated:

> Faced with this threat, the presidents of former Soviet Central Asia, observers believe, could unite around Moscow. But it could be that something else will happen: for example, a successful northward advance by the Taliban. Then it would become difficult to hold the Tajik border on the river Pyandzh [Panj], and at worst we might have to quit the Central Asian republics, which would mean the exodus of ten million Russian-speaking refugees from the region.[17]

It was clear that the Russian leaders were attempting to create a common ground with the CAR and reduce the gap between these republics and Moscow in a level close to the Soviet era. In this case, signing the Tashkent Collective Security Treaty (TCST) on May 15, 1992, can be viewed as a matter of reshaping Russia's historical influence in CAR. But, because of Russia's unrealistic and exaggerated notion of Islamic threat, the TCST treaty has weakened increasingly.

First, the notion of TCST seemed more suspicious to the CAR leaders, and this notion failed to convince the public opinion in these countries. Even though under the TCST the member states conducted a joint military exercise in the Trans-Volga Military District called Pamir coalition army group, they avoided direct involvement in Afghanistan. The secretary of Kazakhstan's National Security Council, Baltash Tursumbayev, called the Russian's rhetoric of the Islamic threat by the Taliban "haste and groundless."[18]

Second, because of the weakness of the Russian rhetoric, Russians themselves felt that under the TCST, they might get dragged into the local conflicts between the CAR members. In this case, Russia could lose the prestige it had achieved since 1992.

Third, Russian leaders noticed that under a collective security they would have an equal vote, and therefore they may not enjoy their strategic interests. Thus, they entered into a bilateral security agreement with each country, thereby weakening the foundation of the TCST. This new approach by Russian leaders sped up when Uzbek President Karimov opted out of the TCST to promote military integration within CAR through the Central Asian Union (CAU). Due to its regional interest, Tashkent rejected the presence of the Russian troops in Tajikistan, but at the same time, Uzbek leaders supported Moscow's struggle against the Islamic fanatics.

Fourth, the downfall of economic conditions in Russia, and its severe impact on the CAR, had increasingly weakened the TCST proposed agenda more than before. Economic deterioration, due to the economic dependency of the CAR economy on the Russian market, became very obvious. This deteriorated situation weakened Russia's ability to maintain its influence in Central Asia and the Caucasus. In October 1997, Georgia, Azerbaijan, Ukraine, and Moldova (GAUM) formed an economic grouping that later moved into a security formation. Uzbekistan has also shown interest in sending its troops to be a part of the GAUM contingent.

Finally, the TCST failed to sort out the local conflicts between the member states. In this case, Russia, the most powerful and influential member of the TCST, not only failed to intervene positively in the dispute between the member states, it has also created a suspicious environment as well.

In reality Russia's main objective was containing the North Atlantic Treaty Organization (NATO). The Russians were very upset by NATO's eastward expansion, and they mounted pressure on Azerbaijan and Georgia to ward off NATO:

> Meanwhile, Moscow is jealously protecting its influence in Armenia, its crucial Trans-Caucasian ally that has recently indicated its desire to keep a balance between relations with Russia and the West. This trend is likely to continue, especially as Moscow's very actions make Baku and Tbilisi ever more desperate for NATO support. Earlier this month [in early 1999], Azerbaijan requested the status as an "aspirant country" to the Atlantic Alliance while President Shevardnadze explicitly declared Georgia's aspiration to NATO membership within five years.[19]

Russia had difficulties convincing the CAR leaders to support their policy against NATO. Above all, Uzbekistan refused openly to support Russia's view on NATO's eastward expansion; instead, Tashkent referred to Russia as imperialistic.

In 1994, the recognition of the Caspian region as one of the richest natural resources in the world attracted the attention of the international oil companies.

The Caspian region is the center of the last great oil rush of the twentieth century, where some 200 billion bbl., or 10 percent of the earth's potential oil reserves, which at today's prices would cost up to U.S. $4 trillion, are located. Among all of the Central Asian countries, Turkmenistan has the fourth largest natural gas reserve in the world. The proposed pipeline would connect the Caspian Sea, Western Siberia, and Kazakhstan to Pakistan, India, and the Asian Pacific countries. The existing pipelines that connect the Central Asian oil to the Novoressisk Russian port on the Black Sea do not have the capacity to carry increased oil production in the region. The United States attempted to avoid Russia's influence over the transportation of the Caspian's natural gas and oil and for this reason supported the construction of underwater pipelines. Such pipelines would connect Turkmenistan to Azerbaijan and Georgia and Turkey to the Mediterranean port of Ceyhan.

After Vladimir Putin was elected president of Russia, the federal troops crashed the Chechen fighters and pushed them into the southern mountains. Putin rallied forces around him as a popular president who wanted to gain back the Russian prestige. A large number of Russian troops and a massive military presence in the northern Caucasus convinced many in Russia that security and order could be reestablished. This development convinced many of the CAR leaders that Russia could help them with their national security. As a result, the political position of the CAR shifted toward more cooperation with Moscow. In response to the economic situation particularly with the Caspian natural resources, President Putin visited Central Asian capitals where he was received respectfully. In the meantime, Russia launched a project called the Blue Stream Pipeline, owned by Russia's Gazprom and Italy's ENI Spa, to ship the Turkmen gas to Turkey.[20] Overall, the concern over the security and economic situation in the CAR reshaped the rivalry and competition between the United States and Russia, indicating the beginning of another Great Game in the twenty-first century.

Russia under Vladimir Putin was able to get closer to the Afghanistan border and get out from the lull of Russia's direct relations with Afghanistan. Russia along with the CAR (except Turkmenistan), Iran, and India reached a common agreement in support of the United Front led by Ahmed Shah Massoud. In a recent statement, Russian Foreign Minister Ivanov expressed the possibility of Russian air strikes in support of the terrorist camps in Afghanistan. He also stated that since Ahmed Shah Massoud is a member of the ousted government of Afghanistan, Russia may consider his request of support against the Taliban regime.

THE UNITED STATES'S POSITION

In 1980, the United States noticed that the struggle of the Afghan people against the Soviets was in the best interest of its regional engagement. Thus, the United States supported the Afghan Mujahideen groups financially as well as militarily, in particular providing the heat-seeking-anti-air missiles known as stingers. Even though the United States has been considered a friendly government by many Afghans, in particular during the Soviet invasion, the U.S. policy toward Afghanistan suffered deeply in the hands of inner agencies of the U.S. government. As a result, U.S. policies toward Afghanistan were faced with three strategic failures in the past 20 years.

First, during the Soviet invasion, the U.S. policy in Afghanistan was clear: to contain the Soviet threat against America's regional and national security. From the early stage of the Soviet invasion, the Carter and then the Reagan administrations assigned the Central Intelligence Agency (CIA) to support the anti-Soviet struggle in Afghanistan. It was the CIA that spent the $3 billion in U.S. aid toward warding off the Soviets in Afghanistan. The CIA under Robert Gates delegated the important task of U.S. decisions to General Zia-ul-Haq and his army circle, in particular with the ISI. The CIA neglected the fact that General Zia and the ISI might have interests that did not coincide with U.S. national security or the people of Afghanistan. For example, under the misleading of the ISI, the CIA considered Hekmatyar to be the most popular Afghan Mujahideen leader. According to Afghan sources, Hekmatyar was busy more with assassination plots against his political opponents and fighting Afghan Mujahideen groups than fighting the Soviets and the Communist regime in Afghanistan. After all, Hekmatyar supported Saddam Hussein during the Gulf War, and his party was associated with the Iran-Contra scandal at the local level. In addition, many of the Islamic fanatics from around the world were channeled via his party to Afghanistan, including those who were involved in the World Trade Center bombing in New York in 1993.[21]

Secondly, even though the Geneva Accord conditioned the withdrawal of the Soviet forces from Afghanistan on an imposed arms embargo to Afghanistan, the CIA continued supplying the Afghan Mujahideen groups who were fighting over the control of Kabul against the Najibullah regime. The ISI channeled most of these supplies of arms and ammunitions to Hekmatyar, who was preparing for a military victory in Kabul. The ISI misguided the CIA into receiving the green light from Washington for such a military victory. This collaboration of CIA with ISI undermined the genuine pattern of political dialogue established in Geneva for a peaceful settlement in Afghanistan. Hekmatyar and the ISI launched a massive military attack to open the way from Jalalabad to capture Kabul. This ill and misconceived military operation caused a large number of casualties, but the Najibullah regime still stood on its feet.

This failed military operation embarrassed the CIA for believing the ISI's misinterpreted analysis regarding the situation in Afghanistan. On the field, the efforts by the Afghan National Commander Council (NCC) toward the creation of a united force and cooperation at the national level were aborted. The aim of such a cooperation was to conduct organized military operations for the control of the cities controlled by the Kabul regime with minimum casualties.

At the same time, the UN-led political dialogue for a peaceful settlement disrupted by the ISI/Hekmatyar-led military operation had developed a confused environment full of suspicion among the armed political groups. In another development the ISI and Hekmatyar in cooperation with Khalqi General Shahnwaz Tani attempted a military coup against Najibullah in March 1990. This military coup caused a severe division along the ethnic lines in the Afghan armed forces. Later, this suspicious development dragged Afghanistan into a bloody civil war that weakened the Najibullah regime and caused the collapse of the state and the disintegration of the central government in Afghanistan.

After pouring $3 billion worth of arms into Afghanistan, the United States decided on a hands-off policy and walked away from Afghanistan when the Najibullah regime disintegrated in 1992. The U.S. policy gave its regional allies, Pakistan and Saudi Arabia, free hands in Afghanistan and made it seem that the democratic administration of President Clinton did not have a coherent policy toward Afghanistan, that Washington had lost direction in Afghanistan. Afghans were furious when the United States walked away and left them in the ruins of a war, in the middle of bloody civil strife.

During President Clinton's first term in the White House U.S. policy toward Afghanistan was very vague. In all his time in office as secretary of state, Warren Christopher never mentioned anything about the Washington policy on Afghanistan. Robin Raphel, undersecretary of state for Afghanistan, endeavored to gain the White House support for an arms embargo through the UN security council, but the White House did not have any political will for her proposal. In March 1996, Senator Hank Brown, with Raphel, held a Senate hearing on Afghanistan and coordinated a three day conference that was attended by the leaders of the Afghan armed factions. At the hearing, Raphel stated that Afghanistan has become a conduit for drugs, crime, and terrorism, and that extremist training camps in Afghanistan were exporting terrorism.[22] One of the prominent speakers in this hearing was Marty Miller, the UNOCAL vice president in charge of the proposed Afghan pipeline project. Yet none of these activities provoked a U.S. commitment toward Afghanistan, and heavy fighting escalated the political environment of Afghanistan.

Thirdly, in October 1994, Washington greeted the rise of Taliban in Afghanistan, and U.S. policy makers viewed the Taliban through their strategic interests: the Taliban would disarm the local armed groups and restore law and order; the Taliban would drive out the international terrorists from Afghanistan; they would end the production of opium and fight narcotic trafficking; they would unite the country and help form a nationally and internationally recognized government in the country; the Taliban would contain Iran and Russia's interests and provide an access route within the CAR to U.S. ally Pakistan; and the Taliban would pave the road toward a settlement with the participation of former King Mohammed Zahir Shah. In 1996, after the Taliban captured Kabul, there were talks of dispatching the U.S. embassy to

Kabul. In a press release, Nicholas Burns, the State Department spokesman, acknowledged that the United States had had contacts with the Taliban regularly in years past as well as in 2000. An editorial comment in the *New York Times* said that the Islamic fundamentalist movement that gained control over much of Afghanistan with its recent string of military victories had brought a measure of stability to the country for the first time in years. Zalmay Khalilzad, a former State Department official who had been in contact with Afghanistan, stated that the United States should actively assist the Taliban because even though it is fundamentalist, it does not practice the anti-U.S.-style fundamentalism of Iran. Others defined the Taliban movement as antimodern rather than anti-Western and said they are restoring traditional society rather than exporting Islam.

UNOCAL lobbied a long time in Washington for support of the Taliban and even recognition for their government in Afghanistan. This lobbying complimented the ISI's analyses to the CIA about the Taliban, that they were ready to capture the whole country. These developments forced the Clinton administration to shape its Central Asian policy and, to avoid Iran, his administration supported the construction of a pipeline via Turkey.[23] UNOCAL hired Robert Oakley and Delta hired Charles Santos, both former U.S. government officials at the time of the jihad in Afghanistan. At the same time, UNOCAL funded a $1.8 million training program for the Center for Afghanistan Studies at the University of Nebraska in Omaha. This program, headed by Thomas E. Gouttierre, established educational and training programs for the pipeline project.[24] In November 1997, a Taliban delegation headed by Mullah Mohammed Ghaus was greeted by UNOCAL representative Marty Miller in Houston. Later, the Taliban met with the State Department's officials and demanded U.S. recognition of the Islamic Emirate of Afghanistan.[25]

NEW SHIFT IN U.S.-AFGHAN POLICY

In the subsequent years, there were three major events that shifted U.S. policy toward Afghanistan from that of a passive stance with no direction toward a limited active and minimum direction. In 1998, fighting against international terrorism became a very sensitive area in the U.S. foreign policy. This sensitivity was the aftermath of wake-up explosions against the U.S. embassies in East Africa. In August 1998, two bomb blasts destroyed the U.S. embassies in Kenya and Tanzania and killed 220 people. These bombings were linked to Osama bin Laden, the Saudi dissident who lived in Afghanistan. President Clinton, facing impeachment due to his sex scandal with Monica Lewinsky, ordered a missile attack on Afghanistan. Seventy cruise missiles hit the training camps of *Al Badr* controlled by bin Laden and the *Khalid Ibn-e-Walid* and *Muawia* camps controlled by the Kashmirian group, *Harkat-ul-Ansar.* Three Yemenis, two Egyptians, one Saudi, one Turk, seven Pakistani, and close to thirty Afghans were killed. Afterwards, in November 1998, the United States offered a $5 million reward for Osama's capture. Bin Laden was enraged over the U.S. strike and he claimed to be seeking to acquire chemical and nuclear weapons to fight the United States. In an interview, bin Laden stated: "It would be sin for Muslims not to try to possess the weapons that would prevent infidels from inflicting harm on Muslims. Hostility towards America is a religious duty and we hope to be rewarded for it by God."[26]

The United States demanded bin Laden's extradition from the Islamic Emirate, but the Taliban rejected the demand. Through the 13129 Executive Order, the United States imposed a sanction on the area controlled by the Taliban in Afghanistan. As the Associated Press reported: "Mullah Mohammed Omar, promised never to hand over bin Laden to the US," and he stated "Even if the whole of Afghanistan is destroyed, we will never deliver Osama. . . . A Muslim can't deliver a Muslim to a non-Muslim."[27] In November 1999, the United Nations Security Council's 1267 resolution declared limited sanctions against the Taliban to press for bin Laden's extradition.

On May 17, 2000, President Clinton charged in a commencement address to the U.S. Coast Guard Academy that bin Laden was behind a bomb plot late in 1999 at millennium celebration sites in America. He emphasized his will to add an extra $300 million for counterterrorism programs like intercepting communications.[28] The activities of the transnational Islamic fanatic organization in Afghanistan drew U.S. attention. Washington became more serious about regional security and cross-border activities of the fanatic organizations. This development caused the United States to move away from the Taliban and make the Islamic Emirate more isolated in the international community.

The Taliban policies on women were interpreted by many Americans as cruel and inhumane. Since the United States claims that the expansion of democracy and the improvement of human rights are important to its foreign policy, the Taliban policy on women was at odds with this claim. In the wake of UNOCAL and Taliban interaction in 1998, the Feminist Majority launched a massive campaign for the rights of women under the Taliban rule and human rights abuses by the Islamic Emirate of Afghanistan. These activities were coordinated by a group of Afghan women led by Ziba Shoresh Shamley and the cooperation of the Revolutionary Women Association of Afghanistan (RWAA). RAWA is a grassroots women's organization and has been active mostly among the Afghan refugees in Pakistan. In September 1998, a grassroots activist group asked the California attorney general to dissolve UNOCAL for its crimes against humanity and the environment in connection to the Taliban in Afghanistan.

Ziba Shoresh's Afghan circle, with the support of the Feminist Majority, launched a petition, signature campaign to support Afghan women and pressure the Clinton administration for a tougher position against the Islamic Emirate of Afghanistan. Three hundred women's groups, trade unions, and human rights delegates signed the petition. In a further development, Mavis Leno, the wife of famous TV host Jay Leno, donated $100,000 toward the cause of Afghan women. Later, the Afghan women's issue was supported by some celebrities in Hollywood resulting in an honor for the plights of the Afghan women after the Oscars in 1999.[29] The condition of the Afghan women concerned the American public opinion and caught the attention of top politicians. In a speech in 1999, Hillary Clinton condemned the Taliban's policies on women. On October 10, 1999, Secretary of State Albright also condemned the Taliban policies on women while she was talking to the U.S. governors in California. She said:

> The only female rights the Taliban appeared to recognize were the rights to remain silent and uneducated, unheard and unemployed. We [the United States] are speaking up on behalf of the women and girls of Afghanistan, who have been victimized by all factions in their country's bitter civil war. The most powerful of those factions, the Taliban, seems determined to drag Afghan women back from the dawn of the 21st century to somewhere close to the 13th. There are those who suggest that all this is cultural and there is nothing we can do about it, I say it is criminal and we each have a responsibility to stop it.[30]

As a result of the U.S. sanction and the pressure by the Feminist Majority, UNOCAL stopped its project in Afghanistan and finally gave an official statement: "UNOCAL will not conduct business with any party in Afghanistan until peace is achieved and a government recognized by international lending agencies is in place. We have neither signed nor negotiated any business deals with any faction within Afghanistan."[31] According to the Center for Afghanistan Study at Nebraska University, UNOCAL also stopped funding programs to train young Afghans to work in the construction of the pipelines via this center in Kandahar, Afghanistan.

Central Asia and the Caucasus have emerged as the Great Game of the twenty-first century between the United States and Russia. Because of the geopolitical position of Afghanistan, there are logical connections between U.S. Afghan policies and those of Central Asia. The regional security and the Caspian oil and gas have provoked U.S. attention to this region. The American oil companies' involvement in the extraction and export of oil and gas formed strong and wealthy lobbying crowds in Washington.

The United States defined the areas of Central Asia and the Caucasus as a zone of American responsibility. The United States has already brought the CAR into its Central Command (Centcom) responsibility. The United States also has signed a defense treaty with Kazakhstan, as well as with Georgia in 1998 that covers U.S. air and marine defense. The U.S. Sixth Fleet flagship visited the Georgian port of Poti in September 1998. It is expected that the Sixth Fleet could penetrate the Caspian Sea.[32] After all, the United States defined the current situation in Afghanistan as a threat to regional security and stability. A senior official of the National Security Council of the United States said: "It's a lethal cocktail of drugs, weapons, Islamic militancy and terrorism [that] is spreading across the region from Afghanistan."[33] It seems as if the United States does not have any other choice than to add Afghanistan into its zone of responsibility and become engaged in Afghanistan.

On July 20, 2000, testimony was heard in the U.S. Senate Foreign Relations Committee. Those that testified included: Karl F. Inderfurth, undersecretary for Afghanistan; Peter Thomsen, former ambassador and special envoy to the Afghanistan Resistance; Ziba Shoresh Shamley, an Afghan women's activist; and Hamid Karzai, the representative of the former Afghan King Mohammed Zahir. In his testimony Karl Inderfurth stated that Afghanistan has become a gateway country, a gateway for some of the worst evils of drugs and violence that daily pass through it en route to other parts of the globe. He rejected the Taliban commitment to a military solution for Afghanistan, and he condemned the human rights abuses in Afghanistan. Inderfurth also emphasized that the Security Council should take more serious steps against the Taliban, including an arms embargo against the Islamic Emirate.[34]

THE PEACE EFFORTS FOR AFGHANISTAN

On October 4, 1997, Uzbekistan introduced a peace proposal for Afghanistan and through this proposal Uzbek Foreign Minister Kamilov addressed the establishment of a contact group comprised of the Afghanistan neighboring states and the Afghan warring factions.[35] In December 1997, Iran conducted a conference to approach a peace negotiation among Afghan factions. During the three-day meeting that many Afghans attended in the city of Isfahan, Iranian Foreign Minister Kamal Kharazi stressed the support of his government for the formation of a coalition government in Afghanistan.[36] Taliban leaders boycotted this conference and have not changed their military and political agendas for the establishment of a government under their leadership. In March 1998, the United Nations started to push a peace settlement in Afghanistan, and in a common approach, the United States and China agreed to ending the Afghan conflict "that involved bringing pressure on rival factions to stop fighting and negotiate peace."[37] This common approach among the international community involved the United States directly in Afghanistan affairs after three decades of war. On April 17, 1998, Washington's representative to the United Nations, Bill Richardson, and Bruce Riedel, Clinton's special assistant, visited Afghanistan. This delegation held talks with Taliban leaders in Kabul and northern alliances in Shabarghan. The warring factions agreed to direct negotiation, a cease-fire, and the release of prisoners of war.[38]

Both sides of the civil war in Afghanistan agreed with the U.S. delegation to establish a steering committee comprised of five Taliban members and nine

Northern Alliance representatives to meet face-to-face in Pakistan.[39] Later, the Taliban insisted on establishing a committee comprised of 20 representatives from each side, and these members were to be only *ulema*, full-time Islamic scholars.[40] The Northern Alliance argued that anyone who is well versed in Islam, including the politicians, should participate in the steering committee. Even though there were many different views on the mechanics of the peace process in the country between the two sides, both the Taliban and the Northern Alliance agreed on several important grounds including a cease-fire, the release of prisoners of war, and direct negotiation. Particularly, these three crucial steps were helping to bring peace to the country. Therefore, the Northern Alliance proposed a three-step forward policy toward peace: "A permanent cease-fire, exchange of prisoners of war, and the opening of trade routes across the war zone."[41]

The peace process created a gap between the Taliban leaders; part of the Kabul-based leaders agreed with the peace process as it continued, but another part of the leadership under Mullah Mohammed Omar rejected the peace process and insisted on a military solution against their opponents in the country.[42] This political gap between the Taliban leaders caused the Taliban representatives (who went to Afghanistan to discuss the Northern Alliance's three-step proposal with their leaders) to not return to the meeting in Pakistan. The next day, Taliban forces attacked the province of Takhar that was controlled by the opposition, and this negative attitude of the Taliban's extreme leaders aborted the spectacular momentum that had been generated for a peaceful settlement.

One of the most significant initiatives of the track-one effort for conflict resolution in Afghanistan was the formation of the Six Plus Two conference in Tashkent, Uzbekistan, during the third week of July 1999. Afghanistan's six neighboring countries—China, Iran, Pakistan, Tajikistan, Turkmenistan, and Uzbekistan—with the participation of Russia and the United States and the active engagement of the United Nations, participated in the Tashkent conference. The Taliban and United Front delegations participated in the conference and met one another as well. Members who attended the Six Plus Two conference discussed a variety of different issues and agreed to stop any military aid to the warring factions as a helpful strategy for the establishment of a broad-based fully representative government in Afghanistan. They also expressed their concerns about the threat of narcotic trafficking as well as the dangers of the rise of fanaticism in the region:

> We express the profound concern of our Governments at the continuing military confrontation in Afghanistan, which is posing a serious and growing threat to regional and international peace and security. We remain committed to a peaceful political settlement of the Afghan conflict, in accordance with relevant provisions of resolutions and decisions of the General Assembly and

the Security Council of the United Nations, and we, in particular, recall the "talking points" and the "points of common understanding," adopted earlier by the countries of the "Six plus Two" group.[43]

Along with the Six Plus Two members, the Taliban and the United Front representatives also discussed the possibilities for an immediate cease-fire and the restoration of peace in Afghanistan.

Many observers including the majority of people in Afghanistan thought the misery of war and destruction was going to end. The Afghan civilian communities inside the country and millions suffering from the humiliation of being refugees in other countries were crying for a peaceful Afghanistan. But, what came from the conference was another multilateral agreement without any enforcement. The irony during the Tashkent conference was that while the Six Plus Two members were signing agreements and rejecting any military solution for the restoration of peace in Afghanistan, both the Taliban and United Front, with the support of their patrons, were preparing for the summer offensives. After the conference ended, Lakhdar Brahimi, special envoy of the United Nations secretary general for Afghanistan, visited Afghanistan and other countries to report the results of the Tashkent conference. Before Brahimi's arrival back to the United Nations, the seasonal fighting between the warring factions started in several fronts. After all, one point of the Tashkent agreement, implemented by warring factions, was an agreement not to block foreign humanitarian aid from reaching each other's territory.[44]

In the last 12 years there has been a continuous effort by Afghans to bring peace and security to their homeland. In 1994, when the central administration was fragmented, Ismail Khan, the famous Afghan Mujahideen chief commander, demilitarized the province of Herat and expanded his peaceful alternative to the north and south of the province. In 1994, Ismail Khan announced a peace conference that he had invited Afghan political leaders and prominent individuals from inside and outside of the country to attend. He sent an Afghan airbus to Europe to transport a large number of Afghans from the United States and Europe to the conference in Herat. Among the prominent Afghans at the conference included Mohammed Yosuff, a former prime minister and distinguished Afghan politician. The conference appointed several working committees to promote cooperation among Afghans for a peaceful settlement.

Even though the attendants of the conference were able to limit the manipulation of *Jamaiat-e-Islami* led by Burhanadin Rabbani, the conference did not include representatives of all warring factions. At the regional and international levels, the conference did not gain the political will of the international community. Soon after, the escalation of war between Gulbadin Hekmatyar and *Hezb-e-Wahdat*-led forces and the government troops around Kabul, as well as the military clashes between General Dostam's forces and those of Ismail Khan, disrupted the outcome of the conference. The rise of the Taliban movement in 1994, their successful military campaign toward Kabul, and the fall of Herat in the summer of 1995 ended the peace-building process inside the country.

Since 1996, Afghan's peace building efforts shifted abroad, mostly in Western Europe and North America. In 1998, Afghans formed a conference in Bonn, Germany. Many prominent Afghan politicians, professionals, and scholars attended, and the conference formed contact committees and planned future sessions. The contact committees of the Bonn conference attracted the attention of many Afghans abroad by forming continuous gatherings. All of these activities encouraged the participation of Afghan's former King Mohammed Zahir, who has lived in exile in Italy since 1973.

In December 1999, the king called for a significant gathering in Rome of prominent Afghans from outside and inside the country. The Rome conference formed several contact committees and sent delegations to Iran, Pakistan, the United States, and European countries. The Rome conference received the support of the United Nations and other countries around the globe. James P. Rubin of the U.S. State Department stated: "The United States welcomes efforts by Afghans, including those undertaken by the former king and other moderates, to bring peace to their country."[45] For the first time, the warring factions, mostly the Islamic United Front for Liberation of Afghanistan (UIFLA), supported the Rome conference, but the Taliban administration rejected the initiative. In July 2000, the former king's delegates traveled to Pakistan where they were met with encouragement by Pakistan foreign minister Abdul Satar. Later, the delegates, headed by Karzai, traveled to Qandahar to meet the Taliban leader and talk about the king's peace initiative. The Taliban argued that due to the current condition in Afghanistan the king's initiative was not practical in Afghanistan. They insisted on their military campaign against the UIFLA led by Ahmed Shah Massoud.[46] The Rome conference was one of the most significant events in the peace-building process, but it did not have the muscle required to create a drastic impact on the warring factions. Like many other activities of the Afghans abroad, the Rome conference had also suffered from the lack of direct participation of Afghans from inside the country.

CONCLUSION

IN THE LAST THREE DECADES, THE POLITICAL CHANGES IN Afghanistan were fundamental and unique. Fundamental, because the continuous and rapid changes in the area of government and leadership had affected the social, political, economic, and cultural lives of the people, massively and collectively. What made these political changes unique were their Afghani characteristics. These characteristics were rooted in the nature of a dynamic force that was created by the mutual engagement of the national ideology with its roots in the political, social, and cultural elements of Afghan society against those groups who desired to remove, relocate, or demonize it. In reality, this dynamic force was the outcome of a clash between those social, political, and cultural values that helped the people of Afghanistan form a nation and shape a history together and those political ideologies that had challenged those values. A clash with such gigantic magnitude created a dynamic force that shattered the nation of Afghanistan as a whole and changed the country's destiny. The engagement of forces was not the aftermath of a peaceful and voluntary interaction of the members of Afghan society; rather, it was the outcome of a continuous chain of violence that erupted involuntarily. Events in Afghanistan intertwined with the regional and international forces that had created harmonic, as well as antagonistic political, social, economic, and military mobilization in the region. Such a mobilization internationalized the problems and prospects in Afghanistan and challenged peace and security in the region.

The Afghan mass revolt began as an uprising without organizational leadership against the brutalities of the PDPA-led regime. The mass revolt caused Soviet intervention and forced Afghanistan into an international battleground. This development injected the regional and international interests in the Afghan conflict and led this conflict to the present civil war.

Almost seven million Afghans were forced to leave the country, and a large percentage of them were influenced by the dominant sociopolitics and culture of the host countries. The landowners became refugees in neighboring countries and lived in the same camps with the farmers. A large percentage of the peasants learned new technical skills while in exile and now have different occupations. Moreover, the farmers who migrated to the cities also began a new way of life, and their children are no longer village boys and girls. There are numerous individuals from the lower and middle social classes who became the military commanders or political leaders. These new leaders and commanders have played a significant role in the formation of a new Afghanistan.

According to the UN report after the Soviet withdrawal, there were 500,000 widows who could not rely on any economic sources other than their own employment.[1] This large number of widows would foster women's participation in the economic and political life of the nation in a new and a more progressive way. Thousands of children lost their parents, and they grew up under the dark influence of war culture, with no parental role model and emotional support. Thousands of teenage boys became not only responsible for their expenses, they also became the caretakers of their mothers and little sisters and brothers. Although the old expression says it takes a village to raise a child, it is not applicable anymore in Afghanistan because the village has been destroyed and its inhabitants are gone. This severe and uncertain sociopolitical environment has a great impact on these Afghan children, and it has challenged what remained from the Afghan tradition and cultural values for the new generation. Indeed, if these children are able to survive the atrocity of the present living conditions in Afghanistan, they will be in a state of psychological trauma from the war for many years ahead.

The most significant remark of the Afghan struggle against the Soviets was the emergence of national solidarity among the people. Afghan ethnic, linguistic, and religious groups enjoyed a very strong common cause, to force the Soviets out, that had not been experienced since the war of independence against the British in 1919. War brought a new way of ethnic, linguistic, religious, and political awareness in this country, but this awareness has been highly politicized. War also forced many Afghans to reach out for security through their ethnic, linguistic, and political ties. In other words, war lightened the ethnic, linguistic, and religious borders, and forced people to live within these boundaries. The members of each ethnic group bore arms and brought a specific territory under their control to secure their community. In addition, during the three decades of war, the prewar political institution that was dominated by the Pushton ethnic group was also destroyed. Ethnic strife between the Pushtons and non-Pushtons to influence the formation of a national government was considered an important factor in the continuation of the present civil war. In the meantime, the continuation of the civil war has proven that Afghan ethnic, linguistic, and religious groups can rule the country only through a cooperative effort, not a militaristic campaign against one another.

Conducting a cooperative effort in Afghanistan needs its own artistic political understandings that fit in the present national, regional, and international realities. One can argue that the arms race in Afghanistan has brought a new way of power sharing and that this arms race itself mobilized Afghan society in a new way. Whether this argument is correct or not, one can agree that the arms race has had a great impact on the formation of the regional powers led by the ex-Mujahideen internal leaders or the ex-government generals. In Afghanistan, the need for a new political mobilization came from a typical social revolution that was not based on class conflicts, yet had a great impact on them. Contrary to Marx and some western scholars such as Skocpol (1979), Leopold and Tilly (1989), who argued that the social class conflict causes the social and political revolution,[2] the Afghan social revolution took place through a chain of mass revolts in the form of political revolution (1978–1979) and developed into a gradual social revolution (1979–1992) with its Afghan-Asiatic characteristic. This development of political and social revolution in Afghanistan disqualified Marx and other political thinkers who argued that social revolution happens only through the social class conflict in human society. Even though these types of arguments stay popular in the academic community around the globe, the Afghanistan political and social revolution has brought unique aspects into this subject, and I hope, one day, this topic gets more attention for in-depth studies.

During these 21 years of war and bloodshed, the people of Afghanistan experienced six governments and more than a half dozen presidents. These governments were run by either the far left politician with a Marxist/Leninist political ideology or the far right conservative with extreme political beliefs. More than one-third of the population was displaced several times, over one million people have been killed, and hundreds have been handicapped. The impact of rapid violence has changed the physical nature of the land and the character of its people. Under these massive waves of mobilization no one was fully able to survive these changes. To scrutinize the massive mobilization indicators in Afghan society one needs to concentrate on the political, economic, and cultural changes.

POLITICAL CHANGES

Two decades of war and violence in Afghanistan had a massive impact on the traditional political system that was based on the national ideology. The structure of this system was based on the principle of *jirga* (tribal or communal council) of Afghan society. In the pre-PDPA coup and Soviet invasion of Afghanistan, Afghan communities participated in the communal or *qawm jirga* and expressed their opinions willingly and freely. In most cases, the community or *qawm* reached an agreeable resolution for the political and social problems and sent their representative through the eldership system to the authorities. Traditionally, Afghanistan has enjoyed the work of highly experienced, skilled, and respectful local leaders to interact and mediate between the central authorities and the local communities. The long years of armed conflict and violent interaction between political forces weakened this important generation of community leaders and made the local communities vulnerable.

When the People's Democratic Party of Afghanistan (PDPA) seized the government in April 1978, the mutual relationship and the relative agreement between the central government and the local communities vanished. Local communities or *Aqwam* became the subject of the leaders of the central government, and they were not able to express their causes freely and willingly. In the time of disagreement, the local communities and *Aqwam* faced the violent forces of the government and the orders directed by the government leaders.

In the Afghan Mujahideen controlled territories, the local communities and *Aqwam* enjoyed, relatively, the process of *jirga* and this drove their support for the local armed Mujahideen groups. But this enjoyment did not last long when the economic and social base of the local communities was destroyed by the massive military campaign of the Soviet and the PDPA armed forces. These military campaigns forced millions of Afghans to leave their villages and towns and take refuge in neighboring countries. This massive displacement and economic devastation changed the balance of the mutual communication and agreement between the local Mujahideen groups and local communities. The arrival of foreign aid to the Mujahideen groups reduced their economic dependencies on the local communities and this aid made the Mujahideen groups superior over the local communities. In the course of time, the local communities received external aid via the local or regional Mujahideen groups, but in times of disagreement with the local commanders this aid could be withheld. This severe situation pushed the local communities further under the influence of the Mujahideen groups. The importance of the local communities became so limited that they were only seen as a source of fighters for the local armed groups who were fighting against the PDPA and the Soviets.

Those Afghans who became refugees in the neighboring countries of Pakistan and Iran were comprised of large displaced groups of people who did not have equal community and township rights with their hosts. These Afghans were subjected to decisions made by their hosts or the Afghan political leaders whose personal lifestyles were far better than those living in the refugee camps. The Afghan refugees, in particular those who lived in the refugee camps, were not able to participate in the decision making process of their daily lives. These refugees also were not able to feed their families and had to look for the hands of those who were controlling the flow of international aid. The monopoly of the international aid by the Mujahideen external front leaders and their political followers, in particular those who were close to the Pakistani and Iranian circles, enabled these leaders to impose their party lines on the refugees. The monopoly of aid and political influence of the political parties over the refugee communities created an environment full of fear and this depressed the people politically.

During the Soviet invasion (1979–1988) the status of political parties and their leadership changed continuously. Both factions of the PDPA, the *Khalqi* and the *Parchami*, faced massive revolts and resistance by the people. These revolts and resistance caused the PDPA factions to disintegrate faster than before. This disintegration resulted in political differences between the two factions and violent confrontations between them. These confrontations encouraged leaders such as Babrak Karmal to enter Afghanistan on a Soviet tank and to accompany the Soviets as they killed his rival, Hafizullah Amin.

The resistance of the masses against the PDPA and its fragmented party organization caused the leaders to deal with national and international issues realistically. The emergence of Najibullah as head of the revolutionary council of the PDPA government and the chairman of the party was intertwined with changes within the Soviet system. This intertwined situation made him open his eyes to the new national, regional, and international developments, particularly: the rise of organized armed political forces led by the Mujahideen internal front; and the Soviet political development under Mikhail Gorbachev's glasnost policy. These developments helped Najibullah move from the far left to the center of the political spectrum in Afghanistan. This political move was the most significant event in the history of the political parties in Afghanistan, and Najibullah was committed to broadening the political and social base of his government by allowing the nonparty individuals to join the government. With the existence of the PDPA militant communists, *Soor Khalqian*, Najibullah formed the *Hezb-e-Watan* with a much more moderate political agenda and changed the name of the government from the Democratic Republic of Afghanistan to the Republic of Afghanistan.

On the part of oppositions, many of the leftist anti-Soviet organizations such as *Rahaei, Akhgar, Satam-e-Meli*, and the more moderate SAMA, melted away in the massive mobilization and lost their political status. Among these groups, SAMA under Abdul Qayom Dadfar (older brother of Abdul Majid Kalakani) continued its activities, albeit sluggishly. SAMA moved out from the influence of a hard-line core with Maoist political ideology toward a moderate and realistic approach dealing with the political situation in Afghanistan. Another secret group with a leftist background called *Raushangar* led by Austad Shoayb criticized Marxist and Leninist doctrines and distributed intellectual literature among the educated Afghans. The core members of this group conducted a massive study on many different subjects such as Marxism, Islam, Afghan History, and international politics. The literature distributed by this group along with the rigid reality in Afghanistan helped many among the leftist circles to leave their radical shells behind and be reborn in the light of the truth with the masses.

Many individuals who were affiliated with the leftist circles joined either the PDPA or the Mujahideen groups and developed a new political ideology that enabled them to participate in the mass mobilization in this country. What remained from leftist political groups (Marxists, Leninists, or Maoists) were a few nuclear circles with isolated activities in Europe.

The external Mujahideen political leaders conducted a massive political organization outside of Afghanistan and attempted to influence the situation inside the country. These parties received large amounts of cash and weapons from states who opposed the Soviet invasion in Afghanistan. The Mujahideen external front recruited thousands of young male Afghans from refugee camps and attracted non-Afghan Muslims from other parts of the world, particularly in the Middle East. The massive organization of these groups in the neighboring countries, particularly in Pakistan, had a significant impact on the political environment of this country. In Afghanistan each of these political groups (seven in Pakistan and eight, smaller, in Iran) attempted to influence the local armed Mujahideen. In this case, parties like *Hezb-e-Islami Hekmatyar* (HIH) attempted to keep their influence through those members who believed in the leadership and the party principle. Other Mujahideen parties attempted to follow the same path in which they were able, in some degree, to implement a similar method, but not as great as HIH. The monopoly over foreign aid and the use of that aid to impose party leadership on the armed Mujahideen inside Afghanistan made the armed groups inside Afghanistan more vulnerable against the Soviet military and political campaigns, and it prolonged the Soviet invasion.

The monopolistic political behavior of the Mujahideen external leaders and the use of aid for the interest of the party rather than the local communities inside the country forced the chief Mujahideen commanders to establish the internal front. The emergence of internal front Mujahideen was a new phenomenon in the Afghans' political world. Soon, the internal front attracted the attention of those who supported the struggle against the Soviets in Afghanistan. These organizations run by the internal front leaders formed their own political and military agendas independently from the external leaders and later formed their own local administration in the areas they controlled. This development limited the influence of the external leaders and their political parties over the local communities inside Afghanistan. In 1983 to 1984, the internal front Mujahideen leaders opened their own offices separately from the offices run by the external front leaders. For example, in 1984, Massoud and Ismail Khan opened their own offices in Pakistan and Iran, which were operated separately from the *Jamaiat-e-Islami Afghanistan* (JIA) led by Burhanadin Rabbani. This practice was followed by other Mujahideen chief commanders such as Abdul Haqh, Mawlawi Haghani, and Nassim Akhondzadah.

The emergence of the internal front Mujahideen organizations and their heroic leaders who were supported by the local communities inside Afghanistan, and the emergence of the Watan Party led by Najibullah, were two significant phenomena that resulted from the massive political mobilization in Afghanistan. Even though both of these political developments were rejected by the extreme communists and extreme Islamic groups, they reshaped the balance of the political power in the country. This new development perpetuated the negative reputation of Najibullah, who had been the head of the brutal Afghan secret police for many years and was known as "the butcher of Kabul," and damaged the positive impact of his reforms severely. This negative reputation contributed largely to the local communities' distrust of the Watan Party. When Najibullah lost control of the Soviet aid for his regime, his government started to disintegrate. Soon, many segments of the government, particularly the armed forces, were absorbed into the regional organization of the internal front of Mujahideen. The expansion of the internal front of Mujahideen and the increase of their influence in large territories, in particular the establishment of the National Commanders Shura (NCS), changed the balance of power toward Mujahideen's influence in Afghanistan. This development caused the collapse of the Najibullah government and the establishment of the Islamic State of Afghanistan (ISA) in 1992. The establishment of ISA under the strong influence of the internal front Mujahideen leaders was a political transition that not only reduced the influence of the external front leaders and their political parties, but also pushed them toward vanishing from the mainstream of the political mobilization in Afghanistan.

The eruption of the civil war between Hekmatyar ISI-supported forces and those led by Burhanadin Rabbani reduced the credibility of the Afghan Mujahideen leaders. This civil war resulted in the emergence of regional political organizations that were different from those before the downfall of the Najibullah government. These new regional powers consisted of a large segment of the previous military and civil administration but were led by famous internal front leaders of Afghan Mujahideen. These regional military and civil administrations, such as the *Nangarhar Shura* led by Haji Abdul Qadir, the *Junbesh-e-Meli* led by General Dostam, the *Shurai Nezar* led by Ahmed Shah Massoud, and the southwest region led by Ismail Khan, were not functioning as parts of the central government.

In 1994, the emergence of the Taliban movement opened another page in the political mobilization of Afghanistan. As the Taliban fighters expanded their control in many parts of the country, they disarmed the local communities and integrated the former military and civil administration into their movement. In the course of four years they defeated the local and regional powers inside Afghanistan, but they also made these powers vanish from the current political map of the country. In their struggle to bring Afghanistan under their strict control, the Taliban controlled more than two-thirds of the country. After the significant military victory of the Taliban movement in Mazar-e-Sharif on August 8, 1998, the only survivors among the regional organizations were the forces led by Ahmed Shah Massoud and the ethnic Hazarah forces in central Afghanistan.

THE ECONOMIC CHANGES

Years of war and violence have destroyed the traditional economic system that was based on agricultural and livestock production. Traditionally, most of the fertile lands were located close to towns that were surrounded by numerous villages. Because of the existence of a traditional transportation system between markets or towns and the villages, it was viable for the populations living in towns and those living in villages to exchange and sell, mutually, their goods and services. Despite this traditional economic system, towns were dependent, economically, on villages. In the remote areas of the country, people maintained a semi-self-sufficient economic system by way of local production.

In 1978, the mass revolts against the PDPA started from the villages and influenced the towns all over the country. The PDPA armed forces controlled the towns but the villages became the main grounds for the formation of guerrilla groups. The formation of anti-PDPA armed groups changed the villages into the military front line against the government. This change, in particular after the Soviet invasion, caused the destruction of the roads and bridges and subsequently, the Soviet-PDPA military machines destroyed the farms. The massive displacement caused millions of people to become external and internal refugees and led to the gradual degradation of farms and irrigation systems in many parts of the country. The deployment of millions of land mines devastated village economies and made numerous areas like ghost towns. As a result of these changes in the economic lives of the people, the towns and in particular the big cities that were controlled either by the PDPA government or by the Mujahideen became dependent on foreign aid.

The economic impact of massive displacement of people from their towns and villages made them disconnected from their economically productive lives. Those who were placed in refugee camps in Pakistan and Iran did not have the facilities to engage in the economy and were not able to use their traditional knowledge and experiences in other fields. Because of this situation, the new generation of these Afghans was also deprived of the knowledge and experience of their ancestors' livelihood of agricultural production and livestock. Those who moved to the cities engaged in economic activities that were different from what they had done in the villages.

All these developments were very rapid and this caused the economy to shift from a productive economy to a war-based economy. The war-based economy was formed mostly with the massive Soviet military and economic support of the PDPA regime and the Islamic countries' and the west's, in particular the United States's, support of the Afghan Mujahideen groups. Despite this war-based economy, the local communities survived if they were connected to one or both sides of the conflict. For thousands of young people, participation in the armed forces, either the PDPA government or the Afghan Mujahideen, became the only way of supporting their families. The meaning of ownership changed dramatically, and owning a rifle was more important than owning production tools. For example, in prewar times, owning a large farm with fertile land and a large group of animals defined the status of wealth in the rural area. In a war-based economy, owning more rifles and other war machines and controlling a larger number of armed men became the main source of wealth. Any local community with larger armed arsenals and more fighters could receive a larger portion of foreign aid. This status of ownership and wealth became very obvious between 1984 and 1988 when the progovernment militia groups emerged as a new political phenomenon in Afghanistan.

During the years of war in Afghanistan, the agriculture sector of the national economy was relatively functional in smaller areas and mostly under the control of the PDPA government. But the agricultural sector was unable to satisfy the local needs as it did during the pre-PDPA period. A large portion of the highly fertile land in the southwest of the country, in particular in Helmand valley, was converted into opium fields. Opium provided the local armed forces, who were fighting against the Soviets, a significant source of financial capacity. But opium production also created an international network of illicit drug production and drug trafficking. The internationalization of the opium production in Afghanistan diverted the primary goal of the cultivation under the supervision of the local Mujahideen commanders. This internationalization of opium production in Afghanistan formed a regional triangle made of war, politics, and drugs that had influenced the politics of the region. Soon the areas where opium had been cultivated became known as the Golden Crescent, the second-highest drug production area in the world after the Golden Triangle in Burma. The emergence of a multi-million-dollar smuggling of transported goods under the Transit Treaty (TT) between Afghanistan and Pakistan has opened a new network of illegal activities in the region. Caravans of goods arrive in Afghanistan under the TT agreement and illegally leave the country through Pakistan, Iran, and Central Asia. This massive smuggling transport network is taking the lead to reshaping the war-based economy in the areas controlled by the Taliban. Those who benefit largely from the Golden Crescent and the illegal transport-network operations are not the Afghan farmers or shopkeepers. The long-term impact of opium production and operation by the illegal transport-network in Afghanistan would be disastrous for the region. The interest groups who form the triangles of war, drugs, and politics in the region are benefiting from the chaotic situation in Afghanistan, and their interest has been rooted in the continuation of war, national or regional conflicts, and a weak and nonfunctional national government in Afghanistan.

All this happens while Afghanistan continues to suffer severely from years of war destruction and regional complicated relations. According to the Human Development Report published by the United Nations Development Programs (UNDP), the physical destruction of Afghanistan by the Soviet invasion and civil war resulted in the following figures:

- The agriculture production percentage decreased to 45 percent as compared to prewar 77 percent.
- The irrigation system in 1987 functioned at 36 percent of its prewar level.

- In 1987, the electrical power generation was only 40 percent of the pre-war level.
- Only 40 percent of the highways were functioning in 1987 as compared to the prewar period.
- Within the telecommunication sector 237 of 245 telephone exchanges were destroyed by 1987.
- By 1987 500,000 homes were severely damaged.
- Only 40 percent of the urban population had safe drinking water in 1987.
- By 1987 there were 7 million refugees outside of the country.
- There were 500,000 widows by 1987.
- By 1987 one out of every six people suffered from some disability caused by the war.
- Life expectancy in 1987 was 42 years.
- The infant mortality rate in 1987 was 296 per 1,000 births.
- The maternal mortality rate in 1987 was 640 per 100,000.
- In 1987 the crude birth rate was 48 per 1,000.
- In 1987 the crude death rate was 28 per 1,000.
- By 1987 only 25 percent of the total population had access to health services.
- In 1987 it was estimated that there were 12 to 15 million unexploded land mines in Afghanistan.[3]

In the areas close to the borders with the former Soviet states, Iran, and Pakistan, such as Herat, Qandahar, and Mazar-e-Sharif, the city populations have increased rapidly in the last 20 years. The majority of these people have been engaged in trades with neighboring countries. The status of trade in these areas has been out of the control of the local authorities, and there have been numerous cross-border routes dominated by illegal traders. A small percentage of people who lived in these cities worked for the government while they also worked in the private sectors to support their families. A large portion of people were fully dependent on the trading of goods and services with the neighboring countries. In the event of regional confrontation, the lower portion of those who are involved in trade would not have any other alternatives to support their families. Indeed, the current war-based Afghan economy led millions to make a living upon bearing arms and fighting in one or the other sides of the war.

THE CULTURAL CHANGE

The Afghanistan cultural status had been one of a unique kind in the region, and this uniqueness has contributed greatly to the cultural identity of its people. The geopolitical location of Afghanistan as the crossroads of ancient civilizations gave the possibility to people with many different ethnic, linguistic, and religious backgrounds to meet and live together for centuries. This geopolitical location also helped these ethnic, linguistic, and religious groups form the nation of Afghanistan. Within a national identity, different ethnic communities were able to build a relatively strong common ground to understand one another and engage in a mutual social and political life. In comparison to other countries in the region, the ethnic, linguistic, and religious interconnection through marriages, in particular, among different Muslim groups, such as Sunnis and Shias, was greater in Afghanistan. This greater social interconnection developed as one of the unique aspects of Afghans' cultural identity, which was different from their neighbors in the Middle East, Central Asia, and the Indian subcontinent.

The Afghanistan geopolitical location also made this country attractive to invaders, who attempted to expand their empire and reach the Indian subcontinent. These kinds of ambitions created an external threat to the people of Afghanistan and forced them to avoid ethnic, linguistic, and religious confrontations from time to time. In the course of history, these diverse social groups had formed the Afghan national ideology that helped them to find positive common ground and survive from internal fragmentation and destruction done by the external forces. Struggling against the invaders helped the social groups to concentrate on the Afghan national ideology, define their common interests, and respect one another. This was one of the main reasons that Afghans with different ethnic, linguistic, and religious backgrounds were able to live peacefully in a village, town, or in a compound in remote areas for centuries.

After the PDPA military coup in April 1978, and the Soviet invasion in December 1979, the Afghan national ideology came under the direct attack of the coup leaders and the Soviets. The PDPA's claim of authority and their political and social reforms were in conflict with the fundamental elements of the Afghan national ideology. The atheist-based political agenda prevented the PDPA leaders from understanding the in-depth role of the Islamic faith in the cultural identity of the Afghan people. The political alignment with the Soviets and operating as a part of the Soviet agenda in Afghanistan was contrary with the notion of national self-determination. The massive prosecution of the political opponents and the use of violence against all social and political forces created a dark environment of fear in which the notion of individual freedom and communal autonomy were suppressed. The radical reforms and brutalities of the PDPA and the Soviet invasion of the country put people in a defensive position. Throughout this, the average population attempted to defend themselves against the radical reforms and the violent campaign of the Soviet forces by holding onto those aspects of their culture that helped them to resist the PDPA and the Soviets. The Islamic notion of Afghan culture clashed against the Marxist interpretation of the PDPA and the Soviets. The nationalistic notion of the Afghan culture appeared face-to-face against the internationalization of the Afghan proletariat by the PDPA and the colonialistic invasion of the

Soviets in Afghanistan. This hostile social, political, and ideological environment had embraced a complex dichotomy of notions that caused the physical clash of forces. In reality, the war in Afghanistan was not only an armed struggle between the PDPA/Soviets and the Mujahideen forces, it was also a cultural clash between the Soviet and the Afghan ways of life.

The clash between the physical and cultural forces of Afghans against the Soviets created a violent approach by each side when dealing with one another. The massive use of violent force by the PDPA and the Soviets watered the seeds of Islamic radicalism in Afghanistan. The emergence of Islamic fundamentalism in Afghanistan was the direct result of this hostile environment created by the PDPA and the Soviets' radical and violent campaign. The rise of Islamic fanaticism in Afghanistan was not the result of a normal sociopolitical strife. The PDPA coup, the Soviet invasion, the existence of the Islamic Republic of Iran, and the General Zia regime in Pakistan gave radical Islam an obvious cause and appearance in Afghanistan. Therefore, the Islamic fundamentalism was a politically motivated force that did not have roots in the social and cultural fabric of Afghanistan.

The waves of refugees in all directions caused the destruction of the social and cultural formation of the local communities. One-third of the total population was in constant movement and migration due to the shift in the front line of the war inside the country. Another large portion of this displaced population were refugees in Pakistan and Iran, who came under the cultural influence of their host communities. The rest of the population who lived in Afghanistan maintained their daily lives under the strict influence of the PDPA regime or the Mujahideen groups. Thousands of Afghans migrated to the other countries, in particular Western Europe, the United States, and Russia, and they are now faced with the cultural influences of the communities where they live.

When the internal front of the Afghan Mujahideen controlled larger areas, they had to respond to the needs of the local communities according to their social and cultural requirement. Since the Islamic fundamentalist groups were following a radical agenda for Afghanistan, they were not able to satisfy the needs of these local communities inside Afghanistan. This development failed the fundamentalist leaders in the formation of proper civil organizations in these areas. In this circumstance, the local Mujahideen commanders met the needs of the local communities and organized their forces in a way to help these communities and protect their social and political values against the Soviets and the PDPA. Practically, the internal front Mujahideen's activities were inspired, more than any other political forces in the country, by the Afghan national ideology. Subsequently, the local communities under the influence of the internal front Mujahideen survived culturally and practiced Afghan cultural traditions more than the Afghans abroad or those under the domination of Soviets.

The emergence of the Taliban and the establishment of the Islamic Emirate of Afghanistan (IEA) was a surprising phenomenon for many observers.

This new phenomenon, in the violent political environment of Afghanistan, sparked hope for order and peace. However, many quickly lost their hope in the dusty field of the militaristic, ethnic, and religious ultra-supremacy approach of the Taliban. The Taliban's rigid policies in the name of Islamic law and Afghan traditions appeared contrary to the Islamic notion in Afghanistan that encourages peaceful co-existence among different ethnic, linguistic, and religious groups. In this Afghan tradition, the exemplary teachings of the leading *Sofies* who devoted themselves to peace and tolerance were valued highly. The Taliban discrimination against women and their rigid behavior against modern values brought their regime closer to the one led by Habibullah Kalakani, known as *Bach-e-Saqaw* in the 1920s. Afghan historians considered Habibullah's regime as a dark chapter in Afghan modern history.

The Taliban alignment with Pakistan and the Arab fanatics such as bin Laden is in conflict with the notion of Afghanistan as an independent nation. The Taliban political agendas have neglected the importance of the national ideology and it has forced Afghanistan in a similar direction as the PDPA did 20 years ago. All these have developed a political environment in which militancy and violence have continued to be the dominant themes of the inside politics of Afghanistan. Many Afghans cheered during the peace conference and tried to imagine a peaceful Afghanistan in the horizon of their wishful thinking, but the burst of rifles and artillery from the fresh assaults brought them back into the reality of their national misery.

Long years of war and violence in Afghanistan and the large amount of displacement, deaths, and migration have had a significant impact on the cultural tradition of the Afghan people. This impact shifted the cultural identity of Afghans in a new direction, different from their prewar cultural status. The war in Afghanistan has mobilized society toward the formation of a new social, political, and cultural order. This new order needs to replace the old order; it also has to direct society in accordance with the current situation. The prospects of peace, security, reconstruction, and the economic development of Afghanistan rely vastly on Afghans and their leadership to form an alternative for the implementation of such a new order. Indeed, this new order has to have profound and lively roots into the Afghan national ideology.

Afghans have a vast source of potential abilities to reconstruct their country; among others, the new Afghan generation, who live in the industrialized countries and have earned professional skills, can play a significant role. The emergence of Afghanistan as a vital bridge between the Central Asian region, the Indian subcontinent, and the Asian Pacific market is a significant development. This development will help Afghans to attract regional cooperation and international investment. In this case, Afghanistan as the gate of Central Asia would have a positive impact in the process of peace, security, and economic development in the region. Yet the continuation of the violent confrontation damages Afghanistan more than any other nation in the region. There are countries in the region, particularly Pakistan, that have benefited from the continuation of the civil war. But, they should know these benefits are based on short-term influence in Afghan politics, and in the long run, they will lose more resources than they receive from the war in Afghanistan.

Indeed, the massive mobilization forced Afghanistan from a peaceful social, political, and cultural life to a hostile, complex, extremely violent, and destructive one. All this occurred without a popular political leadership acceptable to the general public. During these years, the people of Afghanistan have experienced a variety of political parties and leaders who have symbolized their political goals with many different slogans. Afghanis also have witnessed numerous governments and presidents who symbolized their government through the color of the Afghanistan national flag: from communist red, to the radical Islamic green, and to the white flag of the Taliban. But all of these governments and government leaders failed to guide their people into peace and stability. It seems that the political gap between the political leaders and the masses is still wide and deep, and the need for a third movement, different from the radical communists and fanatic Islamists has become greater than before.

Epilogue:
The Afghan Connection
to September 11

THE SEPTEMBER 11, 2001, TRAGIC AND CATASTROPHIC TERRORIST attack in the United States apparently was the result of individuals affiliated with Al-Qaeda, under Osama bin Laden, based in Afghanistan. Thousands of people lost their lives in a matter of hours, and massive destruction and other physical and psychological damages were inflicted; the international system was challenged, as was the post–Cold War concept of global security. The attacks on the United States occurred just two days after two suicide bombers posing as journalists, and apparently under the command of bin Laden, assassinated Ahmed Shah Massoud, the legendary Afghan commander and the most important leader in the forces opposing the Taliban.

Tragic as these events have been, critical is the need to understand the roots of the Islamic radicalism represented by bin Laden, how this radicalism spread into Afghanistan, and what is necessary for these roots to be removed so that the receptive ground is created for a stable Afghanistan that both advances the interests of its people and is a member in good standing of the international community. To explain helps understanding, but is not to condone; accurate diagnosis is the first step in any treatment.

The catastrophe of September 11 has roots in the militant warfare originating in the Middle East. The political, economic, and military engagement of the Western world, especially the United States, has been important in the development of a rigid political environment shaping this new brand of global militancy. The massive imbalance in wealth and economic opportunities between the elites and the average population, the high levels of corruption, the persecution of the political oppositions by the governments supported by the United States, have contributed greatly to the declining social, political, and economic status of Islamic countries, particularly in the Middle East. The conflict between Palestinians and Israelis, the Persian Gulf War and its aftermath, the way the United States handled its engagement against the Soviets and then turned its back on Afghans after they forced the Soviets out of the country, are important factors that contributed to the rise of fanatic Islam. Groups like Al-

Qaeda, who interpret religion in accord to their political agendas, well capitalize on the local grievances and use violence as tactical measures to "reflect" the social, economic, and political problems in these countries. The political goal of these fanatic groups is to establish a theocratic dictatorship such as those in Iran led by Ayatollah Khomaini and in Afghanistan led by Mullah Mohammed Omar, and the rigid political environment in many Islamic countries enabled these groups to emerge as an attractive force and influence societies.

This book was written before the tragic events of September 11, in an effort to increase understanding of Afghanistan's plight. In this epilogue, written in the aftermath of the terrorist attack, a brief review seems warranted, highlighting how Afghanistan's traditional social system was weakened and then undermined by invasion and then external interference, creating the opportunity for external groups to make the country their base.

THE IMPACT OF THE SOVIET INVASION

The traditional social and political institutions of Afghanistan were undermined by the Soviet military intervention in support of its local allies, who had formed the Democratic Republic of Afghanistan against the Afghan Mujahideen. Thousands of villages and towns were destroyed and a large number of the Afghan population was displaced internally and as refugees in neighboring countries. The result of the Soviet-led military campaign was the destruction of the economic base of the country and the shattering of its traditional social and political system. Millions of Afghans who lost their livelihood inside of the country were traumatized while running from front lines, village to village and town to town, and several millions more have been humiliated in the refugee camps in Pakistan and Iran. A large portion of the population became dependent on foreign aid, either via the Soviets or those who were supporting the Afghan resistance groups. The result was that indigenous constraints and restraints were bypassed as groups increasingly drew on external financial and military assistance to pursue their goals, goals further complicated by those providing external support.

When the Soviet troops pulled out of Afghanistan in 1988, the restoration of peace, stability, and communal security was the core interest of the people. Millions of people who lost a loved one in the war, thousands who were maimed, and millions more who had suffered from displacement and humiliation in the refugee camps and other parts of the world dreamed of participating in the reconstruction of the country and living in peace and dignity. The eruption of the civil war after the Soviet withdrawal, especially after the formation of the Islamic State of Afghanistan (ISA) in 1992, destroyed the dream for rebuilding the country. Civil war, which later became a proxy war, with the continuing and expanded role of external actors with their own interests, caused the total destruction of many urban centers such as Kabul, and added thousands of human losses to the million who were lost during the Soviet invasion.

THE U.S. ENGAGEMENT IN AFGHANISTAN

After the Communist coup (1978), and particularly after the Soviet invasion (1979), the United States undertook a massive covert operation, and with Saudi Arabia supported the Afghan Mujahideen by matching aid dollar for dollar. Zbigniew Brzezinski also convinced General Zia-ul-Haq of Pakistan to be the conduit of arms and supply to the Afghan Mujahideen groups inside Afghanistan. The United States allowed the Pakistani to be in charge of the U.S. operation in Afghanistan.[1]

The United States also used Egypt as a base, as the U.S. Air Force transferred military personal and weapons from the Egyptian air bases in Aswan and Qena to Pakistan. President Anwar-al-Sadat of Egypt started a public campaign for supporting the Afghan Mujahideen and his government engaged in recruiting and training volunteers, mostly with Islamic militancy background. Speculations about Sadat's motives of aiding the Afghan Mujahideen included his desire to: gain public support for his government after he signed a peace treaty with Israel in Camp David, which was rejected by many conservative Muslim groups; improve his public image in Egypt and among his Middle Eastern neighbors; and defuse the Islamic militancy threat to his regime. Many of the Egyptian militants were sent to Afghanistan, where they might not survive in the war against the Soviets. In this case, President Sadat would kill two birds with one stone, by appearing to support the fundamentalists and at the same time destroying the movement by effectively sending its participants to their deaths. If this was Sadat's ploy, it backfired, as some of those militants who served in Afghanistan returned to Egypt and formed the Islamic Jihad, one of whose members, Khaled Islambaly, assassinated President Sadat in 1981.

In Pakistan, General Zia sought to influence the future Afghan government, in order both to have a strategic ally against India and to run a militant campaign in the Soviet Central Asia. Since Gulbadin Hekmatyar was affiliated with the *Jamaat-e-Islami of Pakistan* (JIP) led by Qazi Hussein, and was a close ally and personal friend to the ISI generals, Hekmatyar became Zia's man in Afghanistan. This development helped the *Hezb-e-Islami*, Islamic Party of Hekmatyar (HIH), receive around 65 percent of the U.S military and financial aid, and form the most powerful militant organization. In addition, Hekmatyar's close relationship with the Egyptian militant groups helped him receive personal and financial aid from the nongovernmental sources, mostly from conservative elements in various Islamic countries. *Jamaiat-e-Islami* (JIA) led by Burhanadin Rabbani, received the second largest portion of military and financial aid. It was through the HIH, the JIA, and later the *Itahad-e-Islami Sayyaf* (IIS), that non-Afghans received training in Afghanistan.

After the Soviets withdrew their forces from Afghanistan in 1988, the international aid agencies reduced their humanitarian assistance and the UN program for reconstructing Afghanistan fell way short of its target. The Soviet/Afghan war forced half of the Afghan population to become refugees, took over a million lives, and shattered the economic, social, and political system of the country. The United States, the most powerful supporter of the Afghan Mujahideen, turned its back: rather than provide assistance for rebuilding, it left Afghans with a country devastated by war. The U.S. pull-out created a power vacuum: The Afghans did not have the resources to put the country on its feet, making it vulnerable to the interference of neighboring countries, particularly Pakistan. The Pakistani ISI, which had been the agency distributing the U.S. military and financial aid to Mujahideen, supported Hekmatyar in his effort for a military takeover of Kabul. In 1992, Hekmatyar forces under the direct support of the ISI opened fire on the newly established Mujahideen government in Kabul. Thus the internal war in the country was ignited.

From the chaos of this internal war supported by external actors, in 1996 the Taliban captured Kabul and established their Islamic Emirate of Afghanistan (IEA). The United States considered the Taliban a source of stability sharing anti-Iranian interests with Washington. The Clinton administration miscalculated the manifestation of rigid hostility toward modern values among the Taliban forces. The State Department was inclined to consider Taliban rule as the best possible outcome for stability in Afghanistan, while also underestimating the threat posed to both regional stability and international security.[2] Washington optimism also resulted in UNOCAL proposing to use Afghanistan as a transit route for oil and gas produced in Central Asia. This was the reason that the Clinton administration supported the multi-billion-dollar pipeline project that could pump oil and gas from Turkmenistan to Karachi, Pakistan.

From 1998 to 2000, the Clinton administration policy toward Afghanistan was focused on one issue: bringing Osama bin Laden to justice. The U.S. cruise missile attack on August 20, 1998, aimed at assassinating bin Laden and destroying the terrorist camps, was followed by repeated ineffective requests to the Taliban to extradite bin Laden. On August 19, 1999, Washington imposed sanctions that, among other things, affected trade with the Taliban-controlled areas and banned the use of the Afghan airline, Aryana. On November 14, 1999, the United Nations followed the United States and declared an embargo on the Taliban-controlled Afghan airline, and froze the Taliban's assets. Yet in Afghanistan, the western powers' focus on the extradition of bin Laden made him a symbol of defiance against the west. This provided bin Laden an ample opportunity to introduce his jihadic struggle (now against the United States) throughout the world. At the expense of Americans and the people of Afghanistan, he became an antiwestern hero among the Afghan fanatics as well as among the international network of Islamic fundamentalists.

THE RISE OF ISLAMIC FANATICISM
IN AFGHANISTAN

The violent antireligious campaign by the Democratic Republic of Afghanistan (DRA) and later by the Soviets created an environment upon which the Afghan fanatic groups were able to capitalize. The emergence of Islamic fanatics in Afghanistan is not rooted in the social and cultural fabric of the country. Instead, Islamic radicalism was imported by foreign political groups, mostly during the Soviet invasion, who took advantage of the struggle against the Soviets and then, after the Soviet withdrawal, of the disorder within Afghanistan.

For many centuries, Afghanistan was influenced by the teachings of Sufi and Islamic mystic leaders like Khajah Abdullah Anssari, Mawlana-e-Balkhi, Naser Khosrow, Al-Bironi, Khoshhal Khan Khatak, Hamid Baba, and so on. These Sufi leaders encouraged peace, tolerance, and love. These leaders also believed that a human being may enter into the territory of infinite truth, where God's kingdom is, if he or she is able to reach the highest level of love for God. In this case, God is the ultimate truth that has been reflected in His creations, and loving God means loving His creations. The only way that one may reach the highest level of love for God is to be in peace with all those who belong to Him.[3] The influence of the mystic and Sufi teachings in the cultural formation of Afghanistan helped local communities maintain pre-Islamic traditions like the celebration of the new year, and the concept of Pushtonwali (a Pushton way of life that is based on hospitality, honor, and revenge) among the ethnic Pushton. The result of this cultural and traditional social structure was that different religious groups, such as Jews, Hindus, and Sikhs, have lived with the Muslim majority in harmony. This historical social and cultural development was reflected in the modern Afghan constitution, which granted equal rights to all its citizens regardless of their ethnic and religious background.

The separation of state and religion was an important component of national politics in Afghanistan. Historically, Afghanistan was never ruled by religious leaders, and the state leaders were always in charge of the public affairs and the religious institutions were managed either independently or under the auspices of the state. In most cases, the state authorities were in good-faith relationships with the religious institutions, and the religious institutions were supportive of the governmental leader at the times of national crises.

The roots of Afghan Islamic fanatics lie in the political and social environment of the Middle East. In the early 1970s, the Afghan government sent students for higher education to the Middle East, particularly to Egypt. Some of these students attended Al Adhere University in Cairo and were influenced by the political ideology of the Egyptian Muslim Brotherhood, one of the original Islamic fundamentalist groups. Among these Afghan graduates were Burhanadin Rabbani, Abdul Rabe Rassul Sayyaf, and Sibqatollah Mujaddadi, who formed the Afghan Muslim Brotherhood, which was known as *Ikhwan-al-*

Muslimun (IM). These, and others, were to become important leaders in the Mujahideen movement. Above all, Hekmatyar and Rabbani adopted a radical approach toward state and society. After a failed plot against Dauod's regime in 1974, the IM fanatic leaders took refuge in Pakistan and received support from the Pakistani regime under Zulfaghar Ali Bhutto. In the following year, an IM armed force crossed the border into Afghanistan to purge rebellions against Dauod's regime, but the government forces with the help of the local communities crushed them.

During and after the Soviet invasion, Afghan fanatic leaders developed a diabolical image of their opponents, leading to the maximum use of violent force against their political opponents. These fanatic leaders called for jihad against their political opponents. Because these opponents were Muslim, the fundamentalists called them *monafiq*, meaning one who creates divisions among Muslims and acts against God and the *Ummah*, the Muslim community. According to some interpretations, a *monafiq* is worse than those unbelievers who act deliberately as an enemy of Muslims, and is akin to a traitor. For the Afghan fanatic leaders, using religion for their political gain and the total elimination of their opponents was a routine way of doing politics: a large number of prominent Afghan politicians, scholars, and Mujahideen field commanders in Afghanistan were assassinated during and after the Soviet occupation. These assassinations were predominantly carried out by the *Hezb-e-Islamic* Hekmatyar and the fanatic portion of the *Jamaiat-e-Islami* Rabbani, under the watchful eyes of the ISI in Pakistan and in some cases with the collaboration of the Afghan KGB. The secret war and terror campaign by the Afghan Islamic fanatic groups in Afghanistan and in Pakistan forced a large number of Afghan politicians into exile in Europe and North America. This terror campaign and harassment, supported by Pakistan ISI, created openings for those political leaders who agreed with General Zia's forward policy toward Afghanistan. While moderate political leaders like Sayyed Ahmed Gailani, Sibqitollah Mujadadi, and Mohammed Nabi Mohammedi attempted to fight the secret war and terror campaign run by the Afghan fanatics, they were reluctant to resist Pakistan's policies toward Afghanistan. Practically, the Afghan moderate politicians were under double threats—by the Soviet and DRA regime and also by the Afghan fanatics supported by the ISI. During this time, many Afghan nationalists and prominent politicians, like Dr. Mohammed Yosuf, were forced to leave Pakistan, or, like Shamssadin Majroh, were assassinated. The harassment and assassination of the Afghan moderate politicians continued during the Taliban rule in Afghanistan. For instance, in 1999 an unknown armed man assassinated Abdul Ahad Karzai, a prominent Afghan politician in Pakistan near the border of Afghanistan. Karzai was working for the reconciliation process to end the war and militancy in Afghanistan.

The formation of IEA in 1996 took place as a result of the power vacuum created by the internal war started by the Hekmatyar/ISI military campaign in

1992. The Taliban, with the direct support of Pakistan's interior ministry led by General Babar, was able to capitalize on the lack of cohesive central power and national leadership in Afghanistan and bring up to 80 percent of the country under their control. Soon, the Taliban promises for peace and justice faded away, replaced by their harsh policies and cruelties against their political opponents and average Afghans. Their gender apartheid, ethnic cleansing, religious discrimination, violation of international human rights, and the destruction of historical heritage disrupted the individual and social lives of Afghans living in the Taliban-controlled areas. The Taliban's alliance with Pakistan upset many Afghans who considered it a violation of national independence and sovereignty. The Taliban's association with bin Laden and his non-Afghan followers, engaged in hate crimes against ethnic and religious minorities in different parts of the country, generated additional opposition. Taliban rule was a source of cultural shock to Afghan tradition and Islamic values, and a destructive force threatening to Afghans as well as non-Afghans.

OSAMA BIN LADEN AND AL-QAEDA IN AFGHANISTAN

Bin Laden joined the struggle against the Soviet invaders in Afghanistan in 1979, when he was 22. He already had been associated with fanatic circles in Saudi Arabia. Bin Laden was influenced by his professor at the King Abdul Aziz University, Abdullah Azzam, who was affiliated with Egyptian Muslim Brotherhood. Azzam was preaching the notion of pan-Islamism to form an international solidarity among Muslims, and rejecting the pan-Arabism. Azzam, who was very influential in Arabia, left Saudi Arabia in late 1978 and established Maktab al Khidmat, the Serving Center (serving in jihad) in Pakistan, which subsequently developed branches around the world, including in the United States. Azzam preached the formation of an Islamic Khelafat in Afghanistan, meaning a government ruled by *Shari'ah* (Islamic law), interpreted as a pristine form exemplified by the immediate successors of the Prophet Muhammed. He was able to build up an autonomous area in the Kunar Province near the Pakistani border. Azzam's small symbolic Khelafatdom was controlled by his non-Afghan army; he also was unofficial representative of Saudi Arabia's interest among Afghan Mujahideen groups based in Pakistan. When bin Laden joined his mentor in Pakistan, he became the chief financier and major recruiter of the so-called Arab Afghans, or those Arabs who had fought against the Soviets in Afghanistan. Bin Laden was instrumental in bringing construction equipment to build training camps and bunkers, and his projects received U.S. funds.[4] Toward the end of the Soviet invasion, Azzam was assassinated in southeast Afghanistan, and bin Laden took charge of the Maktab al Khidmat ("Service School," symbolically meaning to service jihad). Within the international channel of this organization, he built up Al-Qaeda, "the Base."

In 1990, bin Laden was outraged by the Iraqi invasion of Kuwait, and he proposed to the Saudi king that he and his Arab Afghan friends could protect the kingdom. But the Saudi royal family, who feared the fanatic perspective and influence of bin Laden and his associates, instead asked for help from the United States. Bin Laden was enraged by the deployment of U.S. troops in Saudi Arabia, and he protested against their presence and demanded their withdrawal. This opposition with the Saudi regime and the U.S. troops being there caused him to lose his status as Saudi citizen and he was exiled to Sudan, where he reorganized the Al-Qaeda network and built up training camps. Finally, under U.S./Saudi pressure, he was forced out of Sudan and he arrived in Afghanistan with his three wives, his children, and his associates in early 1996.

In September 1996, the Taliban forces captured Nangarhar province, where bin Laden resided. Bin Laden recognized that the Taliban were going to be the most powerful armed political force in Afghanistan, and he donated U.S. $3 million to the Taliban leaders for their military campaign on Kabul. In the following years, bin Laden's support of the Taliban increased financially and militarily, and this support was cemented by inter-marriage between the bin Laden family and the supreme leader of the Taliban. Bin Laden's familial connection to the Taliban supreme leader and his generous donations to the leadership provided him with the power to influence important areas of the Taliban's domestic and foreign policies. Under this circumstance, bin Laden was able to build up the Al-Qaeda training camps and coordinate his effort around the world.

In 1998, the failed U.S. cruise missile attack against bin Laden's facilities in Afghanistan provided him with worldwide fame, particularly in the Islamic countries. In the Islamic world, particularly in the Middle East, bin Laden's fame confused the borderlines between resistance based on the concept of hope, and militancy and terrorism that relies on the notion of hate. In this confused anti-Western and anti-American political environment, bin Laden declared the formation of The International Islamic Front for Jihad (IIFJ), which was led and coordinated by Al-Qaeda. Al-Qaeda's shapeless organization has allowed it to operate like a multinational corporation capitalizing on the shares and profits of its partners (the IIFJ). The main shareholders of this joint venture are well organized and disciplined groups such as *Jamaat-al-Islamia* and *Al Jihad* in Egypt, *Hezbollah* in Lebanon, *Hammas* in Palestine, *Harkat-ul-Mujahedin* and *Leshkar-e-Anssar* in Pakistan, *Abu Sayyf* in the Philippines, the Islamic Salvation Front in Algeria, the Islamic Movement of Uzbekistan, and many connected cells and units without any known title. By using the Taliban administration as a protective shell, bin Laden has turned Afghanistan into a laboratory for jihad, where Al-Qaeda cadres provide ideological and military training for other devoted militants arriving from different countries. The prevalence of training programs, the Taliban Afghan and Pakistani religious seminaries, and battles against the forces opposed to the

Taliban, made Afghanistan an important source of inspiration for Islamic radicals. The successful militancy movement in Afghanistan, led by their fanatic interpretation of Islamic law *Shari'ah* (which resulted in the formation of the Taliban regime), has set an example for other Islamic militants.

AFGHANISTAN:
A BASE FOR MILITANT WARFARE

In recent years many of the 25,000 non-Afghans who joined the armed struggle against the Soviets have returned to Afghanistan.[5] Along with these fighters, thousands of students from the Pakistani religious schools, *madrasahs*, have arrived in Afghanistan. Many of these students are generally enrolled in these schools at the tender age of six and continue until they turn sixteen, coming from many different countries around the globe to attend. For them, learning about jihad in conjunction with a struggle for social and political justice had been simply theoretical, but the ongoing war in Afghanistan exposed them to the practical and military aspects of jihad. The Bionsi town mosque in Karachi, Pakistan, a stronghold for the Afghan Taliban, claims to have students as well as donations from as many as 45 countries, including Britain, France, Germany, Switzerland, the Philippines, and the United States.

Apart from the students, the rest of the non-Afghan fighters have come from all over of the world, including Egypt, Sudan, Jordan, Palestine, Iraq, Yemen, Algeria, Nigeria, Morocco, Tanzania, the Philippines, China, Britain, and a large number from Central Asia and the Caucasus. In the past five years between 60,000 to 80,000 Pakistanis have fought in Afghanistan, bringing their experience back home.

These combatants are suspected of hijackings, kidnappings, and sectarian killings in India, Pakistan, the Middle East, Africa, Europe, North America, and Central Asia. These fighters are linked with many of the fanatic armed political movements with Afghanistan in one way or another; several fanatic leaders like bin Laden, Jumah Namangani from Uzbekistan, Taher Yuldashev from Kyrgyzstan, Ayman al-Zawahiri from Egypt, and large numbers from the Middle East and South and East Asia were trained in Afghanistan. The activities of these groups have become coordinated and increasingly funded under the structure of the IIFJ.

The Taliban's rigid and militant policies imposed on Afghanistan do not fit within the principle of Afghan national ideology, which has deep roots in the teachings of Islamic mysticism and Sufism and fraternity with other religious groups. These policies also offended the core traditional values that helped Afghans with different ethnic, religious, and linguistic backgrounds to live in peace and form a coexisted nation. The Taliban gender apartheid and disrespect against women has been an offence against the traditional concept of *nang*, honor. Their hate campaign against religious and ethnic minorities has offended the notion of *hamssaiagi*, neighborliness upon which different religious and ethnic groups cared and shared their local resources at the time of crisis. The massive influx of non-Afghan militants who arrived in Afghanistan to support the Taliban and also for training became problematic for the local communities. Under Taliban supervision, these non-Afghan militants have used violence against the local people, and they build their political and military powers within the Taliban-controlled territories. These non-Afghan fighters, along with the Taliban army, have not only broken the traditional norms of Afghan civil societies, they have also committed massive crimes against humanity by beheading and killing prisoners of war (POWs) and massacring thousands of civilians in different parts of the country. In 1998 to 1999, the International Red Cross reported that the Taliban and their non-Afghan army killed thousands of civilians in Bamyan and set fire to about 8,000 houses and shops.

The brutality of the Taliban regime and their non-Afghan militant friends crippled Afghan civil society, and when the recent drought hit the country, people had few resources—whether food or social support—on which to draw. As a result, Afghans became the largest refugee and displaced people in the world. This social instability in Afghanistan diminished the recruitment pool for the Taliban, which relied increasingly on foreign militant fighters and their bin Laden/Pakistani supporters. The Taliban regime has increasingly crept into the organizational framework and political agenda of the IIFJ. According to recent reports, more than 35 percent of the Taliban's armed forces are comprised of non-Afghan nationals. In addition, bin Laden has been consulted on domestic policies including the destruction of Buddha's statues that generated international condemnation. The growing role of bin Laden in the decision-making process within the Taliban leadership was detrimental to the roles of some Taliban leaders, who were considered more pragmatic and moderate.[6] The importance of bin Laden to the Taliban regime is given further evidence if, as appears to be the case, his supporters were responsible for the assassination of Ahmed Shah Massoud, a leader in the anti-Taliban Northern Alliance. The goal behind assassinating Massoud was to decapitate the UIFLA forces and take out an important possible ally for Washington.

AFTER SEPTEMBER 11:
HOPE FOR A NEW AFGHANISTAN

After Massoud's assassination, the UIFLA formed a leadership council to coordinate its political and military operation.[7] As an important step, the UIFLA sent a delegation led by Yunus Qanooni and Haji Qadir, the prominent Pushton leader, to Rome to work on a coalition program with the former king.[8] This coalition program, called the *Loyah Jirgah* Process, is considered the most obvious alternative to have popular support from a strong majority of Afghans. Both the former king and the UIFLA leadership are working hard to form an alternative strong enough to gain the support of the international community and also challenge Pakistan's influence in Afghanistan. In this case, the *Loyah Jirgah* Process appears to be a pragmatic alternative that would legitimize the process for undermining the social base of the Taliban regime, stabilizing Afghanistan, forming a national government, and ending years of war and militancy.

After the terrorist attacks on the United States on September 11, the situation in Afghanistan is receiving increased attention in the international community. This incident impacted the international system and made the industrial western nations look beyond their special interests, and created a sense of solidarity among the world communities. When one understands the connection between what happened in Afghanistan and the Middle East during the last two decades and the September catastrophe in the United States, the importance of the international community taking steps to help Afghanistan rebuild and become stable is clear. In the last ten years the Afghans have been suffering from warfare and fighting terror forces in their land, while using their maximum resources to promote peace and end the war in their homeland. Unfortunately, years of neglect by the international community, especially by Washington, of Afghanistan and the dangers arising from its internal turmoil and the opportunities it created for external groups prevented the international support that Afghans seeking stability needed. The lack of international attention combined with years of political violence resulted in the rise of the Taliban. This development along with the support and influence of Al-Qaeda and IIFJ crippled the ability of Afghans to stand on their feet and defend their social and political rights. The external interference of neighboring countries, especially Pakistan, in supporting the most fanatic elements of Afghan society suppressed the moderate and democratic political forces. In an environment where violence has become the dominant theme of politics, the Afghan local communities have not had the chance to express their will.

The U.S.-led global war on terrorism, particularly dealing with the Taliban and bin Laden, should be viewed and expanded as a constructive engagement to stabilize Afghanistan. The long-term goal of stabilizing Afghanistan should concentrate on the eradication of all terrorist camps, training facilities, as well as all of their financial and logistical means in Afghanistan. Afghans and non-Afghans alike who have been involved in terrorist activities must be apprehended and brought to justice, either in the United States or in their native countries. Under the auspices of the United Nations, assistance should be provided to the Afghans to move toward the establishment of a stable government that respects human rights and is consistent with accepted international norms. For this important reason, the United States can promote a constructive dialogue between all those forces that support the war on terrorism and military warfare in Afghanistan on the basis of Afghan self-determination. This effort needs the United States's direct support to help Afghans form a broad coalition comprised of different ethnic and religious groups within the country and abroad. Traditionally, Afghans have solved their local and national crises by convening the *Loyah Jirgah* (grand assembly). Within the *Loyah Jirgah*, delegates representing different ethnic, religious, and linguistic groups have the chance to decide on the future government of Afghanistan. Indeed, the participation of former King Zahir Shah in a future *Loyah Jirgah* as a neutral national figure will help the reconciliation process and direct Afghanistan toward building peace and reconstructing the country.

Deploying American-led ground troops in Afghanistan would be considered an invasion of Afghanistan and would cause tragic results, both for Americans and for the people of Afghanistan, while a heavy bombing campaign would only drive more Afghans and other Muslims into bin Laden's camps. If the U.S. military hits Afghanistan without having much effect on the terrorist networks, it will be a second victory for bin Laden after the September 11 attacks on American soil. Forming a coalition among Afghans, which may be joined by some Taliban-defector-commanding leaders in a coordinated effort with the U.S.-led forces, seems a pragmatic military approach. In this coalition, the UIFLA (also known as the Northern Alliance), which has pockets of resistance to the Taliban in the north, west, central, and east of Afghanistan, can play an important role. Even though the UIFLA had lost its main leader, Ahmed Shah Massoud, with U.S. aid the Afghan alliance could mobilize their forces within Afghanistan in a short period of time. A coordinated effort of Afghan and U.S. efforts from different directions would damage the military machine of the Taliban and of bin Laden and would destroy all the facilities used by the terrorist networks. Under the auspices of the United Nations, the people of Afghanistan could elect their representatives for the great assembly (*Loyah Jirgah*) to appoint a transitional government for Afghanistan and participate in a free election. Achieving the political, military, diplomatic, and humanitarian goals of the war on terrorism and of stabilizing Afghanistan would end the control of the Taliban, destroy the terrorist headquarters on the ground, and would cause the defection of their military commanders, while convincing the more pragmatic Taliban leaders to join this effort. Those who remain would have no other option but to agree with the goals of stabilizing Afghanistan or lose their military and financial strengths and finally surrender. Finally, at long last, after tremendous suffering, Afghanistan would return to its neutral status as a transit route connecting Central Asia to the Indian subcontinent.

NOTES

CHAPTER 1

1. Cordovez, Diego and Selig S. Harrison: *Out of Afghanistan* (Oxford: Oxford University Press, 1995), p. 26.
2. Lifschults, Lawrence: *Pakistan Times*, Islamabad, February 12, 1989, p. 23.
3. Wakmen, Mohammed A.: *Afghanistan, Non-Alignment and the Super Powers* (New York: Radiant Publisher, 1985), p. 5.
4. UNDP, *Action plan for immediate rehabilitation of Afghanistan* (New York: UN Publication, 1993), vol. 1, p. 7.
5. Wilber, Donald N.: *Afghanistan* (New York: Human Relation Press, 1980), p. 56.
6. Jawad, Nassi: *Afghanistan: a Nation of Minorities* (London: The Minority Rights Group, Brixton, 1992), p. 9.
7. Dupree, Louis: *Afghanistan in the 1970s* (New York: Praeger Publisher, Inc., 1974), p. 14.
8. *The Holy Qur'an* (Al Madonna: Madonna Publication, 1986), Surah 42, Aya 38, Aya 159, and Sura 3.
9. Ghobar, Ghulam Mohammed: *Afghanistan dar Massir Tarikh* (Kabul, Matba'ah Daulati, 1978), p. 80.
10. Ibid., p. 90.
11. Ibid., p. 277.
12. Anthony, Arnold and Rosanna Klass: "Afghanistan Communist Party and the Fragmented PDPA," in *Afghanistan, the Great Game Revisited* (New York: Freedom House, 1987), p. 135.
13. Hugh, Beattie: *Afghanistan Studies* (London: Society for Afghanistan Studies, British Academy, 1982), vol. 3 and 4, p. 44.
14. Interview with Mr. Abdul Wassil (Wardak), the former *woleswal* of Enjeel, Herat, and the former governor of the Province of Parwan. He now resides in Connecticut.
15. Klass, Rosanna: *Afghanistan, the Great Game Revisited* (New York: Freedom House, 1987), p. 205.
16. Dupree, Louis: *Afghanistan in the 1970s* (New York, Praeger Publisher, Inc., 1974), p. 4.
17. Hugh, Beattie: *Afghanistan Studies* (London: Society for Afghanistan Studies, British Academy, 1982), vol. 3 and 4, p. 44.
18. Ghobar, Ghulam Mohammed: *Afghanistan dar Massir Tarikh* (Kabul: Matba'ah Daulati, 1978), p. 468.
19. Kakar, Hassan: *Trends in Modern Afghan History* (1974), p. 4.
20. Vartan, Gregorian: *The Emergence of Modern Afghanistan: Political Reforms and Modernization* (California: Stanford University Press, 1969), p. 361.

CHAPTER 2

1. Ilpyong, Kim J.: *Mass Mobilization Politics and Techniques Developed in the Period of the Chinese Soviet Republic* (Washington: University of Washington Press, 1996), p. 86.
2. Fischer, Louis: *The Life of Mahatma Gandhi* (New York: Harper and Brothers Press, 1985), p. 14.
3. Green, Philip: *"Democracy,"* Robert Michael, *"Political Parties"* (New Jersey: Humanities Press, 1993), p. 68.
4. My personal notes, Afghanistan, Herat, 1982–1984.
5. UNDP, *Action plan for immediate rehabilitation of Afghanistan* (New York: UN Publication, 1993), vol. 1, p. 34.
6. There are two words that people, particularly, Dari (Farsi) speaking communities, pronounce similarly: 1) *"Ghazi"* with ghain; 2) *Ghazi* with ghaf. *Ghazi* with ghain means victor. Historically, the term *"Ghazi"* has a deep root in the traditional life of Afghans. During the three Afghan-British wars (1884–1919), the term *Ghazi* became very popular, and individuals like Amir Akber Khan, the son of Dost Mohammed Khan, became the head of the *Ghazian* (plural of *Ghazi*) against the British. At that time individuals who committed to be *Ghazian* became professional freedom fighters and a handful of these crossed the border from Afghanistan into India to take part in the Indian people's struggle against British rule in this subcontinent.
7. From 1988 to 1992, the situation was a continuous civil war in Afghanistan between the former Mujahideen groups and Soviet supported government. From 1992–1994, the fight between the Islamic Government of Afghanistan and the opposition rival groups, particularly the Islamic Party of Hekmatyar, prevented a national leadership. From 1996 to 2000, the war between the Taliban forces and the High National Defense Council under General Abdul Rashid Dostam and Ahmed Shah Massoud prevented the formation of a united political leadership in Afghanistan.
8. Cordovez, Diego and Selig S. Harrison: *Out of Afghanistan* (Oxford: Oxford University Press, 1995), p. 34.
9. Hobbes, Thomas: *Leviathan or the matter, form and power of a Commonwealth*, ed. Michael Oakeshott (New York: Collier Books, 1962), p. 138.
10. Ibid., p. 138.
11. Anthony, Arnold and Rosanna Klass: "Afghanistan's Divided Communist Party," in *Afghanistan, the Great Game Revisited*, ed. Rosanna Klass (New York: Freedom House Press, 1987), p. 135.
12. "The Truth About Afghanistan" (Moscow: Novosti Press Agency Publishing House, 1986), p. 4A.

CHAPTER 3

1. Anthony, Arnold and Rosanna Klass: "Afghanistan's Communist Party: the Fragmented PDPA," *Afghanistan, the Great Game Revisited* (New York: Freedom House, 1987), p. 135.
2. Wakmen, Mohammed: *Afghanistan, Non-Alignment and the Super Powers* (Pakistan, Islamabad, 1985), p. 4.
3. Ibid., p. 5.
4. The People's Democratic Party of Afghanistan (Kabul, Afghanistan: State Publishing House, 1978).

5. Watkins, Mary: *Afghanistan, Land in Transition* (New Jersey: Princeton, 1963), p. 29.

6. According to local and international sources, the Soviet secret operation in Afghanistan was comprised of two sections: 1) the civilian operation led by the KGB that concentrated on civil officers of the Afghan government and non-government elements; and 2) the military operation led by GRU that concentrated on the military officers, in particular, those who were sent to military schools and training programs in the East Block. These operations also were divided into two major mechanisms: 1) recruiting Afghans as individuals and politically and ideologically preparing them to work toward the regional interest of the Soviets. This did not mean that these individuals were involved in intelligence operations and became spies. Many of these individuals had their own political ambitions and personal characteristics with strong nationalist sentiments. But being a part of the general Soviet operation in the region in the long run categorized them on the side of the Soviets. Therefore, the KGB and the GRU, attempting to benefit from the work of an individual by direct connection, were thought to have the political and ideological loyalty to the Soviet leadership. In this case, there were individuals like Hafizullah Amin, who had their own circle in Afghanistan, and individuals who were working not as a group, like Colonel Abdul Qader, who was nurtured by the GRU (Cordovez and Harrison, 1995, p. 26), and Jallalar, a long-term high-ranking official of the Afghan government. In many circumstances, these individuals had a great deal of experience in public affairs and were highly qualified professionals able to have significant influence on the shape of government policies. 2) The KGB and GRU were Recruiting individuals who were able to establish their own circle within the party or their ethnic and linguistic groups. Among the *Pushtons* was Hafizullah Amin; among *Hazaras*, Abdul Karim Missaq; and among Tajiks, Babrak Karmal.

7. Ibid., p. 138.

8. Ibid., p. 141.

9. Arnold, Anthony and Rosanna Klass: "Afghanistan's Communist Party: the Fragmented PDPA," in *Afghanistan, the Great Game Revisited* (New York: Freedom House, 1987), p 141.

10. Ibid., p. 135.

11. Ibid., p. 46.

12. After the Soviet army withdrew from Afghanistan, PDPA changed the title and ideological agenda of the party to "Homeland Party" and tried to represent the modern and traditional elements of nation politics. But this reform happened after more than a decade of bloodshed, especially, and the PDPA leaders contributed directly to the destruction of the country and also were responsible for the death of one and a half million Afghans. Therefore, such political reform could not rescue the deterioration of the PDPA's regime.

13. Arnold, Anthony and Rosanna Klass: "Afghanistan's Divided Communist Party," in *Afghanistan, the Great Game Revisited*, ed. Rosanna Klass (New York: Freedom House Press, 1987), p. 135.

14. Sen Gupta Bhabani: *Afghanistan Politics, Economics and Society* (London: 1985), p. 33.

15. Ibid., p. 34

16. Ibid., p. 58.

17. Arnold, Anthony and Rosanna Klass, "Afghanistan's Divided Communist Party," in *Afghanistan, the Great Game Revisited*, ed. Rosanna Klass (New York: Freedom House Press, 1987), p. 142.

18. Ibid., p. 143.
19. Ibid., p. 144.
20. To the best of my knowledge, I have not seen any evidence that there were finan-cial ties between the Soviet regime and the PDPA before the 1978 coup. But there is evidence that the Soviet operation especially provided financial support to groups such as the PDPA before seizing government power directed through secondary connections. In the case of PDPA, if it was not direct, it may have hap-pened through the Indian Communist Party (ICP), National Party in Pakistan, and the Revolutionary People Party of Iran. In general, the financial support by the Soviets to the parties who believed the Soviet Union to be the center of the socialist world was dependent on 1) the geopolitical importance of the country and 2) the influence of the party among the people. These two issues would be the indicators for the Soviet planners in this particular matter to support the party financially either as a whole or just the leaders.
21. Ibid., p. 144.
22. Siddg, Noorzoy M: "Soviet Economic interests and Policies in Afghanistan," in *Afghanistan, the Great Game Revisited*, edited by Rosanna Klass (New York: Free-dom House Press, 1987), p. 7.
23. Arnold, Anthony and Rosanna Klass: "Afghanistan's Divided Communist Party," in *Afghanistan, the Great Game Revisited*, ed. Rosanna Klass (New York: Freedom House Press, 1987), p. 145.

CHAPTER 4

1. Cordovez, Diego and Selig S Harrison: *Out of Afghanistan* (New York: Oxford University Press, 1995), p. 17.
2. Ibid., p. 18.
3. Ibid., pp. 17–24.
4. Ibid., p. 27.
5. Hyman, Anthony: *Afghanistan under Soviet Domination* (New York: Macmillan Academic & Professional, Ltd., 1992), p. 77.
6. Arnold, Anthony and Rosanna Klass: "Afghanistan's Communist Party: The Fragmented PDPA," in *Afghanistan, the Great Game Revisited*, ed. Rosanna Klass (New York: Freedom House, 1987), p. 138.
7. Rubin, Barnet: "Human Rights in Afghanistan," in *Afghanistan, the Great Game Revisited*, ed. Rosanna Klass (New York, Freedom House Press, 1978), p. 336.
8. Hyman, Anthony: *Afghanistan under Soviet Domination* (New York: Macmillan Academic and Professional Ltd., 1992), p. 81.
9. Arnold, Anthony and Rosanna Klass: "Afghanistan's Communist Party: the Frag-mented PDPA," in *Afghanistan, the Great Game Revisited* (New York: Freedom House Press, 1987), p. 146.
10. Hyman, Anthony: *Afghanistan under Soviet Domination* (New York: Macmillan Academic and Professional Ltd.), p. 85.
11. Saur means April, therefore, Saur Revolution = April Revolution.
12. Hyman, Anthony, *Afghanistan under Soviet Domination* (New York: Macmillan Academic and Professional Ltd.), p. 83.
13. Rubin, Barnett R.: "Human Rights in Afghanistan," in *Afghanistan the Great Game Revisited*, ed. Rosanna Klass (New York: Freedom House Press, 1987), p. 337.
14. Hyman, Anthony: *Afghanistan under Soviet Domination* (Macmillan Academic and Professional Ltd.), p. 85.

15. Bhabani, Sen Gupta: *Afghanistan Politics, Economics and society* (London: 1985), p. 48.

16. *The Truth About Afghanistan* (Moscow: Novesti Press Agency Publishing House, 1986), p. 151.

17. Bhabani, Sen Gupta: *Afghanistan Politics, Economics and Society* (London: 1985), p. 49.

18. *The Truth About Afghanistan* (Moscow: Novesti Press Agency Publishing House, 1986), p. 149.

19. UN, Coordinator for Humanitarian and Economic Assistance Programs Relating to Afghanistan, Geneva, September 1988, p. 91.

20. Hyman, Anthony, *Afghanistan under Soviet Domination* (New York: Macmillan Academic & Professional, Ltd., 1992), p. 93.

21. Ibid., p. 94.

22. During the Herat Mass Revolt, I lived in Herat city and witnessed many parts of the city while it was involved in the uprising and the clash between the PDPA armed units and the rebels. I worked with a group of local community activists trying to assist wounded people by collecting clean bed sheets to use as bandages.

23. I interviewed Colonel Abdul Aziz, the chief of the artillery unit. I also interviewed Major Ismail Kahn, in charge of the anti-air artillery unit, who became one of the most important internal front leaders of the Mujahideen against the Soviets and the DRA regime. Ismail Khan became the governor of Herat in 1992 until Herat was captured by the Taliban forces in 1995.

24. In 1983, I interviewed an officer of this commando unit after he was surrounded by a local Mujahideen group in Kushk, Herat. Since not releasing his legal name was one of the conditions of the interview, I will keep my promise. "It was early morning that we started the mission," he said, "we rushed into the helicopters; soon, we were in the northwest of Herat, and we surrounded the villages." He continued "we separated men from women and children; and we brought all the men in the back of the farmlands, and line them up. The head of my unit asked me to follow him; he pulled the trigger of his Kalakove (an advanced automatic machine gun) while walking across the back of the line of the villagers." He continued with tears, "The officer (the head of the unit) was screaming Tofang (rifle), and I was changing the magazine while replacing the empty rifle with the loaded one."

25. Amin, Saikal, and William Maley: *Regime Change in Afghanistan* (Boulder: Westview Press, 1991), p. 23.

26. Hyman, Anthony: *Afghanistan under Soviet Domination* (New York: Macmillan Academic & Professional, Ltd., 1992), p. 95.

27. *The Truth About Afghanistan* (Moscow: Novesti Press Agency Publishing House, 1986), p. 148.

28. Urban, Mark: *War in Afghanistan* (London: The Macmillan Press, 1990), p. 30.

29. Mohammed Siddieq, Noorzoy: "Soviet Economic Interests and Politics in Afghanistan" in *Afghanistan the Great Game Revisited*, ed. Rosanna Klass (New York: Freedom House Press, 1987), p. 83.

30. Ibid., p. 18.

31. Urban, Mark: *War in Afghanistan* (London: The Macmillan Press, 1990), p. 36.

32. Ibid., p. 23.

33. Ibid., p. 28.

34. Ibid., p. 27.

35. Ibid., p. 24.

36. Cordovez, Diego and Selig S. Harrison: *Out of Afghanistan* (New York: Oxford University Press, 1995), p. 41.

37. Ibid., p. 42.
38. Ibid., p. 43.
39. Ibid., p. 44.
40. Gorbachev declared the Soviet invasion a "bloody wound" that was created by Brezhnev's failure in Afghanistan.

CHAPTER 5

1. Cordovez, Diego and Selig, S. Harrison: *Out of Afghanistan* (Oxford: Oxford University Press, 1995), p. 365.
2. Personal notes, 1987–1988.
3. In 1983, I was traveling in Pakistan along the eastern border of Afghanistan. I met two Pushton men from the Chetral district who migrated from Afghanistan years ago. These two men were on their way to Iran to participate in a religious school in Qoum (the religious center of Iran). They were practicing Shia Islam, and proclaiming that their whole sub-tribe in the Chetral district are Shia.
4. Nassim, Jawad: *Afghanistan a Nation of Minorities, the Minority Right Groups* (London: Manchester Free Press, 1992), p.9.
5. Ibid., p. 11.
6. Ibid., p. 13
7. Ibid., p.12.
8. Ibid., p.11.
9. Diego, Cordovez and Selig, S. Harrison: *Out of Afghanistan* (Oxford: Oxford University Press, 1995), p. 26.
10. In December 28, 1929, King Amanollah's government was faced with an armed insurgency led by Habibollah (*Bachah Saqhah*), a Tajik from north of Kabul. Habibullah was able to enter Kabul and seize power for a short period of time and ended King Amanollah's rule. From: Mir Gholam Mohammad Ghobar: *Afghanistan dar Massire Tarikh* (Tehran: Markaz Nashr Enghallab, 1987), p. 821.
11. The eldership system does not mean a system comprised of old people. To became an ethnic or communal leader or the head of a *Qawm* in Afghanistan it is not necessary for an individual to be aged. There are many middle aged and young adults ages 30 to 40 who became the head of a *Qawm*. For example, when the ethnic and communal council elected Ahmed Shah Abdali as the head of the Afghanistan state, he was the youngest individual among the ethnic and communal leaders.
12. Farhang, Mir Mohammad Saddigh: *Saddigh: Afghanistan Dar Panj Qarn-e-Akhir* (Afghanistan in the Last Five Centuries) in Persian (Iran-Mashhad: Derakhshesh Publication, 1992), p. 114.
13. Ibid., p. 327.
14. Editorial article, *Enghalab-e-Saur* (Kabul: Governmental Press, June 28, 1978), p. 1.
15. Ibid., p. 4.
16. The PDPA leadership announced the military coup of April 1978 as a democratic revolution. Because this coup occurred in the mouth of Saur (April), the second month of the Afghani calendar, they called it the Saur revolution.
17. Barth, Fredrik: *Ethnic Groups and Boundaries, The Social Organization of Cultural Difference* (Boston: Little, Brown, and Co. 1969), p. 9.
18. Taubman, Philip: "Afghan Truce Said to Begin, But Kabul Claim Is Doubted," *New York Times*, January 15, 1988, p. A1
19. From 1980 to 1982, I worked closely with a local Mujahideen group around the city of Herat. The massive air and ground military operations and the pressure of

shortages destroyed many local Mujahideen groups. The group I was working with lost its main commander in a military operation, Engineer Asghar, and many personnel, while the shortage of food forced us to find, wash, and then eat the bread we threw away during the previous days. The lack of doctors and medicine made us see, helplessly, many civilians and members of our group die. The lack of ammunition and weapons made the Soviet fire power superior over the Mujahideen. The Soviets and the DRA forces severely punished any village that provided even some bread or nourishment.

20. Diego, Cordovez and Selig S. Harrison: *Out of Afghanistan* (Oxford: Oxford University Press, 1995), p. 154.

21. Haqqani, Husain: "Rise and Fall of Karmal," *Far Eastern Economic Review*, December 4, 1986, p. 26.

22. Joseph, Newman, J. R.: "The Future of Northern Afghanistan," *Asian Survey*, vol. 28, no. 7. July 1988, p. 733.

23. Coll, Steve: "Afghan Leader Defies Predictions of Demise," *The Washington Post*, May 4, 1991, p. A14.

24. These opinions about Khalighyar came from individuals who knew him through family connections or had worked with him previously. Most of them were suspicious of his role in the RSA government but the majority of them stated that he is a knowledgeable person and knows Afghan history pretty well. (Personal notes from 1987.)

25. In 1988, I was present when a messenger of Khalighyar reached Ismail Khan in the western part of Herat. Ismail Khan rejected any form of cooperation and returned the messenger without any positive response. He was furious and extremely upset and verbally called Khalighyar and Najibullah murderers who destroyed the country and killed millions of their fellow countrymen. (Personal notes from 1987 to 1988). Around this time, my father informed me that when Najibullah's/Khalighyar's messenger reached him in exile, he also rejected any cooperation with Kabul's regime.

26. Taubman, Philip: "Afghan Truce Said to Begin, But Kabul Claim Is Doubted," *The New York Times*, January 15, 1988, p. A.

27. Coll, Steve: "Afghan Leader Defies Predictions of Demise," *The Washington Post*, May 4, 1999, p. A14.

28. Personal notes from 1987 to 1988.

CHAPTER 6

1. Newman, Joseph J.: "The Future of Northern Afghanistan," *Asian Survey*, vol. 28, no. 7. July 1988, p. 730.

2. Ibid., p. 732.

3. Ibid., p. 733.

4. For many people it is not clear whether Mihanparast was a Soviet or an Afghan citizen. At one time he worked as a high-ranking officer of the Afghan government (vice chairman of the Council of Ministers and the minister of electrical energy of Afghanistan). Another time, he worked as the deputy of the Economic Advisory Section of the Soviet Embassy in Kabul and the deputy general consul of the Soviet Union in Balkh.

5. Ibid., p. 731.

6. Ibid., p. 734.

7. Ghobar, Mir Gholam Mohammad: *Afghanistan Dar Masir-e-Tarikh* (Tehran: Markaz Nashr Enghallab, 1978), p. 910.

8. Personal interview in 1984 with Colonel Abdul Aziz, a former teacher of the *Harbi Pohanzai* (the Military Academy) and a famous Mujahideen commander in Shindand, in the Mujahideen controlled area near Shindand.
9. Newman, Joseph J.: "The Future of Northern Afghanistan," *Asian Survey*, vol. 28, no. 7, July 1988, p. 737.

CHAPTER 7

1. Frederick, Barth: "Cultural Wellsprings of Resistance in Afghanistan," in *Afghanistan, Great Game Revisited*, ed. Rosanna Klass (New York: Freedom House, 1987), p. 187.
2. Abdul, Rashid: "The Afghanistan Resistance," in *Afghanistan the Great Game Revisited*, ed. Rosanna Klass (New York: Freedom House, 1987), p. 209.
3. Ibid., p. 210.
4. In my trips to Pakistan between 1982 and 1986, I witnessed many of these local Mujahideen groups who were desperately waiting to get weapons and ammunitions. I interviewed many of the staffs and commanders of these groups.
5. In 1981, Zahir, an aid to Kamal Khan and later Qafar Khan, both main field commanders of *Jamaiat Islami Burhanadin*, presented me official documents written by the JIA's chief officers in Mashahd and Tehran ordering hit campaign and military attacks against the forces of Shir Agha Chongar from *Harkat-e-Islami Mohammedi*.
6. In the fall of 1984, as I organized medical support for the Mujahideen groups in northwest Afghanistan, I witnessed many groups from the ethnic Hazaras who were running away from the Mujahideen's internal fighting in the central part of the country. These groups were exhausted and each one had a horror story to tell of their flight to Iran.
7. At that time I was affiliated with a local political circle, and no member of that group was connected to anyone on the outside or received external aid. We donated money or collected from the volunteers, mostly in the private sector. I also participated in the mass revolt of Herat. My participation in the revolt, like many other members of the group, was not planned by the group; it was our feeling and sentiment for doing so. As a local resistance group, we knew there would be an uprising, but no one knew when and how. To the best of my knowledge, it was like a wave that starts from a small interaction of wind and water then gets bigger and greater. On the third day of the revolt, when the 17th army division broke out and opened fire on the PDPA leadership and the Soviet advisors in the base, I, with some of my friends, approached one of the villages nearby to see what was going on and also to sneak out ammunitions and rifles. We got into an armored vehicle with a lieutenant and two soldiers and headed toward the city. On the way, while we were busy taking apart a heavy machine gun from the top of the vehicle, I asked the lieutenant, "Who is your leader?" "We don't have leader, I was in charge of my unit, we just joined the other unit to punish those who wanted to sell us to the Soviets," he yelled at me.
8. Roy, Olivier: *Islam and Resistance in Afghanistan* (Cambridge: Cambridge University Press, 1986), p. 133.
9. Newman, Joseph, J: "The Future of Northern Afghanistan," *Asian Survey*, vol. 28, no. 7, July 1988, p. 738.
10. Rubin, Barnett: *The Fragmetation of Afghanistan* (New Haven: Yale University Press, 1995), p. 234.
11. Simpson, John: "The Rare Stone that Buys Guns," *World Monitor*, vol. 3, September 1990, pp. 16–18.

12. Personal interview with Engineer Ballal, Massoud representative in the south-west to Ismail Khan in 1987.

13. Rubin, Barnett: *The Fragmentation of Afghanistan* (New Haven: Yale University Press, 1995), p. 239.

14. Afzal, Mohammad, *Neda-ei-Sangar* (The Front Line Call) (Herat: monthly journal of the Southwest Mujahideen lead by Ismail Khan, October 1987), p. 1.

15. Personal notes,1986–87.

16. Rubin Barnett: *The Fragmentation of Afghanistan* (New Haven: Yale University Press, 1995), p. 241.

CHAPTER 8

1. Saikal, Amin and William Maley: *Regime Change in Afghanistan* (Oxford, Oxford University Press, 1994), p. 119.

2. Ahmed, Rashid: "Friendless Foe," *Far Eastern Economic Review*, vol. 150, October 25, 1990, p. 18.

3. Henry, Kamm: "Muslim Insurgents Attacking Kabul," *The New York Times*, October 13, 1990, p. 6.

4. Krauss, Clifford: "U.S. Renews Hope for Afghan Peace," *The New York Times*, October 15, 1990, p. A3.

5. Hollon, Eliza Van: *Afghanistan, A Year of Occupation* (Washington, D. C.: Department of State, February 1981), Special Report no. 79, p. 3.

6. *The Washington Post*, April 13, 1982, p. A9.

7. Personal notes from 1984–1986.

8. *The Washington Post*, June 4, 1982, p. A15.

9. *Time*, July 5, 1982, p. 39.

10. Ahmed Rashid: "$3 billion Economic Aid, Military Sales Package," *Pakistan Times*, Islamabad, June 16, 1981, pp. 1, 5.

11. In the fall 1987, Mohammed Zahir Azimi, chief Commander of Harkat Islami Mohsseni in Herat, was angry about the hardship that the Iranian government imposed on his activities among the Afghan refugees. Commander Zahir told me that Iranian sources were not happy about the military and financial aid he had received during his recent trip to Pakistan.

CHAPTER 9

1. During the Soviet invasion of Afghanistan, there were many Afghans who were active inside the local Mujahideen forces and not affiliated with the Pakistan and Iran-based Afghan political parties. These political activists were engaged in day-to-day politics in Afghanistan. Most of them were loyal only to the regional commanders and provided these commanders their organized opinion and thoughts on many different issues. In the course of several years, any time I traveled to different provinces I was able to interview and talk with these types of individuals. Most of these political activists were disappointed with the external front leaders while struggling against the Afghan communist regime.

2. In 1987, I was with Ismail Khan in the western part of Herat, and he was fully convinced that the Afghan leaders in Pakistan or Iran were not capable of creating an alternative for Afghanistan. In a meeting with Commander Allawadin Khan, the second person after Ismail Khan who just arrived from his trip to Pakistan, I understood that what was going on in Pakistan was designed by ISI and Saudi's intelligent service to put Afghan leaders into a so-called exiled govern-

ment by using financial resources and military aid. In particular, ISI and Saudi Arabia wanted to select each of the leaders in a government position according to their loyalty to the general and special interests in Afghanistan.

3. In 1987, Commander Allawadin Khan told me that the wireless radios they received from Pakistan channels were distributed in a way so that each kind of radio can only operate within a specific region, and for long-range communication each region has to connect through the Pakistani base station to reach other regions. He stated that the ISI and Afghan leaders were against any network of communication between the major commanders. In the following months, the major commanders trained staff to build the communication bridge between them.

4. Ahmed, Rashid: "Friendless Foe," *Far Eastern Economic Review*, October 25, 1990, p. 19.

5. Steve, Coll and James Rupet: "Afghan Rebels Veto Drive for Kabul," *The Washington Post*, November 28, 1990, pp. 27, 28.

6. "Praise Allah and Pass the Ammunition," *U. S. News & World Report*, November 12, 1990, p. 54.

7. Personal notes from 1982–1984.

8. According to my observation, only in the province of Herat were many major militia commanders receiving military and financial aid from Pakistan-based Afghan political leaders: militia commanders like Shir Agha Chonger (1980–1982) from HEI led by Mohammedi; Turan Rassul (1984–1986) and Jamah Gull Pahlawan (1984–1989) from HIH led by Hekmatyar; and Aamer Said Ahmed and Gholam Yahya Siawshan (1984–1989) from JIA led by Rabbani.

9. Rubin, Barnett R.: *The Fragmentation of Afghanistan* (New Haven: Yale University, 1995), p. 253.

10. Ahmed, Rashid: "Friendless Foe," *Far Eastern Economic Review*, October 25, 1990, p. 18.

11. Ibid., p. 25.

CHAPTER 10

1. Wolesmal, Mohammed Hassan: "Interview with General Safi," *Mujahed Wollas*, vol. 16, no. 240, August 1997, pp. 1, 4.

2. Sandy Gall: An Interview with Commander Ahmed Shah Massoud, *Asian Affairs Journal, The Royal Society Asian Affairs*, vol. 25 (old service vol. 81, part II), June 1994, pp. 141–142.

3. Ibid., p. 149.

4. Rashid, Ahmed: "Advantage Rabbani," *Far Eastern Economic Review*, July 7, 1994, p. 22.

5. Ibid.

6. Ibid.

CHAPTER 11

1. In Arabic the word Talib can combine with different adjective like Talib-u-Ilm, the knowledge seeker, to which the Taliban leaders' name refers.

2. Aabha, Dixit: "Origin, Ideology and Strategy of Taliban," *The Pioneer*, June 11, 1997, p. 4.

3. Singh, S. K.: *Hindustan Times*, February 1995.

4. Aabha, Dixit: "Origin, Ideology and Strategy of Taliban," *The Pioneer*, June 11, 1997, p.3.

5. Ibid., p. 3.
6. Singh, S. K.: *Hindustan Times*, February 1995.
7. Aabha, Dixit: "Origin, Ideology and Strategy of Taliban," *The Pioneer*, June 11, 1997, p. 4.
8. "Law and Order in Afghanistan," *The Taliban Islamic Movement*, editorial, June 20, 1998, p. 1.
9. Magnus, Ralph H.: "Afghanistan in 1996," *Asian Survey*, vol. 37, no. 2, February 1997. p. 112.
10. Ibid. p. 113.
11. Personal notes, Afghanistan, 1984.
12. "The Truth about Taliban," *Taliban in Perspective*, in Persian, November 1, 1995, pp. 1–23.

CHAPTER 12

1. "The Truth about Taliban," *Taliban in Perspective*, in Persian, November 1, 1995, pp. 1–23.
2. Thor, John: "Dahlburg," *The Guardians*, November 24, 1995, p. 5.
3. Tokhi, Owais: "Yong Boys' True Jihad," *AFP reporter* in Karachi, August 10, 1997.
4. "The Truth about Taliban," *Taliban in Perspective*, in Persian, November 1, 1995, p. 10.
5. Davis, Anthony: "A Brotherly Vendetta," *Asiaweek*, December 1996, p. 14.
6. Ibid.
7. Ibid.
8. Ibid.
9. Ibid.
10. Rashid Ahmed: "Afghan Taliban have $100 million war chest," *Academic*, AFP, February. 18, 2000, p. 6.
11. Ibid., p. 1.
12. Ibid., p. 2.

CHAPTER 13

1. Rashid, Ahmed: "Dangerous Liaisons," *Far Eastern Economic Review*, April 16, 1998, p. 28.
2. Cooper, Kenneth J.: "Afghanistan Cultivates Islamic State but Ignores Illicit Harvest," *Washington Post*, May 11, 1997, p. A22.
3. Khan Emel: "Taliban Leaders and the New Government," *Frontier Post*, Pakistan, February 24, 1995.
4. Author's conversation with Abdul Hakim Mujahid Noorullah Zadran and Taliban representative at the UN in New York, March 2000.
5. Yusufzai, Rahimullah: "Massive changes in Taliban Government," *Jang News*, October 28, 1999, p. 4.
6. Mullah Abdul Salam Rakiti, a military man, kidnapped several Pakistanis, including a deputy commissioner, militiamen, and Chinese engineers, from Balochistan in retaliation for the arrest of his brother by Pakistani authorities.
7. Radio Shariah, "The Islamic Emirate of Afghanistan," October 28, 1999.
8. Fairbanks, Charles: "Strategy & Governmental Organization" *Comparative Strategy*, vol. 6 no. 3, 1987, p. 23.
9. Webber, Max: *Wirtschaft und Gesellshaft*, in Gerth and Mills, op. Cit., p. 196.

10. Personal notes, Herat, summer 1995.

11. Personal interview with several medical doctors at Herat's main hospital, Herat, summer 1995.

12. Rashid, Ahmed: "Hope for Peace in Kabul," *Far Eastern Economic Review*, July 1, 1994, p. 22.

13. The Islamic Conference of Herat for Peace in Afghanistan, in Persian, July 1994.

14. The Islamic Conference of Herat for Peace in Afghanistan, in Persian, July 1994.

15. Personal notes, Herat, 1987.

16. *The Aims & Goals of Jamait-e-Islami Afghanistan*, printed in Pakistan, 1983, p. 4.

17. Mossbah and his group became famous as Ikhwani Shia.

18. Personal interview (July 1995) in Herat with an officer of the Afghan Intelligent Service, who insisted on remaining anonymous.

19. "Dustam Made a Deal," *Afghan News*, vol. 11, no. 9, August 1995, p. 7

20. Personal interview (July 1997) with a close member of commander Nasir's family who fought with him against the Taliban forces, and now he and his family are refugees in Birjund, Iran. He requested that his name not be mentioned.

21. Nasseri, Waiss, Telephone interview with Ismail Khan, September 9, 1995, Hamburg, Germany.

22. Economist Intelligence Unit: *Report on Afghanistan*, 4th Quarter 1995, p. 11.

23. Kalilzad, Zalmay (an Afghan-born, U.S. citizen) is Director of Strategy, Doctrine and Force Structure of Project Air Force and Director of the Greater Middle East Studies Center at the RAND Corporation. "Afghanistan in 1995," *Asian Survey*, vol. 36, no. 2. February 1996, p. 191.

24. "Uzbek General Helps the Taliban," Reuters, September 7, 1995, 04:16 AET.

25. Ibid.

26. Crossette, Barbara: "Kabul Under Taliban," *The New York Times*, International, September 26, 1996, p. A3.

27. Moosa, Muhammad: "The Taliban Movement and Their Goals," from Darul Ifta-e-Wal Irshad, Peshawar, Pakistan, 7th Moharram 1417 (June 20, 1998).

CHAPTER 14

1. Moosa, Muhammad "The Taliban Movement and Their Goals," from *Darul Ifta-e-Wal Irshad*, Peshawar, Pakistan, 7th Moharram 1417 (June 20, 1998).

2. Ibid.

3. Ibid.

4. Laghari, Nazeer and Mufti Jameel Khan, Interview with the Ameerul M'umineen, Peshawar, Pakistan, June 1998.

5. Moosa, Muhammad "The Taliban Movement and Their Goals," from *Darul Ifta-e-Wal Irshad*, Peshawar, Pakistan, 7th Moharram 1417 (June 20, 1998).

6. Ibid.

7. Rashid, Ahmed: "Scourge of God," *Far Eastern Economic Review*, August 7, 1997, p. 52.

8. Burns, John: "Islamic Rule Weighs Heavily for Afghans," *The New York Times*, September 24, 1997, p. A6.

9. Moosa, Muhammad "The Taliban Movement and Their Goals," from *Darul Ifta-e-Wal Irshad*, Peshawar, Pakistan, 7th Moharram 1417 (June 20, 1998).

10. Burns, John: "From the Chaos of the Cold War, Afghanistan Inherits Brutal New Age" *The New York Times*, February 14, 1996, p. A1, A8.

11. Ibid.

12. Ibid.

13. Rashid, Ahmed: "Austere Beginning," *Far Eastern Economic Review*, October 17, 1996, p. 19.
14. Ibid.
15. "Fears Fighting in North of Kabul," *The Hartford Courant*, Associated Press, October 31, 1996, p. 4.
16. Goodman, Anthony: "The Afghan Taliban Opposition Offers Cease-Fire," *Reuters*, October, 31, 1996.
17. "New Wave of Refugees in Kabul," *Reuters*, January 21, 1997.

CHAPTER 15

1. "Ethnic Cleansing in North Afghanistan," *Reuters*, November 20, 1998.
2. Cooper, Kenneth J.: "Taliban Short Victory in the North," *Washington Post Foreign Service*, June 4, 1997, p. A25.
3. "A Short Biography of the Martyred Leader, Abdul Ali Mazari," *Hazara Press*, India, June 1998, p. 3.
4. Cooper, Kenneth J.: "Taliban Short Victory in the North," *Washington Post Foreign Service*, June 4, 1997, p. A25.
5. "By the Herald," *Hazara Press*, June 1998, p. 1.
6. "New Waves of Refugees in Northern Afghanistan," *The New York Times*, May 4, 1997, p. 13.
7. Davis, Anthony: "The U.N. is probing incidents of mass murder," *Nations*, June 19, 1998, p. 1.
8. *CNN Television Interactive*, World News, June 3, 1997.
9. Ibid.
10. This information is based on personal interviews with Hazarah political activists who wanted to remain anonymous.
11. "Massoud Forces Blocked the Taliban Advance," *The Irish Times*, May 30, 1997, p. 1.
12. "Afghan Warring Factions Talking Peace," *Reuters*, September 18, 1997.
13. Koshan, M. Qawi: "Northern Alliance Should Avoid Hekmatyar," *Omaid Weekly* (Persian), vol. 7, no. 322, June 22, 1998, p. 1.
14. Interview with Gulbadin Hekmatyar, *Missaq Issar* (Persian), vol. 45, no. 5, April 26, 1998, p. 1, 3.
15. Hekmatyar's Talk at Balkh University, Mazar-e-Sharif, *Missaq Issar* (Persian), May 15, 1998, p. 12.
16. Davis, Anthony: "A Brotherly Vendetta," *The New York Times*, December 1996, p. 2.
17. "Afghan Opposition's New Strategy," *Reuters*, June 12, 1997.
18. The Associated Press: "Afghan Oppositions New Military Front," *The Hartford Courant*, March 20, 1997, p. A16.
19. "Mass Execution in Northern Afghanistan," *The Economist*, August 8, 1998, p. 38
20. Radio Sharia, August 8, 1998, 8 P.M., local time.
21. Ibid.
22. Maulawi Mahboob-u-Rahman, Taliban's Spokesperson in Pakistan, August 13, 1998.
23. "Taliban Greeted by the Local Commanders," *The Frontier Post*, August 13, 1998, p. 4.
24. Clover, Charles: "Taliban Forced Sweep into Opposition's Last Redoubts," *The New York Times*, August 13, 1998, p. 6.
25. Gubar, Ghulam Mohammed: *Afghanistan Dar Masir-e-Tarikh*, Persian (Kabul: State Publication, 1981), p. 643.

CHAPTER 16

1. Dunphy, Harry: "2 Afghan battle over an embassy," *The Inquirer,* May 29, 1997, p. 4.
2. *BBC World Service,* November 30, 1997.
3. *Reuters,* November 18, 1997, 6:32 P.M.
4. NNI, Islamabad, February 28, 2000.
5. Rashid, Ahmed: "Taliban Inc.," *Far Eastern Economic Review,* August 7, 1997, p. 16.
6. Ibid.
7. Ibid.
8. UNOCAL: "Official position on Afghanistan pipeline project," 1998.
9. Rashid, Ahmed: "Taliban Inc.," *Far Eastern Economic Review,* August 7, 1997, p. 15.
10. Ibid.
11. Ali, Lila: "Pak-Afghan-CAS rail link feasibility ready," *Business Recorder,* April 23, 2000, p. 3.
12. Menaker, Drusilla: "Iran Waging Quiet War on Drug Traders mostly Solo Effort May Help to Ease Isolation From West," *The Dallas Morning News,* February 20, 2000, p. 2.
13. Quaglia, Signor: "United Nations Drug Control Program in Afghanistan," *UN Special Report,* August 11, 1979.
14. "Organized Crime in Pakistan," IDSA, Strategic Analysis, vol. 23, no. 5, August 1999, pp. 719–747.
15. Rashid, Ahmed: "Afghan Taliban have 100 million dollar war chest," *Academic,* and *AFP,* Feb. 18, 2000, p. 5.
16. Webber, Max: *Economy and Society,* ed. Guenther Roth and Claus Wittich (1980), p. 225.
17. Burns, John F.: "Islamic Rule Weighs Heavily for Afghans," *The New York Times,* September 24, 1997, p. 6.
18. Ibid.
19. Rashid, Ahmed: "Scourge of God," *Far Eastern Economic Review,* August 7, 1997, pp. 52–53.
20. Ibid.
21. Ibid.
22. Ibid.
23. Cooper, Kenneth: "Taliban Islamic-Code," *The Washington Post,* March 11, 1998, p. 4.
24. Ibid.

CHAPTER 17

1. "Islamic Threats on the Southern Borders," *The Communist Tajikistana,* May 13, 1988.
2. Warikoo, K.: "Afghanistan Factor in Tajikistan's Crisis," *Tajikistan Times,* May 1994.
3. Some Afghan politicians argued that the formation of a joint-government between the Mujahideen and the Watan Party, probably, was the best practical alternative for the establishment of a central government in Afghanistan.
4. Huntington, Samuel P.: *The Clash of Civilizations and the Remarking of World Order* (New York: Simon & Schuster, 1996), p. 247.
5. When the Taliban seized Kabul in 1996, Gulbadin Hekmatyar has moved his headquarter to Iran. Hekmatyar and the JIA Ikhwanis rejected the participation

of the former Afghan king in the peace process and they condemned his *Loyah Jirga* initiative as an American plot.

6. Warikoo, K., "Afghanistan Factor in Tajikistan's Crisis," *Tajikistan Times*, May 1994.
7. "The important of Uzbekistan Security" *Inside Central Asia*, no. 141, September 30 to October 6, 1996, p. 1.
8. Ibid.
9. BBC, Summary of World Broadcasts, May 28.
10. "China Resumes Flights to Kabul," *Far Eastern Economic Review*, March 11, 1999, p. 14.
11. Sirrs, Julie R.: "Report on Foreign POW's Held by the Anti-Taliban Forces," *International Committee for Red Cross*, October 1999.
12. Dawisha, Adeed and Karen Dawisha: *The Making of Foreign Policy in Russia and the New States of Eurasia* (New York, M. E. Sharpe, 1995), pp. 215–245.
13. Shevtsova, Lilia: *Yeltsin's Russia* (Washington, D.C.: Carnegie Endowment for International Peace, 1999), pp. 107–126.
14. "The important of Uzbekistan Security" *Inside Central Asia*, no. 141, September 30 to October 6, 1996, p. 1.
15. "Containing the Islamic Threat is Important for National Security," Interfax New Agency report, October 1, 1996.
16. Radio Shariat, Kabul, Afghanistan, May 31, 1997, 6pm.
17. *Rassiskaia Gazeta*, October 1, 1997.
18. Pope, Hugh: "Moscow Lures Back Central Asia," *The Wall Street Journal*, May 22, 2000, p. 4.
19. Cornell, Svante: *Of Small Nations and Great Powers: A Study of Ethnopolitical Conflict in the Caucasus* (New York: St. Martin's Press, 1999), p. 6.
20. Pope, Hugh: "Moscow Lures Back Central Asia," *The Wall Street Journal*, May 22, 2000, 4.
21. Bergen, Peter and Richard Mackenzie: "Terror Nation: US Creation?" *CNN Presents*, January 16, 1993.
22. Raphel, Robin: Testimony to the Senate Foreign Relations Subcommittee on the Near East and South Asia, May 11, 1996.
23. Nelan, Bruce W.: "The Rush for Caspian Oil," Time, May 4, 1998, p. 41.
24. "Odd Partners in UNO's Afghan Project," *Omaha World Herald*, October 26, 1997.
25. Caroline Lee: "Oil barons court Taliban in Texas," *Sunday Telegraph*, December 14, 1997.
26. "Bin Laden's Anti-American Decrees," *Time*, January 11, 1999.
27. "Taliban Leader Rejected Osam's Extradition," Associated Press, Islamabad, Pakistan, March 1999.
28. Holland, Steve: "Clinton charges Bin Laden behind bomb plot," *Reuters*, May 17, 2000.
29. Waxman, Sharon: "A Cause Unveiled, Hollywood Women Have Made the Plight of Afghan Women their Own," *The Washington Post*, March 30, 1999, p. 4.
30. BBC News, October 6, 1999, at 16:00 GMT.
31. UNOCAL Position Statement, "UNOCAL in Afghanistan : Policy on Proposed Central Asian Pipeline Project," April 1998.
32. "The U.S. Six Flag Ship Visits Caucasus," Times of Central Asia, April 8, 1999.
33. "US to counter terrorism in Afghanistan," *The Nation Group*, 1999.
34. The U.S. Senate Foreign Relation Committee, Testimony on Afghanistan, Washington D.C., July 20, 2000.

35. Kinzer, Stephen: "Uzbek offer Plan to End Afghan War," *The New York Times*, October, 4, 1997, p. 6.
36. *BBC News*, December 1, 1997, at 16:00 GMT.
37. Glacomo, Carol: "The United States and China Support Peace Settlement in Afghanistan," *Reuters*, April 9, 1998.
38. "The U.S Broking Peace in Afghanistan," *The New York Times*, April 18, 1998, p. A4.
39. Singh, Ajay & Anthony Davis: "Afghan Warring Faction Meet Face to Face," *Asiaweek Hompage*, May 22, 1998.
40. Ibid.
41. Ibid.
42. Ibid.
43. Samad, Omar: "Tashkent Declaration on Fundamental Principles for a Peaceful Settlement of the Conflict in Afghanistan," *Afghan Azady Radio*, Washington, D.C., July 21, 1999.
44. Khattak, Afrsiab: "The Failure of Tashkent Conference," *Weekend Post*, July 28, 1999, p. 11.
45. Rubin, James: Press Statement, U.S. Department of State, Washington D.C., March 13, 1999.
46. Farooq, Omar: "Taliban Reject Plan to Convene Loya Jirga," Jang, *The News*, July 16, 2000.

CONCLUSION

1. Clover, Charles: "Taliban Forced Sweep into Opposition's Last Redoubts," *The New York Times*, August 13, 1999, p. 12.
2. Skocpol, Theda: *State and Social Revolution* (Cambridge: Harvard University Press, 1979), p. 5.
3. UNDP: "Action Plan for Immediate Rehabilitation of Afghanistan," vol. 1 (New York: United Nations, 1993), pp. 11–17.

EPILOGUE

1. Cogan, Charles C.: "Partners in Time, the CIA and Afghanistan," *World Policy Journal*, New York, Summer 1993, vol. X, no. 2, pp. 373–374.
2. Phillips, James: "Defusing Terrorism at Ground Zero: Why a New U.S. Policy Is Needed for Afghanistan." The Heritage Foundation *Background*, July 12, 2000, p. 13.
3. Nicholson, Reynold: *Introduction to Rumi*, trans. Ovaness Ovanessian (Tehran: Nashr-I-Nay, Publication), 1987, p. 130.
4. Beyer, Lisa: "The Most Wanted Man in the World."
5. Weaver, Mary Anne: "The Real Bin Laden," *The New Yorker*, January 24, 2000.
6. Report of the Secretary General: "The situation in Afghanistan and its Implications for International Peace and Security," August 17, 2001, p. 9.
7. Telephone conversation with Mohammed Younus Qanoni, a member of the UIFLA leadership council.
8. Telephone conversation with Haroon Amin, the UIFLA liaison in Washington, D.C.

BIBLIOGRAPHY

Afzal, Mohammed: *Neda-i-Sangar* (The Front Line Call), Herat: a monthly journal of the Southwest Mujahideen lead by Ismail Khan, October 1987.

The Aims & Goals of Jamiat-e-Islami Afghanistan (in Persian), Pakistan: Jamiat-Islami Press, 1983.

Apter, David E. and Nagayo Sawa: *Against the State*, Cambridge: Harvard University Press, 1984.

Arnold, Anthony and Rosanna Klass: "Afghanistan's Divided Communist Party," in *Afghanistan, the Great Game Revisited*, ed. Rosanna Klass, New York: Freedom House Press, 1987.

Barth, Fredrik: *Ethnic Groups and Boundaries*, Boston: Little, Brown, 1969.

Burns. John F.: "From the Chaos of the Cold War, Afghanistan Inherits Brutal New Age," *The New York Times*, February 14, 1996.

Burns, John F.: "Islamic Rule Weighs Heavily for Afghans," *The New York Times*, September 24, 1997.

Clover, Charles: "Taliban Forced Sweep into Opposition's Last Redoubts," *The New York Times*, August 13, 1998.

Coll, Steve: "Afghan Leader Defies Predictions of Demise," *The Washington Post*, May 4, 1990.

Coll, Steve and James Rupet: "Afghan Rebels Veto Drive for Kabul," *The Washington Post*, November 28, 1990.

Cooper, Kenneth J.: "Afghanistan Cultivates Islamic State but Ignores Illicit Harvest," *The Washington Post*, Foreign Service, May 11, 1997.

———: "The Opposition Forces Claimed Victory," *Washington Post*, Foreign Service, June 4, 1997.

Cordovez, Diego and Selig S. Harrison: *Out of Afghanistan*, London: Oxford University Press, 1995.

Crossette, Barbara: "Pakistan Accused Afghan Communists for Bomb Blasts," *The New York Times*, International, September 26, 1996.

Dahl, Robert A.: *Modern Political Analysis*, New Jersey: Englewood Cliffs, Prentice Hall, 1991.

Dahlburg, John Thor: "New Communist Leader In Kabul," *Gardian*, Nov. 24, 1995.

Davis, Anthony: "A Brotherly Vendetta," *Asiaweek*, December 13, 1996.

———: "The U.N. is Probing Incidents of Mass Murder," *Nations*, June 19, 1998.

Dixit, Aabha: "Origin, Ideology and Strategy of Taliban," *The Pioneer*, June 11, 1997.

Dunphy, Harry: "2 Afghan battle over an embassy," *The Inquirer*, May 29, 1997.

Dupree, Louis: *Afghanistan in the 1970s*, New York: Praeger Publisher, Inc., 1974.

"Editorial," *Enghalab-e-Saur*, Kabul: Governmental Press, June 28, 1978.

Farhang, Mir Mohammad Saddigh: *Afghanistan in the Last Five Centuries* (in Persian), Iran-Mashhad: Derakhshesh Publication, 1992.

Fischer, Louis: *The life of Mahatma Gandhi*, New York: Harper and Brothers Press, 1985.

Gall, Sandy: "An Interview with Commander Ahmed Shah Massud," *Asian Affairs Journal, the Royal Society Asian Affairs*, vol. 25 (old service vol. 81, part II, June 1994).

Ghobar, Ghulam Mohammed: *Afghanistan dar Massir Tarikh*, Kabul: Matba'ah Daulati, 1978.

Gilpin, Robert: *The Political Economy of International Relations*, Princeton: Princeton University Press, 1987.

Goodman, Anthony: "Taliban Enforce Sharia in Kabul," *Reuters*, October 31, 1996.

Green, Philip: *Democracy*, New Jersey: Humanities Press, 1993.

Haqqani, Husain: "Rise and Fall of Karmal," *Far Eastern Economic Review*, December 4, 1986.

Hazara Press: "A Short Biography of the Martyred Leader, Abdul Ali Mazari," June 1998.

Hugh, Beattie: *Afghanistan Studies*, vol. 3 and 4, London: Society for Afghanistan Studies, British Academy, 1982.

Hyman, Anthony: *Afghanistan under Soviet Domination*, New York: Macmillan Academic and Professional, Ltd., 1992.

Jawad, Nassim: *Afghanistan a Nation of Minorities*, Brixton, London: The Minority Rights Group, 1992.

Kakar, Hassan: Trends in Modern Afghan History, 1974.

Kalilzad, Zalmay: "Afghanistan in 1995," *Asian Survey*, vol. 36, no. 2. February 1996.

Kamm, Henry: "Muslim Insurgents Attacking Kabul," *The New York Times*, October 13, 1990.

King J., Ilpyong: *Mass Mobilization Politics and Techniques Developed in the Period of the Chinese Soviet Republic*, Washington: University of Washington Press, 1969.

Kinzer, Stephen: "Uzbek Offers Plan to End Afghan War," *The New York Times*, October 4, 1997.

Klass, Rosanna, ed.: *Afghanistan, the Great Game Revisited*, New York: Freedom House Press, 1987.

Koshan, Mohammed Qawi: "Afghan Opposition Should Not Trust Hekmatyar," *Omaid Weekly* (Persian), vol. 7, no. 322, June 22, 1998.

Krakovski, Elie: "Afghanistan, The geopolitical Implications of Soviet Control," in *Afghanistan, the Great Game Revisited*, ed. Rosanna Klass, New York: Freedom House Press,1987.

Krauss, Clifford: "U.S. Renews Hope for Afghan Peace," *The New York Times*, October 15, 1990.

Laghari, Nazeer and Mufti Jameel Khan: "Interview with the Ameerul M'umineen," Peshawar, Pakistan, *Frontier Post*, June 1998.

Lifschults, Lawrence: "Corruption in Pakistan," *Pakistan Times*, February 12, 1989.

Magnus, Ralph H.: "Afghanistan in 1996," *Asian Survey*, vol. 37, no. 2, February 1997.

Moosa, Muhammad: "The Taliban Islamic Movement," Peshawar, Pakistan: *Darul Ifta-e-Wal Irshad*, June 20, 1998.

Nasseri, Waiss: "Telephone interview with Ismael Khan," Hamburg, Germany, September 9, 1995.

Newman, Joseph Jr.: "The Future of Northern Afghanistan," *Asian Survey*, vol. 28, no. 7, July 1988.

Noorzoy, Mohammed Siddg: "Soviet Economic interests and Policies in Afghanistan," in *Afghanistan, the Great Game Revisited*, ed. Rosanna Klass, New York: Freedom House Press, 1987.

Office of the UN: *Coordinator for humanitarian and economic assistance programs relating to Afghanistan*, Geneva, September, 1988.

PDPA Central Committee: *The PDPA Charter*, Kabul: State Publication Center, 1979.

Personal notes, Afghanistan, from 1982 to 1989.

"Praise Allah and Pass the Ammunition," *U. S. News & World Report*, November 12, 1990.

Qur'an, Al Madonna: Madonna Publication, 1986.

Rashid, Ahmed: "Advantage Rabbani," *Far Eastern Economic Review*, July 7, 1994.

————: "Austere Beginning," *Far Eastern Economic Review*, October 17, 1996.

————: "Dangerous Liaisons," *Far Eastern Economic Review*, April 16, 1998.

————: "Friendless Foe," *Far Eastern Economic Review*, vol. 150, October 25, 1990.

————: "Scourge of God," *Far Eastern Economic Review*, August 7, 1997.

————: "Taliban Inc.," *Far Eastern Economic Review*, August 7, 1997.

Roy, Olivier: *Islam and Resistance in Afghanistan*, Cambridge: Cambridge University Press, 1986.

Rubin Barnett R.: *The Fragmentation of Afghanistan*, New Haven: Yale University Press, 1995.

————: "Human Rights in Afghanistan," in *Afghanistan Great Game Revisited*, ed. Rosanna Klass, New York: Freedom House Press, 1987.

Saikal, Amin and William Maley: *Regime Change in Afghanistan*, Boulder: Westview Press, 1991.

Sen Gupta, Bhabani: *Afghanistan Politics, Economics and Society*, Oxford: Oxford University Press, 1985.

Simpson, John: "The Rare Stone that Buys Guns," *World Monitor*, vol. 3, September 1990.

Singh, Ajay and Anthony Davis: "New Fighting in Northern Afghanistan," *Asiaweek Hompage*, May 22, 1998.

Singh, S. K.: New Change in Afghan Government," *Hindustan Times*, February 14, 1995.

Skocpol, Theda: *State and Social Revolutions*, Cambridge: Harvard University Press, 1979.

Taubman, Philip: "New Waves of Refugees in Northern Afghanistan" *The New York Times*, Jan. 15, 1988.

Thomas Hobbes: *Leviathan or the Matter, Form and Power of a Commonwealth*, ed. Michael Oakeshott, New York : Collier Books, 1962.

Tohid, Owais: "Soviet Pullout From Afghanistan," *Afghan Free Press*, Karachi: August 10, 1997.

The Truth About Afghanistan, Moscow: Novosti Press Agency Publishing House, 1986.

"The Truth about Taliban," *Taliban in Perspective* (a Taliban's Publication in Persian), November 1, 1995.

"$3 billion Economic Aid, Military Sales Package," *Pakistan Times*, Islamabad: June 16, 1981.

UNDP: *Action plan for immediate rehabilitation of Afghanistan*, vol. 1, New York: 1993.

UNOCAL: "Official position on Afghanistan pipeline project." www.unocal.com, 1998.

Urban, Mark: *War in Afghanistan*, London: The Macmillan Press Ltd. 1990.

Van Hollon, Eliza: "Afghanistan, A Year of Occupation," Special Report no. 79. Washington, D.C.: Department of State, February 1981.

Wagstaff, Jeremy: "Taliban Captured Bagram," *Reuters:* October 25, 1996.

Wakmen, Mohammed A.: *Afghanistan, Non-Alignment and the Super Powers*, New York: Radiant Publisher, 1985.

Watkins, Bradley Mary: *Afghanistan Land in Transition*, New Jersey: Princeton, 1963.

Wilber, Donald N.: *Afghanistan*, New York: Human Relation Press, 1988.

Wolesmal, Mohammed Hassan: "The Road to Law and Order," *Mujahed Wollas:* vol. 16, no. 240, August 1997.

INDEX